SENECA'S *THYESTES*

AMERICAN PHILOLOGICAL ASSOCIATION

TEXTBOOK SERIES

Gilbert W. Lawall, Editor

NUMBER 11
SENECA'S *THYESTES*
Edited with Introduction
and Commentary by
R. J. Tarrant

SENECA'S *THYESTES*

Edited with Introduction
and Commentary by

R. J. Tarrant

Scholars Press
Atlanta, Georgia

SENECA'S *THYESTES*

Edited with Introduction
and Commentary by
R. J. Tarrant

© 1985
The American Philological Association
Reprinted 1998

Library of Congress Cataloging in Publication Data

Seneca, Lucius Annaeus, ca. 4 B.C.–65.
   Seneca's Thyestes

    (Textbook series / American Philological
Association ; no. 11)
   Latin text with commentary in English.
   Bibliography : p.
   Includes index
   I. Tarrant, R. J. (Richard John). 1945–   . II. Title.
III. Title: Thyestes. IV. Series: Textbook series
(American Philological Association) ; no. 11.
PA6664.T5 1985 872'.01   85-10917
ISBN 0-89130-870-9 (alk. paper)
ISBN 0-89130-871-7 (alk. paper: paperback)

Printed in the United States of America
on acid-free paper

CONIVGI OPTIMAE

CONTENTS

PREFACE

Although the *Thyestes* is widely acknowledged to be one of Seneca's most powerful tragedies, there has until now been no modern commentary on the play in any language. My principal aim has thus been to make this extraordinary work more widely accessible and so contribute to a greater appreciation of its quality. The *Thyestes* seems to me an even better and richer play now than it did when I embarked on this commentary; I hope that the pleasure I have had in exploring it will be reflected in what I have written, and that my enthusiasm will offer some compensation for my failures of understanding.

Like other volumes in the APA Textbook Series, this book is primarily designed to meet the needs of students; I have specifically tried to keep in mind readers with some experience of Latin poetry but no prior acquaintance with Senecan drama. As a result technical and philological discussion has been held to a minimum, along with references to specialized literature, especially in languages other than English; where possible, lexical and syntactical explanations are keyed to the reference works most readily available to students (e.g., *OLD* rather than *TLL*); notes on textual problems have been placed in brackets for the convenience of readers who may wish to bypass or defer them. At the same time, I hope that my detailed interpretation of the play will be of interest to scholarly readers. I have given particular attention to Seneca's masterful deployment of language, an aspect of his writing still not adequately recognized and one that a line-by-line commentary is uniquely able to display.

While working on this book I have received much help of various kinds, which it is now my pleasant duty to acknowledge. Successive chairmen of the APA's Committee on Publications and of its Editorial Board for Textbooks have shown remarkable forbearance toward an often exasperating author; I owe special thanks to Gilbert Lawall for his skill in finally extracting a manuscript from me and for his painstaking care in preparing it for the printer. Elaine Fantham and John Fitch provided detailed and helpful comments on the entire book, and allowed me early access to the products of their own Senecan researches. As in the past, Otto Zwierlein has given me the benefit of his opinion on problems of text; he has also most generously shown me the relevant sections of his forthcoming OCT edition of the tragedies. Colleagues and students both in Toronto and at Harvard have listened patiently to my inchoate ideas, supplied me with useful information, and saved me from at least some of my blunders; I am particularly grateful to Lyn Straka for her probing but sympathetic criticisms. A number of my lexical notes have profited from consultation of the files of the *Thesaurus linguae latinae* on microfilm at the Institute for Advanced Study, Princeton; I wish to thank Professor J. F. Gilliam for granting me permission to use this material and Professor G. W. Bowersock for his help in making my stay at the Institute both beneficial and enjoyable. In preparing the final typescript I have had the willing and skillful assistance of Louise Di Giacomo, Lenore Savage, and Juliet Shelmerdine. My wife steadfastly, if misguidedly, refuses to admit that she has done anything to merit mention in this preface, so I must let the dedication suggest the extent of my gratitude to her.

Cambridge, Massachusetts
April 1985

ABBREVIATIONS AND SHORT TITLES

AG	Allen and Greenough, *A New Latin Grammar* [numbers indicate sections]
AJP	*American Journal of Philology*
ANRW	*Aufstieg und Niedergang der römischen Welt* (Berlin, 1972–)
Bell	A. J. Bell, *The Latin Dual and Poetic Diction* (Oxford, 1923)
Canter	H. V. Canter, *Rhetorical Elements in the Tragedies of Seneca* (University of Illinois Studies in Language and Literature 10 [1925])
CHLL	*Cambridge History of Latin Literature*, ed. E. J. Kenney and W. V. Clausen (Cambridge, 1982)
CP	*Classical Philology*
Fantham	*Seneca's Troades: A Literary Introduction with Text, Translation, and Commentary*, by Elaine Fantham (Princeton, 1982)
HSCP	*Harvard Studies in Classical Philology*
Leo, *Obs.*	Friedrich Leo, *De Senecae tragoediis observationes criticae* (Berlin, 1878)
OCD²	*The Oxford Classical Dictionary* (Second edition, Oxford, 1970)
OLD	*Oxford Latin Dictionary* (Oxford, 1968–82)
Otto	A. Otto, *Die Sprichwörter der Römer* (Leipzig, 1890)
RE	F. Pauly and G. Wissowa, eds., *Real-Encyclopädie der klassischen Altertumswissenschaft* (Stuttgart, 1893–)
Roscher	W. H. Roscher, *Ausführliches Lexicon der griechischen und römischen Mythologie* (Leipzig, 1884–1937)
Schanz-Hosius	M. Schanz and C. Hosius, *Geschichte der römischen Literatur*, vol. 2 (4th ed., Munich, 1935)
Seidensticker	Bernd Seidensticker, *Die Gesprächsverdichtung in den Tragödien Senecas* (Heidelberg, 1969)
TAPA	*Transactions and Proceedings of the American Philological Association*
TLL	*Thesaurus linguae latinae* (Leipzig, 1900–)
Zwierlein, *Rezitationsdramen*	Otto Zwierlein, *Die Rezitationsdramen Senecas* (Meisenheim am Glan, 1966)
Prolegomena	————, *Prolegomena zu einer kritischen Ausgabe der Tragödien Senecas* (Mainz, 1984)

Note on citations:

(1) In general, ancient texts are cited according to the short forms used in standard lexica. For Seneca's short moral treatises, however, I

have preferred abbreviations of their individual titles (*Prov.* = *De Providentia, etc.*) to the collective title *Dialogi.*

(2) In references to Seneca's *Agamemnon,* the addition of "(n)" to a line-number indicates that further information may be found in the note on that line in my edition (Cambridge, 1976).

INTRODUCTION

A. SENECA'S LIFE AND CAREER[1]

Information about Seneca's career is relatively abundant, but very unevenly distributed. During the last fifteen years of his life he was one of the most important men in Rome, and he figures prominently in historical accounts of that period—in Suetonius, Dio Cassius, and above all in Tacitus, who found Seneca an absorbing and challenging subject. The first fifty years are much less well documented, and Seneca's own prose works, although to a large extent ostensibly personal, are oddly uninformative about the details of his life; his concern was with moral generalities rather than with autobiography, and so he reveals less about himself than Cicero, Horace, or even Ovid.

Lucius Annaeus Seneca was born at Cordoba in southern Spain, probably between 4 and 1 B.C.[2] He was brought to Rome when scarcely out of infancy,[3] and seems to have had no further connection with his native country. Seneca belonged to a wealthy equestrian family, several of whose members attained recognition in literary or public life. His nephew, the son of his retiring younger brother Mela, was the phenomenally gifted poet Lucan, and his older brother Novatus (later called by his adoptive name Gallio) makes a brief appearance in the *Acts of the Apostles* (18.12–17) as the proconsul of Achaea who declined to involve himself in theological disputes between Paul and the Jewish community of Corinth. Seneca's father, also named L. Annaeus Seneca (ca. 55 B.C.–ca. A.D. 40), combined the skills of a prosperous landowner with a keen interest in literary pursuits. His writings included a history of Rome (now lost), but he is best known for a voluminous and unusual memoir, a record of the declaimers he had heard at Rome and elsewhere, compiled in his last years for the edification of his sons.[4]

---

[1] Useful digest of information in *OCD*[2] 976–77 (by A. Ker and L. D. Reynolds); fuller accounts by M. T. Griffin in *Seneca*, ed. C. D. N. Costa (London, 1974), 1–38, and (with detailed treatment of disputed points) in *Seneca: A Philosopher in Politics* (Oxford, 1976), 29–66—referred to below as "Griffin (1974)" and "Griffin (1976)" respectively. The dates given for Seneca's prose works are, except where noted, those supported by Griffin (1976), 395–411.

[2] The date is calculated from Seneca's only explicit statement about his age, in *Epist.* 108.22 *in primum Tiberii Caesaris principatum iuventae tempus inciderat.*

[3] *Cons. Helv.* 19.2.

[4] The work is extant in a severely mutilated form: for five of the ten books of *Controversiae* only excerpts are preserved, and only a single set of *Suasoriae* survives from a

The schools of declamation that so fascinated Seneca's father provided Seneca himself with his training in rhetoric, and the imprint of the declamatory style can be seen in all his writing, poetry as well as prose. (See below, pp. 19–22.) Declamation may also have given Seneca his first exposure to moral philosophy, since ethical reflections, often in the form of vigorous denunciation of contemporary vice, were an indispensable item in a declaimer's repertory. A specific influence in this direction was exerted by Papirius Fabianus, who combined distinction as a rhetor with serious philosophical interests; nearly fifty years after hearing him declaim, Seneca could still vividly recall the impression Fabianus had made through the refinement and dignity of his manner.[5] This admiration may have made Seneca receptive to Papirius' blend of Stoic and Pythagorean doctrines; at any rate Seneca now embraced moral philosophy with characteristic fervor, and even began to practice vegetarianism as a means to simplicity of life. This conspicuous asceticism did not please Seneca's father, who felt the practical Roman's distaste for philosophy, and before long the younger Lucius was persuaded to return to a more traditional style of living.[6]

Poor health, along with paternal pressure, may have recalled Seneca from the rigors of abstinence. At about this time, when he was in his early twenties, he suffered a severe attack of the wasting disease (probably a form of tuberculosis) from which he would never be entirely free.[7] To recuperate he went to Egypt, where his mother's stepsister was the wife of the prefect C. Galerius.[8] After a stay of several years he returned with them to Rome in 31 (Galerius died in a shipwreck en route) and began a somewhat belated political career by standing for the quaestorship; his aunt, though by nature shy and withdrawn, exerted herself successfully on his behalf.[9]

---

collection of unknown size. The remains are now accessible in the excellent Loeb edition of M. Winterbottom (Cambridge, Mass., 1974; 2 vols.).

[5] *Epist.* 40.12, 52.11, 100 *passim.* Fabianus' works included treatises on political philosophy (*Epist.* 100.1 *civilium libri*) and natural science (*libri causarum naturalium, De animalibus*), cf. Schanz-Hosius 2.359.

[6] *Epist.* 108.22; nor, Seneca wryly added, did he fiercely resist his father's urging (*nec difficulter mihi ut inciperem melius cenare persuasit*). Abstinence from meat had become suspect with Tiberius' prohibition of foreign religious observances; Seneca's vegetarian phase may therefore be placed in or shortly before A.D. 19.

[7] *Epist.* 78.1. His condition, Seneca later claimed, was so serious that he often contemplated suicide (*ibid.*, 2).

[8] *Cons. Helv.* 19.2.

[9] *Ibid.*

The quaestorship brought Seneca into the Senate, and made him eligible for higher office. His progress, though, was not notably rapid: by the time Gaius (called "Caligula") had been succeeded by Claudius in 41, Seneca had held the offices of aedile and *tribunus plebis* but had not yet advanced to the praetorship.[10] Insecure health may have held him back, perhaps also imperial disfavor. Seneca's rhetorical brilliance had begun to attract notice, and Gaius, who took a deluded pride in his own eloquence, would not have looked kindly on a potential rival. Suetonius records his scornful descriptions of Seneca's speeches as "mere classroom exercises" and "sand without lime."[11] Dio goes further, and relates that in 39 Gaius, enraged when Seneca pleaded a case with particular flair, ordered him executed, relenting only when advised by one of his mistresses that Seneca was expected to die of consumption before long.[12] The story could be fiction, or a romantic garbling of events; some have thought, for example, that Seneca had been involved in a conspiracy against Gaius exposed in 39.[13] What is clear is that by this time Seneca was prominent enough to seem worth liquidating.

Seneca escaped disaster under Gaius only to encounter it at the hands of his successor. Late in 41 he was implicated in the prosecution of Gaius' sister Julia Livilla for adultery. In all likelihood the accusation was prompted by Claudius' wife, the domineering Valeria Messalina; the reasons for her hostility to Seneca are not obvious, and Livilla may have been the real target of her enmity.[14] The charge, whether true or false,[15] cannot have been incredible; Seneca must therefore have been moving regularly in the highest levels of society. The Senate voted the death penalty, but Seneca was once again spared, perhaps through the intervention of Gaius' other sister, Julia Agrippina;[16] the sentence was commuted to banishment, and Seneca left Rome for Corsica. His disgrace was the final blow in a series of personal misfortunes: his father had died not long before, and more recently he had lost a young son and perhaps also his wife.[17]

---

10 Tac. *Ann.* 12.8.3. Griffin (1976), 44–51, instead defers the start of Seneca's political activity, placing his quaestorship in 37 or later. It has also been suggested that Seneca's political career was held up in the 30s by his family's associations with the disgraced Sejanus; cf. Z. Stewart, *AJP* 74 (1953), 70–85.

11 *Cal.* 53.2 *lenius comptiusque scribendi genus adeo contemnens, ut Senecam tum maxime placentem commissiones meras componere et harenam sine calce diceret.*

12 Dio 59.19.7.

13 See Griffin (1976), 53–56.

14 As suggested by Dio 60.8.5.

15 Tacitus implies disbelief by his use of *iniuria* at *Ann.* 12.8.3 (see n. 21); Dio, almost unrelievedly hostile to Seneca, accepts the truth of the charge (61.10.1).

16 When Agrippina intervened on Seneca's behalf in 49, he was already *memor beneficii* (Tac. *Ann.* 12.8.3); for the connection with 41, see Griffin (1976), 52 n. 4, 60.

17 *Cons. Helv.* 2.4–5. It cannot be determined whether Pompeia Paulina, Seneca's wife

With his political hopes apparently shattered, Seneca returned to philosophy as a solace for his losses and an outlet for his energies. He had already published at least one work of a philosophical nature, a letter of consolation to a noble lady named Marcia on the death of her son. On Corsica he developed and perfected the role of Stoic moralist and teacher that he would play for the rest of his life; when he returned to Rome in 49, it was with a reputation for wisdom as well as eloquence.[18] The products of these years include two other *consolationes*, one comforting his mother Helvia for the irreplaceable loss of his presence, the other directed to Polybius, a powerful freedman in the service of Claudius, a fawning piece of flattery and a faintly disguised appeal for pardon and recall. Seneca also started work on a more ambitious treatise, a study of irrational passions (*De ira*) in which he took an author's delayed revenge on Gaius by depicting him as an archetype of sadistic cruelty and deranged egomania.[19] Other works, not precisely dated, may also come from this period, such as the lost biography of his father (*De vita patris*), the lost *De remediis fortuitorum* (a suitable subject for a Stoic in exile), and conceivably the *De brevitate vitae*, addressed to Pompeius Paulinus, the father of Seneca's (second?) wife.[20] There was time as well for less serious pursuits (*leviora studia*, *Cons. Helv.* 20.1), among which Seneca would have included poetry— even tragedy. (See below, p. 12.)

After eight years, Seneca's exile was ended by a shift in Roman dynastic politics. Messalina was overthrown and executed in 48, and in the following year Claudius married Julia Agrippina, whose son by her earlier marriage to Cn. Domitius Ahenobarbus was then eleven years old. Agrippina hoped to secure the succession for her child in preference to Britannicus, Claudius' own son by Messalina, who was slightly more than three years his junior. If the young Nero was to be groomed for power, no more suitable guide and adviser could be imagined than Seneca. He was already thought to be well disposed to Agrippina and resentful toward Claudius; arranging his recall would make him an even more willing instrument of her ambitions, while the public would approve the restoration of an eminent man of letters.[21]

So the Senate, which had condemned Seneca to death, now voted his rehabilitation. At Agrippina's urging he was designated praetor for 50,

---

at the time of his death, was also the mother of this son, or whether both infant and mother perished in childbirth; see F. Giancotti, *Cronologia dei 'Dialoghi' di Seneca* (Turin, 1957), 111–31, Griffin (1976), 55–57 (inclining to the latter view).

[18] This seems a natural inference from Tacitus' phrase *ob claritudinem studiorum eius* (*Ann.* 12.8.3).

[19] *De ira* 1.20.8–9, 2.33.3–6, 3.18–19.5.

[20] Griffin, *JRS* 52 (1962), 105, 108–9, argued that the essay was written when Paulinus was *praefectus annonae*, a position he held from roughly mid-48 to 55.

[21] Tac. *Ann.* 12.8.3.

and he began instructing Nero first in rhetoric, later in ethics. Meanwhile, Agrippina's hopes for her son were being quickly fulfilled: he was adopted as Claudius' heir in 50, and four years later, on Claudius' death by poisoning, he was proclaimed as his successor.

Nero's accession altered Seneca's role and enhanced his influence; while continuing to teach the young *princeps*, he became as well an intimate adviser to the new regime. One of his functions was to serve as Nero's principal speechwriter (a position that had not existed under previous emperors); in Nero's first days as emperor Seneca composed both the remarks he made when presented to the praetorian guard[22] and the formal *laudatio* of Claudius that he later delivered in the Senate.[23] Seneca now acquired the traditional emblems of high prestige—he took a suffect consulship in 56, the year after his brother Gallio had held the same position—, but official honors counted for relatively little compared to the influence he could exert as Nero's confidant. Only one other person outside the imperial family had an equal ability to shape policies and decisions, S. Afranius Burrus, the prefect of the praetorian guard whose support was now essential for an emperor's survival. Seneca and Burrus shared power with uncommon harmony,[24] and used their authority to hold both the ambitions of Agrippina and Nero's wilder impulses in check. The first five years of Nero's reign, when their control of events was most secure, were later held up as a model of wise and stable administration.[25] Seneca's political responsibilities did not halt his activity as a philosopher. Soon after Nero became emperor (in 55/56), Seneca addressed to him a substantial treatise on the proper behavior of a ruler (*De clementia*, originally in three books, of which only the first and the opening of the second survive); slightly later came a longer work, a seven-book discussion of the morality of giving and receiving (*De beneficiis*). Other writings located with probability in these years include *De constantia sapientis*, *De tranquillitate animi*, and *De otio* (all addressed to Annaeus Serenus), and *De vita beata* to his brother Gallio. Whether any of the lost ethical works, such as the *De officiis*, *De amicitia*, or the *Exhortationes*, were also composed in this crowded period is not certain. On the other hand, one work of a quite different character can be securely fixed to the first months of Nero's principate, a genuinely

---

[22] Dio 61.3.1.

[23] Tac. *Ann.* 13.3.2.

[24] Tac. *Ann.* 13.2.2 *hi rectores imperatoriae iuventae et (rarum in societate potentiae) concordes diversa arte ex aequo pollebant.*

[25] Aurelius Victor *Caes.* 5.2 (cf. *Epit. de Caes.* 5.2) *quinquennium tamen tantus* [sc. Nero] *fuit . . . uti merito Traianus saepius testaretur procul differre cunctos principes Neronis quinquennio.* On the meaning of *quinquennium Neronis*, see F. A. Lepper, *JRS* 47 (1957), 95–103, Griffin (1976), 424.

funny satire on Claudius' deification—the *Apocolocyntosis* or "Pumpkini-fication" of Claudius[26]—that was at once an attack on the abuses of the previous ruler and an advertisement of the virtues to be looked for in his successor.[27]

The rewards of association with Nero did not come without cost to Seneca's reputation or, perhaps, to his conscience. His quickly-won prominence made him a natural target of envy and resentment, and even such a generally detested figure as P. Suillius Rufus, tried for extor-tion in 58, could win some response by sneering at the prodigious wealth that a provincial philosopher had amassed in four years of imperial friendship.[28] The glaring discrepancy between Seneca's personal fortune and his Stoic professions of detachment from material things was clearly a source of embarrassment to him; he addressed the issue in *De vita beata*, taking the comfortable view that a philosopher can enjoy and make good use of riches without the risk of being corrupted. It is harder to judge how much uneasiness Seneca felt at another consequence of his position, the necessity of acting as apologist for Nero's crimes. The mur-der of Claudius was soon followed by that of Britannicus in 55 and of Agrippina in 59; all of Seneca's skill could not prevent the official lies from sounding more hollow on each new occasion. The *laudatio* for Claudius had touched off laughter,[29] but the speech in which Nero justi-fied Agrippina's death prompted a deeper revulsion, directed at Seneca even more than at his master.[30]

As Nero grew older, he became less amenable to restraining influ-ences. Three years after the murder of Agrippina, Burrus died (some said he had been poisoned),[31] and Seneca found himself isolated and outmaneuvered by new advisers like Ofonius Tigellinus, all too ready to win Nero's favor by encouraging his basest instincts. In an attempt to extricate himself, Seneca asked Nero for permission to retire from his service; the request was formally denied, but from 62 onward Seneca did

---

[26] The title contains a pun on ἀποθέωσις and κολοκύντη (= *cucurbita*, a pumpkin or gourd) whose precise meaning is not clear (exhaustive discussion by M. Coffey in *Lustrum* 6 [1961], 247–54), but which probably plays on the association of that vegetable with hollowness, and by implication, slow-wittedness. (An English rendering might be "Claudius the Gourd.") Seneca's authorship of the work has been doubted (perhaps because of the liveliness of its humor) but is virtually guaranteed by Dio 60.35.3. On auth-orship and title see now the edition of P. T. Eden (Cambridge, 1984).

[27] A further purpose was to promulgate the *fable convenue* that Claudius had died of natural causes; cf. Griffin (1974), 20.

[28] Tac. *Ann.* 13.42 (Tacitus notes that Suillius was condemned, *haud tamen sine invidia Senecae*).

[29] Tac. *Ann.* 13.3.2.

[30] Tac. *Ann.* 14.11.4.

[31] Tac. *Ann.* 14.51.1

largely withdraw from active involvement in the affairs of the court.[32] In 64, after the disastrous fire at Rome for which Nero was widely blamed, Seneca again offered his resignation and the surrender of most of his fortune. Nero accepted Seneca's money, but still withheld permission to retire. In a pointed display of independence, Seneca pleaded illness and refused to leave his rooms for some time.[33] The virtual end of his political activity left Seneca once again free for philosophy; between 62 and 65 he composed the two largest of his surviving works, the *Naturales Quaestiones* (originally in eight books, of which six are now complete and two fragmentary) and the series of *Epistulae morales* to Lucilius, 124 of which remain from a once greater number.[34]

In the spring of 65 Seneca's fertile retirement was cut short. According to Tacitus, Nero had for some time wanted to rid himself of Seneca's disapproving presence, and had even tried unsuccessfully to remove him by poisoning.[35] When a plot to assassinate Nero headed by C. Calpurnius Piso was uncovered in April of 65, Seneca's connections with Piso and with some of the other conspirators gave the emperor his chance.[36] Twice before Seneca had been placed under sentence of death, but this time there was no reprieve, only the opportunity to die by his own hand rather than face execution. In his writings Seneca had often held up death as the supreme test and proof of virtue,[37] and he now set about his own end determined to leave behind a model of philosophical resolution. No detail was omitted: there were bracing words for his disconsolate pupils, reluctant acceptance of his wife's desire to die with him, sufficient strength in the last painful moments to dictate a final statement, even a cup of hemlock taken straight from Plato's *Phaedo*. Tacitus' account—one of the great death-scenes of ancient literature—captures both the strain of theatrical contrivance and also the genuine courage, affection, and tranquillity of the protagonist.[38]

Reactions to Seneca have varied widely from his own time onward.[39]

---

[32] Tac. *Ann.* 14.56.6.

[33] Tac. *Ann.* 15.45.5.

[34] He also began work on a synthesis of his ethical views, referred to as *moralis philosophiae libri* or *volumina* (*Epist.* 108.1, 109.17).

[35] Tac. *Ann.* 15.45.6, 60.3.

[36] Tac. *Ann.* 15.60.4–61.5. On Seneca's involvement in the plot, Griffin (1974), 25–28. Tacitus knew of reports that, had the conspiracy succeeded, Piso would have been eliminated and Seneca made emperor (*Ann.* 15.65.1).

[37] E.g., *B.V.* 7.3 *tota vita discendum est mori*, *Epist.* 26.4–6 *ille laturus sententiam de omnibus annis meis dies*, etc., 70.6, 77.20 *quomodo fabula, sic vita . . . quocumque voles desine; tantum bonam clausulam impone.*

[38] Tac. *Ann.* 15.62–63.

[39] Ancient testimony is collected by W. Trillitzsch, *Seneca im literarischen Urteil der Antike* (Amsterdam, 1971; 2 vols.); see also Griffin (1976), 427–44; on views of Seneca's style see below, p. 22.

He inspired loyalty and devotion in those closest to him,[40] and both his
writing and his manners were highly attractive to his contemporaries.[41] In
one respect even his severest critics have had to acknowledge him as a
master: no satirist ever brought a sharper eye to the exposure of vice and
folly.[42] Yet many have been repelled by his apparent readiness to compromise his principles, by his scandalous wealth, and by his service to a vicious
emperor. It may be that, for all his admissions of failure and imperfections,
Seneca was too confident of his virtue and too willing to believe in the
wisdom of his actions fully to recognize the ambiguities of his position. One
is even tempted to wonder if the character of Thyestes in this play, whose
aspirations to a life of withdrawal and simplicity are not strong enough to
withstand the attractions of power, may in some measure represent what
Seneca knew, or feared, about himself.[43] The contradictions remain, however they may be accounted for, but these traces of weakness are also part
of Seneca's curious appeal, since they suggest, behind the confident pose of
the sage and preacher, the more sympathetic figure of a fallible and
uncertain human being.

B. SENECA'S TRAGEDIES

THE CORPUS OF SENECAN TRAGEDY

The plays attributed to Seneca are preserved in two forms, corresponding to the two main classes of the manuscript tradition (below, pp.
36–37). One branch (called "E") contains nine plays, in the following
order: *Hercules [Furens], Troades, Phoenissae, Medea, Phaedra, Oedipus, Agamemnon, Thyestes, Hercules [Oetaeus]*.[44] The other (known as
"A") has ten plays, the nine found in E plus the historical tragedy
Octavia. The A branch also presents the plays in a different order and in
some cases with different titles: *Hercules Furens, Thyestes, Thebais* [=
Phoenissae], *Hippolytus* [= *Phaedra*], *Oedipus, Troas* [= *Troades*],
Medea, Agamemnon, Octavia, Hercules Oetaeus. Modern editors gener-
ally follow the order and titles of E (while placing *Octavia* last); there is

---

[40] His wife Pompeia Paulina was prevented by Nero from dying with him, and lived on
laudabili in maritum memoria (Tac. *Ann.* 15.64.2); his posthumous supporters also
included the historian Fabius Rusticus and the author of the tragedy *Octavia* (on which
see below, p. 9). Juvenal expected no disagreement in asking *libera si dentur populo
suffragia, quis tam / perditus ut dubitet Senecam praeferre Neroni?* (8.211–12).

[41] The popularity of Seneca's style was deplored by Quintilian (10.1.125 *tum autem
solus hic fere in manibus adulescentium fuit*); cf. also Tacitus *Ann.* 13.3.2 *fuit illi viro
ingenium amoenum et temporis eius auribus accommodatum*. The best description of
Seneca's personal charm, a blend of rectitude and graciousness, emerges from Tacitus'
phrase *comitas honesta* (*Ann.* 13.2.2).

[42] Quint. 10.1.129 *in philosophia parum diligens, egregius tamen vitiorum insectator fuit*.

[43] See 446–70, 487.

[44] The first and last plays in E are simply titled *Hercules*.

no way of knowing if this reflects Seneca's own arrangement—or even whether he arranged his plays for publication as a body—, but the variant titles in A are obviously unauthentic,[45] and there is no reason to invest A's order with any more authority.

At various times doubts have been raised about the authenticity of several plays in the collection, but at present only the *Octavia* and the *Hercules Oetaeus* remain under serious suspicion. The two cases are quite different. Few scholars would now maintain Seneca's authorship of the *Octavia*; the case against it appears convincing both on external grounds (the play seems to allude to the circumstances of Nero's death in 68, when Seneca had been dead for three years) and also on grounds of style and form, which show more divergences from Senecan idiom than can be easily explained.[46] It was probably composed soon after Nero's death[47] by a writer under strong Senecan influence, who almost certainly never intended it to pass for a work of Seneca. By contrast there is no clear agreement about the *Hercules Oetaeus*. It reproduces the manner and form of Senecan tragedy much more closely than the *Octavia*, and even skeptics must admit that its style is at times indistinguishable from that of the genuine plays; on the other hand, it can hardly be a finished work of Seneca, not only because of its enormous length (1996 lines, as against a high of 1344 in the eight undisputed plays), but also because it echoes many Senecan phrases in an inept way—usually a strong indication of spuriousness.[48] It might be an inferior poet's elaboration of material that Seneca had begun to cast in dramatic form.[49]

---

[45] *Troas* and *Thebais* are impossible titles for tragedies (the latter possibly suggested by the title of Statius' epic), and *Hippolytus* is less satisfactory than *Phaedra* as an indication of that play's central focus. The defining epithets of the Hercules-plays, *Furens* and *Oetaeus*, may also be later accretions, required when the un-Senecan *Oetaeus* was added to the corpus (see next paragraph).

[46] See most recently M. E. Carbone, *Phoenix* 31 (1977), 48–67; C. J. Herington, *CHLL*, 530–32. It is fair to add, however, that Senecan authorship still finds supporters, for example in L. Y. Whitman's edition and commentary (Bern, 1978; reviewed by O. Zwierlein in *Gnomon* 52 [1980], 713–17).

[47] A more precise date (late in 68) is supported by T. D. Barnes, *Museum Helveticum* 39 (1982), 215–17; see also P. Kragelund, *Prophecy, Populism, and Propaganda in the Octavia* (Copenhagen, 1982), 49–52.

[48] Cf. W. H. Friedrich, "Sprache und Stil des *Hercules Oetaeus*," *Hermes* 82 (1954), 51–84, B. Axelson, *Korruptelenkult: Studien zur Textkritik der unechten Seneca-Tragödie "Hercules Oetaeus"* (Lund, 1967).

[49] The *Phoenissae* is anomalous for a different reason: it lacks choral odes and looks more like a set of independent dramatic episodes than a conventional drama, even an incomplete one, cf. *HSCP* 82 (1978), 229–30.

DATING OF THE TRAGEDIES[50]

Although many of Seneca's works cannot be dated with precision, this problem is particularly acute in the case of the tragedies: in the absence of firm evidence, scholars have placed some or all of them in every phase of Seneca's career, from his youth to the final years of retirement. Seneca makes no reference to the plays in his prose works, one of several examples of a disjunction between his philosophical writing and other sectors of his life. Other ancient writers are hardly more informative: the first explicit reference to a Senecan play is in Quintilian (9.2.8, quoting *Medea* 453), the next a century later in the grammarian Terentianus Maurus.[51] The plays do not overtly mention contemporary persons or events; veiled topical allusions have often been suggested, but no dating based on them has won general acceptance.[52] In short, there are no securely attested facts to serve as points of reference; all arguments are to some extent speculative, and the best that a discussion can hope to achieve is not proof, but plausibility.

The most reliable inferences are perhaps those based on imitations of Senecan tragedy in other works of Latin literature. The similarities between the plays and Lucan's *De bello civili*, for example, are too close and too numerous to be the result of coincidence, and in many places Lucan has clearly been influenced by Seneca rather than vice-versa.[53] It seems reasonable to conclude that all of Seneca's plays were written before Lucan began work on his epic, which was probably not earlier than 60 and not later than early 63.[54] Evidence of this kind also produces a terminus for one play: Seneca's own *Apocolocyntosis*, written shortly after Claudius' death in October 54, contains what looks like a deliberate echo and parody of the *Hercules Furens*.[55]

---

[50] The most recent discussion, in Fantham, 9–14, is also one of the fullest and most balanced; among earlier treatments note M. Coffey, *Lustrum* 2 (1957), 149–51, my edition of *Agamemnon* (Cambridge, 1976), 6–7 (dogmatically sceptical).

[51] This and other *testimonia* are registered in the editions of R. Peiper and G. Richter (Teubner [Leipzig], 1902), xxiv–xxx, and G. Viansino (Paravia [Turin], 1965), v. 1, 103–6.

[52] The leading proponent of this approach has been O. Herzog, in *RhM* 77 (1928), 51–104; for criticism, see Coffey, 150, Fantham, 13–14 (although she accepts the reference to the *lusus Troiae* in *Tro.* 777–79 as yielding a *terminus post quem* of 47 for *Troades*). E. Lefèvre (*ANRW*, forthcoming) has argued that the *Oedipus* alludes to Nero's murder of Agrippina. For a possible contemporary reference in *Thyestes* see note on 629–30.

[53] Cf. C. Hosius, "Seneca und Lucan," *NJb* 145 (1892), 337–56. For instances in *Thyestes* cf. notes on, e.g., 358–59, 370, 574–75. See also Zwierlein, *Prolegomena*, 246–48.

[54] The chronology of Lucan's writings raises problems that cannot be pursued here; on the whole I follow the judicious conclusions of F. M. Ahl, *Lucan* (Ithaca, 1976), 41–42, 343 n. 13, 352–53.

[55] Cf. O. Weinreich, *Senecas Apocolocyntosis* (Berlin, 1923), 62, 112. The most striking verbal parallel is perhaps *Apoc.* 12.3.3 *resonet tristi clamore forum* and *HF* 1108 *resonet maesto clamore chaos*. (The mock-dirge of the *Apocolocyntosis* also resembles the *kommos*

No other play can be assigned a precise *terminus ante quem* in this way; it would therefore be very useful to know the place of *HF* in the order of composition.[56] Attempts to arrive at a relative chronology on the basis of shared themes, phrasing, and verse technique have been generally unproductive,[57] but a recent study by J. G. Fitch may represent a breakthrough.[58] Fitch has calculated for each play the percentage of strong sense-pauses occurring within the line rather than at line-end: the degree of variation extends from a minimum of 32.4% in *Agamemnon* to a maximum of 57.2% in *Phoenissae*. On the assumption (true for Sophocles and Shakespeare) that higher percentages reflect greater flexibility in handling the verse-form and therefore later date, the plays break down into three groups: I *Agamemnon* (32.4), *Phaedra* (34.4), and *Oedipus* (36.8); II *Medea* (47.2), *Troades* (47.6), and *HF* (49.0); III *Thyestes* (54.5) and *Phoenissae* (57.2). This classification coincides nicely with groupings suggested by common elements of dramatic technique[59] or metrical practice;[60] one detail of meter in particular lends striking support to part of Fitch's division. Poets of the first century A.D. became progressively freer in shortening the final *o* in certain classes of words, including nouns of the third declension, adverbs like *aliquando*, and the first person singular forms of verbs in the present and future tenses.[61] What had not been previously noticed is that Seneca's practice in this regard differs significantly in *Thyestes* and *Phoenissae* from that seen in the other six plays, showing a marked preference for the shortened forms, especially in first person singular verbs.[62] This shift in technique strongly suggests that *Thyestes* and *Phoenissae* were Seneca's last plays, and also that some time intervened between their composition and that of the other six tragedies.

---

of Hecuba and the Trojan chorus in *Troades*.) A similar argument could be made concerning *Agamemnon* and the first Einsiedeln Eclogue, written in the first years of Nero's reign, but the verbal parallels are not decisive (cf. *Ag.* 330–41 and *Ecl. Eins.* 1.22–33).

56 The order of plays in the two branches of the manuscript tradition (on which see above, p. 8) seems to bear no relation to their chronological sequence; compare the *Dialogi*, where the earliest work, the *Cons. Marc.*, is in the middle of the collection.

57 Fantham 12–13. Fantham has herself attempted to show that *Agamemnon* follows *Troades* (*CJ* 77 [1981–82], 118–29), a conclusion at odds with the chronology tentatively adopted here.

58 *AJP* 102 (1981), 289–307.

59 For example, the plays of "Group I" account for eight of the nine places where a Chorus follows an ode with a transition to the next act (Fitch, 306); other instances in the notes on *Thy.* 107, introductory note to Act IV.

60 *Oedipus* and *Agamemnon* are the only plays containing polymetric choruses; if Fitch's theory is correct, this was a feature of Seneca's early plays that he soon abandoned.

61 The standard study is R. Hartenberger, *De o finali* (diss. Bonn, 1911).

62 Fitch, 303–5. The figures for *Thy.* and *Pho.* are 10 long/36 short and 5 long/42 short respectively; among the other six plays the greatest preponderance of shortened final *o* is in *Tro.*, with 8 long/12 short. The figures for first person singular verb forms are: *Ag.* 1, *Pha.* 4, *Oed.* 1, *Med.* 5, *Tro.* 2, *HF* 5, *Thy.* 18, *Pho.* 27.

If Fitch's relative chronology is accepted, the bulk of Seneca's work in tragedy was probably completed by 54, the latest date at which the *HF* can have been written. Nothing prevents placing the composition of all the plays some time before this date, perhaps during Seneca's years on Corsica, when by his own account he varied philosophical reflection with lighter pursuits.[63] There is in fact reason to believe that Seneca had acquired a name as a tragedian not long after his return from exile in 49. Quintilian recalls that as a raw youth (*iuvenis admodum*) he heard Seneca debating with Pomponius Secundus in *praefationes* over a nicety of tragic diction.[64] Quintilian would not have qualified as a *iuvenis* before 50, and since Pomponius was away in Germany for 50 and part of 51, the end of 51 is the earliest feasible date for the dispute. Seneca may therefore have been writing tragedies at this time, although that is not the only inference that could be drawn from Quintilian's testimony: it is also possible that Seneca was holding recitations of plays he had written while in exile but which had not yet been published in Rome, or even that his remarks on Pomponius were made incidentally during the introduction to a non-dramatic work. What does seem certain is that by the early 50s Seneca could disagree publicly with a well-known tragedian on a point of style and expect his views to be taken seriously; this suggests that Seneca was himself a dramatist of some standing at the time.

The result of the discussion so far is to show that no play of Seneca can be decisively dated after the accession of Nero in 54, and that there is instead good reason to place at least some of Seneca's dramatic activity before that date. There is, however, one item of evidence that might point in a different direction. In 62, when Tigellinus and others were blackening Seneca's name to Nero, one of their insinuations was that Seneca had started to turn out works of poetry (*carmina*) more frequently once Nero had conceived a liking for them.[65] In Tacitean usage *carmina* can denote dramatic poetry[66]—although the word could as easily refer to lyric or epigram—, and it has been suggested that the jibe of Seneca's detractors alludes to a late renewal of his interest in tragedy.[67] This idea could now be combined with Fitch's evidence for a

---

[63] *Cons. Helv.* 20.1, cf. above, p. 4. One could add that the works securely dated to the years of exile are quite few, especially in light of Seneca's obvious capacity for writing at great speed.

[64] Quint 8.3.31 *nam memini iuvenis admodum inter Pomponium ac Senecam etiam praefationibus esse tractatum an 'gradus eliminat' in tragoedia dici oportuisset*; discussion in C. Cichorius, *Römische Studien* (Leipzig, 1922), 426–29. The *praefationes* referred to are the remarks made by the author or performer before the recitation of a new literary work. (See below, p. 13.)

[65] Tac. *Ann.* 14.52.3 *obiciebant etiam . . . carmina crebius factitare, postquam Neroni amor eorum venisset*.

[66] Cf. *Ann.* 11.13.1 of Pomponius Secundus: *is carmina scaenae dabat*.

[67] So (with due caution) C. J. Herington in *CHLL*, 871.

break between Seneca's first six plays and *Thyestes* and *Phoenissae* to produce an approximate date of 60–62 for the last two plays. The hypothesis is no more than possible, but there is an undeniable fascination in the thought that *Thyestes*, which contains Seneca's most harrowing depiction of pathological tyranny, might have been composed toward the end of his days in the court of Nero.[68]

PERFORMANCE[69]

The Athenian dramatists of the fifth century B.C. composed their plays for public performance, on a specific occasion and usually under their own direction. In Rome the situation was quite different. It is true that the Romans, following the Hellenistic Greeks, classed tragedy with epic as the most prestigious of literary genres. The theater in Rome, however, never attained the high esteem it had enjoyed in Greece, and a close involvement with the stage would have been thought positively dishonorable for a Roman of high social standing. As a consequence, at least as early as the Augustan period some Roman writers seem to have composed tragedies without regard to stage performance: Ovid, for example, claimed never to have written for the theater (*Tr.* 5.7.27 *nil equidem feci, ut tu scis ipse, theatris*), which suggests that his *Medea* was not intended for theatrical production. The place of the theater was partially taken over by public recitations, at which an author or professional reader would deliver all or part of a new composition to an invited audience.[70] Recitation of a tragedy did not preclude stage performance: Seneca's contemporary Pomponius Secundus first sought his friends' opinion at a recitation, then tested their criticisms against the response of a wider public in the theater.[71] For other writers, though, like Curiatius Maternus as depicted in Tacitus' *Dialogus*, recitation seems to have been the only form of public performance expected or desired, providing an occasion to advertise new work and to solicit friendly criticism before releasing the text for publication.[72]

Where do Seneca's tragedies fit in this picture? No external evidence connects Seneca with the theater, whereas the young Quintilian heard him and Pomponius Secundus debate a point of tragic language in the introductory remarks before a recitation—not conclusive proof that the

---

68 The reference to the Alans in 629–30 might also support a date in the late 50s or early 60s; see note *ad loc.*

69 For more detailed discussion see Zwierlein, *Rezitationsdramen*; Fantham, 34–49.

70 The practice of recitation was introduced at Rome by Asinius Pollio, perhaps as early as the 30s B.C. (Sen. *Contr.* 4. *pr.* 2); the custom was quickly adopted by poets (cf. Ovid *Tr.* 4.10.57–58, recalling his first public readings in the mid-20s B.C.) and was well established for all genres of literature by the end of Augustus' life, cf. Suet. *Aug.* 89.

71 Pliny *Epist.* 7.17; cf. Fantham, 7.

72 *Dial.* 2.1–3.3.

tragedies were recited, but an indication that Seneca did use the recital-hall to bring new work before the public.[73]

The evidence of the plays themselves is more abundant, but harder to interpret.[74] Many scholars of the last century, following the lead of August Wilhelm Schlegel, held up what they saw as the plays' rhetorical excesses, lack of taste, and general artificiality as arguments against their having been written for the theater. Defenders of stage production have countered by pointing to the undeniable theatrical power of many Senecan scenes and by arguing that standards of taste and effectiveness derived from Attic tragedy may not be relevant to Roman drama of the first century A.D. The debate has grown more sophisticated,[75] but it has not been, and indeed cannot be, definitively settled: we simply know too little about what was or was not acceptable to theater audiences of Seneca's time to prove that his plays were not theatrically viable. It can be said, though, that Senecan drama shows a lack of concern for theatrical realities that goes considerably beyond what is attested for any phase of ancient stage-history. The setting can fluctuate without warning (as in *Troades*); absent characters appear at a moment's notice (e.g., Calchas in *Tro.* 351–53, Medea's children in *Med.* 843–45), and figures on stage just as abruptly vanish (e.g., Cerberus, who has a cameo part in *HF* 593–615, the Trojan chorus in *Agamemnon*); action that would be visible to a theater audience is elaborately narrated (e.g., the signs of Cassandra's possession in *Ag.* 710–19), while significant entrances and exits are reduced to dumb-shows by a shorthand style of description (e.g., Agamemnon's reception by Clytaemestra in *Ag.* 778–81, Pyrrhus' silent entrace and exit in *Tro.* 999–1003, the arrival of Hippolytus' body in *Phaedra*, only signalled by an offhand reference in 1158 *planctus . . . supra corpus invisum*[76]). Taken one by one, each of these features might be reconciled with the possibility of theatrical performance, and it should also be added that some plays pose fewer problems in this respect than others: *Thyestes*, for example, is much more traditional in its dramatic technique, and potentially more effective

---

[73] Quint. 8.3.31; above, p. 12.

[74] Zwierlein, *Rezitationsdramen*, 9–11, gives a convenient survey of earlier views.

[75] Some recent views (in addition to Fantham's well-rounded discussion): E. Lefèvre, *Gnomon* 40 (1968), 782–89; B. Walker, *CP* 64 (1969), 183–87; W. M. Calder III, *CP* 70 (1975), 32–35; W. M. S. Russell, in *Papers of the Radio Literature Conference* (Durham, 1978), 1–26 (all supporting stage-production). In *HSCP* 82 (1978), 213–63, I have tried to relate Senecan dramaturgy to theatrical developments between the fifth century and his own time (without arguing that Seneca wrote for the theater); below, pp. 16–17.

[76] Far more serious dramatic inconsistencies have been found in this scene, e.g., by Zwierlein (*Rezitationsdramen*, 13–23); it does look as though an actable staging can be worked out only by convicting Seneca either of loose writing (if *ab altis tectis* 1154 means "from the lofty palace" and not the expected "from the rooftop") or else of poor management of stage-space (if Phaedra laments over Hippolytus' body while pointlessly standing on the palace roof).

as a stage-play, than, say, *Troades* or *Phaedra*. On the whole, though, I think it probable that Seneca conceived his plays without regard for the restraints of theatrical production.[77]

In her recent discussion of this question, Elaine Fantham has noted that some aspects of Senecan dramaturgy which point away from the theater—for example, the frequent absence of textual cues to identify speakers—would also cause difficulty for a recitalist; she also stresses the problems a single performer would face in rendering passages of rapid dialogue (such as, e.g., *Thy.* 257–59). Our almost complete ignorance of recitation procedure makes these objections hard to assess, but they do not seem insurmountable. A reader might, for example, have prefaced each scene with the names of the speaking characters in it, and a skilled performer could surely distinguish various characters by changes of voice-quality and delivery. Some passages would admittedly lack the impact that a second or third voice could provide, but this limitation is inherent in the nature of recitation and must therefore have been accepted by the Roman writers and audiences who made this such a popular form of literary entertainment.[78]

But to pose the question exclusively in terms of theatrical performance vs. recitation is to obscure an essential fact. Whatever form of public exposure Seneca may have planned for his tragedies could only have been the beginning of their career, a preliminary to the ultimate goal of publication.[79] Most of Seneca's contemporaries would have encountered the plays as texts for reading—not, though, for silent perusal, for it should be recalled that "throughout antiquity books were written to be read aloud, and that even private reading often took on some of the characteristics of a modulated declamation."[80] Perhaps only in those private performances could ancient readers—or their modern counterparts—appreciate the language of Senecan drama in all its intricate richness.

---

[77] This is not to deny the possibility that the plays *were* acted in Seneca's lifetime, perhaps for small audiences in great private houses or at court (as suggested by W. M. Calder III, *CP* 70 [1975], 32–35).

[78] See Fantham, 240–41 (arguing that Seneca wrote with recitation in mind); elsewhere (48) she tentatively suggests that Seneca read only selected passages of the plays, or else gave dramatic readings in cooperation with others. Both ideas have their attractions but also their difficulties: there is no evidence for recitation by more than one reader (as Fantham notes, 47), and on her own showing this division of roles would not remove all the awkwardnesses of a recited performance; on the other hand, a recitation that omitted rapid exchanges of dialogue like *Med.* 158–73 or *Thy.* 248–60 would deprive the plays of some of their most sensational and effective passages.

[79] A point well stressed by Fantham, 48–49.

[80] E. J. Kenney in *CHLL*, 11.

BACKGROUNDS TO SENECAN TRAGEDY

Seneca's position as the only Roman tragedian whose works have survived complete has often caused his plays to be interpreted exclusively as Roman equivalents of classical Greek tragedy. Even when such comparisons are made without prejudice, they can give only a partial impression of Senecan drama's peculiar character, since they neglect the important non-theatrical elements in Seneca's background: his rhetorical training, his philosophical interests, and his profound familiarity with Augustan poetry. The following pages try to show briefly what each of these has contributed to the unique amalgam that is Senecan tragedy.

The Dramatic Tradition

A Roman writing in the middle of the first century A.D. could look back on half a millennium of tragic drama, from the "classical" period of Greek tragedy in the fifth century B.C., dominated then as now by the figures of Aeschylus, Sophocles, and Euripides, to the development of Roman tragedy under their influence in the second and first centuries B.C., and finally to the mature Roman tragedy of the Augustan period. Just how much Seneca knew of these earlier phases of dramatic history and in what ways they shaped his own approach to tragedy are still matters of dispute.[81] Seneca's prose works reveal only a limited and superficial acquaintance with earlier drama, but this might be simply one more way in which Seneca's moral writing fails to disclose the full range of his knowledge or interests. On the evidence of the plays themselves, most scholars today believe that Seneca had read widely in both Greek and Roman tragedy and that his use of his predecessors was eclectic and independent.

Certainly Seneca's tragedies are not translations or even free adaptations of Greek models, like the comedies of Plautus and Terence or the tragedies written in the Republican period by Ennius, Pacuvius, and Accius. Seneca looked to the Greek classics for plots, characters, and general notions of dramatic treatment, but in the writing of individual scenes and even in larger matters of structure and organization his plays are essentially original compositions.

In particular Seneca's ideas of dramatic form do not derive immediately from classical Greek tragedy.[82] On a number of points Senecan dramatic technique is closer to that of fourth-century New Comedy than

---

[81] Short discussion and bibliography in my edition of *Agamemnon*, 8–14. I have modified some of the views expressed there, partly in response to the criticism of C. J. Herington, *Phoenix* 32 (1978), 270–75. Fantham, 3–9, offers a brief survey of Roman tragedy up to and including Seneca's time.

[82] This and the following paragraph summarize arguments elaborated in *HSCP* 82 (1978), 213–63.

to the practice of fifth-century tragedy; not because Seneca was directly influenced by Comedy, but because Comedy, being better preserved than the tragedy of the same period, reveals the direction in which both forms were evolving in the fourth and third centuries B.C. The most obvious of these features is the five-act structure that Senecan tragedy usually observes, a Hellenistic canon of form prescribed by Horace in his *Ars Poetica* (189–90) and shown by papyrus discoveries to have been standard in the comedies of Menander. This stricter concept of dramatic structure coincides with a change in the use of the Chorus: in Seneca the Chorus retains some vestiges of its former role as an actor—it takes part in dialogue if there is no second actor to do so, as in Act IV of *Thyestes* (623-788)—, but on the whole its function is confined to dividing the acts by choral odes, and Seneca often seems to treat it as absent during the dialogue portions, like the interlude-chorus of New Comedy. The parallel with Comedy also includes some stage conventions, such as the extended aside (cf. *Thy.* 491–507) and the monologue by an entering character which is not heard by others on stage and so can be considered almost a soliloquy (cf. *Thy.* 404–20, 423–28).

Seneca probably encountered these and other post-classical elements of dramatic technique in the work of earlier Roman tragedians, either Republican or Augustan. In some respects, though, the form of Senecan tragedy bears an unmistakable post-Augustan stamp. The debt of the Augustans is clearest in the area of meter: Seneca's dialogue meter is the iambic trimeter of Ovid and Varius, not the looser *senarius* of Republican drama, and many of his choral lyrics are drawn from the *Odes* of Horace. (See below, pp. 31–32). Seneca may well have known and occasionally imitated the work of the Republican dramatists—he can hardly have failed to appreciate the rhetorical vigor of Accius—, but it seems likely that the Augustans decisively influenced his notions of how a tragedy should look and sound.

Augustan Poetry[83]

The part played by Ovid, Varius, and their contemporaries in shaping Seneca's ideas of tragedy was only one of the ways in which Augustan

---

[83] The links between Senecan tragedy and Augustan poetry have never been systematically explored, and almost all existing discussions are narrowly focused and uncritical in method. These include: B. ter Haar Romeny, *De auctore tragoediarum quae sub Senecae nomine feruntur, Vergilii imitatore* (diss. Leiden, 1877), J. Spika, *De imitatione Horatiana in Senecae canticis chori* (Programmrede, Vienna, 1890), H. L. Cleasby, *De Seneca tragico Ovidii imitatore* (diss. Harvard, 1907), J. Charlier, *Ovide et Sénèque. Contributions à l'étude de l'influence d'Ovide sur les tragédies de Sénèque* (diss. Brussels, 1954), C. K. Kapnukajas, *Die Nachahmungstechnik Senecas in den Chorliedern des Hercules Furens und der Medea* (diss. Leipzig, 1930), R. B. Steele, "Some Roman Elements in the Tragedies of Seneca," *AJP* 43 (1922), esp. 15–23.

poetry affected his work. Seneca's memory was filled with phrases and lines from Vergil, Horace, and Ovid, and the influence exerted on him by these Roman "classics" was deep and pervasive. The Augustans, though, offered Seneca much more than a quarry of poetic diction and phraseology. A more general debt to Augustan epic—to the *Aeneid* and the *Metamorphoses*—can be seen in the narrative passages in which Senecan drama so notably abounds; in extended reports such as the great storm in *Agamemnon* (421–578) or Hercules' journey to the underworld in *HF* (658–829), and also in curiously full descriptions of on-stage action such as *Med.* 382–90 or *Ag.* 710–19. When Seneca's characters denounce extravagance and luxury or praise the simple life, they regularly do so in images taken from Horace's *Odes*;[84] Horatian coloring is especially strong in the choral lyrics, where it is often heightened by metrical similarity. Augustan poetry also provided models of characterization: Seneca's portrayals of emotionally divided characters draw repeatedly on Vergil's depiction of Dido in *Aeneid* IV[85] and also on the passionate women of Ovid's *Heroides* and *Metamorphoses*,[86] and Ovid's story of Procne and Tereus (*Met.* 6.424–674, especially 609–66) contributed much to Seneca's treatment of Atreus' revenge—in fact, Seneca goes so far as to make Atreus himself seem aware of the parallel (cf. 272–77).

Seneca's verbal borrowings from Augustan poetry are of several kinds. Many isolated verbal echoes were probably not meant to be noticed by an audience, and indeed Seneca himself may not have been aware of them as borrowings. An example of this sort of fleeting echo is Tantalus' question *in quod malum transcribor?* (13), which resembles a line of Ovid's *Ibis* (187) where *transcribere* is used of "re-assigning" the punishments of notorious underworld figures.[87] In a number of places, though, Seneca alludes to his Augustan predecessors in a way that seems to invite comparison. When the Fury prays that Tantalid children "die evilly and be still more wickedly born" (*liberi pereant male, / peius tamen nascantur*, 41–42), her words carry added force for the reader or listener who recognizes them as Seneca's "capping" of Manilius' epigram on the children of Medea, *male conceptos partus peiusque necatos* (3.13); similarly, Atreus' prediction that dire poverty will overcome Thyestes' reluctance to return home, *egestas tristis ac durus labor / . . . subigent virum* (303–304), will only make its full impact if it is seen as a knowing adaptation of a famous line from the *Georgics: labor omnia vicit / improbus et duris urgens in rebus egestas* (1.145–46).[88]

---

[84] See notes on, e.g., *Thy.* 350–57, 452, *Ag.* 96, 105.

[85] E. Fantham, *Greece and Rome* 22 (1975), 1–10.

[86] Some references in Costa's notes on *Med.* 863–65, 926ff., 939ff., Fantham on *Tro.* 642–62, my notes on *Ag.* 132ff., *HSCP* 82 (1978), 262–63.

[87] For other examples see notes on 66–67, 80, 152, 173, 337, 567–71, 655–56.

[88] See also notes on, e.g., 104, 117–18, 144, 319, 399, 707–11, 865–66, 1010 and below,

Sometimes the relationship between Seneca's text and an Augustan model is yet more complex: not only is the allusion meant to be observed, but the differences of tone or point of reference between the original and Seneca's revision are an integral part of Seneca's meaning.[89] The most telling example in *Thyestes* comes at the start of the Messenger's report (641–64), where the palace of Atreus is described in terms clearly meant to recall the palace-temple of Latinus in *Aeneid* 7.170–91—except that what, in Vergil was a symbol of benign and venerable authority appears in Seneca as a monument to crime and tyranny. Once the connection is noticed, and once a reader or listener recalls that Vergil's account was seen as a tacit allusion to Augustus' palace on the Palatine, it is hard not to infer that Seneca too is making an implicit comment on contemporary Rome, and that his evocation of Vergil bitterly points up the gap between Augustan ideals and the imperial realities of his own time.[90]

Declamation Oratory[91]

Near the end of the Republican era, an important change was taking place in the Roman system of education. It had for some time been the practice for young men, after learning the basics of reading and writing and spending several years in the study of Greek and Latin literature, to complete their formal schooling with a training in rhetoric. The rhetorical education of Cicero's time was essentially practical, aimed at developing the skills needed for effective speaking in a courtroom or deliberative assembly; it included exercises in arguing general propositions, or "theses" (e.g., "should a man marry?" or "is it ever right to tell a lie?"), and others based on actual or invented situations from law, history, or mythology (sometimes called *causae*), but these were considered merely preliminary to the true practice of oratory, which required direct experience of the conditions of public speaking. The shift of emphasis which took hold in the early Augustan period and which remained dominant for several generations thereafter entailed a narrowing of the range of

p. 21, for similar adaptation of language from declamatory sources (note too Sen. *Contr* 2.2.8, *Suas*. 3.4–7, 6.27 for instances of conscious imitation of earlier writers).

[89] This style of "intertextual" or allusive reading is well established in current criticism of Latin poetry from Catullus to Ovid; for example, it informs much of D. O. Ross, Jr.'s book *Backgrounds to Augustan Poetry: Gallus, Elegy, and Rome* (Cambridge, 1975), and for a recent specimen of the approach cf. R. F. Thomas, "Catullus and the Polemics of Poetic Reference," *AJP* 103 (1982), 144–64. Its revelance to post-Augustan literature has not been overlooked (Lucan's inverted references to the *Aeneid* being an obvious instance), but much remains to be done.

[90] See notes *ad loc*. and for other examples see on 40–45, 369–79, 958, 134, 252–53, 269–70, 409–10, 804–12.

[91] The standard treatment is S. F. Bonner, *Roman Declamation* (Berkeley, 1949), which may now be complemented by D. A. Russell, *Greek Declamation* (Cambridge, 1983).

techniques and a more "scholastic" approach; becoming more and more
detached from the realities of courtroom or Senate, it cultivated fluency
and cleverness to the detriment of solid argument, genuine persuasive-
ness, or simple common sense. Two forms of exercise claimed the bulk of
the student's attention: the *controversia*, or invented legal case about
which arguments were to be constructed for both prosecution and
defense, and the *suasoria*, in which a figure of history or mythology was
given advice for or against a particular course of action (e.g., "should the
Spartans at Thermopylae retreat?" or "should Cicero save his life by
burning his speeches against Antony?"). The cases chosen for *controversiae* showed a marked preference for the unlikely and the lurid,
being largely populated by disinherited children, rapists, and pirates in
dizzying combinations.[92] In both *controversia* and *suasoria* the search
for novelty led to ever greater extremes of contrivance and forced subtlety; these tendencies were aggravated by the public character of
declamatory exhibitions, at which leading practitioners would vie for the
applause of the assembled students and guests.

The effects of declamatory training on Latin literature can be seen
as early as Ovid, who was himself a skilled performer in the *suasoria*,
but they are perhaps nowhere more evident than in the writings of
Seneca and his father. The elder Seneca arrived in Rome in the late 40s
B.C., just as the new rhetorical style was gaining acceptance, and came
immediately under its spell; seventy years later, he drew on his prodigious memory and his unquenchable zest for the form to compile an
invaluable collection of *controversiae* and *suasoriae*, packed with substantial citations from scores of declaimers and punctuated by his own
pithy and sometimes penetrating criticisms. The work was carefully
studied by his son Lucius, and this encyclopaedic knowledge of declamation can only have strengthened the impact that his own rhetorical education had made on his style.

Seneca's declamatory background reveals itself in several ways. The
most obvious is near-verbatim borrowing of *mots* from his father's collection, often with an attempt to improve on the original.[93] The
declaimer-poet Cornelius Severus had tried to capture the mood of soldiers on the eve of battle, enjoying what might be their last meal:
"stretched out on the grass, they said 'this day is mine,'" *hic meus
est . . . dies* (i.e., this day at least belongs to me, whatever tomorrow

---

[92] A particularly choice specimen (*Contr.* 1.7): "The Tyrannicide the Pirates Let Go. [Chil-
dren must support their parents, or be imprisoned.] A man killed one of his brothers, a tyrant.
The other brother he caught in adultery and killed despite the pleas of his father. Captured
by pirates, he wrote to his father about a ransom. The father wrote a letter to the pirates,
saying that he would give double if they cut off his hands. The pirates let him go. The father
is in need; the son is not supporting him." (Winterbottom's translation.)

[93] Cf. Leo, *Obs.*, 152–53, *Ag.* 35–36 (n).

may bring; *Suas.* 2.12). Seneca turned this rather lame epigram to a much more interesting purpose in his *Medea,* where the title character has been given a day's grace before going into exile and takes the opportunity to destroy her husband's new wife and to kill her own two children. As she prepares to murder the second child, she urges herself to enjoy her revenge to the full, without haste: *meus dies est, tempore accepto utimur* (1017). For the reader or listener who caught the allusion, the bold twist given to Severus' phrase would deepen the chilling impact of Medea's words.

A more general legacy of declamation, and one that Seneca shares with many other writers of the Empire, is an attraction to certain moralizing themes (called *loci communes* or "commonplaces"), such as the caprice of Fortune or the anxieties of city life;[94] Thyestes' praise of poverty in Act III (446–70) is clearly indebted to this practice. Seneca also shows the influence of another form of declamatory set-piece, the extended description of a scene; a storm, for example, or a lavish palace, a tyrant's torture-chamber or a drunken orgy.[95] The prominence given these genre-scenes helps to account for the length of the *descriptiones* in Seneca's messenger-speeches, of which *Thy.* 641–82 is an outstanding example.[96]

The most important effect of declamation oratory on Seneca, though, is stylistic. The declaimer often had to address themes that had become threadbare from repeated handling, to catch and hold the attention of an experienced or even jaded audience. As a result, the declamatory style was noted above all for its frequent and sharply pointed epigrams, or *sententiae*. A *sententia* need not be a gnomic statement, although many *sententiae* were in generalizing form, like Atreus' pronouncement that "you only avenge crimes by outdoing them" (*scelera non ulcisceris, / nisi vincis, Thy.* 195–96). The essential element is an arresting use of language, often with a paradoxical shift of meaning or a parallelism that couples ideas not normally combined. Examples can be found in almost every Latin writer of the Empire. There is Ovid's Narcissus who, when he discovers he is in love with his own reflection, utters "an unprecedented wish for a lover—I wish that I and my beloved were apart" (*Met.* 3.467 *votum in amante novum—vellem quod amamus abesset*); or Lucan's description of Rome under the Triumvirs as "a condominium with three owners" (1.85 *facta tribus dominis communis Roma*); or Juvenal's way of asserting the security of the poor, "the empty-handed traveler can whistle in the robber's face" (10.22 *cantabit vacuus coram latrone viator*); or Tacitus' summing-up of the emperor Galba, "no one would have doubted his ability

94 Bonner, 60–62.
95 Bonner, 58–60.
96 Note also, for example, the enormous storm-narrative in *Ag.* 421–578 (the centerpiece of the play in more than one sense) and the underworld-description in *HF* 658–829.

to rule, had he never been emperor" (*Hist.* 1.49.4 *omnium consensu capax imperii, nisi imperasset*). As for Seneca, every page of his prose works could supply instances. Two almost at random: the account of mid-day gladiatorial games in *Epist.* 7.3, introduced with the remark "all the previous [i.e., morning] combats were acts of mercy" (*quidquid ante pugnatum est, misericordia fuit*; cf. *Med.* 903–904, *Thy.* 744–45), and the delightfully apt comment on Cicero's praise of his consulship—"not without cause, but without end" (*non sine causa, sed sine fine, BV* 5.1).

The declamatory element in Seneca's writing has been largely responsible for the loss of favor he has suffered in the last century; in particular it lies behind the dismissive characterization of his work as "rhetorical." To an extent these negative reactions may be justified. Seneca's fondness for pointed *sententiae* can give his prose a static, disjointed quality (Caligula's "sand without lime"), and his strokes of verbal brilliance, at first invigorating, can become wearisome through sheer abundance (hence Macaulay's remark that reading Seneca in large quantities was "like living on nothing but anchovy sauce").[97]

Like Ovid, Seneca was often unable or unwilling to restrain his extraordinary cleverness, but, again like Ovid, he could use his rhetorical skill with greater subtlety than he is usually given credit for. His tragic style fully exploits the *sententia*'s capabilities as a structural device, varying the pace of long speeches and siting the strongest epigrams for maximum effect. In *Thyestes* he goes still further, and makes the contrast between Atreus' and Thyestes' use of the pointed style an indicator of the differences in their temperaments.[98]

Stoic Philosophy[99]

Seneca's prose works contain not the slightest hint that he was also a tragedian. The reverse, however, is not true: the tragedies are unmistakably the work of a writer imbued with Seneca's particular philosophical

[97] "Essay on Bacon" (1836), quoted in W. C. Summers's Macmillan edition of *Select Letters* (London, 1910), cxii. I relegate to the decent obscurity of a footnote the more pungent verdict of Dr. Kettel, a seventeenth-century President of Trinity College, Oxford, who, according to John Aubrey, "was wont to say that Seneca writes as a Boare does pisse, *scilicet* by jirkes." It is interesting that attacks on Seneca's style from Caligula onwards have been couched in vivid metaphors of which Seneca himself might have strongly approved.

[98] Below, 44–45.

[99] For other brief treatments and surveys of earlier work see Fantham, 15–24; N. T. Pratt, *Seneca's Drama* (Chapel Hill, 1983), 73–81; M. Coffey, *Lustrum* 2 (1958), 151–60 (especially useful on German scholarship 1925–1955). [Add now E. Lefèvre, "Die philosophische Bedeutung der Seneca-Tragödie am Beispiel des 'Thyestes'," *ANRW* II.32.1 (due to appear in 1985).] The most accessible discussions of Stoic doctrine in English are J. M. Rist, *Stoic Philosophy* (Cambridge, 1969); F. H. Sandbach, *The Stoics* (London, 1975); and Pratt, *op. cit.*, 35–72.

outlook. The importance of philosophy in Senecan drama has long been acknowledged, though described in very different ways: in the last forty years the plays have been analyzed both as a systematic exposition of Stoic doctrine and as an indictment of Stoicism's failure to account for the world as it is.[100] Philosophical readings of the tragedies, whatever their direction, have often been reductive, slighting the plays' poetic elements and taking too little account of Seneca's exuberant philosophical eclecticism. It may be more useful to speak of basic concerns common to the dramatist and the philosopher.

For Seneca, philosophy was essentially a moral rather than a metaphysical pursuit. Its object was to show human beings the way to live, to insulate them from the disturbances of the world outside and the still more threatening forces within them, and above all to teach them to accept and even to welcome their inevitable death. Ethical concerns are also at the heart of Senecan drama: a chorus of the *Oedipus* may describe destiny in orthodox Stoic terms as "an intertwined chain of causes" (*quae nexa suis currunt causis*, 990), and the last ode of the *Thyestes* may picture the end of the world as postulated by Stoic physics (830-74), but it is in their attitudes to human behavior that the tragedies most clearly show the imprint of Seneca's version of Stoicism.

The central issue of Senecan moral philosophy is the control of the passions (*affectus*) and the attainment of inner peace through rational conformity with nature; this emotional control allows those who possess it to confront all misfortune with courage and equanimity. But although Seneca has left several impressive descriptions of the Stoic ideal or *sapiens*, the bulk of his moral writing is concerned with those who in various ways fall short of that goal. Seneca has few rivals, ancient or modern, in the observation of neurosis—of the divisive and crippling effects of desire, fear, and above all anger, the most destructive of the passions and the subject of Seneca's most extended study of emotional pathology, the treatise *De ira*.[101]

This fascination with the dark corners of the psyche is also evident in Senecan tragedy; the opportunity to portray human beings under extreme emotional pressure may in fact have been tragedy's strongest attraction for Seneca. In any event he takes full advantage of drama's potential for exploring psychological conflict. There is, of course, nothing specifically Stoic in depicting the struggle of reason and passion; this is a leading theme both in Euripides and in the two greatest works of Augustan literature, the

---

[100] The approaches, respectively, of B. Marti, "Seneca's Tragedies: A New Interpretation," *TAPA* 76 (1945), 216-45, and J. Dingel, *Seneca und die Dichtung* (Heidelberg, 1974).

[101] For parallels between the analysis of *ira* in this treatise and Seneca's dramatic portrayal of passion, see notes on 190-91, 267-86, 268, 283-84; also K. Trabert, *Studien zur Darstellung des Pathologischen in den Tragödien des Seneca* (diss. Erlangen, 1953).

Aeneid and the *Metamorphoses*. What Stoicism contributed to Seneca's handling of the issue was a greater precision of psychological analysis and an enlarged conception of passion's destructive capability. His characters' souls are anatomized in a detail never before attempted, not even by Ovid or Euripides; as they agonize over a fateful decision they are shown, as it were, in slow motion, and allowed to note the symptoms of their condition with clinical exactness.[102] Seneca's choice of characters also shows a strong predilection for the deviant. The *sapiens* is glimpsed only at a distance, in an off-stage figure like Astyanax in *Troades* or in passages of choral lyric (cf., e.g., *Thy.* 348–90, a reflection on the Stoic concept of the *sapiens* as true king). For his central figures, Seneca turns to the interesting failure or the complex maladjustment. He devotes special attention to divided characters, people with some claim to virtue or at least some stirrings of principle who must contend with the temptations of the world or of their own emotions.[103] In most cases the struggle ends in defeat: Phaedra is overcome by her untamed desires, Hippolytus by his refusal to accept adult sexuality, Clytaemestra by her weakness, Agamemnon (in *Troades*) and Theseus by their need to assert authority, Andromache by her attachment to her loved ones, Thyestes by his susceptibility to the rewards of power. Only Hercules in *HF*, after confronting the violent forces within himself and his still more devastating sense of guilt, arrives in the end at what seems to be a victory of survival.[104] A special place is occupied by two protagonists, Medea and Atreus, who represent what might be called a Stoic's nightmare, the human person fully under the control of the madness of *ira*. These figures act with a resolution and single-mindedness that make them perverted mirror-images of the *sapiens*, and just as the *sapiens* achieves a sort of divinity through perfect harmony with the divine order of the universe, so these characters concentrate into themselves a power of evil that is literally cosmic in its destructive effects.[105]

What was Seneca trying to accomplish with these portraits of disturbed and even deranged personalities? The most likely answer is that he was exploiting the emotional directness of dramatic poetry to make

---

[102] Cf. *Pha*. 177–85, *Ag*. 131–40, *Med*. 926–28, 939–44, *Tro*. 642–62, *Thy*. 267–86.

[103] In Stoic terms several of these characters might qualify as *proficientes* or "those making progress," i.e., toward wisdom. Seneca provides a typology of this class in *Epist.* 75.8–18; his description of the *secundum genus* (13 *qui et maxima mala et adfectus deposuerunt, sed ita ut non sit illis securitatis suae certa possessio; possunt enim in eadem relabi*) is especially appropriate to Thyestes, cf. Lefèvre (above, n. 99).

[104] Even this is not beyond dispute, cf. J. G. Fitch, *Hermes* 117 (1979), 240–48.

[105] "Literally cosmic" because Stoics thought of the universe as a single organism, all of which could be affected by a violent disturbance at any particular point. Ancient evidence on this doctrine (known as *sympatheia*) is collected in Pease's notes on Cic. *Div.* 2.34, *N.D.* 3.28; it was applied to the understanding of Senecan drama in an important article by Otto Regenbogen, "Schmerz und Tod in den Tragödien Senecas," *Vorträge der Bibliothek Warburg 1927/8*, 167–218 (= *Kleine Schriften* [Munich, 1961], 411–64.

his audiences feel the appalling consequences of passion, that the shock
and revulsion aroused by his most effective scenes were meant to be the
stimulus to moral awareness and growth.[106] This explanation may correspond with Seneca's own understanding of his motives, but it omits one
significant fact. Seneca's most terrifyingly evil characters, Medea and
Atreus, are also his most memorable dramatic creations.[107] There is
something splendid about their energy and force of personality, shown
above all in their unflagging mastery of language; next to them their
victims, though morally more complex, seem pallid or contemptible. The
fascination exerted by powerful evil is a recurring phenomenon in literature (Lucan's Caesar and Milton's Satan are two of the better-known
instances); it is striking proof of the commonplace that a work of art can
never be fully accounted for by the artist's conscious intentions. Seneca's
Stoic convictions may have led him to probe the extremes of human
behavior, but his artistic response to that challenge contains more than
was dreamt of in his philosophy.[108]

STYLISTIC FEATURES

No comprehensive study of the style of Senecan tragedy has yet
been made,[109] and this would indeed be a formidable task, since
Seneca's tragic style does not lend itself to simple characterization. Despite Seneca's extensive debt to Ovid, for example, his poetry resembles
Ovid's hardly at all, except for a shared delight in brilliant elaboration of
ideas. Even Seneca's own prose makes a clearer and more distinct
impression than his dramatic poetry. The tendencies that dominate the
prose works—epigrammatic brevity, directness, lack of complex
subordination, use of colloquial language—can all be paralleled in the
tragedies, but there they form part of a richer and more complex
stylistic repertory. Seneca's tragic diction encompasses both high-flown
grandiosity reminiscent of Accius and also the plainest of everyday

[106] For Seneca's views on the moral value of poetry, cf. W. S. Maguinness, "Seneca and
the Poets," *Hermathena* 88 (1956), 81–98. This interpretation of Senecan drama has been
especially popular in German scholarship of the last half-century; see for example,
F. Egermann, "Seneca als Dichterphilosoph," *Neue Jahrbücher* 3 (1940), 18–36,
U. Knoche, "Senecas Atreus, Ein Beispiel," *Das Antike* 17 (1941), 60–76, and (with
greater sophistication) much of the work of Eckard Lefèvre.
[107] Fantham, 18.
[108] The sympathy that Seneca evokes for some emotionally disturbed characters (Phaedra,
for example) is another indication that his plays cannot be understood in narrowly moral-
istic terms.
[109] Seneca's use of tropes and figures has been exhaustively catalogued by Canter, and
there is much information on his syntax and morphology in Fantham, 92–103 (along with
some brief, but well-chosen remarks of a more general nature on pages 33–34); much of
Gordon Williams, *Change and Decline* (Berkeley, 1978), 213–32 is also relevant to Seneca.

speech, and his phrasing similarly ranges from near-periodic fullness to the clipped and even fragmentary.[110] Such extremes could be accommodated within a style that nonetheless gave an overall impression of consistency, but this does not appear to have been Seneca's aim; in many places it seems that jarring shifts in linguistic level are part of the intended effect. In Thyestes' last long speech, for example, the juxtaposition of the rolling period *tu, summe caeli rector . . . fulminibus exple* (1077–87) and the disjointed phrases that follow (*causa . . . mala sit mea* 1087–88) is as startling as the contrast between the grandiloquence of *trisulco flammeam telo facem / per pectus hoc transmitte* (1089–90) and the prosiness of the nearby *si minus* (1089) and *nil queror* (1095). The significance of these variations in particular passages is open to dispute,[111] but their presence is beyond question. At a more general level, Seneca's frequent use of pointed expressions (*sententiae*)[112] produces a comparable result. To be successful, a *sententia* must carry a higher verbal charge than the surrounding context and must to some extent take the audience by surprise. Seneca often heightens these effects by preceding *sententiae* with unpointed lead-in lines and following them with a new start at a lower level of intensity, thus increasing the listener's sense of discontinuity and inequality.[113]

Fluidity of linguistic level is one of several aspects of Senecan poetry which require a complex response from its audience. Another is Seneca's tendency to cross clear physical images with more abstract or conceptual[114] terms, as when Tantalus describes his punishment as that of "parched thirst" and "gaping hunger" (4–6 *siti / arente, fame / hiante*), with *sitis* and *fames* appearing instead of, e.g., *guttur* and *os*. Some of these passages mingle description and analysis, replacing an object or action with a term that points up its significance or result, e.g., 777 *merseris . . . diem* [= *solem*], 743 *per utrumque vulnus moritur* [= *sanguinem effundit*], 1044 *ferro liberis detur via* [= *ferro pectus reseretur*]. In others the speaker's emotions drive out purely descriptive language, as when Atreus uses *generis invisi indoles* to mean "Thyestes' children" (492) or when Thyestes refers to the flesh of his sons within his body as a *clusum nefas* struggling to get free (1041). Similar effects are produced when figurative and literal language are coupled in unexpected ways, e.g., 819–20 *fumantes . . . iubas mergere ponto* and

---

[110] For examples of these extremes see, e.g., 74–81, 225–35 versus 321.

[111] I have suggested that in this case the stylistic inconsistency underscores Thyestes' failure to control his situation; by contrast the sudden changes of level at 245–46 and 784–88 seem to reflect the speaker's full command of language.

[112] For definition and examples see above, pp. 21–22.

[113] See notes on 11–12, 192, 205, 417–20, 917–18, 1050, 1067. This feature of the *sententia* was pointed out by Quintilian: *subsistit omnis sententia ideoque post eam utique aliud est initium* (8.5.27).

[114] This useful term is Fantham's (34).

840-41 *vincet . . . sui / fratris habenas*, where the synecdoches *iuba* = *equus* and *habenae* = *currus* are thrown into bizarre prominence by the surrounding words.[115] On occasion both literal and non-literal senses are simultaneously present, in a form of *double entendre*. One of Atreus' most powerful lines is of this kind, when he pictures his revenge as *ingesta orbitas / in ora patris* (282–83); Atreus here anticipates both a physical act ("thrusting Thyestes' dead children into his mouth") and its psychological consequences ("hurling his childlessness in his face," cf. 890–91). (This is only one variety of *double entendre*, a device that Seneca often uses as a vehicle for irony, both conscious and unconscious, and which is largely responsible for the impression of density that his dramatic style creates.[116])

The product of these traits is a style that is paradoxically compressed yet ornate and elaborate, rich in sensory and emotive stimuli but often lacking in clear pictorial images.[117] For an audience it is a demanding, even a wearying style; only the occasional passage of choral lyric offers a respite from the relentless pressure, and these moments of relaxation (such as the end of the second chorus, 391–403) are as a result all the more welcome. For the troubled characters who populate Seneca's plays, however, this intense, restless, and discordant style is a natural medium of expression.

METER[118]

The basic metrical division in Senecan tragedy, as in its Greek antecedents, is between spoken ("dialogue") and sung ("lyric") sections. The lyric element comprises the choral odes and the occasional arias (or "monodies") sung by individual characters, such as Thyestes' drinking-song in the last act of this play (920–69). All other parts of the play are in dialogue meter.

Dialogue

The dialogue meter of Senecan drama is essentially that used by the Greek tragedians, with a number of differences in detail. It is based on

---

[115] See also notes on 787 *ab ortu*, 861 *pinnata . . . spicula*.

[116] For some examples see on 431–33, 928–33, 971–72, 982–83. The greatest concentration of *double entendres* is found in the first meeting of Atreus and Thyestes, where they function as a verbal sign of the uneasy relations of the brothers; cf. 510–11, 530–31, 535, 539, 544–45.

[117] These features, plus the cultivation of "unnatural" perspectives mentioned earlier, largely account for the label "mannerist" that has been applied to Seneca's writing in recent criticism; see on 152–75 for further discussion and examples.

[118] This sketch is intended only as a practical aid to reading and scansion; for fuller expositions of Senecan metrical practice see Fantham, 104–15; Zwierlein, *Prolegomena*, 182–230; L. Strzelecki, *De Senecae trimetro iambico quaestiones selectae* (Cracow, 1938). On lyric meters see, e.g., D. S. Raven, *Latin Metre* (London, 1965), 133–50.

the iambus, a metrical unit consisting of two elements in the order short-
long (◡ –). The iambus has a metrical "beat" or *ictus* that falls on the
long second element (sometimes marked ◡ ⊥); this element is called the
arsis, and the unstressed first element is known as the *thesis*. A full line
of tragic dialogue is made up of six iambic "feet," and is therefore sometimes called a *senarius*, but Seneca's practice shows that, like the Greek
dramatists, he thought of this meter as containing three pairs of iambi
rather than six independent feet. Each pair of iambi (◡ – ◡ –) is called
an iambic metron, and the entire line is thus referred to as an iambic
trimeter.

A strict iambic trimeter would have the following form:

$$\text{◡ – ◡ – } | \text{ ◡ – ◡ – } | \text{ ◡ – ◡ –}$$

This pure form, however, is practically nonexistent in Senecan dialogue
and literally does not occur in the whole of *Thyestes*. Just as the dactylic
hexameter at several points allows a choice between a dactyl (– ◡◡) and
a spondee (– –), so the iambic trimeter permits a wide range of choice
between iambi and other metrical units. The patterns of variation are set
out below; for ease of reference I shall occasionally speak of a trimeter as
having twelve "elements" or "positions" (see the schema below).

There are two basic ways in which pure iambs can be replaced by
other metrical forms: by substituting a long syllable for the short first syllable, or *thesis* (producing – – for ◡ –), and by "resolving" a long
syllable into its metrical equivalent of two short syllables (– = ◡◡). At
some places in the trimeter both types of variation may operate within a
single "foot": for example, at the beginning of the line (positions 1–2), as
well as a pure iamb one may find a spondee (– –, with long *thesis*), an
anapest (◡◡ –, with the long *thesis* resolved), a dactyl (– ◡◡, with long
thesis and resolved *arsis*), or a proceleusmatic (◡◡◡◡, with both long
thesis and *arsis* resolved).[119] A different form of substitution is limited to
the last element (position 12), which may be either a long or a short
syllable; in other words, the sixth "foot" of each trimeter may be either
an iamb (◡ –) or a pyrrhic (◡◡).[120] This final syllable is often called
anceps (i.e., "doubtful" or "ambiguous" in quantity); in metrical notation
it is indicated by an x.

Described in the abstract, the Senecan trimeter may sound daunt-
ingly complex, but in practice the meter is not inordinately difficult.
This is because substitutions are governed by certain clear guidelines and

[119] The proceleusmatic is restricted to the first metron and is very rare even there (only
at 289 in *Thyestes*).
[120] A short syllable may have been permitted at the end of the line because a pause at
this point (even if minimal or nonexistent in actual delivery) provided the necessary
lengthening.

also because within the range of possible forms Seneca shows marked preferences for a few patterns which recur so often as to become quickly familiar.

The most important principle regulating Seneca's trimeters is the different treatment given to the two halves of the iambic metron. In the first half of each metron (i.e., in the first, third, and fifth "feet," or at positions 1, 5, and 9) the *thesis* is much more often long or resolved than short, whereas in the second half (i.e., in the second, fourth, and sixth "feet," or at positions 3, 7, and 11) a short *thesis* is mandatory and is never replaced by a long syllable or its resolved equivalent. [This is the single most striking difference between the Senecan trimeter and the *senarii* of early Latin tragedy. In Republican tragedy it is possible to replace an iamb with a spondee in every "foot" except the last, so that lines with the shape – – – –   – – – –   – – ∪ – are not uncommon, cf., e.g., Acc. 411 R^2 *primum ex immani victum ad mansuetum applicans*. Seneca's restriction on the number of permissible spondees allows the iambic rhythms to be more clearly heard and also produces a less ponderous line.[121]] The final metron shows this difference between odd and even "feet" in its most pronounced form: Seneca virtually eliminates the short *thesis* in the first half (at position 9), permitting only the long and resolved forms, and also avoids resolution of the following *arsis* (position 10), so that the only possible patterns at the end of the line are – – ∪ x and ∪∪ – ∪ x.[122] The near-uniformity in the last metron, coming after the much more diverse patterns found earlier in the line, gives each verse the feeling of a strong close.[123]

Combining the fixed and variable elements of the Senecan trimeter yields the following complete schema:

1	2	3	4	5	6	7	8	9	10	11	12
⏓	⏔	∪	⏔	⏓	⏔	∪	⏔	⏔	–	∪	⏓

The best way to illustrate the particular forms favored by Seneca is to reproduce a short sketch of text with metrical notation. Here are the opening twelve lines of the *Thyestes*: resolved syllables are marked ‿ and elisions are indicated below the line (e.g. 1 *sede ab*). To the right of each line are references to one or two other lines in the play with the same metrical form; the figures in square brackets give the total number of

[121] It seems quite likely that this refinement was introduced by Augustan writers of tragedy, cf. *HSCP* 82 (1978), 258.
[122] Seneca here carries further a tendency seen in the *senarii* of Republican drama, where an iambic fifth "foot" is not favored, and is positively avoided when the sixth "foot" is filled by an iambic word or sense-unit—the so-called "Bentley-Luchs law."
[123] This effect is reinforced by certain restrictions on word-shape at the end of the trimeter, for which see Fantham, 105–106.

lines of this type in the *Thyestes*.[124]

1 Quis inferorum sede ab infausta extrahit   (6, 16 [46])

2 avido fugaces ore captantem cibos,   (21, 28 [61])

3 quis male deorum Tantalo visas domos   (10, 14 [23])

4 ostendit iterum? peius inventum est siti   (7–9, 11, 48 [29])

5 arente in undis aliquid et peius fame   (25, 52 [47])

6 hiante semper? Sisyphi numquid lapis   (= 1)

7 gestandus umeris lubricus nostris venit   (= 4)

8 aut membra celeri differens cursu rota   (= 4)

9 aut poena Tityi qui specu vasto patens   (= 4)

10 visceribus atras pascit effossis aves   (= 3)

11 et nocte reparans quidquid amisit die   (= 4)

12 plenum recenti pabulum monstro iacet?   (13, 15 [210])

The six patterns found in these lines account for more than half of all the trimeters in the play, and one of them (line 12), in which all the permitted substitutions of long for short syllables are made, occurs in more than a quarter of the play's dialogue. The most popular variety not seen in this sample shows resolution at the start of the third metron (position 9); as seen in line 24, *umbra et penates impios furiis age*, it appears 69 times, with 19 further occurrences containing a pure iamb at the start of the first (13) or second (6) metron. The remaining forms can all be worked out on the basis of the principles outlined above.

Each of the twelve lines scanned here also exhibits the most common form of *caesura* (i.e., word-break within a metron) in Seneca's trimeters, after the first element of the second metron (= position 5). In metrical notation the *caesura* is marked by a double vertical line (‖): e.g., *quis inferorum ‖ sede*, etc. Line 13 contains the play's first example of the other (much less common) main form of *caesura*, in the fourth foot (= after position 7): *in quod malum transcribor?* ‖ *o*, etc. Both *caesurae* can also appear in the same line, as in 2: *avido fugaces* ‖ *ore* ‖ *captantem cibos*.

Because the Senecan trimeter leans so heavily toward spondaic rhythms where these are permitted, lines with several resolved long syllables stand out in contrast. Of the 14 trimeters in *Thyestes* containing

---

124 The figures are based on a scansion of the text as printed in this edition, setting aside the incomplete line 100 and several other lines where the text is doubtful (47, 58, 272, 302, 745, and 1008); this leaves a total of 760 trimeters.

three or more resolutions, most coincide with moments of high emotion, where a sudden rush of short syllables effectively mirrors the feeling of the content. Note, e.g., 33 *repetantque profugos; dubia violentae domus,* in the Fury's vision of ceaseless crime, 267 *nescioquid animus maius et solito amplius,* as Atreus eagerly grasps the shape of his revenge, and 1040 *hoc est quod avidus capere non potuit pater,* as Thyestes despairingly surveys the remains of his children.

Lyric

Unlike his dialogue, Seneca's lyrics owe almost nothing of their form to their Greek antecedents. There is no trace in Seneca of the strophic responsion on which most Greek choral song is based. A few of his odes are constructed in stanzas, but for the most part Senecan lyrics are stichic—that is, a single basic meter is used in every line of a section or even an entire ode. The individual meters are based on Roman adaptations of Greek lyric patterns; Horace (the *Odes* in particular) seems to have been Seneca's most important model.

The lyrics of the *Thyestes* offer relatively few difficulties. Although four lyric meters appear in the play, three of them consist of a single pattern repeated without variation, and even the fourth does not approach the trimeter in the complexity of its form.

Chorus I (122–75)

> First asclepiad: – – – ∪∪ – – ∪∪ – ∪ x

This is the meter of Horace *C.* 1.1 (*Maecenas atavis*) and 3.30 (*Exegi monumentum*). As in Horace, there is consistent word-break after the sixth syllable.

> 122 Argos de superis si quis Achaicum
> 123 Pisaeasque domos curribus inclitas

Chorus II (336–403)

> Glyconic: – – – ∪∪ – ∪ x

Glyconics are not used by Horace as an independent metrical form, but they are a constituent element in several of his asclepiad-based stanzas, e.g., *C.* 1.5 (*Quis multa gracilis*), as the third line of each stanza: 3 *cui flavam religas comam.*

> 336 Tandem regia nobilis
> 337 antiqui genus Inachi

Chorus III (546–622)

Sapphic hendecasyllable: – ∪ – – – ∪∪ – ∪ – x
with an adonius in the final line (622): – ∪∪ – x

These are the constituents of Horace's sapphic stanza (as in, e.g., *C.* 1.22 *Integer vitae*), each of which comprises three hendecasyllables and an adonius. There is consistent word-break after the fifth syllable of the hendecasyllable (as is normal in Horace's first three books of *Odes*).

546 Crēdăt hŏc quĭsquăm? fĕrŭs īllĕ ĕt ācĕr

547 nĕc pŏtēns mēntĭs trŭcŭlēntŭs Ātrĕŭs

622 tūrbĭnĕ vērsăt.

Chorus IV (789–884) and Thyestes' Monody (920–69)

Anapestic dimeter: ∪∪ – ∪∪ – | ∪∪ – ∪∪ x
with occasional monometers: ∪∪ – ∪∪ x (cf. 829, 969)

The anapaestic dimeter is Seneca's most popular lyric form and also the most varied in its patterns. Like the iambic trimeter, it is rarely seen in its pure form (in *Thyestes* only at 923, 938, and 968). Several substitutions are permitted, as follows: – for ∪∪ in each half of each metron, and ∪∪ for – in the first half of each metron. The complete scheme is therefore ⏗ ⏗ ⏗ – | ⏗ ⏗ ⏗ x (for the monometer ⏗ ⏗ ⏗ x). Seneca does not, though, allow a run of four successive short syllables anywhere in the line, thereby avoiding the sequence dactyl-anapest (–∪∪ ∪∪–). For each metron, therefore, the possible combinations are (in order of decreasing frequency): dactyl-spondee (– ∪∪ – –), spondee-anapest (– – ∪∪ –), spondee-spondee(– – – –), anapest-anapest (∪∪ – ∪∪ –), and anapest-spondee (∪∪ – – –). Of these the first two are by far the most common, accounting for between half and three-fifths of the metra in these two sections of the play. Word-break between metra is consistently observed; elision and hiatus are avoided at this point.

Anapestic dimeters were used in Greek tragedy to accompany the first entrance of the Chorus (the *parodos*, cf., e.g., Aesch. *Ag.* 40–103) and also its departure from the orchestra at the end of the play (the *exodos*, cf., e.g., Eur. *Alc.* 1159–63); as a result they are sometimes called "marching anapests." The meter found a broader range of uses in Roman tragedy before Seneca, where it was employed both for choral odes at any point in the play (cf. Acc. 289–91 R[2]) and for, emotional arias (monodies) by individual actors; one of the two surviving lines of Ovid's *Medea* is from an anapestic monody sung by Medea: *feror huc illuc, ut plena deo* (cf. Sen. *Suas.* 3.7).

A short section of the final ode should suffice to illustrate the typical forms of Senecan anapests:

789 Quo, terrarum superumque parens, (SS AA)

790 cuius ad ortus noctis opacae (DS DS)

791 decus omne fugit, quo vertis iter (AA SA)

792 medioque diem perdis Olympo? (AA DS)

793 cur, Phoebe, tuos rapis aspectus? (SA AS)

[Note: for possible modifications of this view of Seneca's anapests, see Appendix I.]

LATER HISTORY OF THE TRAGEDIES[125]

At no time during the thirteen centuries after Seneca's death were his tragedies among the most popular works of Latin literature. Through the end of Antiquity, however, they seem to have been known to most well-educated writers, both pagans like Statius, Martial, Tacitus, Juvenal, and (probably) Claudian and Christians like Augustine, Jerome, and Sidonius Apollinaris. Indeed it was through the work of a Christian writer, in the many echoes-of Seneca's choral odes in Boethius' *Consolation of Philosophy*, that the words and themes of Senecan drama became most widely, though indirectly, familiar to the Middle Ages. From the sixth to the twelfth century the plays were almost entirely unknown; they re-emerge from the shadows only at the end of the twelfth century, in northern France and perhaps in circles associated with the University of Paris. Knowledge of the text first spread to England, then to Italy. By the end of the thirteenth century scholars in northern Italy were writing introductions to the plays and treatises on Senecan tragic meter; one of these early humanists, Albertino Mussato, also produced the first imitation of a Senecan drama since Antiquity, a tragedy of contemporary Italian politics called the *Ecerinis*. In the early fourteenth century knowledge of the tragedies grew beyond a narrow group of scholars. A sign of this wider acceptance is an exchange of letters from about the year 1314 between Cardinal Niccolò Albertino da Prato, a prominent figure at the court of Pope John XXII in Avignon, and Nicholas Trevet, a Dominican scholar resident at Blackfriars, Oxford; the cardinal noted the current interest in Senecan drama and asked Trevet to provide a full commentary that would make these unfamiliar and difficult works accessible to a broader educated public. Trevet's thorough, if numbingly elementary, gloss accomplished its purpose, and contributed to the great expansion of popularity the tragedies enjoyed for the next two centuries. Thousands of manuscript copies were turned out (mostly in Italy) of which several hundred still survive, and

---

125 A slightly fuller account is given in *Texts and Transmission*, ed. L. D. Reynolds (Oxford, 1983), 378–81.

Senecan drama at last acquired the secure position of a standard text, the exemplar of ancient tragedy to be placed beside the long-established figures of Plautus and Terence. The itinerant players who arrive at Elsinore in the second act of *Hamlet*, for whom "Seneca cannot be too heavy nor Plautus too light" (2.2.400–401), typify the Renaissance view of Seneca's classic status.

It is not surprising that Senecan tragedy should have so deeply impressed readers of the later Middle Ages, when knowledge of Greek in Europe was quite limited and the Attic dramatists were little more than names. It is harder to explain why many of the most learned critics of the sixteenth century, who could make direct comparisons between Seneca and his Greek predecessors, accorded Senecan drama an esteem that now seems greatly exaggerated. The most influential treatise on poetry of the century, the *Poetices libri septem* of Julius Caesar Scaliger (Lyons, 1561), ranked Seneca as the equal of any of the Greeks in *maiestas* and as superior to Euripides in *cultus* and *nitor*.[126] Similar judgments were delivered by other eminent theorists of the time. One of these, Giovanni Battista Giraldi Cintio, gives an especially clear idea of what the high Renaissance prized so highly in Seneca: in a treatise of 1543, Giraldi writes that Seneca surpassed all the Greeks in "prudence, gravity, decorum, dignity, and *sententiae*," and in a comparison of Seneca's *Troades* with Euripides' play he gives Seneca higher marks for "majesty, the depiction of the emotions, the observation of behavior, and the liveliness of the *sententiae*."[127] The recurring stress on "gravity" and "majesty," on elegance (*cultus*) and point (*sententiae*), shows that the sixteenth-century preference for Seneca was largely based on stylistic familiarity; to writers whose taste had been formed by Latin models, Seneca's command of rhetorical technique and the overt moralizing of his lyrics made him seem accessible and therefore attractive. His clearly articulated dramatic structure would also have commended him to an age in which Horace's *Ars Poetica* and overliteral readings of Aristotle's *Poetics* constituted the dominant canons of dramatic form.

The influence of Senecan drama was as strong in sixteenth-century England as it was on the Continent, though the forms it took were different.[128] Besides being studied and imitated in learned circles, at the

---

[126] "Seneca . . . quem nullo Graecorum maiestate inferiorem existimo; cultu vero ac nitore etiam Euripide maiorem" (*Poet.* VI.6).

[127] *Discorso . . . intorno al comporre delle comedie e delle tragedie*, ed. C. G. Crocetti (Milan, 1973), 184, 205, 210.

[128] Among the most useful of the many treatments of Senecan influence in this period are the introduction to J. W. Cunliffe's *Early English Classical Tragedies* (Oxford, 1912); F. L. Lucas, *Seneca and Elizabethan Tragedy* (Cambridge, 1927); T. S. Eliot's essay "Seneca in Elizabethan Translation," reprinted in *Selected Essays* (London, 1951), 65–105; and C. J. Herington's essay "Senecan Tragedy," *Arion* 5 (1966), 422–71.

Universities and the Inns of Court, Seneca's plays also exerted a direct influence on the popular theater, in part through a series of translations by various hands published between 1559 and 1567 and reprinted in collected form in 1581. In their flamboyant sound-effects and pounding rhythms, these translations are vivid evidence of the freshness with which the early Elizabethans responded to Seneca's poetry. Here, for example, is Jasper Heywood's version of *Thy.* 9–10 *aut poena Tityi, semper accrescens iecur / visceribus atras pascit effossis aves*: "or shal my paynes be Tytius panges th'encreasing liver still, / whose growing guttes the grawing gripes and fylthy foules do fyll?"[129] In a sense, though, the Elizabethan translations of Seneca represent a poetic dead end. The future of English dramatic poetry lay elsewhere, in the unrhymed iambic pentameter which was just beginning to be used when the work of Heywood and his colleagues appeared. In a short thirty years this new form had developed into a medium of unprecedented subtlety, and the part that Seneca played in this process may well be his most important legacy as a dramatist. The key figures in the evolution of blank verse—Kyd, Marlowe, and the young Shakespeare—had all read some Seneca in Latin at school, and direct echoes and borrowings of Senecan lines can be discovered throughout their works.[130] Seneca's largest contribution, though, was a less specific one: he provided a model of dramatic verse that was both vigorous and flexible, rich in imagery but still direct and pungent. Marlowe and Shakespeare were greater poets and greater dramatists, but their genius would not have attained the form it did without Seneca as a precedent and example.

After about 1600 Seneca's prestige as a dramatist began to decline. He is still a significant influence on the French classical tragedy of the seventeenth century, but even there he counts for less than the Greek tragedians, whose standing continued to rise at Seneca's expense in subsequent centuries, as knowledge and appreciation of Greek culture increased. The most severe blow to Seneca's reputation came from nineteenth-century Romanticism, by whose standards everything about his work appeared repellently artificial. The present century has been more receptive: Seneca's departures from naturalism and his dark, even nihilistic view of life no longer disqualify him from being taken seriously as an artist.[131] Senecan drama may never again exert a profound and widespread influence, as it did during the Renaissance, but for the moment at least it has found readers for whom its themes and modes of expression are, if anything, disconcertingly familiar.

---

129 Heywood was translating a text different from the one printed in modern editions, with the variant *semper accrescens iecur* for *qui specu vasto patens* in line 9.
130 For examples see notes on 168, 246, 250–54, 259, 269–70.
131 Precisely these aspects of Senecan drama were in fact highlighted in the most important production of a Senecan play in recent years, Peter Brook's *Oedipus* of 1967 (in an English version by Ted Hughes).

MANUSCRIPTS AND EDITIONS[132]

More than 400 manuscript copies of Seneca's tragedies survive, the vast majority dating from the 14th and 15th centuries and most of these still not thoroughly studied.[133] This enormous body of testimony seems to derive ultimately from two copies, or possibly two editions, of Seneca's plays produced in late Antiquity (i.e., the 4th or 5th centuries A.D.).[134] One of these ancient texts is the source of the earliest surviving manuscript, written in northern Italy toward the end of the eleventh century and since the 1490s in the Laurentian Library in Florence (Biblioteca Medicea Laurenziana, plut. lat. 37.13). This manuscript was first systematically used in the edition of J. F. Gronovius (Leiden, 1661), who dubbed it the "codex Etruscus" (i.e., Florentine); today it is still known as the "Etruscus" or E. E is the only representative of its branch of tradition with independent authority; it is in turn the ancestor of a group of 14th-century Italian manuscripts (FMN in the diagram below), whose testimony is only helpful in places where E itself has been damaged or corrected. Nearly all other manuscripts descend from a second ancient text, which differed from the E-branch in the order and some of the titles of the plays (above, p. 8).[135] Manuscripts based on this second ancient copy begin to appear in northern France at the end of the twelfth century, in England soon thereafter, and in Italy by the end of the thirteenth century. This strain of transmission (called "A" by modern scholars) became the dominant form of the text in the 14th and 15th centuries, although many A manuscripts were more or less carefully compared with texts related to E, producing a large group of hybrid (or "contaminated") manuscripts. In most places the testimony of A can be recovered from four of its best representatives: on the one hand, Paris Bibliothèque nationale lat. 8260 (13th century, called P) and Bibl. nat. lat. 8031 (15th century, called T), which belong to a rare but superior subgroup (known as δ), and on the other, Cambridge Corpus Christi College 406 (13th century, called C) and El Escorial T.III.11 (late 13th century, called S), the purest surviving specimens of a second A subgroup (β), to which nearly all the later medieval copies belong.

The relationships of the manuscripts named above can be shown on the following simplified *stemma*:

[132] Fuller accounts in my edition of *Agamemnon*, 23–94, also (with corrections) in L. D. Reynolds, ed., *Texts and Transmission* (Oxford, 1983), 378–81; Fantham, 116–24; Zwierlein, *Prolegomena*.

[133] A handlist by A. P. MacGregor is forthcoming in *ANRW*.

[134] Fragments of a third ancient copy are extant in Milan Bibl. Ambrosiana G 82 sup. (= S.P. 9.13–20), written probably in Italy in the 5th century. The Ambrosian fragments do not include any lines from *Thyestes*.

[135] The immediate ancestor of the A family also differed from E in containing the *Octavia*, but this might have been a relatively late insertion.

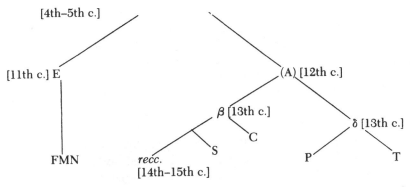

These affiliations (which are fairly stable) furnish an editor with some guidance in constructing a text of the tragedies. When, for example, E PT agree against CS or—as happens much less often—E CS agree against PT, the minority reading is probably an error of β or δ respectively, and may therefore be disregarded. On the other hand, any reading attested either in E or in PTCS (= A) is at least potentially ancient, and must therefore be assessed on its intrinsic merits, i.e., conformity with Senecan style and suitability to the context. In practice E is the more reliable branch; it is in particular much less prone than A to interpolation, i.e., deliberate rewriting of obscure or difficult passages.[136] In hundreds of places, however, A preserves what look like original readings that have been corrupted in E, so E's overall superiority may only be invoked to settle a choice between readings of roughly equal merit. When E and A agree, they do not necessarily yield the reading of Seneca's original text, but only that of the ancient copies from which they derive; editors must still judge whether this consensus reflects the original or whether an emendation is required.[137] This is an issue on which scholars are rarely in full agreement, which explains why no single edition of a classical text is likely to be accepted as definitive.

The editions of Seneca's tragedies in common use today are those of Friedrich Leo (Berlin, 1878; the basis of the Loeb text of F. J. Miller, Cambridge, Mass., 1917), the Teubner text of Rudolf Peiper and Gustav Richter (Leipzig, 1902), and the most recent critical text, by Gian Carlo Giardina (Bologna, 1966). None of these editions reports the readings of T, and only Giardina reports the testimony of PCS. For these and other reasons a new critical text is very much needed; fortunately, the long-awaited Oxford Classical Texts edition by Otto Zwierlein should soon be available.

---

[136] For examples of interpolation in A see notes on 180–82, 469, appendix of variants at lines 9, 439, 526.

[137] The places where late manuscripts offer readings superior to the consensus of EA (cf., e.g., *Thy.* 355, 487, 624, 652, 731, 1070) are probably instances of successful conjecture rather than evidence for independent survival of ancient readings.

For this edition I have constructed a new text on the basis of Giardina's reports of E PCS, adding the readings of T from my own collation of a microfilm copy. [Note: T has been heavily and skillfully corrected by a second hand. The corrections are sometimes difficult to make out on microfilm; my reports are consequently at times tentative (and should in all cases be checked against Zwierlein's OCT).]

Orthography

In general I have followed the principles used in my text of *Agamemnon* (set out on pp. 363–68 of the edition), aiming for consistency on each single point (e.g., *natus* everywhere, although the Mss vary between *natus* and *gnatus*). In one respect, however, I have adopted a different approach. It seems clear that in formal speech and poetry of the first century A.D. both the *-is* and *-es* forms of the accusative plural of i-stem third declension nouns and adjectives were in normal use, and that the choice of one form rather than another was determined by considerations of euphony (cf. the remarks of the scholar Valerius Probus quoted by Aulus Gellius 13.21). I have therefore admitted accusative plurals in *-is* where they have manuscript attestation and where they seem to harmonize with their surroundings (cf., e.g., 44 *omnis* and 107 *fontis*); whether I have come closer to Seneca's own practice by doing so is, of course, open to question.

C. *THYESTES*

THE MYTH

Seneca took it for granted that his audience would be thoroughly familiar with the mythic plots of his plays; he therefore reduced expository passages to a minimum and alluded freely to events before and after the action of the plays themselves. The following factual outline may be useful in giving modern readers some of this sense of prior familiarity.[138] (Numbers in parentheses denote references in the text of the play.)

Tantalus, king of Sipylus in Phrygia and a son of Zeus, had two children, Pelops and Niobe, by his wife Dione, a daughter of Atlas. He was granted the privilege of joining the gods at their feasts, but he incurred their enmity by abusing this honor, either by stealing the divine ambrosia and nectar to share with mortals, by revealing the gods' secrets (91–93), or by serving them the flesh of Pelops (144–49). He was condemned to eternal punishment in the underworld, either with a rock

---

[138] The main mythographical sources are "Apollodorus" *Epitome* 2.1–14 (with Frazer's extensive notes) and "Hyginus" *fab.* 82–88. Other useful discussions in A. C. Pearson's *Fragments of Sophocles* s. vv. *Atreus* and *Thyestes*; F. Bömer's commentary on Ovid *Met.* 6.173.

perpetually suspended above him (cf. 153) or by being placed in a stream with fruit-trees over his head and having the water and fruit constantly elude his efforts to reach them (149–75).

Pelops as a young man came as a suitor to Hippodamia, the daughter of Oenomaus, ruler of Pisa in Elis. Having been warned by an oracle that he would be killed by a son-in-law, Oenomaus had decreed that any suitor wishing to marry Hippodamia must first defeat him in a chariot-race. (Oenomaus' horses were a gift from Ares and therefore invincible.) Pelops arranged for Myrtilus, Oenomaus' charioteer, to sabotage the king's chariot, promising in return to share his own kingdom with him (139–43, 659–61).[139] Oenomaus was killed in the race, and Pelops won Hippodamia. On the homeward journey he disposed of Myrtilus by drowning him in what then became known as the Myrtoan Sea, then returned to Elis as Oenomaus' successor, enlarging his kingdom to include much of southern Greece and calling it the Peloponnese after himself.

Pelops had many children, among them Atreus and Thyestes. Atreus married Aerope and had two sons, Agamemnon and Menelaus. Aerope fell in love with Thyestes and committed adultery with him (46–47, 239, 1103), and when the two brothers competed for the throne of Mycenae, Aerope assisted her lover Thyestes. Victory in the contest turned on the possession of a miraculous ram with golden fleece; this was owned by Atreus but was stolen by Aerope and given to Thyestes, who thus obtained control of Mycenae and banished Atreus (32–36, 42–43, 225–37).[140] After a time the situation was reversed: Atreus regained power and drove Thyestes into exile (37–38).[141] Determined to avenge the wrongs done to him by Thyestes, Atreus lured him and his sons[142] back to Mycenae by feigning a desire to be reconciled; he then killed the children and served their flesh to their unwitting father.

Thyestes fled Mycenae and inquired of Apollo's oracle how he might take revenge on Atreus. He was told that he could only produce an avenger by mating with his own daughter (41–42, 46–47). The prophecy was fulfilled either at Sicyon (Hyg. 88.3) or at the court of Thesprotus in

[139] So "Hyginus" (84.4); "Apollodorus" attributes Myrtilus' treachery to his passion for Hippodamia (who was in turn infatuated with Pelops).

[140] The original significance of the ram is obscure, cf. Frazer on "Apollodorus" Epit. 2.11. Seneca's description in Thy. 225–31 suggests that its possession was a guarantee of sovereignty for a Pelopid; could Pelopis (225) imply that it had once belonged to Pelops?

[141] According to "Apollodorus" (Epit. 2.12), Zeus assisted Atreus in regaining power by causing the sun to set in the East at his bidding. The more familiar significance of the sun's reversal is at least as old as Sophocles, cf. Anth. Pal. 9.98.2.

[142] The number and names of the children vary: "Apollodorus" gives three names (Aglaus, Callileon, and Orchomenus), "Hyginus" only two, Tantalus and Plisthenes. Seneca has these plus an unnamed puer, cf. 731–43. Neither mythographical source need reflect an early tradition; cf. Fraenkel on Aesch. Ag. 1605, n. 2.

Epirus, where Thyestes had found refuge; he encountered his daughter Pelopia and raped her, probably without realizing her identity. The child that Pelopia conceived was exposed at birth, found and reared by herdsmen, and given the name Aegisthus; he eventually discovered his parentage and killed Atreus, in some versions also restoring the kingdom of Mycenae to Thyestes. Later he joined with Clytaemestra in killing Atreus' son Agamemnon on his return from the Trojan War (43–46).

DRAMATIC VERSIONS BEFORE SENECA

The house of Tantalus provided Greek dramatists with one of their favorite themes, and no part of the saga was as often treated as the strife between Atreus and Thyestes. Sophocles wrote at least two plays on the subject, an *Atreus* and the play usually called *Thyestes in Sicyon*; Euripides wrote a *Thyestes*, a *Plisthenes* (dealing with Thyestes' efforts to avenge the loss of his children), and a third play, *The Cretan Women*, in which both Thyestes and Aerope appeared; plays with the title *Thyestes* or *Aerope* are recorded for several other Greek tragedians (Agathon, Chaeremon, Carcinus, Cleophon, Diogenes, Apollodorus of Tarsus). The legend was equally popular among Roman dramatists before Seneca: Ennius wrote a *Thyestes* and Accius an *Atreus* (both well known to Cicero, who quotes from each several times), and Accius may have handled a later phase of the story in his *Pelopidae*; from the Augustan period we know of Varius' *Thyestes* and a play with the same title by Gracchus (named together by Ovid in *Pont.* 4.16.31); the *Atreus* of Mamercus Aemilius Scaurus belongs to the reign of Tiberius (Dio 58.24.3–4 claims that it grievously offended the emperor); finally there was an *Atreus* by Pomponius Secundus, quite possibly written within a few years of Seneca's play.

Unfortunately, not one of this large corpus of pre-Senecan plays survives in more than fragments.[143] In several cases what remains can be plausibly related to more than one phase of the Tantalid saga, and only for Accius' *Atreus* does the evidence reveal even the broad outlines of the treatment. Sophocles' *Atreus*, which is generally agreed to have covered much the same ground as Seneca's play, has disappeared virtually without trace, unless its influence is to be seen in Accius' handling. Euripides' *Thyestes* is almost as intangible: the fragments do not show whether the play dealt with Atreus' revenge and the banquet or with a later episode; a line in Aristophanes' *Acharnians* (433) suggests that Thyestes appeared on stage in rags, but this detail would fit equally well with his return from exile as in Seneca (cf. 524–26) or with his arrival,

[143] The basic discussion is still A. Lesky, "Die griechischen Pelopidendramen und Senecas Thyestes," *Wiener Studien* 43 (1922/3), 172–98 (though Lesky's attempt to identify Euripides as Seneca's main source presses the evidence too far).

disgraced and polluted, at the court of Thesprotus. A similar ambiguity surrounds the plot of Ennius' *Thyestes* (perhaps an adaptation of Euripides' play); thanks to Cicero, however, we can at least see that Thyestes' role contained passages of considerable power, among them an urgent appeal to a chorus of "strangers" (*hospites*) not to come near him in his polluted state (349–51 V^2 = 293–95 J) and an impassioned denunciation of Atreus that imagined for him a horrible death and mutilation at sea (362–65 V^2 = 296–99 J).

The most frustrating of these losses is Varius' *Thyestes*, by all accounts an outstandingly good play and potentially the strongest single influence on Seneca's treatment.[144] Only one line is securely attributed to it, the trimeter *iam fero infandissima, iam facere cogor*, spoken by Atreus according to Quintilian (3.8.45). It is usually assigned to a scene corresponding to Seneca's second act (176–335), in which Atreus justified his planned revenge on Thyestes (see specifically Sen. *Thy.* 201–202 and note *ad loc.*).[145] This attribution, though, rests on the premise that the banquet was the *dénouement* of Varius' play, as it is in Seneca (and Accius), and this assumption, though plausible, cannot be proven true; indeed, Eckard Lefèvre has recently offered an alternative reconstruction that sets the play after the *cena*, ending with Atreus' death at the hands of Aegisthus.[146] Even if Lefèvre's view is not accepted,[147] there is no secure basis for regarding Varius as the model for any particular aspect of Seneca's play.[148]

Only in the case of Accius' *Atreus* does enough survive to let us go beyond generalities, enough in fact to allow most of its scenes to be sketched out with some confidence; what emerges is a play which overlaps with Seneca's to a remarkable extent, both in general outline and in some specific details.[149] It began with an expository prologue (perhaps spoken by a god or some other figure not involved in the action) which

---

144 The play enjoyed lasting renown as a classic of Roman drama, cf. Quint. 10.1.98, Tac. *Dial.* 12.6.

145 The proud entrance-lines of an Atreus quoted by Seneca at *Epist.* 80.7 have also been plausibly referred to this play: *en impero Argis; regna mihi liquit Pelops, / qua ponto ab Helles atque ab Ionio mari / urgetur Isthmos.* (More speculatively, cf. Sen. *Contr.* 1.1.21 = *inc. inc. fab.* 212 R².)

146 *Der Thyestes des Lucius Varius Rufus: Zehn Überlegungen zu seiner Rekonstruktion* (Akademie der Wissenschaften und der Literatur, Mainz; Abhandlungen der Geistes- und Sozialwissenschaftlichen Klasse, 1976.9).

147 See the comments of H. D. Jocelyn, *Gnomon* 50 (1978), 778–80; R. J. Tarrant, *CR* n.s. 29 (1979), 149–50.

148 One might suggest that the prominence of Aerope as a tragic character in Ovid *Tr.* 2.391–92 and Quintilian 11.3.73 implies a substantial role for her in Varius' play (so Wilamowitz, quoted by Lefèvre, 9–10).

149 On the structure (particularly the conclusion) of Accius' *Atreus* see now O. Zwierlein, *Hermes* 111 (1983), 121–25.

included a detailed genealogy of Atreus (Serv. Auct. on Verg. *Aen.* 8.130) and an account of Pelops' winning of Hippodamia (197 R^2); it probably went on to narrate Thyestes' adultery with Aerope, the theft of the golden ram, Atreus' expulsion and return to power, and Thyestes' present exile. There followed, as in Seneca, a scene in which Atreus brooded over his grievances against Thyestes and worked out his plan of revenge (198–213 R^2), described in general terms by Cicero: *ille funestas epulas frati comparans nonne versat huc et illuc cogitatione rationem?* (*N.D.* 3.68). In all likelihood an underling served as a foil to Atreus, and it was probably an objection from this character (along the lines of Sen. *Thy.* 204–205 *fama te populi nihil / adversa terret?*) that provoked from Atreus the most famous line in all of Accius, the splendidly tyrannical *oderint, dum metuant* (quoted three times each by Cicero and Seneca, and "capped" by Seneca's Atreus in *Thy.* 206–207 *facta domini cogitur populus sui / tam ferre quam laudare*). Atreus then left the stage and Thyestes arrived with his children, to whom he offered sage advice on the burdens of power (215–16 R^2) and the snares that lie in wait for the upright (214 R^2). These remarks suggest that Thyestes was suspicious of Atreus' good will; perhaps, again as in Seneca, his sons overcame his misgivings.[150] No trace survives of the first encounter between the brothers, and we next pick up the thread with the Messenger relating Atreus' preparation of the children's flesh: *concoquit / partem vapore flammae, veribus in foco / lacerta tribuit* (220–22 R^2, cf. Sen. *Thy.* 765–67, 770).[151] The banquet may well have been presented on stage; one fragment (217–18 R^2) has Atreus ordering that no one should sit with Thyestes or share his food, and another, admittedly uncertain in attribution, may preserve part of the moment of recognition, with Thyestes suspecting that he has eaten his children and Atreus wryly answering, "I wouldn't think of lessening your worries by denying it" (*numquam istam imminuam curam infitiando tibi*, 233 R^2).[152] The banquet touched off the traditional disturbance in the heavens, one of the play's most noted incidents (schol. Ovid *Ibis* 427) and the subject of its only surviving lyrics, three lines of excited anapests (223–25 R^2) usually given to the Chorus but conceivably belonging to Thyestes: *sed quid tonitru turbida torvo / concussa repente aequora caeli / sensimus sonere?* (cf. Sen. *Thy.* 992–95). The play ended with Thyestes

---

[150] This might be the place for fr. 234^{bis}R^2, specifically attributed to the *Atreus* by a scholiast on Verg. *G.* 1.1: *probae etsi in segetem* [= terram] *sunt deteriorem datae / fruges, tamen ipsae suapte natura enitent.* A comforting argument advanced by one of Thyestes' sons?

[151] Perhaps also fr. 219 R^2 *epularum fictor, scelerum fratris delitor* (though the text is uncertain).

[152] So R. G. M. Nisbet on Cic. *Pis.* 82; this placement, however, requires emending the attribution in Asconius, who gives the line to Thyestes.

aghast at Atreus' deception and helplessly bewailing his own disgrace (227, 231–32 R²), while Atreus reminded him of his earlier crimes (228 R²).[153]

From this brief survey it appears that the disposition of scenes and some of the elements of character-depiction in Seneca's *Thyestes* follow an outline used at least by Accius (if not by Varius as well), and possibly worked out as early as Sophocles or Euripides. This adherence to tradition may help to explain why the *Thyestes* fits more comfortably within the conventions of the ancient stage than most Senecan tragedies, but it does not lessen the originality of the play or its status as an authentically Senecan creation.

SENECA'S *THYESTES*[154]

The *Thyestes* is an extraordinarily cohesive play, in which all the elements of drama—plot, character, setting, language—work together to produce an impact of shattering power. The following paragraphs comment briefly on some of the means by which Seneca achieves this remarkable integration.

The play's title denotes its most complex character, and also the figure whose downfall furnishes the leading action, but it is Atreus and Thyestes, and not Thyestes alone, who constitute its true center of interest. Although the brothers meet on stage in only two scenes, they are linked throughout the play, in the Messenger's narrative (682–788), the Fury's foreshadowing (54–62), and above all in each other's thoughts (176–335, 412–16, 473–86, 491–507, 885–919). As befits brothers, Atreus and Thyestes are both alike and yet different. They share a longing for power and a lack of moral inhibition that mark them as true descendants

---

153 Two fragments assigned to the *Atreus* by Ribbeck and others seem not to belong: (1) 233 R² *ecquis hoc animadvortet? vincite!*, cited by Cicero *De or.* 3.217 as an example of *iracundia*, but not necessarily from the *Atreus* (so also Zwierlein, *op. cit.*, 122–23); (2) 229–30 R² *ipsus hortatur me frater ut meos malis miser / manderem natos*, which seems to be spoken by Thyestes recounting his deception to others (perhaps in Accius' *Pelopidae?*). On the other hand, three unplaced lines of Accius (657–59 R²) in high emotive style, lamenting the Tantalid drive to self-destruction, might form part of Thyestes' shocked reaction in the final scene: *quisnam Tantalidarum internecioni modus / paretur? aut quaenam umquam ob mortem Myrtili / poenis luendis dabitur satias supplici?*

154 For other general treatments of the play cf. C. J. Herington, *CHLL* 524–29; N. T. Pratt, *Seneca's Drama* (Chapel Hill, 1983), 103–107; C. P. Segal, *Antike und Abendland* 29 (1983), 183–86; and the articles by Boyle, Calder, Gigon, Hine, Knoche, Poe, and Steidle listed in the Bibliography. [To these may now be added E. Lefèvre, "Die philosophische Bedeutung der Seneca-Tragödie am Beispiel des 'Thyestes'," *ANRW* II.32.1 (due to appear in 1985), which offers an acute analysis of the character of Thyestes and a generous sampling of earlier work on the play.] On imagery cf. N. T. Pratt, "Major Systems of Figurative Language in Senecan Melodrama," *TAPA* 94 (1963), 199–234.

of Tantalus and Pelops (cf. on 2 *avido . . . ore*, 53, 133–37, 339–42, 1011–12). But while both are drawn to power, its attractions are different for each. Thyestes associates power with the rewards and comforts of high status (cf. 455–67), which he claims to despise but which he cannot in the end resist (cf., e.g., 470, 542–43, 920–37). For Atreus, on the other hand, the trappings of rule are of no interest whatever; to him power means only one thing, the ability to impose one's will on others, preferably against their bitter opposition (205–18). This portrayal of the brothers gives new meaning to the traditional story of Atreus' revenge. That Thyestes participates actively in his own undoing becomes a vindication of Atreus' control over him (277–78, 285–86),[155] while the form of Atreus' vengeance makes Thyestes' fatal weakness, his physical appetites, a fitting instrument of his destruction.

With superb economy, Seneca suggests the essential features of Atreus and Thyestes in their opening lines. Here is Atreus: *ignave, iners, enervis, et (quod maximum / probrum tyranno rebus in summis reor) / inulte* (176–78); restless and dissatisfied, but clear in his aims, sharply aware of his position as a *tyrannus*, and determined to avenge any slight to his control. Now Thyestes: *optata patriae tecta et Argolicas opes / miserisque summum ac maximum exulibus bonum, / tractum soli natalis et patrios deos / (si sunt tamen di) cerno* (404–407); outwardly joyful, but already showing signs of doubt (*si sunt tamen di*) and unwittingly confessing the attraction to wealth that will be his ruin (*optata tecta et . . . opes*; see note *ad loc.*). In wording as well, these two entrance lines form a scrupulously contrasted pair. Each brother places a qualifying phrase with *maximus* after his opening words (*quod . . . reor, miserisque . . . bonum*), a shared mannerism that sets off the more significant differences. Atreus' self-indictment mounts steadily in force, with sound reinforcing sense, from *ignave* to *iners* to *enervis*; then, after tension has been heightened by the delaying phrase *quod . . . reor*, the reason for his scorn finally becomes clear in the pointed and unexpected *inulte*. Here, as throughout the play, Atreus' strength of will and singleminded pursuit of his goals are reflected in his command of language; he is a virtuoso rhetorician, whose verbal powers are an expression—in a sense, the most complete expression—of his personality.[156] Thyestes' language is equally indicative; his phrases seem to strive toward a climax that never arrives, while sounding ironic undertones of which he remains unaware (404, also 409–10 *nobilis / palmam paterno . . . curru tuli*). From his first words the audience is led to see

---

[155] For the same reason Thyestes' lack of awareness (and so of resistance) deprives Atreus of his keenest pleasure, cf. 1054–68.

[156] The language of Atreus can be seen as a masterful embodiment, in Senecan terms, of Cicero's prescription for the speech of anger: *aliud . . . vocis genus iracundia sibi sumat, acutum, incitatum, crebro incidens* (*De or.* 3.216).

Thyestes' lack of self-knowledge, his internal divisions, and his disastrous weakness of will. This distinction in the brothers' use of language forms an essential part of Seneca's character-portrayal. Atreus is consistently the master of language, Thyestes its victim; words are for one a weapon, for the other a trap.

The minor figures of the drama all participate to some degree in the central conflict. Tantalus and the Fury do so most obviously, since their struggle parallels and symbolically anticipates Atreus' victory over Thyestes. In their various ways the attendant who fails to restrain Atreus' cruelty and in the end pledges wholehearted support and the messenger who overcomes his horror at speaking and comes finally to exult in the atrocity he relates each manifest the eventual triumph of evil over all resistance. The Chorus's relation to the action is more complex, but its lyrics follow a basically similar line of development. The first ode expresses a belief in divine justice (149–51) and a hope for release from impious rulers (132–37). In the middle odes, despite the appearance of concord between Atreus and Thyestes, the Chorus turns inward in search of true power (*regnum*), but the idyllic vision of untroubled withdrawal (393–400) is soon overshadowed by thoughts of ceaseless change and an unknowable future (596–622). The final ode confronts the prospect of universal disaster, salvaging a voluntary death from the ruins of a collapsing world (875–84). The Chorus is no more able than the other characters to halt the progress of *ira* or to escape its consequences, but the breadth of its perspective and the dignity of its ultimate response give the play its only moments of moral sanity.[157]

Thyestes is unusual among Seneca's plays for the prominence it gives to the physical setting. From the play's first speech, when Tantalus declares that Tartarus will never lack for criminals "while the house of Pelops stands" (22), the *domus* is a constant dramatic presence, its impious potency rendered visible by Tantalus' polluting touch (101–103, cf. also 53; later 190–91, 404, 625, 641–82, 901–902). In the final scene the *domus* is even, as it were, brought on stage, as Thyestes is seen within it reclining at his dreadful banquet (902–903, 908–969). The stage-picture here brilliantly reflects the significance of the action, since the *domus* (which is also the *arx*, cf. 641) represents the royal status that both brothers long for (*cupidi arcium* 342). In his opening speech Atreus prays "that this royal palace of great Pelops collapse on me, as long as it falls as well on my brother" (190–91). His wish is in a sense fulfilled, since the power symbolized by the *domus* lures Thyestes to his doom and drives Atreus himself into madness.

---

[157] The Chorus's sentiments take on added weight because of the remarkably personal language in which they are uttered: each ode except the first ends with a striking shift to the first person, cf. 393–400, 621–22, 875–84 (and notes *ad locc.*).

The most comprehensive source of the play's coherence is its imagery, a thickly interwoven network of motifs that encompasses all the figures and themes of the drama. Some images point up distinctions between characters, as when Atreus and Thyestes are each described as "dripping" (*madidus*), one with gore (734) and the other with hair-oil (780). Animal-imagery is applied with similar precision: the Tantalids generally are called "bestial" (*ferus*, cf. 136, 150), but Atreus is consistently depicted as a predator (497–503, 707–11, 732–36), Thyestes as a hunted victim (286–87, 491, see on 413–14).[158] The connections between Tantalus and his descendants also provide the basis for the profusion of words denoting "fullness" and "emptiness" in the prologue and opening chorus (cf. note on 22 *complebo*), which foreshadows the brothers' pursuit of "fullness" in differing senses (cf. 253–54 *impleri iuvat / maiore monstro*, 890–91 *implebo patrem / funere suorum*), a satiety that provokes a horrified "emptiness" in the surrounding world (892 *caelum vacat*). More specific links between Tantalus and Thyestes account for several appearances of the motif of "flight" or "escape": Tantalus longs to escape the Fury's compulsion (83), but is finally made to "follow" (100), just as Thyestes, though he wishes to flee back into exile (412, 428), in the end uneasily "follows" his sons (489). In the final scene Thyestes, having failed to seize his earlier opportunity, seems haunted by thoughts of flight, escape, and freedom (cf. 922–23, 1003, 1042, 1044), while in reality he comes to resemble Tantalus more closely, a figure of painful fixity from whom things run (Tantalus 2, 69, 154, 172; Thyestes 986, 1021, 1070, especially 1016–17).

Other images are not linked to individual characters but cluster around the play's central themes. Several of them operate on both the literal and metaphorical level, thereby underscoring the importance of these themes while at the same time glossing their significance. The idea of violent fragmentation, for example, takes in Atreus' dismemberment of his victims (cf. 760 *divisum secat*, 1039 *rupta fractis cruribus vestigia*), the figurative rupturing of moral ties that produced it (179 *fas omne ruptum*), and the fracture of the natural order that it in turn calls forth (cf. 777 *ruptum . . . diem*).[159] Similarly the notion of an oppressive weight applies both to Thyestes in his abominable fullness (781 *gravis . . . vino*, 910 *vino gravatum . . . caput*, 1000 *onus*, 1050–51 *natos premo / premorque natis*) and also to the outer world, weighed down by the resulting darkness (see on 787 *gravis*). The concept of "extinction" shows the connection of the moral and physical realms at its clearest, since the realization of the Fury's wish

---

[158] The motif of "uncertainty" or "hesitation" is also applied to both brothers, but in different situations, cf. 422, 490 versus 709–14, 724–25.

[159] In counterpoint to this image is that of an equally unnatural linking, as for example in 466–67 *somno dies / Bacchoque nox iungenda*, 979 *totum . . . turba iam sua implebo patrem;* see on 433 *componit artus*.

ius . . . omne pereat (48) is the annihilation of cosmic order (813 *solitae mundi periere vices*). The most complex single pattern of imagery surrounds the play's crucial action: the victory of evil over all attempts to resist or evade it. On the level of verbal imagery this theme is reflected in the many references to unwillingness (cf., e.g., 420 *moveo nolentem gradum*, 565 *invitus . . . ensis*, 770 *[ignis] invitus ardet*, 896 *die nolente*, 965 *nolo infelix*, 985–86 *nolunt manus / parere*), ordering or commanding (cf. 165 *[fames] iubet*, 769 *iussus pati moram*, 943–44 *quid flere iubes . . . dolor?*), and enduring (cf. 158 *nec patiens morae*, 198, 767, 1000 *impatiens onus*; see on 470, 931). Here too Tantalus and Thyestes show a close resemblance; each has to be prodded to act against his judgment, and this parallel finds its verbal expression in the imperative *perge* addressed to each (23, 490); Atreus, on the other hand, is the instigator of action rather than its object, and so he applies this sort of pressure to himself (890 *pergam*, 892 *perge*). Atreus in fact provides the most pregnant statement of this theme, when he announces his aim to make his subjects "will what they would not" (*quod nolunt velint* 212). Only the gods escape Atreus' efforts at compulsion (893–95), but they maintain their freedom by a withdrawal so complete as to seem tantamount to nonexistence.[160]

A still more pervasive image runs through the play, of which several of the motifs mentioned so far can be seen as particular aspects. From the first words of the prologue, where Tantalus finds himself forcibly removed from his usual place of torment (*quis . . . sede ab infausta extrahit* 1), Seneca's language repeatedly depicts a disjointed world, in which things do not remain in their normal position[161] and in which customary boundaries fail to hold good. At the level of plot this confusion of realms is represented by the unnatural outbreak of night (777, cf. also 677–79 and perhaps 466–67) and also by the intrusion of the lower world into the world of the living (1–122, 668–78, cf. 804–12). (It could be added that Thyestes' action is itself a perverse mingling, both of what is and what is not proper nourishment, cf. 917 *mixtum suorum sanguinem*, and also of the living and the dead, cf. 1041–47, 1090–92.) Simile and allusion extend the theme further, breaking down the distinction between "civilized" and "barbarous" (627–32, 1047–50) and even between human and animal (707–12, 732–37). All these violations of order emanate from a single source, the *ira* of Atreus. *Tantum potest quantum odit*, says Thyestes with greater truth than he realizes (483): "his power is as great as his hatred." That hatred is itself

---

160 This theme too operates on a literal and a figurative level, so that, for example, Thyestes' statement "the gods have fled" (*fugere superi*, 1021) describes both the absence of celestial light and also the disappearance of divinely sanctioned norms of morality. (For a comparable double sense see on *aras . . . extinguens* 742.)

161 This may be the reason for the remarkable prominence of words for "wandering" (*errare, vagare, vagus*); see, for example, on 282, 631, 1068–69. On "boundary violation" in Senecan tragedy see now Segal, *op. cit.* (p. 43, n. 154).

without limit (26, 255–56, 1053–54), and so it has the strength to overturn all boundaries, throwing the very cosmos into anarchic confusion.

The world of the *Thyestes* is bizarre and nightmarish, but it is not the product of mere fantasy. In its externals it is, in fact, curiously similar to Seneca's own, a world of *Lares, Penates,* and *Quirites* (264, 775, 396), of rooftop gardens and heated bathing-pools (464–66), where Parthians and Alans threaten the margins of empire (382–84, 603, 629–30) and rulers chosen by Jupiter bestow diadems on obedient client-kings (599). In this patently Roman context Seneca's Atreus—a vicious and demented tyrant whose megalomania extends to self-deification[162]—cannot have failed to strike audiences as disturbingly familiar. The obvious links are with "Caligula," whom Seneca had depicted in similar terms in the *De ira*[163] and who could safely be held up to Nero as an *exemplum* of all that was abhorrent in a ruler. The play might carry other, more subversive contemporary allusions; by their nature, though, any hostile references to Nero would need to be so well concealed as to be, at this distance, beyond certain discovery.[164] What does seem clear is that Seneca's portrait of Atreus draws some of its unique conviction from Seneca's first-hand observation of absolute power.

In the end, though, the play derives its power from an ability to reflect and clarify the enduring facts of human experience. Its vision of life is even by tragic standards painfully bleak. It portrays a world where belief in a benign providence seems a delusion and ambition merely another form of folly, where the highest aspirations possible are a life of peaceful obscurity or, failing that, a freely chosen death, and where even this modest degree of control is rarely attained. At the heart of the play, in the portraits of Atreus and Thyestes, lies an anguished sense of the fragility of reason and order, a dreadful awareness of what human beings can be led to do and to suffer by the irrational forces within them. These concerns do not represent the sum of life, but they are real, and they have not lost their meaning in the second half of the twentieth century. The vision of the *Thyestes* may even seem appallingly prophetic in an age when, as never before in history, paranoiac suspicion and the unbounded drive for power can literally consume the world.

---

[162] Cf. 712–13, 885, 911; for Atreus' madness cf. 547 *nec potens mentis,* 682 *furens.*

[163] Above, p. 4.

[164] One possible candidate: the reference to poisoning in 453 *venenum in auro bibitur,* although a commonplace (and therefore unsuspicious), could carry an additional resonance if, as seems plausible on other grounds (above, p. 13), the play was written after the death of Britannicus in 55. The story of Atreus and Thyestes had already been made the basis for "invective against palace and dynasty" and "maxims of subversive statecraft" (R. Syme, *Tacitus* [Oxford, 1958], 362) and would serve a similar purpose for Curiatius Maternus under Vespasian, cf. Tac. *Dial.* 3.3.

THYESTES

PERSONAE

TANTALI UMBRA
FURIA
ATREUS
SATELLES
THYESTES
TANTALUS filius eius
PLISTHENES tacitus
NUNTIUS
CHORUS ARGIVORUM

The conventional act divisions are not part of the text as transmitted by
the manuscripts; they are therefore printed within brackets.

[PROLOGUE/ACT I]

TANTALI UMBRA—FURIA

TANTALI UMBRA

Quis inferorum sede ab infausta extrahit
avido fugaces ore captantem cibos,
quis male deorum Tantalo visas domos
ostendit iterum? peius inventum est siti
arente in undis aliquid et peius fame   5
hiante semper? Sisyphi numquid lapis
gestandus umeris lubricus nostris venit,
aut membra celeri differens cursu rota,
aut poena Tityi, qui specu vasto patens
visceribus atras pascit effossis aves   10
et nocte reparans quidquid amisit die
plenum recenti pabulum monstro iacet?
in quod malum transcribor? o quisquis nova
supplicia functis durus umbrarum arbiter
disponis, addi si quid ad poenas potest   15
quod ipse custos carceris diri horreat,
quod maestus Acheron paveat, ad cuius metum
nos quoque tremamus, quaere; iam nostra subit
e stirpe turba quae suum vincat genus
ac me innocentem faciat et inausa audeat.   20
regione quidquid impia cessat loci
complebo; numquam stante Pelopea domo
Minos vacabit.

FURIA

Perge, detestabilis
umbra, et penates impios furiis age.
certetur omni scelere et alterna vice   25
stringatur ensis. nec sit irarum modus
pudorve, mentes caecus instiget furor,
rabies parentum duret et longum nefas
eat in nepotes. nec vacet cuiquam vetus
odisse crimen; semper oriatur novum,   30

nec unum in uno, dumque punitur scelus,
crescat. superbis fratribus regna excidant
repetantque profugos; dubia violentae domus
fortuna reges inter incertos labet;
miser ex potente fiat, ex misero potens   35
fluctuque regnum casus assiduo ferat.
ob scelera pulsi, cum dabit patriam deus,
in scelera redeant, sintque tam invisi omnibus
quam sibi. nihil sit ira quod vetitum putet.
fratrem expavescat frater et natum parens   40
natusque patrem; liberi pereant male,
peius tamen nascantur; immineat viro
infesta coniunx; bella trans pontum vehant,
effusus omnis irriget terras cruor,
supraque magnos gentium exultet duces   45
Libido victrix; impia stuprum in domo
levissimum sit facinus; et fas et fides
iusque omne pereat. non sit a vestris malis
immune caelum; cur micant stellae polo
flammaeque servant debitum mundo decus?   50
nox alta fiat, excidat caelo dies.
misce penates, odia caedes funera
accerse et imple Tantalo totam domum.
ornetur altum columen et lauro fores
laetae virescant, dignus adventu tuo   55
splendescat ignis; Thracium fiat nefas
maiore numero. dextra cur patrui vacat?
[nondum Thyestes liberos deflet suos;]
ecquando tollet? ignibus iam subditis
spument aena, membra per partes eant   60
discerpta, patrios polluat sanguis focos,
epulae instruantur; non novi sceleris tibi
conviva venies. liberum dedimus diem
tuamque ad istas solvimus mensas famem.
ieiunia exple, mixtus in Bacchum cruor   65
spectante te potetur; inveni dapes
quas ipse fugeres. siste, quo praeceps ruis?

TANTALI UMBRA

Ad stagna et amnes et recedentes aquas
labrisque ab ipsis arboris plenae fugas.
abire in atrum carceris liceat mei   70
cubile, liceat, si parum videor miser,

mutare ripas; alveo medius tuo,
Phlegethon, relinquar igneo cinctus freto.
quicumque poenas lege fatorum datas
pati iuberis, quisquis exeso iaces 75
pavidus sub antro iamque venturi times
montis ruinam, quisquis avidorum feros
rictus leonum et dira Furiarum agmina
implicitus horres, quisquis immissas faces
semiustus abigis, Tantali vocem excipe 80
properantis ad vos; credite experto mihi,
amate poenas. quando continget mihi
effugere superos?

FURIA

Ante perturba domum
inferque tecum proelia et ferri malum
regibus amorem, concute insano ferum 85
pectus tumultu.

TANTALI UMBRA

Me pati poenas decet,
non esse poenam. mittor ut dirus vapor
tellure rupta vel gravem populis luem
sparsura pestis? ducam in horrendum nefas
avus nepotes? magne divorum parens 90
nosterque, quamvis pudeat, ingenti licet
taxata poena lingua crucietur loquax,
nec hoc tacebo; moneo, ne sacra manus
violate caede neve furiali malo
aspergite aras. stabo et arcebo scelus— 95
quid ora terres verbere et tortos ferox
minaris angues? quid famem infixam intimis
agitas medullis? flagrat incensum siti
cor et perustis flamma visceribus micat.
sequor. 100

FURIA

Hunc, hunc furorem divide in totam domum;
sic, sic, ferantur et suum infensi invicem
sitiant cruorem. sentit introitus tuos
domus et nefando tota contactu horruit.
actum est abunde. gradere ad infernos specus 105
amnemque notum; iam tuum maestae pedem

terrae gravantur. cernis ut fontis liquor
introrsus actus linquat, ut ripae vacent
ventusque raras igneus nubes ferat?
pallescit omnis arbor ac nudus stetit   110
fugiente pomo ramus, et qui fluctibus
illinc propinquis Isthmos atque illinc fremit,
vicinā gracili dividens terra vada,
longe remotos latus exaudit sonos.
iam Lerna retro cessit et Phoronides   115
latuere venae nec suas profert sacer
Alpheos undas et Cithaeronis iuga
stant parte nulla cana deposita nive
timentque veterem nobiles Argi sitim.
en ipse Titan dubitat an iubeat sequi   120
cogatque habenis ire periturum diem.

CHORUS

Argos de superis si quis Achaicum
Pisaeasque domos curribus inclitas,
Isthmi si quis amat regna Corinthii
et portus geminos et mare dissidens,   125
si quis Taygeti conspicuas nives,
quas cum Sarmaticus tempore frigido
in summis Boreas composuit iugis,
aestas veliferis solvit Etesiis,
quem tangit gelido flumine lucidus   130
Alpheos, stadio notus Olympico,
advertat placidum numen et arceat,
alternae scelerum ne redeant vices
nec succedat avo deterior nepos
et maior placeat culpa minoribus.   135
tandem lassa feros exuat impetus
sicci progenies impia Tantali;
peccatum satis est. fas valuit nihil
aut commune nefas. proditus occidit
deceptor domini Myrtilus, et fide   140
vectus qua tulerat nobile reddidit
mutato pelagus nomine; notior
nulla est Ioniis fabula navibus.
exceptus gladio parvulus impio
dum currit patrium natus ad osculum,   145
immatura focis victima concidit
divisusque tua est, Tantale, dextera

mensas ut strueres hospitibus deis.
hos aeterna fames persequitur cibos,
hos aeterna sitis, nec dapibus feris   150
dercerni potuit poena decentior.
stat lassus vacuo gutture Tantalus,
impendet capiti plurima noxio
Phineis avibus praeda fugacior;
hinc illinc gravidis frondibus incubat   155
et curvata suis fetibus ac tremens
alludit patulis arbor hiatibus.
haec, quamvis avidus nec patiens morae,
deceptus totiens tangere neglegit
obliquatque oculos oraque comprimit   160
inclusisque famem dentibus alligat.
sed tunc divitias omne nemus suas
demittit propius pomaque desuper
insultant foliis mitia languidis
accenduntque famem, quae iubet irritas   165
exercere manus; has ubi protulit
et falli libuit, totus in arduum
autumnus rapitur silvaque mobilis.
instat deinde sitis non levior fame;
qua cum percaluit sanguis et igneis   170
exarsit facibus, stat miser obvios
fluctus ore petens, quos profugus latex
avertit sterili deficiens vado
conantemque sequi deserit. hic bibit
altum de rapido gurgite pulverem.   175

[ACT II]

ATREUS—SATELLES

ATREUS

Ignave, iners, enervis et, quod maximum
probrum tyranno rebus in summis reor,
inulte; post tot scelera, post fratris dolos
fasque omne ruptum questibus vanis agis
iratus Atreus? fremere iam totus tuis   180
debebat armis orbis et geminum mare
utrimque classes agere, iam flammis agros
lucere et urbes decuit ac strictum undique

micare ferrum. tota sub nostro sonet
Argolica tellus equite; non silvae tegant 185
hostem nec altis montium structae iugis
arces; relictis bellicum totus canat
populus Mycenis; quisquis invisum caput
tegit ac tuetur, clade funesta occidat.
haec ipsa pollens incliti Pelopis domus 190
ruat vel in me, dummodo in fratrem ruat.
age, anime, fac quod nulla posteritas probet,
sed nulla taceat. aliquod audendum est nefas
atrox, cruentum, tale quod frater meus
suum esse mallet. scelera non ulcisceris, 195
nisi vincis. et quid esse tam saevum potest
quod superet illum? numquid abiectus iacet?
numquid secundis patitur in rebus modum,
fessis quietem? novi ego ingenium viri
indocile; flecti non potest—frangi potest. 200
proinde antequam se firmat aut vires parat,
petatur ultro, ne quiescentem petat.
aut perdet aut peribit; in medio est scelus
positum occupanti.

SATELLES

       Fama te populi nihil
adversa terret?

ATREUS

       Maximum hoc regni bonum est, 205
quod facta domini cogitur populus sui
tam ferre quam laudare.

SATELLES

       Quos cogit metus
laudare, eosdem reddit inimicos metus;
at qui favoris gloriam veri petit,
animo magis quam voce laudari volet. 210

ATREUS

Laus vera et humili saepe contingit viro,
non nisi potenti falsa. quod nolunt velint.

SATELLES

Rex velit honesta; nemo non eadem volet.

ATREUS

Ubicumque tantum honesta dominanti licent,
precario regnatur.

SATELLES

    Ubi non est pudor   215
nec cura iuris sanctitas pietas fides,
instabile regnum est.

ATREUS

    Sanctitas pietas fides
privata bona sunt; qua iuvat reges eant.

SATELLES

Nefas nocere vel malo fratri puta.

ATREUS

Fas est in illo quidquid in fratre est nefas.   220
quid enim reliquit crimine intactum aut ubi
sceleri pepercit? coniugem stupro abstulit
regnumque furto; specimen antiquum imperi
fraude est adeptus, fraude turbavit domum.
est Pelopis altis nobile in stabulis pecus,   225
arcanus aries, ductor opulenti gregis.
huius per omne corpus effuso coma
dependet auro, cuius e tergo novi
aurata reges sceptra Tantalici gerunt;
possessor huius regnat, hunc tantae domus   230
fortuna sequitur. tuta seposita sacer
in parte carpit prata, quae cludit lapis
fatale saxeo pascuum muro tegens.
hunc facinus ingens ausus assumpta in scelus
consorte nostri perfidus thalami avehit.   235
hinc omne cladis mutuae fluxit malum;
per regna trepidus exul erravi mea,
pars nulla generis tuta ab insidiis vacat,
corrupta coniunx, imperi quassa est fides,
domus aegra, dubius sanguis est. certi nihil   240

nisi frater hostis. quid stupes? tandem incipe
animosque sume. Tantalum et Pelopem aspice;
ad haec manus exempla poscuntur meae.
profare, dirum qua caput mactem via.

SATELLES

Ferro peremptus spiritum inimicum expuat.   245

ATREUS

De fine poenae loqueris; ego poenam volo.
perimat tyrannus lenis; in regno meo
mors impetratur.

SATELLES

Nulla te pietas movet?

ATREUS

Excede, Pietas, si modo in nostra domo
umquam fuisti. dira Furiarum cohors   250
discorsque Erinys veniat et geminas faces
Megaera quatiens. non satis magno meum
ardet furore pectus, impleri iuvat
maiore monstro.

SATELLES

Quid novi rabidus struis?

ATREUS

Nil quod doloris capiat assueti modum;   255
nullum relinquam facinus et nullum est satis.

SATELLES

Ferrum?

ATREUS

Parum est.

SATTELES

Quid ignis?

ATREUS

Etiam nunc parum est.

SATELLES

Quonam ergo telo tantus utetur dolor?

ATREUS

Ipso Thyeste.

SATELLES

Maius hoc ira est malum.

ATREUS

Fateor. tumultus pectora attonitus quatit   260
penitusque volvit; rapior et quo nescio,
sed rapior. imo mugit e fundo solum,
tonat dies serenus ac totis domus
ut fracta tectis crepuit et moti Lares
vertere vultum—fiat hoc, fiat nefas   265
quod, di, timetis.

SATELLES

Facere quid tandem paras?

ATREUS

Nescioquid animus maius et solito amplius
supraque fines moris humani tumet
instatque pigris manibus; haud quid sit scio,
sed grande quiddam est. ita sit. hoc, anime, occupa.   270
dignum est Thyeste facinus et dignum Atreo;
uterque faciat. vidit infandas domus
Odrysia mensas—fateor, immane est scelus,
sed occupatum; maius hoc aliquid dolor
inveniat. animum Daulis inspira parens   275
sororque (causa est similis); assiste et manum
impelle nostram. liberos avidus pater
gaudensque laceret et suos artus edat.
bene est, abunde est; hic placet poenae modus
tantisper. ubinam est? tam diu cur innocens   280
versatur Atreus? tota iam ante oculos meos

imago caedis errat, ingesta orbitas
in ora patris—anime, quid rursus times
et ante rem subsidis? audendum est, age;
quod est in isto scelere praecipuum nefas,   285
hoc ipse faciet.

SATELLES

Sed quibus captus dolis
nostros dabit perductus in laqueos pedem?
inimica credit cuncta.

ATREUS

Non poterat capi,
nisi capere vellet; regna nunc sperat mea.
hac spe subibit gurgitis tumidi minas   291
dubiumque Libycae Syrtis intrabit fretum,   292
hac spe minanti fulmen occurret Iovi,   290
hac spe, quod esse maximum retur malum,
fratrem videbit.

SATELLES

Quis fidem pacis dabit?
cui tanta credet?

ATREUS

Credula est spes improba.   295
natis tamen mandata quae patruo ferant
dabimus, relictis exul hospitiis vagus
regno ut miserias mutet atque Argos regat
ex parte dominus. si nimis durus preces
spernet Thyestes, liberos eius rudes   300
malisque fessos gravibus et faciles capi
praecommovebunt. hinc vetus regni furor,
illinc egestas tristis ac durus labor
quamvis rigentem tot malis subigent virum.

SATELLES

Iam tempus illi fecit aerumnas leves.   305

ATREUS

Erras; malorum sensus accrescit die.
leve est miserias ferre, perferre est grave.

SATELLES

Alios ministros consili tristis lege.

ATREUS

Peiora iuvenes facile praecepta audiunt.

SATELLES

In patre facient quidquid in patruo doces;   310
saepe in magistrum scelera redierunt sua.

ATREUS

Ut nemo doceat fraudis et sceleris vias,
regnum docebit. ne mali fiant times?
nascuntur. istud quod vocas saevum asperum
agique dure credis et nimium impie,   315
fortasse et illic agitur.

SATELLES

              Hanc fraudem scient
nati parari?

ATREUS

             Tacita tam rudibus fides
non est in annis; detegent forsan dolos.
tacere multis discitur vitae malis.

SATELLES

Ipsosque, per quos fallere alium cogitas,   320
falles?

ATREUS

            Ut ipsi crimine et culpa vacent.
quid enim necesse est liberos sceleri meo
inserere? per nos odia se nostra explicent— ⌉
male agis, recedis, anime; si parcis tuis,

parces et illis. consili Agamemnon mei 325
sciens minister fiat et fratri sciens
Menelaus adsit. prolis incertae fides
ex hoc petatur scelere; si bella abnuunt
et gerere nolunt odia, si patruum vocant,
pater est. eatur—multa sed trepidus solet 330
detegere vultus, magna nolentem quoque
consilia produnt; nesciant quantae rei
fiant ministri. nostra tu coepta occule.

SATELLES

Haud sum monendus; ista nostro in pectore
fides timorque, sed magis claudet fides. 335

CHORUS

Tandem regia nobilis,
antiqui genus Inachi,
fratrum composuit minas.
    Quis vos exagitat furor,
alternis dare sanguinem 340
et sceptrum scelere aggredi?
nescitis, cupidi arcium,
regnum quo iaceat loco.
regem non faciunt opes,
non vestis Tyriae color, 345
non frontis nota regia,
non auro nitidae trabes.
rex est qui posuit metus
et diri mala pectoris,
quem non ambitio impotens 350
et numquam stabilis favor
vulgi praecipitis movet,
non quidquid fodit Occidens
aut unda Tagus aurea
claro devehit alveo, 355
non quidquid Libycis terit
fervens area messibus,
quem non concutiet cadens
obliqui via fulminis,
non Eurus rapiens mare 360
aut saevo rabidus freto
ventosi tumor Hadriae,
quem non lancea militis,

non strictus domuit chalybs,
qui tuto positus loco   365
infra se videt omnia
occurritque suo libens
fato nec queritur mori.
    Reges conveniant licet,
qui sparsos agitant Dahas,   370
qui rubri vada litoris
et gemmis mare lucidis
late sanguineum tenent,
aut qui Caspia fortibus
recludunt iuga Sarmatis,   375
certet Danuvii vadum
audet qui pedes ingredi
et (quocumque loco iacent)
Seres vellere nobiles;
mens regnum bona possidet.   380
nil ullis opus est equis,
nil armis et inertibus
telis, quae procul ingerit
Parthus, cum simulat fugas,
admotis nihil est opus   385
urbes sternere machinis
longe saxa rotantibus;
[rex est qui metuit nihil,
rex est qui cupiet nihil;]
hoc regnum sibi quisque dat.   390
    Stet quicumque volet potens
aulae culmine lubrico;
me dulcis saturet quies,
obscuro positus loco
leni perfruar otio,   395
nullis nota Quiritibus
aetas per tacitum fluat.
sic cum transierint mei
nullo cum strepitu dies,
plebeius moriar senex.   400
illi mors gravis incubat
qui, notus nimis omnibus,
ignotus moritur sibi.

[ACT III]

THYESTES—TANTALUS—PLISTHENES tacitus

THYESTES

Optata patriae tecta et Argolicas opes
miserisque summum ac maximum exulibus bonum,   405
tractum soli natalis et patrios deos
(si sunt tamen di) cerno, Cyclopum sacras
turres, labore maius humano decus,
celebrata iuveni stadia, per quae nobilis
palmam paterno non semel curru tuli.   410
occurret Argos, populus occurret frequens—
sed nempe et Atreus. repete silvestres fugas
saltusque densos potius et mixtam feris
similemque vitam. clarus hic regni nitor
fulgore non est quod oculos falso auferat;   415
cum quod datur spectabis, et dantem aspice.
modo inter illa, quae putant cuncti aspera,
fortis fui laetusque; nunc contra in metus
revolvor. animus haeret ac retro cupit
corpus referre; moveo nolentem gradum.   420

TANTALUS

Pigro (quid hoc est?) genitor incessu stupet
vultumque versat seque in incerto tenet.

THYESTES

Quid, anime, pendes, quidve consilium diu
tam facile torques? rebus incertissimis,
fratri atque regno, credis ac metuis mala   425
iam victa, iam mansueta et aerumnas fugis
bene collocatas? esse iam miserum iuvat.
reflecte gressum, dum licet, teque eripe.

TANTALUS

Quae causa cogit, genitor, a patria gradum
referre visa? cur bonis tantis sinum   430
subducis? ira frater abiecta redit
partemque regni reddit et lacerae domus
componit artus teque restituit tibi.

THYESTES

Causam timoris ipse quam ignoro exigis;
nihil timendum video, sed timeo tamen. 435
placet ire, pigris membra sed genibus labant
alioque quam quo nitor abductus feror.
sic concitatam remige et velo ratem
aestus resistens remigi et velo refert.

TANTALUS

Evince quidquid obstat et mentem impedit 440
reducemque quanta praemia expectent vide.
pater, potes regnare.

THYESTES

Cum possim mori.

TANTALUS

Summa est potestas—

THYESTES

Nulla, si cupias nihil.

TANTALUS

Natis relinques.

THYESTES

Non capit regnum duos.

TANTALUS

Miser esse mavult esse qui felix potest? 445

THYESTES

Mihi crede, falsis magna nominibus placent,
frustra timentur dura. dum excelsus steti,
numquam pavere destiti atque ipsum mei
ferrum timere lateris. o quantum bonum est
obstare nulli, capere securas dapes 450
humi iacentem! scelera non intrant casas,
tutusque mensa capitur angusta scyphus;

venenum in auro bibitur—expertus loquor.
malam bonae praeferre fortunam licet.
non vertice alti montis impositam domum   455
et imminentem civitas humilis tremit,
nec fulget altis splendidum tectis ebur
somnosque non defendit excubitor meos;
non classibus piscamur, et retro mare
iacta fugamus mole, nec ventrem improbum   460
alimus tributo gentium; nullus mihi
ultra Getas metatur et Parthos ager;
non ture colimur nec meae excluso Iove
ornantur arae; nulla culminibus meis
imposita nutat silva, nec fumant manu   465
succensa multa stagna, nec somno dies
Bacchoque nox iungenda pervigili datur.
sed non timemur, tuta sine telo est domus,
rebusque parvis magna praestatur quies.
immane regnum est posse sine regno pati.   470

TANTALUS

Nec abnuendum, si dat imperium deus,
nec appetendum est. frater ut regnes rogat.

THYESTES

Rogat? timendum est; errat hic aliquis dolus.

TANTALUS

Redire pietas unde summota est solet,
reparatque vires iustus amissas amor.   475

THYESTES

Amat Thyesten frater? aetherias prius
perfundet Arctos pontus et Siculi rapax
consistet aestus unda, et Ionio seges
matura pelago surget et lucem dabit
nox atra terris; ante cum flammis aquae,   480
cum morte vita, cum mari ventus fidem ⌐
foedusque iungent.   ⌐

TANTALUS

Quam tamen fraudem times?

THYESTES

Omnem. timori quem meo statuam modum?
tantum potest quantum odit.

TANTALUS

In te quid potest?

THYESTES

Pro me nihil iam metuo; vos facitis mihi   485
Atrea timendum.

TANTALUS

Decipi cautus times?

THYESTES

Serum est cavendi tempus in mediis malis;
eatur. unum genitor hoc testor tamen:
ego vos sequor, non duco.

TANTALUS

Respiciet deus
bene cogitata. perge non dubio gradu.   490

ATREUS—THYESTES
TANTALUS—PLISTHENES taciti

ATREUS

Plagis tenetur clausa dispositis fera;
et ipsum et una generis invisi indolem
iunctam parenti cerno. iam tuto in loco
versantur odia; venit in nostras manus
tandem Thyestes, venit, et totus quidem.   495
vix tempero animo, vix dolor frenos capit.
sic, cum feras vestigat et longo sagax
loro tenetur Umber ac presso vias
scrutatur ore, dum procul lento suem
odore sentit, paret et tacito locum   500
rostro pererrat; praeda cum propior fuit,
cervice tota pugnat et gemitu vocat
dominum morantem seque retinenti eripit.
cum sperat ira sanguinem, nescit tegi;
tamen tegatur. aspice, ut multo gravis   505

squalore vultus obruat maestos coma,
quam foeda iaceat barba. praestetur fides—
fratrem iuvat videre. complexus mihi
redde expetitos. quidquid irarum fuit
transierit. ex hoc sanguis ac pietas die　　　510
colantur, animis odia damnata excidant.

THYESTES

Diluere possem cuncta, nisi talis fores.
sed fateor, Atreu, fateor, admisi omnia
quae credidisti. pessimam causam meam
hodierna pietas fecit; est prorsus nocens　　　515
quicumque visus tam bono fratri est nocens.
lacrimis agendum est. supplicem primus vides,
hae te precantur pedibus intactae manus;
ponatur omnis ira et ex animo tumor
erasus abeat. obsides fidei accipe　　　520
hos innocentes, frater.

ATREUS

　　　A genibus manum
aufer meosque potius amplexus pete.
vos quoque, senum praesidia, tot iuvenes, meo
pendete collo. —squalidam vestem exue,
oculisque nostris parce et ornatus cape　　　525
pares meis, laetusque fraterni imperi
capesse partem. maior haec laus est mea,
fratri paternum reddere incolumi decus;
habere regnum casus est, virtus dare.

THYESTES

Di paria, frater, pretia pro tantis tibi　　　530
meritis rependant. regiam capitis notam
squalor recusat noster et sceptrum manus
infausta refugit. liceat in media mihi
latere turba.

ATREUS

Recipit hoc regnum duos.

THYESTES

Meum esse credo quidquid est, frater, tuum. 535

ATREUS

Quis influentis dona fortunae abnuit?

THYESTES

Expertus est quicumque quam facile effluant.

ATREUS

Fratrem potiri gloria ingenti vetas?

THYESTES

Tua iam peracta gloria est, restat mea;
respuere certum est regna consilium mihi. 540

ATREUS

Meam relinquam, nisi tuam partem accipis.

THYESTES

Accipio. regni nomen impositi feram,
sed iura et arma servient mecum tibi.

ATREUS

Imposita capiti vincla venerando gere;
ego destinatas victimas superis dabo. 545

CHORUS

Credat hoc quisquam? ferus ille et acer
nec potens mentis truculentus Atreus
fratris aspectu stupefactus haesit.
nulla vis maior pietate vera est;
iurgia externis inimica durant, 550
quos amor verus tenuit, tenebit.
ira cum magnis agitata causis
gratiam rupit cecinitque bellum,
cum leves frenis sonuere turmae,
fulsit hinc illinc agitatus ensis, 555
quem movet crebro furibundus ictu

sanguinem Mavors cupiens recentem,
opprimit ferrum manibusque iunctis
ducit ad pacem Pietas negantes.
   Otium tanto subitum e tumultu   560
quis deus fecit? modo per Mycenas
arma civilis crepuere belli.
pallidae natos tenuere matres,
uxor armato timuit marito,
cum manum invitus sequeretur ensis,   565
sordidus pacis vitio quietae.
ille labentes renovare muros,
hic situ quassas stabilire turres,
(ferreis) portas cohibere claustris)
ille certabat, pavidusque pinnis   570
anxiae noctis vigil incubabat.
[peior est bello timor ipse belli.]
iam minae saevi cecidere ferri,
iam silet murmur grave classicorum,
iam tacet stridor litui strepentis;   575
alta pax urbi revocata laetae est.
   Sic, ubi ex alto tumuere fluctus,
Bruttium Coro feriente pontum,
Scylla pulsatis resonat cavernis
ac mare in portu timuere nautae   580
quod rapax haustum revomit Charybdis,
et ferus Cyclops metuit parentem
rupe ferventis residens in Aetnae,
ne superfusis violetur undis
ignis aeternis resonans caminis,   585
et putat mergi sua posse pauper
regna Laertes Ithaca tremente.
si suae ventis cecidere vires,
mitius stagno pelagus recumbit;
alta, quae navis timuit secare   590
hinc et hinc fusis speciosa velis,
strata ludenti patuere cumbae,
et vacat mersos numerare pisces
hic, ubi ingenti modo sub procella
Cyclades pontum timuere motae.   595
   Nulla sors longa est. dolor ac voluptas
invicem cedunt; brevior voluptas.
ima permutat levis hora summis.
ille qui donat diadema fronti,
quem genu nixae tremuere gentes,   600

cuius ad nutum posuere bella
Medus et Phoebi propioris Indus
et Dahae Parthis equitem minati,
anxius sceptrum tenet et moventes
cuncta divinat metuitque casus   605
mobiles rerum dubiumque tempus.

    Vos quibus rector maris atque terrae
ius dedit magnum necis atque vitae,
ponite inflatos tumidosque vultus.
quidquid a vobis minor expavescit,   610
maior hoc vobis dominus minatur;
omne sub regno graviore regnum est.
quem dies vidit veniens superbum,
hunc dies vidit fugiens iacentem.

    Nemo confidat nimium secundis,   615
nemo desperet meliora lassis.
miscet haec illis prohibetque Clotho
stare Fortunam, rotat omne fatum.
nemo tam divos habuit faventes,
crastinum ut posset sibi polliceri;   620
res deus nostras celeri citatas
turbine versat.

[ACT IV]

NUNTIUS—CHORUS

NUNTIUS

Quis me per auras turbo praecipitem vehet
atraque nube involvet, ut tantum nefas
eripiat oculis? o domus Pelopi quoque   625
et Tantalo pudenda!

CHORUS

Quid portas novi?

NUNTIUS

Quaenam ista regio est? Argos et Sparte, pios
sortita fratres, et maris gemini premens
fauces Corinthos, an feris Hister fugam
praebens Alanis, an sub aeterna nive   630

Hyrcana tellus, an vagi passim Scythae?
quis hic nefandi est conscius monstri locus?

CHORUS

Effare, et istud pande, quodcumque est, malum.

NUNTIUS

Si steterit animus, si metu corpus rigens
remittet artus. haeret in vultu trucis   635
imago facti. ferte me insanae procul,
illo, procellae, ferte, quo fertur dies
hinc raptus.

CHORUS

        Animos gravius incertos tenes.
quid sit quod horres ede et auctorem indica;
non quaero quis sit, sed uter. effare ocius.   640

NUNTIUS

In arce summa Pelopiae pars est domus
conversa ad Austros, cuius extremum latus
aequale monti crescit atque urbem premit
et contumacem regibus populum suis
habet sub ictu. fulget hic turbae capax   645
immane tectum, cuius auratas trabes
variis columnae nobiles maculis ferunt.
post ista vulgo nota, quae populi colunt,
in multa dives spatia discedit domus;
arcana in imo regio secessu iacet,   650
alta vetustum valle compescens nemus,
penetrale regni, nulla qua laetos solet
praebere ramos arbor aut ferro coli,
sed taxus et cupressus et nigra ilice
obscura nutat silva, quam supra eminens   655
despectat alte quercus et vincit nemus.
hinc auspicari regna Tantalidae solent,
hinc petere lassis rebus ac dubiis opem.
affixa inhaerent dona; vocales tubae
fractique currus, spolia Myrtoi maris,   660
iunctaeque falsis axibus pendent rotae
et omne gentis facinus. hoc Phrygius loco
fixus tiaras Pelopis, hic praeda hostium

et de triumpho picta barbarico chlamys.
fons stat sub umbra tristis et nigra piger 665
haeret palude; talis est dirae Stygis
deformis unda, quae facit caelo fidem.
hinc nocte caeca gemere ferales deos
fama est, catenis lucus excussis sonat
ululantque manes. quidquid audire est metus 670
illic videtur; errat antiquis vetus
emissa bustis turba et insultant loco
maiora notis monstra. quin tota solet
micare silva flamma, et excelsae trabes
ardent sine igne. saepe latratu nemus 675
trino remugit, saepe simulacris domus
attonita magnis. nec dies sedat metum;
nox propria luco est, et superstitio inferum
in luce media regnat. hinc orantibus
responsa dantur certa, cum ingenti sono 680
laxantur adyto fata et immugit specus
vocem deo solvente. quo postquam furens
intravit Atreus liberos fratris trahens,
ornantur arae—quis queat digne eloqui?
post terga iuvenum nobiles revocat manus 685
et maesta vitta capita purpurea ligat.
non tura desunt, non sacer Bacchi liquor
tangensque salsa victimam culter mola;
servatur omnis ordo, ne tantum nefas
non rite fiat.

CHORUS

Quis manum ferro admovet? 690

NUNTIUS

Ipse est sacerdos, ipse funesta prece
letale carmen ore violento canit;
stat ipse ad aras, ipse devotos neci
contrectat et componit et ferro parat,
attendit ipse; nulla pars sacri perit. 695
lucus tremescit, tota succusso solo
nutavit aula, dubia quo pondus daret
ac fluctuanti similis, e laevo aethere
atrum cucurrit limitem sidus trahens,
libata in ignes vina mutato fluunt 700
cruenta Baccho, regium capiti decus

bis terque lapsum est, flevit in templis ebur.
movere cunctos monstra, sed solus sibi
immotus Atreus constat atque ultro deos
terret minantes iamque dimissa mora 705
adsistit aris, torvum et obliquum intuens.
ieiuna silvis qualis in Gangeticis
inter iuvencos tigris erravit duos,
utriusque praedae cupida, quo primum ferat
incerta morsus (flectit hoc rictus suos, 710
illo reflectit et famem dubiam tenet)—
sic dirus Atreus capita devota impiae
speculatur irae. quem prius mactet sibi
dubitat, secunda deinde quem caede immolet.
nec interest, sed dubitat et saevum scelus 715
iuvat ordinare.

CHORUS

Quem tamen ferro occupat?

NUNTIUS

Primus locus, ne desse pietatem putes,
avo dicatur; Tantalus prima hostia est.

CHORUS

Quo iuvenis animo, quo tulit vultu necem?

NUNTIUS

Stetit sui securus et non est preces 720
perire frustra passus. ast illi ferus
in vulnere ensem abscondit et penitus premens
iugulo manum commisit; educto stetit
ferro cadaver, cumque dubitasset diu
hac parte an illa caderet, in patruum cadit. 725
tunc ille ad aras Plisthenem saevus trahit
adicitque fratri. colla percussa amputat;
cervice caesa truncus in pronum ruit,
querulum cucurrit murmure incerto caput.

CHORUS

Quid deinde gemina caede perfunctus facit? 730
puerone parcit, an scelus sceleri ingerit?

NUNTIUS

Silva iubatus qualis Armenia leo
in caede multa victor armento incubat
(cruore rictus madidus et pulsa fame
non ponit iras, hinc et hinc tauros premens   735
vitulis minatur dente iam lasso impiger)—
non aliter Atreus saevit atque ira tumet
ferrumque gemina caede perfusum tenens,
oblitus in quem fureret, infesta manu
exegit ultra corpus, ac pueri statim   740
pectore receptus ensis e tergo exstitit.
cadit ille et aras sanguine extinguens suo
per utrumque vulnus moritur.

CHORUS

O saevum scelus!

NUNTIUS

Exhorruistis? hactenus si stat nefas,
pius est.

CHORUS

An ultra maius aut atrocius   745
natura recipit?

NUNTIUS

Sceleris hunc finem putas?
gradus est.

CHORUS

Quid ultra potuit? obiecit feris
lanianda forsan corpora atque igne arcuit?

NUNTIUS

Utinam arcuisset! ne tegat functos humus
nec solvat ignis, avibus epulandos licet   750
ferisque triste pabulum saevis trahat.
votum est sub hoc quod esse supplicium solet;
pater insepultos spectet. o nullo scelus
credibile in aevo quodque posteritas neget!

erepta vivis exta pectoribus tremunt 755
spirantque venae corque adhuc pavidum salit;
at ille fibras tractat ac fata inspicit
et adhuc calentes viscerum venas notat.
postquam hostiae placuere, securus vacat
iam fratris epulis. ipse divisum secat 760
in membra corpus, amputat trunco tenus
umeros patentes et lacertorum moras,
denudat artus durus atque ossa amputat;
tantum ora servat et datas fidei manus.
haec veribus haerent viscera et lentis data 765
stillant caminis, illa flammatus latex
candente aeno iactat. impositas dapes
transiluit ignis inque trepidantes focos
bis ter regestus et pati iussus moram
invitus ardet. stridet in veribus iecur, 770
nec facile dicam corpora an flammae magis
gemuere. piceos ignis in fumos abit,
et ipse fumus, tristis ac nebula gravis,
non rectus exit seque in excelsum levat;
ipsos Penates nube deformi obsidet. 775
o Phoebe patiens, fugeris retro licet
medioque ruptum merseris caelo diem,
sero occidisti! lancinat natos pater
artusque mandit ore funesto suos;
nitet fluente madidus unguento comam 780
gravisque vino; saepe praeclusae cibum
tenuere fauces. in malis unum hoc tuis
bonum est, Thyesta, quod mala ignoras tua;
sed et hoc peribit. verterit currus licet
sibi ipse Titan obvium ducens iter 785
tenebrisque facinus obruat taetrum novis
nox missa ab ortu tempore alieno gravis,
tamen videndum est; tota patefient mala.

CHORUS

Quo, terrarum superumque parens,
cuius ad ortus noctis opacae 790
decus omne fugit, quo vertis iter
medioque diem perdis Olympo?
cur, Phoebe, tuos rapis aspectus?
nondum serae nuntius horae
nocturna vocat lumina Vesper, 795

nondum Hesperiae flexura rotae
iubet emeritos solvere currus,
nondum in noctem vergente die
tertia misit bucina signum;
stupet ad subitae tempora cenae 800
nondum fessis bubus arator.
quid te aetherio pepulit cursu?
quae causa tuos limite certo
deiecit equos? numquid aperto
carcere Ditis victi temptant 805
bella Gigantes? numquid Tityos
pectore fesso renovat veteres
saucius iras? num reiecto
latus explicuit monte Typhoeus?
numquid struitur via Phlegraeos 810
alta per hostes et Thessalicum
Thressa premitur Pelion Ossa?
    Solitae mundi periere vices.
nihil occasus, nihil ortus erit.
stupet Eoos assueta deo 815
tradere frenos genetrix primae
roscida lucis perversa sui
limina regni; nescit fessos
tinguere currus, nec fumantes
sudore iubas mergere ponto. 820
ipse insueto novus hospitio
Sol Auroram videt occiduus,
tenebrasque iubet surgere nondum
nocte parata; non succedunt
astra, nec ullo micat igne polus, 825
non Luna gravis digerit umbras.
    Sed quidquid id est, utinam nox sit!
trepidant, trepidant pectora magno
percussa metu,
ne fatali cuncta ruina 830
quassata labent iterumque deos
hominesque premat deforme chaos,
iterum terras et mare cingens
et vaga picti sidera mundi
natura tegat. non aeternae 835
facis exortu dux astrorum
saecula ducens dabit aestatis
brumaeque notas, non Phoebeis
obvia flammis demet nocti

Luna timores vincetque sui 840
fratris habenas, curvo brevius
limite currens; ibit in unum
congesta sinum turba deorum.
hic qui sacris pervius astris
secat obliquo tramite zonas, 845
flectens longos signifer annos,
lapsa videbit sidera labens;
hic qui nondum vere benigno
reddit Zephyro vela tepenti,
Aries praeceps ibit in undas, 850
per quas pavidam vexerat Hellen;
hic qui nitido Taurus cornu
praefert Hyadas, secum Geminos
trahet et curvi bracchia Cancri;
Leo flammiferis aestibus ardens 855
iterum e caelo cadet Herculeus;
cadet in terras Virgo relictas,
iustaeque cadent pondera Librae,
secumque trahent Scorpion acrem;
et qui nervo tenet Haemonio 860
pinnata senex spicula Chiron
rupto perdet spicula nervo;
pigram referens hiemem gelidus
cadet Aegoceros frangetque tuam,
quisquis es, urnam; tecum excedent 865
ultima caeli sidera Pisces.
monstraque numquam perfusa mari
merget condens omnia gurges;
et qui medias dividit Ursas,
fluminis instar lubricus Anguis 870
magnoque minor iuncta Draconi
frigida duro Cynosura gelu,
custosque sui tardus plaustri
iam non stabilis ruet Arctophylax.
    Nos e tanto visi populo 875
digni, premeret quos everso
cardine mundus? in nos aetas
ultima venit? o nos dura
sorte creatos, seu perdidimus
solem miseri, sive expulimus! 880–81
abeant questus, discede, timor:
vitae est avidus quisquis non vult
mundo secum pereunte mori.

[ACT V]

ATREUS

Aequalis astris gradior et cuncta super   885
altum superbo vertice attingens polum.
nunc decora regni teneo, nunc solium patris.
dimitto superos; summa votorum attigi.
bene est, abunde est, iam sat est etiam mihi—
sed cur satis sit? pergam et implebo patrem   890
funere suorum. ne quid obstaret pudor,
dies recessit; perge dum caelum vacat.
utinam quidem tenere fugientes deos
possem, et coactos trahere ut ultricem dapem
omnes viderent; quod sat est, videat pater.   895
etiam die nolente discutiam tibi
tenebras, miseriae sub quibus latitant tuae.
nimis diu conviva securo iaces
hilarique vultu; iam satis mensis datum est
satisque Baccho; sobrio tanta ad mala   900
opus est Thyeste. turba famularis, fores
templi relaxa, festa patefiat domus.
libet videre, capita natorum intuens,
quos det colores, verba quae primus dolor
effundat aut ut spiritu expulso stupens   905
corpus rigescat. fructus hic operis mei est;
miserum videre nolo, sed dum fit miser.
aperta multa tecta conlucent face;
resupinus ipse purpurae atque auro incubat,
vino gravatum fulciens laeva caput.   910
eructat. o me caelitum excelsissimum,
regum atque regem! vota transcendi mea.
satur est; capaci ducit argento merum—
ne parce potu; restat etiamnunc cruor
tot hostiarum. veteris hunc Bacchi color   915
abscondet; hoc, hoc mensa cludatur scypho.
mixtum suorum sanguinem genitor bibat;
meum bibisset. ecce, iam cantus ciet
festasque voces, nec satis menti imperat.

THYESTES

Pectora longis hebetata malis,   920
iam sollicitas ponite curas.
fugiat maeror fugiatque pavor,

fugiat trepidi comes exilii
tristis egestas, rebusque gravis
pudor afflictis. magis unde cadas   925
quam quo refert. magnum, ex alto
culmine lapsum stabilem in plano
figere gressum; magnum, ingenti
strage malorum pressum fracti
pondera regni non inflexa   930
cervice pati, nec degenerem
victumque malis rectum impositas
ferre ruinas. sed iam saevi
nubila fati pelle, ac miseri
temporis omnis dimitte notas;   935
redeant vultus ad laeta boni,
veterem ex animo mitte Thyesten.
　　　Proprium hoc miseros sequitur vitium,
numquam rebus credere laetis;
redeat felix fortuna licet,   940
tamen afflictos gaudere piget—
quid me revocas festumque vetas
celebrare diem, quid flere iubes,
nulla surgens dolor ex causa?
quid me prohibes flore decenti   945
vincire comam? prohibet, prohibet!
　　　Vernae capiti fluxere rosae,
pingui madidus crinis amomo
inter subitos stetit horrores,
imber vultu nolente cadit,   950
venit in medias voces gemitus.
maeror lacrimas amat assuetas,
flendi miseris dira cupido est;
libet infaustos mittere questus,
libet et Tyrio saturas ostro   955
rumpere vestes, ululare libet.
　　　Mittit luctus signa futuri
mens, ante sui praesaga mali;
instat nautis fera tempestas,
cum sine vento tranquilla tument—   960
quos tibi luctus quosve tumultus
fingis, demens? credula praesta
pectora fratri; iam, quidquid id est,
vel sine causa vel sero times.
　　　Nolo infelix, sed vagus intra   965
terror oberrat, subitos fundunt

oculi fletus, nec causa subest.
dolor an metus est? an habet lacrimas
magna voluptas?

ATREUS—THYESTES

ATREUS

Festum diem, germane, consensu pari   970
celebremus; hic est, sceptra qui firmet mea
solidamque pacis alliget certae fidem.

THYESTES

Satias dapis me nec minus Bacchi tenet.
augere cumulus hic voluptatem potest,
si cum meis gaudere felici datur.   975

ATREUS

Hic esse natos crede in amplexu patris.
hic sunt eruntque; nulla pars prolis tuae
tibi subtrahetur. ora quae exoptas dabo
totumque turba iam sua implebo patrem.
satiaberis, ne metue. nunc mixti meis   980
iucunda mensae sacra iuvenilis colunt;
sed accientur. poculum infuso cape
gentile Baccho.

THYESTES

           Capio fraternae dapis
donum; paternis vina libentur deis,
tunc hauriantur—sed quid hoc? nolunt manus   985
parere, crescit pondus et dextram gravat;
admotus ipsis Bacchus a labris fugit
circaque rictus ore decepto fluit.
en ipsa trepido mensa subsiluit solo;
vix lucet ignis; ipse quin aether gravis   990
inter diem noctemque desertus stupet.
quid hoc? magis magisque concussi labant
convexa caeli; spissior densis coit
caligo tenebris noxque se in noctem abdidit;
fugit omne sidus. quidquid est, fratri precor   995

natisque parcat, omnis in vile hoc caput
abeat procella. redde iam natos mihi!

ATREUS

Reddam, et tibi illos nullus eripiet dies.

THYESTES

Quis hic tumultus viscera exagitat mea?   1000
quid tremuit intus? sentio impatiens onus
meumque gemitu non meo pectus gemit.
adeste, nati, genitor infelix vocat,
adeste. visis fugiet hic vobis dolor
—unde obloquuntur?

ATREUS

                Expedi amplexus, pater;
venere. natos ecquid agnoscis tuos?   1005

THYESTES

Agnosco fratrem. sustines tantum nefas
gestare, Tellus? non ad infernam Styga
tenebrasque mergis rupta et ingenti via
ad chaos inane regna cum rege abripis?
non tota ab imo tecta convellens solo   1010
vertis Mycenas? stare circa Tantalum
uterque iam debuimus. hinc compagibus
et hinc revulsis, si quid infra Tartara est
avosque nostros, hoc tuam immani sinu
demitte vallem nosque defossos tege   1015
Acheronte toto. noxiae supra caput
animae vagentur nostrum et ardenti freto
Phlegethon harenas igneus tostas agens
exilia supra nostra violentus fluat.
—immota Tellus pondus ignavum iaces?   1020
fugere superi.

ATREUS

                Iam accipe hos potius libens
diu expetitos; nulla per fratrem est mora.
fruere, osculare, divide amplexus tribus.

THYESTES

Hoc foedus? haec est gratia, haec fratris fides?
sic odia ponis? non peto, incolumes pater   1025
natos ut habeam; scelere quod salvo dari
odioque possit, frater hoc fratrem rogo:
sepelire liceat. redde quod cernas statim
uri; nihil te genitor habiturus rogo,
sed perditurus.

ATREUS

                    Quidquid e natis tuis   1030
superest habes, quodcumque non superest habes.

THYESTES

Utrumne saevis pabulum alitibus iacent,
an beluis scinduntur, an pascunt feras?

ATREUS

Epulatus ipse es impia natos dape.

THYESTES

Hoc est deos quod puduit, hoc egit diem   1035
aversum in ortus. quas miser voces dabo
questusque quos? quae verba sufficient mihi?
abscisa cerno capita et avulsas manus
et rupta fractis cruribus vestigia;
hoc est quod avidus capere non potuit pater.   1040
volvuntur intus viscera et clusum nefas
sine exitu luctatur et quaerit fugam.
da, frater, ensem (sanguinis multum mei
habet ille); ferro liberis detur via.
negatur ensis? pectora illiso sonent   1045
contusa planctu—sustine, infelix manum,
parcamus umbris. tale quis vidit nefas?
quis inhospitalis Caucasi rupem asperam
Heniochus habitans quisve Cecropiis metus
terris Procrustes? genitor en natos premo   1050
premorque natis; sceleris est aliquis modus.

ATREUS

Sceleri modus debetur ubi facias scelus,
non ubi reponas. hoc quoque exiguum est mihi.
ex vulnere ipso sanguinem calidum in tua
defundere ora debui, ut viventium   1055
biberes cruorem; verba sunt irae data
dum propero. ferro vulnera impresso dedi,
cecidi ad aras, caede votiva focos
placavi, et artus, corpora exanima amputans,
in parva carpsi frusta et haec ferventibus   1060
demersi aenis, illa lentis ignibus
stillare iussi; membra nervosque abscidi
viventibus, gracilique traiectas veru
mugire fibras vidi et aggessi manu
mea ipse flammas. omnia haec melius pater   1065
fecisse potuit. cecidit in cassum dolor;
scidit ore natos impio, sed nesciens,
sed nescientes.

THYESTES

              Clausa litoribus vagis
audite maria, vos quoque audite hoc scelus,
quocumque, di, fugistis; audite inferi,   1070
audite terrae, noxque Tartarea gravis
et atra nube, vocibus nostris vaca
(tibi sum relictus, sola tu miserum vides,
tu quoque sine astris); vota non faciam improba.
pro me nihil precabor (et quid iam potest   1075
pro me esse?); vobis vota prospicient mea.
tu, summe caeli rector, aetheriae potens
dominator aulae, nubibus totum horridis
convolve mundum, bella ventorum undique
committe et omni parte violentum intona,   1080
manuque non qua tecta et immeritas domos
telo petis minore, sed qua montium
tergemina moles cecidit et qui montibus
stabant pares Gigantes, hac arma expedi
ignesque torque; vindica amissum diem,   1085
iaculare flammas, lumen ereptum polo
fulminibus exple. causa, ne dubites diu,
utriusque mala sit. si minus, mala sit mea;
me pete, trisulco flammeam telo facem
per pectus hoc transmitte. si natos pater   1090

humare et igni tradere extremo volo,
ego sum cremandus. si nihil superos movet
nullumque telis impios numen petit,
aeterna nox permaneat et tenebris tegat
immensa longis scelera; nil, Titan, queror,   1095
si perseveras.

ATREUS

Nunc meas laudo manus,
nunc parta vera est palma; perdideram scelus,
nisi sic doleres. liberos nasci mihi
nunc credo, castis nunc fidem reddi toris.

THYESTES

Quid liberi meruere?

ATREUS

Quod fuerant tui.   1100

THYESTES

Natos parenti—

ATREUS

Fateor, et, quod me iuvat,
certos.

THYESTES

Piorum praesides testor deos.

ATREUS

Quid coniugales?

THYESTES

Scelere quis pensat scelus?

ATREUS

Scio quod queraris; scelere praerepto doles,
nec quod nefandas hauseris angit dapes,   1105
quod non pararis. fuerat hic animus tibi
instruere similes inscio fratri cibos

et adiuvante liberos matre aggredi
similique leto sternere. hoc unum obstitit:
tuos putasti.

THYESTES

Vindices aderunt dei;   1110
his puniendum vota te tradunt mea.

ATREUS

Te puniendum liberis trado tuis.

COMMENTARY

PROLOGUE/ACT I (1-121)

The scene is set in front of the palace of Argos. In the predawn twilight the ghost of Tantalus appears, alarmed to find himself removed from his place of punishment in the underworld. He suspects that his descendants are about to surpass him in evil, and his fears are confirmed by a Fury who orders him to infect the house with his own impious spirit. Tantalus is horrified at the prospect of future crime unfolded by the Fury, and pleads to be allowed to resume his traditional torment. Ignoring his appeal, the Fury overcomes his resistance by inflaming the hunger and thirst with which Tantalus is eternally afflicted. His task of pollution accomplished, Tantalus is driven back to Tartarus as the upper world revolts at his unnatural presence.

Greek dramatists used the prologue to inform the audience of the background to the play and prepare them for the action to follow; the prologues of Greek tragedy are, of course, much more than versified plot-summaries, but they always perform this basic function. In many of Seneca's opening scenes, however, the element of exposition is inconspicuous or even absent: the Fury's long speech, for example, darkly alludes to past and future crimes of the Tantalids (32-48) and even foreshadows the *dénouement* of the play (54-62), but nothing in it would give an audience any notion of the conflicts between Atreus and Thyestes that have led to the present situation. For Seneca the main purpose of the prologue is to set the mood of the drama and to anticipate its leading themes: it is less an introduction than a microcosm of the play.

Thus in *Thyestes* the prologue creates an atmosphere of anxiety and disorientation. The intrusion of a figure from hell is the first of many signs that the normal boundaries of the upper and lower world will not be maintained (cf. 262-65, 668-78, 804-809, 1011-19), and the disturbances of nature with which the scene ends are a miniature version of the chaos unleashed at the climax of the action (776-884). At the verbal level, the prologue establishes virtually all the motifs and images that bind the play together: in the first twelve lines alone Seneca clusters references to displacement, greedy longing, flight or escape, perverted feasting and satiety, and the surpassing of normal limits.[1] In a broader form of anticipation, the conflict of wills between Tantalus and the Fury is a symbolic enactment in advance of the struggle between Atreus and Thyestes. Like Thyestes, Tantalus attempts to withstand the power of evil but is in the end defeated by his own appetites; on the other hand, the Fury resembles Atreus both in her insatiable lust for crime and in the ferocious vitality of her language. These connections are so close that it seems fair to regard Tantalus and the Fury as in part dramatized metaphors, embodiments of the inherited passions that drive Atreus and Thyestes.[2]

---

[1] See notes on 1 *extrahit*, 2 *avido* and *fugaces*, 4-5 *peius . . . aliquid*, 12 *plenum . . . pabulum*. On connections between the prologue and the rest of the play, see also Harry Hine, "The Structure of Seneca's *Thyestes*," *Papers of the Liverpool Latin Seminar* 3 (1981), 259-75.

[2] A similar point could be made about Vergil's treatment of Allecto in *Aeneid* VII 323-571 (an episode that has influenced the *Thyestes* prologue at several points; see on 23

The scene has no obvious model in extant Greek or Roman tragedy. Its closest parallel is in Euripides' *Heracles* 822-73, where Iris forces the reluctant Lyssa (= Madness) to infect Heracles; although this scene comes at the mid-point of the play, it has some of the features of a prologue and has often been described as a "second prologue."[3] Elsewhere in Seneca the most obvious similarities are with the prologue of *Agamemnon*, spoken by the ghost of Thyestes; probably an earlier work than the *Thyestes*,[4] the *Agamemnon* prologue is more straightforwardly expository and less subtle in its characterization. A nearer approach to the techniques of *Thyestes* can be seen in the prologue to *HF*, which contains both a vivid portrait of the embittered Juno and, in her unleashing of the powers of hell against Hercules, a symbolic foreshadowing of the play's central action.[5]

Thyestes is alone among Seneca's plays in having a prologue that is a true dialogue.[6] The dialogue-form, and the clash of wills that it embodies, is another way in which the prologue mirrors the shape of the play as a whole: every act contains an *agon* of a different kind, a new attempt to restrain or resist the power of evil; each of these efforts is as futile as that of Tantalus, and so each phase of the play confirms the prologue's depiction of a world in which all customary norms have ceased to operate.

1-13 Quis . . . transcribor?: the anxious questions establish a mood of uneasy foreboding; compare 623-25, 627-32 below.

1 extrahit: Tantalus feels displaced from his normal setting (a motif that recurs throughout the play, see above, p. 47).

2 avido . . . cibos: instead of using his name, Tantalus identifies himself by his most distinctive feature, his punishment. The line closely resembles the description of Tantalus in *Ag.* 20 *aquas fugaces ore decepto appetit*, but *avido* stresses Tantalus' insatiable longing, the trait that links him to his descendants: most obviously Thyestes, the *avidus pater* of 277 and 1040, but also Atreus in his lust for revenge (cf. 709 *cupida*), and both brothers in their desire for power (342 *cupidi arcium*). The connection is translated into physical terms at the end of this scene, when Tantalus infects the house with his own *furor* and thirst (101-103).

fugaces . . . cibos: a conventional motif in descriptions of Tantalus (cf. Ovid *Am.* 2.2.43 *poma fugacia*, Sen. *Ag.* 20 [previous note], ps-Quint. *Decl.* 12.28 *fugacibus cibis elusus*), but also the first appearance of the pervasive theme of "flight/escape" (see above, p. 46).

3-4 quis . . . iterum: probably = *quis ostendit iterum Tantalo male visas domos deorum?* ("who shows Tantalus a second time the homes of the gods he saw to his ruin?"). The disjointed word-order, especially the placing of *male*, may reflect Tantalus' distress at finding himself again in the upper world. [The A Mss read *vivas* for *visas* (i.e., *quis*

---

detestabilis, 52 *misce*, 84-85, 85-86, 96-100, 105): the "reality" of the Fury as a character in the epic does not prevent her from bearing a symbolic significance (i.e., as the physical manifestation of the destructive emotions of Turnus and Amata).

[3] See Bond *ad loc.*, who notes the similarity of the *Heracles* scene to the prologue of *Prometheus Bound*, where Hephaestus is compelled to fasten Prometheus to his rock.

[4] See above, p. 11.

[5] On this function of the prologue see Jo-Ann Shelton, *CSCA* 8 (1975), 257-69. The resemblances between *Thyestes* and *HF* become even stronger if Juno is seen as a manifestation of Hercules' own irrational drives, as is done by many recent writers; for an opposing view, cf. O. Zwierlein, *Senecas Hercules im Lichte kaiserzeitlicher und spätantiker Deutung* (Mainz, 1984).

[6] The prologue of *Oedipus* comprises a long monologue and a brief concluding exchange (1-81, 81-109); the long scene between Oedipus and Antigone that opens *Phoenissae* (1-319) cannot usefully be called a prologue.

deorum male ["cruelly"] *ostendit iterum Tantalo vivas domos?*), but *vivae domus* for "abodes of the living" (Miller) is unparalleled and unlikely. It is syntactically possible to combine *quis deorum* and make *male . . . visas domos* refer to the palace of Argos, but Tantalus in fact ruled at Sipylus in Phrygia (cf. 662–63), and the scene loses part of its point if he is simply returning to a former home rather than infecting his descendants' kingdom with his criminal spirit.]

　　male . . . visas: i.e., Tantalus' earlier sight of these *domus* led to disaster, cf. Ovid *Her.* 7.54 *expertae totiens tam male . . . aquae*, *Ibis* 265 (of Polymestor) *qui . . . oculis caruit per quos male viderat aurum*.

　　deorum . . . domos: the "home of the gods" is the sky, here standing for the upper world in general, cf. *Pha.* 1150–51 *caelum superosque Theseus / spectat*, *HF* 585–86 (the command to Orpheus) *tu non ante tuam respice coniugem / quam cum clara deos obtulerit dies* [if the text is sound; cf. O. Zwierlein, *Würzburger Jahrbücher* n.s. 4 (1978), 143–45]. This phrase is unusually specific in naming the *domus*; perhaps we are meant to recall that the gods received Tantalus at their banquets (above, p. 68). [There could also be an ironic appropriateness in *deorum . . . domos*, since Atreus will soon declare himself a god and his palace a temple, cf. on 713, 902.]

　　Tantalo: self-dramatizing; Tantalus has a sense of his own notoriety (cf. 53).

4–13 Tantalus wonders if some new punishment has been devised for him; he asks if anything can be worse than his own perennial hunger and thirst and reviews the torments of the other famous sinners.

　　Tantalus, Sisyphus, Tityos, and Ixion were fixtures of the literary underworld long before Seneca (all but Ixion are present at *Odyssey* 11.576–600), but Tantalus' fear of changing places with another member of the group is a novel treatment of the commonplace; the idea is used for comic effect in *Apoc.* 14–15, and for other Senecan adaptations of the topic cf. *Med.* 743–49, *Pha.* 1229–34, *Ag.* 15–22 (nn). The notion contributes to the play's pervasive theme of disruption; not even in the underworld can established order be counted on to remain intact.

　　The passage is subtly shaped to fit its context: Tityos is placed last and treated with more detail than Sisyphus or Ixion, so that the description ends with the image of a perverted feast (12).

　　4–5 peius . . . aliquid: dread of (or longing for) something worse or greater than what normally constitutes a limit runs through the play, cf. 252–56, 272–75, 744–52, 1052–68. (Elsewhere in Seneca cf., e.g., *Ag.* 29, *Med.* 19–20, *Oed.* 18, 828.)

　　4–6 siti / arente . . . fame / hiante: the successive line-breaks between noun and modifier verbally depict Tantalus' separation from food and drink (while the strong enjambments suggest his ceaseless craving for them).

　　4–5 siti / arente in undis: the wording is close to Ovid *Am.* 3.7.51 *sic aret mediis taciti vulgator in undis*, but shows a typically Senecan mix of abstract and concrete: he omits the pictorially exact *mediis* and makes thirst rather than Tantalus the referent of *arente*. The same is true of *fame / hiante*, since *hiare* is normally used of persons or gaping mouths, cf., e.g., Curt. 4.16 *profluentes aquas hianti ore captantes*.

　　6–7 Sisyphi . . . venit: "can it be that (*numquid*) Sisyphus' stone is coming to my shoulders, to be carried by them"; *umeris* is to be taken both with *venit* and as dat. of agent with *gestandus*: see on 467 *iungenda*.

　　In the most common version of Sisyphus' punishment, he eternally rolls a huge stone to the top of a hill, from which it rolls back again (cf. *Od.* 11.593–600, Lucr. 3.1000–1001, *Ag.* 16–17 [n]). Here, though, *gestandus umeris* points to the rarer alternative in which

Sisyphus carries the stone to the top of the hill, where it slips from his grasp, cf. *HF* 751 *cervice saxum grande Sisyphia sedet, Apoc.* 14.3, Roscher 4.963–66.

6 numquid: here *numquid* implies anxiety; a negative answer is hoped for but cannot be confidently assumed (so also in 805, 807, 810). Its use by Atreus in 197–98 is more overtly rhetorical. [Seneca is the only classical writer who freely uses *numquid* in high poetry (13 instances, three more in *HO*). In general *numquid* introducing a direct question was treated as a colloquialism: it is absent from Cicero's speeches, Livy and Tacitus, love-elegy, Horace's lyrics, Vergil, and Ovid's *Metamorphoses*, and frequent in comedy, Horace's *Satires*, Petronius, and above all Senecan prose (more than 75 occurrences!). (See also J. B. Hofmann, *Lateinische Umgangssprache*³ [Heidelberg, 1951], 162, 203, who cites the replacement of *num* by *numquid* as an example of the colloquial preference for longer and more colorful forms.) Seneca may have taken his cue from Ovid, who admits *numquid* sporadically in his late elegiacs, cf. *F.* 4.7, *Tr.* 5.6.9, *Pont.* 2.9.23, and—if by Ovid—*Her.* 16.367, 21.84, 177. It is also conceivable that the usage existed in Republican tragedy, and that Seneca revived it as an item of tragic diction.]

8 aut . . . rota: "or the swiftly turning wheel pulling the limbs in opposite directions" (the punishment of Ixion).

differens: a strong word, used of men tied to horses and pulled apart, cf. Verg. *Aen.* 8.643, Livy 4.33.10.

rota: understand *venit* from 7, in a slightly altered sense ("come to me as my punishment").

9 poena Tityi: an introductory phrase signaling the more elaborate treatment given Tityos. Seneca follows Vergil in *Aen.* 6.595–600, stressing the regeneration of the liver and the unending feast of the birds; his wording, though, is highly original, with several bold phrases and a skillful interplay of abstract and concrete language.

qui specu vasto patens: probably "who lies spread open with a huge cavity" (*specus* = Tityos' gouged-out entrails, the *effossa viscera* of 10); for *specus* in this sense cf. Verg. *Aen.* 9.700 *specus atri vulneris* and the close parallel in Pliny *N.H.* 34.41 (the Colossus of Rhodes) *vasti specus hiant defractis membris.* [The phrase could also be rendered "who lies spread out in a huge cave"—cf. *HF* 718–19 *hic vasto specu / pendent tyranni limina*—, but this would lessen the horror Tantalus means to evoke.]

patens: *patere* is not often applied to a person; it suggests both Tityos' enormous bulk (the traditional nine *iugera* of *Aen.* 6.596) and the constant "openness" of his wound, cf. Cael. *ap.* Cic. *Fam.* 8.17.2 *nec . . . videmini intellegere qua nos pateamus* ("lie open to attack"), Sen. *Med.* 966 *pectus en Furiis patet.*

10 visceribus atras pascit effossis aves: a carefully balanced distribution of adjectives and nouns, with the verb in the center; the pattern could be notated AbCaB, with AB representing nouns, ab the corresponding adjectives, and C the verb. Similar arrangements are found in epic and elegy; the most famous (abCAB) has since the time of Dryden been called the "Golden Line." (For further details see E. Norden's commentary on *Aeneid* VI, Anhang 3; L. P. Wilkinson, *Golden Latin Artistry* [Cambridge, 1963], 215–17; C. Conrad, *HSCP* 69 [1965], 234–41.) Seneca uses such mannered lines to round off a section within a long speech (e.g., 452), to mirror the content of a line in its form (113), to heighten the expressive effect of a powerful image (cf. also 44), and to suggest a speaker's conscious manipulation of language (cf. 231, 786, 908).

[**visceribus:** a sixteenth-century emendation for *vulneribus*, supported by the imitation in *HO* 947 *effodiat avidus hinc et hinc vultur fibras.*]

aves: the plural implies the Homeric picture of Tityos tormented by two vultures (*Od.* 11.578–79) rather than Vergil's single bird (*Aen.* 6.597).

11 et . . . die: this relatively colorless line offers a respite from the densely-packed wording of 9–10 and a lead-in to the pointed language of 12.

12 plenum . . . pabulum: the twist of perspective that turns a person into a "meal" (for which cf. *HF* 227) foreshadows the central action of the play; *plenum* also links the image to the fate of Thyestes, cf. 890–91 *implebo patrem / funere suorum*, 979, above, p. 46.

recenti . . . monstro: the birds return each day with appetites refreshed, cf. Ovid *Met.* 2.63–64 *mane recentes . . . equi*, 8.370 *fidens . . . recentibus armis* (the Calydonian boar's newly-sharpened tusks).

monstro: collective singular; compare Verg. *Aen.* 3.214 *tristius haud illis* (i.e., the Harpies) *monstrum*. On *monstrum* see also 867 below.

plenum . . .iacet: "he lies there, a full meal for the hungry creature"; *monstro* is dat. of interest or advantage, cf. AG 376.

13 in quod malum transcribor?: "to what punishment am I being re-assigned?" The verb is first attested in this sense in Augustan poetry (cf. Verg. *Aen.* 5.750, 7.422, Ovid *Met.* 7.173, *Ibis* 187) and appears in prose of the next generation, cf. Val. Max. 2.7.9, 15, Sen. *Epist.* 4.2, *N.Q.* 1 *pr.* 17. Seneca may have had the *Ibis* passage in mind, since Ovid's *in te transcribet veterum tormenta virorum* also refers to the famous sinners of the underworld.

malum: a euphemism for "punishment" or "torture," cf. *Tro.* 349, *Oed.* 518–19, *Ag.* 959.

13–15 o quisquis . . . disponis: the apostrophe is indefinite (*quisquis*) because Tantalus does not know the source of this disturbance (*nova* is emphatic, taking up the idea of change in *transcribor*). The vague language also makes it possible to take Tantalus' words as an unwitting description of Atreus, who will inflict *nova supplicia* on the dead, cf. especially 749–53.

13–20 The solemn invocation (*o . . . disponis*) and the relative clauses that follow (*quod . . . horreat, quod . . . paveat, ad cuis metum . . . tremamus*) build up great anticipation, which is then released in a surprising twist: we expect Tantalus to say "if there is any punishment more severe than the one I suffer, I confess that I deserve to bear it," but instead he concludes "if a worse punishment exists, get it ready since a greater criminal is coming."

14 functis: "the dead" (= *defunctis*), condensed from *vita functi* ("those finished with life"), a usage popular with Seneca (cf. *Med.* 999, *Oed.* 240, 579) and Statius (cf. *Theb.* 2.15, 4.511, 12.137).

15 ad poenas: *ad* here signifying purpose, cf. *OLD* s.v., #44–46.

16–18 quod . . . tremamus: the conventional rhetoric of the first two clauses is "topped" by the unexpected shift in the third; Tantalus regards himself as less easily horrified than Cerberus or Acheron, cf. *HF* 1223–24 *si quod exilium latet / ulterius Erebo, Cerbero ignotum et mihi*.

16 custos: of Cerberus in Verg. *Aen.* 6.424, Sen. *Tro.* 404; as in the *Troades* passage, Seneca moves Cerberus from his Vergilian post by the Styx to a position outside the dungeon of Tartarus (see Fantham *ad loc.*).

17 Acheron: standing for "the underworld" generally, as in Verg. *Aen.* 7.312 *flectere si nequeo superos, Acheronta movebo*; see on 1016 below.

ad . . . metum: "at the frightful prospect"; for this use of *ad* cf. *OLD* s.v., #33, Sen. *N.Q.* 2.59.11 *pavescis ad caeli fragorem*, Tac. *H.* 2.68 *Vitellius . . . ad omnis suspiciones pavidus*. See also on 936 *ad laeta*.

18 subit: "is arising," cf. Ovid *Met.* 1.114 *subiit argentea proles*.

19-20 vincat . . . faciat . . . audeat: the subjunctives are characterizing, with a suggestion of result, cf. AG 535, 537 and n. 1; "a *turba* that will surpass its ancestors" etc.

19 turba: "a brood," the members of a family seen as a closely-linked group, cf. 979 *turba iam sua implebo patrem* (*turba* = Thyestes' children), *Cons. Marc.* 15.2 *Augustus amissis liberis nepotibus exhausta Caesarum turba adoptione desertam domum fulsit*. The word refers most obviously to Atreus and Thyestes, but since a *turba* normally numbers more than two (as is clear from Ovid's witty *nos duo turba sumus* of Deucalion and Pyrrha, *Met.* 1.355), Tantalus is probably including more remote descendants such as Aegisthus and Agamemnon, cf. 42–46.

quae suum vincat genus: the first appearance of the important theme of "outdoing" previous standards of crime, cf. 134–35, 195–96, 625–26, 1013–16.

20 me innocentem faciat: Tantalus means that he will appear *innocens* by comparison with what his descendants will do, but for a stronger effect Seneca omits any qualifying idea; cf. Sen. *Contr.* 1.2.8 *inter tot tanto maiora scelera virginem stuprare innocentia est.* See also above, p. 22.

inausa audeat: perhaps deliberate sound-play, with *au* in two successive metrical *sedes*.

21 quidquid . . . cessat loci: "whatever space is not being used"; *cessare* is "to be inactive," perhaps by analogy with untilled fields, cf. Verg. *G.* 1.71, Ovid *F.* 4.617.

loci: partitive gen. after *quidquid*, cf. AG 346 (a) 3.

22 complebo: Tantalus assumes responsibility for the crimes of his race (18–19 *nostra . . . e stirpe*), displaying a typically Senecan warped pride in their accomplishments.

complebo: images of fullness and emptiness play an important part in *Thyestes*, especially in the prologue and finale: note *plenum pabulum* 12, *arboris plenae* 69, *ieiunia exple* 65, *imple* 53, *impleri* 253, *implebo* 890, 979, and *vacare* 57, 108, 892, *vacuus* 152. (The force of *vacare* in 23 and 29 is different—cf. 593, 759—, but those occurrences help establish the word as significant.) Here a direct causal link can be made out: Thyestes' unnatural "fullness" validates Tantalus' claim that his descendants will keep Tartarus fully occupied.

23 Minos vacabit: Seneca often makes a striking phrase end early in the line, throwing it into even greater prominence; cf. 32 *crescat*, 62 *epulae instruantur*, 90 *avus nepotes*, also note on 204.

Minos: named as the judge with jurisdiction over the damned, as (e.g.) in Prop. 3.19.27 *Minos sedet arbiter Orci*, *Ag.* 23, Stat. *Theb.* 4.530–32.

vacabit: "will be idle/unemployed," cf. Ovid *F.* 2.18 *pacando si quid ab hoste vacat*, 3.87.

23–67 The Fury's speech is one of Seneca's most powerful pieces of writing, a sustained evocation of evil ceaseless in its operation and all-encompassing in its effects. The intensity of the Fury's language and the cosmic scope of her vision produce an almost Shakespearian effect; compare, for example, Lear's "tremble, thou wretch / that hast within thee undivulged crimes / unwhipp't of justice" etc. (3.2.49–59), or in a more overtly Senecan idiom the tirade of the Bishop of Carlisle in *Richard II* 4.1.129–49 (and see on 40–41, 44, 52).

23 Perge: "go on," spoken to one who wavers in an activity already begun, cf. 490 and 892 below, *Tro.* 1002, *Med.* 566, *HF* 75.

detestabilis: the Fury loathes her own agent; compare Verg. *Aen.* 7.327–28, of the Fury Allecto: *odit et ipse pater Pluton, odere sorores / Tartareae monstrum.*

24 age: "torment," cf. *Pha.* 541–42 *quaeque succensas agit / libido mentes.*

furiis: abl. of instrument with *age*, cf. Verg. *Aen.* 10.68 *Cassandrae impulsus furiis*, Ovid *F.* 6.489 *hinc agitur furiis Athamas, Ibis* 161.

25 certetur: impersonal passive ("let the struggle be carried on"), suggesting a conflict of unlimited scope; cf. *Ira* 2.9.1 *certatur ingenti quidem nequitiae certamine* ("men struggle in a mighty rivalry of wickedness," Basore).

alterna vice: "by turns" (i.e., let A attack B and then let B retaliate against A); cf. *Ag.* 44 *sanguine alterno*, 77 *scelus alternum* (n), 133 below *alternae scelerum . . . vices.*

26 stringatur ensis: a generic expression for violent attack; cf. *dare sanguinem*, 340 below.

26–27 nec sit irarum modus / pudorve: the Fury significantly begins with *ira*, the most destructive of the passions (*Ira* 1.1.1 *hunc . . . affectum . . . maxime ex omnibus taetrum ac rabidum*) and the primary motive force in the play (cf. 180, 519, 713, 1056).

26 irarum: obj. gen. with both *modus* ("a limit on anger") and *pudor* ("shame at committing acts of anger"); for the latter cf. *VB* 26.6 *pudor peccandi*, Hor. *Epist.* 1.18.24 *paupertatis pudor.*

modus: the notion of limit or boundary is often denied in Senecan drama (cf. *Tro.* 812, *Med.* 397, *Ag.* 691–92), and nowhere more consistently than in *Thyestes*, cf. 255, 1051–52. See also on 4–5.

[**nec**: the Mss divide between *nec* (E) and *ne* (A), each of which makes acceptable sense; *ne* would set off the rejection of *pudor* and *modus*, but a subordinate clause seems out of place in this relentlessly linear speech.]

28–29 longum nefas / eat in nepotes: "let long-lasting evil pass into succeeding generations." For *longus* of protracted anxieties or diseases cf. Ovid *Met.* 9.275 *curae*, Sen. *Contr.* 10.5.4 *tabes*, Pliny *NH* 22.129 *morbus*. In this context *ire in* might suggest the spread of an illness, cf. Lucr. 6.1207 *in nervos huic morbus et artus / ibat*, Luc. 7.543–44 *semel ortus in omnis / it timor.*

29–30 nec vacet . . . crimen: "let no one have leisure to feel disgust at an old crime"; *vacare* with infinitive, cf. 593, Ovid *Met.* 6.585 *nec flere vacat.*

30 semper oriatur novum: a wish fulfilled by Atreus, cf. 254 *quid novi . . . struis?*

31 nec unum in uno: "many in one" (Miller), a riddling phrase referring either to Atreus' murder of several children (a crime that is both "one" and "more than one"), cf. 57 *maiore numero*, or else to his dismemberment of the children, which by insane logic turns each of his victims from "one" to "several"; cf. *Med.* 474 *scelere in uno non semel factum scelus*. [For similar juggling cf. *HF* 487 *nec unus una Geryon victus manu*.]

31–32 dumque punitur scelus / crescat: a thought restated by Atreus, *scelera non ulcisceris / nisi vincis* (195–96).

32–53 After the general phrases of 25–32 *crescat*, which lay down the rules, so to speak, of Tantalid behavior, the Fury turns to a more specific, though still allusive, survey of the family's history. The references range from the past through the present to the distant future, and at times can be applied to more than one episode in the saga (see on 42–43, 46–47)—an ingenious way of portraying the ingrained criminality of the house.

32–36 superbis . . . ferat: the Fury looks first at the struggle for power between Atreus and Thyestes (the *superbi fratres* of 32) and depicts their shifting fortunes with four successive statements of the same idea (*superbis . . . profugos; dubia . . . labet; miser . . . potens; fluctu . . . ferat*)—a verbal equivalent to their restless alternations of position. (At a more detailed level note the shift from *regna* as subject in 32 to *regnum* as object in 36.)

32 excidant: "fall out of the hands of," cf. Ovid *Met.* 2.602–603 *pariter vultusque deo plectrumque colorque / excidit.*

33 repetantque profugos: the language fits both Atreus and Thyestes, each of whom returned to power from exile (above, p. 39).

repetant: perhaps echoed at 412, where Thyestes urges himself to seek out exile again (*repete silvestres fugas*).

34 reges . . . incertos: "insecure kings," cf. Cic. *Rep.* 1.27 *levis fructus, exiguus usus, incertus dominatus.* Atreus and Thyestes are specific instances of the unreliability of all external power, cf. 391–92 *potens / aulae culmine lubrico.*

35 miser . . . potens: sudden transformations of status were usually attributed to god or fortune (here *casus* seems to be the force responsible), cf. Hor. *C.* 1.34.12–14 *valet ima summis / mutare et insignes attenuat deus, / oscura promens*, Juv. 7.197–98 *si Fortuna volet, fies de rhetore consul; / si volet haec eadem, fies de consule rhetor* ("rhetoricians of the empire were particularly moved by Fortune's power to bring men down to professorships"—Nisbet-Hubbard on Hor. *C.* 1.34.12). It is interesting that the Fury treats *miser* and *potens* as opposites (*miser* almost = *humilis*, as at 938), whereas the subsequent action suggests that they are nearly synonymous.

36 fluctu . . . assiduo: for the metaphor cf. Soph. *Trach.* 112–19, Sen. *Contr.* 1.1.10 *divitias, quas huc atque illuc incertae fortunae fluctus appellet*, Val. Max. 6.2.1.

37 cum dabit patriam deus: *deus* is both general ("god" as a near-equivalent for fate or fortune, as in Hor. *C.* 1.34.13 cited above, also 621–22 below) and specific, the oracle of Apollo that prescribed incest as the only way Thyestes could obtain revenge on Atreus (above, pp. 39–40).

dabit patriam: condensed from *dabit reditum in patriam*.

38 in scelera: "for the purpose of crime," cf. Ovid *Am.* 2.10.12 *non fuit in curas una puella satis?*, *Ag.* 99–100 *placet in vulnus / maxima cervix*. The double-edged wording could describe either one who returns to commit crimes (as in the later case of Aegisthus) or, as with Thyestes, a return which serves another's crime.

38–39 sintque . . . sibi: the elements of the phrase appear in the opposite of the expected order, a characteristic Senecan inversion (see on 207) which here throws the hatred of the family for itself into greater prominence. At one level *sibi* refers to the hostility of one member of the line for another, but it also suggests the loathing of oneself that results from consciousness of evil. Seneca's Aegisthus in *Agamemnon* is keenly aware of his tainted ancestry (note 233 *non est poena sic nato mori*), and in this play Thyestes comes to see himself as a *vile caput* (996). Note also *Med.* 933–35 *scelus est Iason genitor et maius scelus / Medea mater . . . pereant, mei sunt.* For Seneca this dissatisfaction with oneself is a sign of a disordered spirit (*Tranq.* 2.10 *invitus aspicit se sibi relictum*).

39 nihil . . . putet: a restatement of 26–27 *nec . . . pudorve* (*pudor* is what leads one to regard certain actions as forbidden), designed to lead into the specific manifestations of *ira* in the following lines. The personification of *ira* is a way of depicting the hold it exercises over its victims; they are so fully in its grip that *ira* itself seems to perform their actions. The wording of this line combines elements of Ovid *Met.* 5.273 *vetitum est adeo sceleri nihil* and 6.25 *nihil est quod victa recusem.*

40–46 These lines rework Ovid's account of the Iron Age in *Met.* 1.144–50 (quoted in *De ira* 2.9.2 and evoked again in *Pha.* 553–57):

> vivitur ex rapto; non hospes ab hospite tutus,
> non socer a genero; fratrum quoque gratia rara est.
> imminet exitio vir coniugis, illa mariti;
> lurida terribiles miscent aconita novercae;
> filius ante diem patrios inquirit in annos.
> victa iacet pietas, et virgo caede madentes
> ultima caelestum terras Astraea reliquit.

The most obvious feature of Seneca's adaptation is that Ovid's symptoms of universal depravity have become the actions of a single family; *frater, vir,* and *coniunx* all specifically refer to events in this history of the Tantalids. But Seneca has not abandoned Ovid's universal perspective: as the Fury proceeds, the effects of the family's crimes become progressively more general (44 *effusus omnes irriget terras cruor,* 48 *ius . . . omne pereat*), until not even heaven is exempt from disruption. Seneca re-interprets Ovid's vision of moral collapse to fit a new context; instead of a common degeneracy, an infection spreading outward from a single source. (It is tempting to connect this outlook with the play's reflections on the corrupting influence of despotic power; see above, p. 48.) In one respect Seneca might even claim to have surpassed his model: the move from earth to heaven in 48–51 is paralleled in *Met.* 1.151 (*neve foret terris securior arduus aether . . .*), but while the transition in Ovid remains purely artificial, in Seneca it is fully integrated with its immediate context and with the action of the play as a whole.

40–41 natum . . . patrem: "sons fearing fathers" could apply to Pelops and Tantalus (cf. 144–48), and "fathers fearing sons" might describe Thyestes, who recognized his son Aegisthus just in time to escape being killed by him (cf. Hyg. 88). The juxtaposition of words denoting family relationships underlines the perversion of blood-ties, cf. 90 *avus nepotes*; *Ag.* 32, 166 (n); D. J. Mastronarde, *TAPA* 101 (1970), 302. Compare *Richard II* 4.1.140–41 "tumultuous wars / shall kin with kin and kind with kind confound."

41–42 liberi . . . nascantur: i.e., Atreus' murder of Thyestes' children will be surpassed by the incest of Thyestes and his daughter that produces Aegisthus; the point is made explicitly in *Ag.* 27–30, esp. 28 *maius aliud ausa* [sc. *Fortuna*] *commisso scelus.* The reversal of the normal superiority of birth over death resembles Ovid's introduction to the story of Myrrha in *Met.* 10.314–15 *scelus est odisse parentem; / hic amor est odio maius scelus.* Seneca may have been inverting Manilius' line on Medea's children, *male conceptos partus peiusque necatos* (3.13). For another pointed use of *nascor* see 313–14.

42–43 immineat . . . coniunx: "let a wife have threatening designs on her husband"; based on Ovid *Met.* 1.146 *imminet exitio vir coniugis, illa mariti*, with *exitio viri* (for which cf. *Pha.* 855 *morti imminet*) replaced by the more compressed *viro*. The less explicit wording permits a double reference, to Atreus' wife Aerope who plotted against him with Thyestes (above, p. 39), and to Clytaemestra's murder of Agamemnon.

43 bella trans pontum vehant: another potential double reference, since later events of the story of Thyestes and Atreus took place in other parts of Greece (above, p. 40), while 44–46 clearly alludes to the Trojan War, in which the Greek forces were led by Atreus' sons Menelaus and Agamemnon.

44 irriget: the metaphor with *irrigo* is not attested before Seneca, but for *rigo* cf. Verg. *Aen.* 12.308 *sparso late rigat arma cruore*, 11.698; later cf. Stat. *Th.* 4.375 *sanguine Dircen irriguam* and *Richard II* 4.1.137 "the blood of English shall manure the ground."

45 supra . . . magnos . . . duces: *duces* is probably a rhetorical plural (see on 1014 *avos*) referring to Agamemnon, whose infatuation with Briseis and Cassandra was a notorious example of love's dominion over the mighty, cf. Hor. *C.* 2.4.7–8 *arsit Atrides medio in triumpho / virgine rapta*, Ovid *Am.* 1.9.37–38 *summa ducum* [compare *magnos . . . duces*] *Atrides visa Priameide fertur / Maenadis effusis obstipuisse comis*. For Agamemnon's status cf. *Ag.* 39 *ductor . . . ducum* (n).

gentium: "peoples" or "nations," cf. on 461, 648 below.

45–46 exultet . . . Libido victrix: the personification of *libido* is not purely conventional (Ovid, for example, does not use it), and functions like that of *ira* (see on 39); *libido* is consistently spoken of in personal terms in *Phaedra*, where it is an important motive force, cf. 206–207 *tunc illa magnae dira fortunae comes / libido subit*, also 195–96, 541–42, 981.

46–47 impia . . . sit: probably another double reference, to Aerope and to Clytaemestra, who committed adultery with Aegisthus (called *stuprum* in *Ag.* 1009, Prop. 3.19.20–21).

47 levissimum . . . facinus: *levissimum* is predicative, "let adultery be the most trivial/insignificant crime in the impious house." The dismissal of crimes normally thought heinous is a typical Senecan gesture, cf. *Pho.* 270 *leve est paternum facinus*, *Med.* 905–907 *faxo sciant / quam levia fuerint . . . quae commodavi scelera*. [*facinus* is Bentley's conjecture for the manuscript reading *fratris*, which would qualify *fas*, *fides*, and *ius*, and which would entail punctuating after *levissimum*. The combination *fratris fas* is without parallel; if the sense is "the laws governing relations between brothers," *fratrum* seems required, on the analogy of *fas bellantium* (Just. 39.3.8) or *fas gentium* (Tac. *Ann.* 1.42). The alternative is to understand *fratris* as possessive, "a brother's [i.e., Atreus'] sense of *fas*" etc.; this—and indeed any reference to brothers—seems too restrictive for this point in the Fury's speech, when universal consequences are being invoked.]

et fas et fides: the pairing recalls Roman legal formulae, cf. Livy 1.9.13 *per* [i.e., *contra*] *fas ac fidem decepti*, 29.24.3 *neve fas fidem . . . fallat*.

48 ius . . . omne: *omne* refers to *fas* and *fides* as well as to *ius*; this emotive use of *omnis* is normal in horrified reactions to events, cf. Cic. *Att.* 1.16.6 *si iudicium est triginta homines . . . ius ac fas omne delere*, Verg. *Aen.* 3.55 *fas omne abrumpit*, Sen. *Contr.* 1.2.8 *piratas . . . quibus omne fas nefasque lusus est*, 179 below *fas . . . omne ruptum*. With characteristic perversity, the Fury welcomes the prospect of moral collapse; compare Medea in *Med.* 900 *fas omne cedat, abeat expulsus pudor*.

48–51 The disturbance of the heavens that the Fury calls for will take place later in the play, 776–88, 789–884. It forms the external counterpart to the moral chaos that precedes and provokes it; compare *ius . . . pereat* here with *solitae mundi periere vices* 813, *mundo . . . pereunte* 884. (On the Stoic background of this idea see above, p. 24.)

49 cur micant stellae polo: the time just before dawn is often the dramatic setting for the action of Greek tragedy (where it corresponded to the real circumstances of performance) and, as a set convention, for Seneca as well, cf., e.g., *HF* 123–24, *Oed.* 1–5, *Ag.* 53–56.

polo: *polus* here just = "sky," a common usage especially in poetry.

50 flammae . . . decus: it seems best to take *flammae* with *stellae*, "why do the fiery rays (of the stars) maintain the glory owed to the world?"

debitum mundo decus: the idea that the heavenly bodies owe light to the world may be based on a witty line of Ovid, *Met.* 4.196–97 (of the sun) *virgine figis in una / quos mundo debes oculos.* Seneca gives it more weight, the thought of obligation suggesting the well-ordered cosmos that the Fury wishes to see disrupted.

decus: a characteristic Senecan use of an abstraction in place of a concrete term (e.g., *lux*). The combination *servare decus* appears in Ovid *Met.* 13.481 *casti . . . decus servare pudoris*, but here *decus* means "attractiveness" or "splendor" rather than "honor," cf. *OLD* s.v. #5, Ovid *Met.* 3.422–23 *impubesque genas et eburnea colla decusque / oris*, Pha. 829 *regium in vultu decus gerens*.

52 misce: "throw into confusion," perhaps suggested by Verg. *Aen.* 7.348 (of Allecto) *quo furibunda domum monstro permisceat omnem.*

odia caedes funera: accumulations of nouns or adjectives in asyndeton were a popular feature of early Latin high style, cf., e.g., Acc. 415 R^2 *exul inter hostis exspes expers desertus vagus* (compare Sen. *Med.* 21); Senecan examples are collected in Canter 169–70. The device can be used simply for resonant effect, but here Seneca puts it to a more subtle purpose, accelerating the pace just before a climactic *sententia* (*imple Tantalo totam domum*); compare *Ag.* 47–48 for a similar sequence. Shakespeare's Bishop of Carlisle once again displays a genuine Senecan fervor: "disorder, horror, fear, and mutiny / shall here inhabit" (*Richard II* 4.1.142–43).

53 [accerse: the MSS divide between *accerse* (E S) and *arcesse* (PTC); at *Oed.* 823 the division is between *accersite* (E PTC) and *arcessite* (S). Both forms are attested in ancient MSS (*accerso* predominates in Verg. *Aen.* 5.746 and 6.119, *arcesso* in *G.* 4.224 and *Aen.* 10.11; see further *TLL* 2.448.50–78), and both are adopted by editors of Seneca's prose works, cf. *Ira.* 3.12.1, *Epist.* 74.33 (*arcesso*) *VB* 12.2, *Epist.* 69.6 (*accerso*). I print *accerse* because E is generally more careful than A in spelling, and because at *Oed.* 823 euphony commends *accersite* after *propere*.]

Tantalo: the name is used with a sense of what "Tantalus" stands for, perhaps both generically (= a spirit of wickedness) and specifically (= a precedent for killing children for this purpose, cf. 62–63). Such self-conscious use of names is frequent in Seneca, and is most prominently seen in the title character of *Medea* (8, 166 *Medea superest*, 171 *Medea—fiam*, 910 *Medea nunc sum*); also *Tro.* 569, 614 (Ulixes), 863 (Helen), and later in this play 180 (Atreus) and 476 (Thyestes and Atreus). In Latin poetry there was precedent in Ovid, cf. *Her.* 6.156 *Medeae Medea forem* (spoken by Hypsipyle), but self-awareness and self-dramatizing were part of Roman life as well as its literature, cf. Servius Sulpicius Rufus *ap.* Cic. *Fam.* 4.5.5 *denique noli te oblivisci Ciceronem esse* (not that there was ever much danger of that), Plut. *Caes.* 38.3, 60.5, Luc. 5.581–86).

Shakespeare's famous "I am Antony yet" (*A. and C.* 3.13.92–93) catches the Roman note perfectly, cf. also 3.13.185–86 "since my lord / is Antony again, I will be Cleopatra."

54–62 The last part of the Fury's speech is its most specific section, a detailed forecast of the *dénouement*. The opening lines illustrate Seneca's practice of starting a new section with unpointed and straightforward language; the first *sententia* arrives in 56–57 *Thracium fiat nefas / maiore numero*.

54–55 ornetur . . . virescant: garlanding the palace is a sign of rejoicing at the apparent concord between Atreus and Thyestes. The details have a Roman coloring: branches of bay were used to decorate Roman houses on festive occasions, cf. Juv. 10.65 *pone domi laurus*, 6.51–52 with Courtney's note.

54 altum columen: collective singular, cf. 232, 736.

55 dignus: ironic use of *dignus* is frequent in Seneca, cf. 271 below, *Oed.* 977 *thalamis digna nox . . . meis, Tro.* 863, *Pha.* 853, *Ag.* 34 (n).

56 Thracium . . . nefas: the fate of Thyestes' children has an antecedent in the story of Procne, who killed her son Itys to punish her husband Tereus for raping her sister Philomela; Tereus was Thracian and the murder is set in Thrace, hence *Thracium nefas*. Atreus is himself aware of Procne's actions as a precedent (see on 272–77)—another way in which he resembles the Fury (see above, p. 85, and next note).

57 maiore numero: i.e., three children rather than one will be involved. For this quantitative measurement of crime or revenge cf. *Ag.* 22 (the ghost of Thyestes speaks) *sed ille nostrae pars quota est culpae senex?* (i.e., how small does Tantalus' crime—serving Pelops to the gods—seem by comparison with Thyestes'), *Med.* 954–57, 1008–1011.

dextra cur patrui vacat?: "why is the uncle's [= Atreus'] hand empty/idle?" The Fury's impatience resembles that of Atreus, cf. 280–81 *tam diu cur innocens / versatur Atreus?* The technique by which a prologue figure experiences in advance a situation that will develop later in the play is also used in *Agamemnon* (compare 48–52 with 226–33), and more subtly in *Medea* (compare, e.g., 48–55 with 904–25).

58–59 ecquando tollet?: "will he ever raise it?" (i.e., will Atreus ever lift his hand to strike Thyestes' children?); cf. *attollit . . . manum* in Stat. *S.* 2.5.21. The Fury impatiently anticipates what the Messenger will relate as accomplished fact; this and the previous question are prompted by Atreus' hesitation before striking the first blow (712–16), which elicits the Chorus' inquiry *quem tamen ferro occupat?* In her next words (*ignibus iam subditis* etc.) the Fury moves beyond the murders to the preparation of the children's flesh (cf. 755–72). [The interpretation given here is controversial and assumes that line 58 is spurious. (Early editors often referred *ecquando tollet* to Atreus while retaining 58, but the change of subject seems very harsh.) If the line is kept, the passage will run as follows: "Why is the uncle's hand idle? Thyestes is not yet bewailing his children; when will he remove (*tollet*) them?" (Line 58 could also be taken as a question without altering the basic sense.) This sequence of thought contains an obvious illogicality—Thyestes cannot bewail his children before they have been "removed," i.e., destroyed—, but this is not a serious objection, since the connection between the events is close enough to forestall ambiguity. The use of *tollere* is more difficult; Thyestes will never in fact "remove" his children in the sense of killing them, and although he will in a grisly way "raise" them (i.e., lift their flesh to his lips), nothing in the later descriptions of the event gives this idea the verbal grounds it requires. Furthermore, the plainness of 58, especially the use of Thyestes' name, seems at odds with the charged and allusive tone of its surroundings.]

59 ecquando: the final *o* is short, as with *quando* in 82 below, *Pho.* 520, *Pha.* 673, *HO*

1531, 1769, 1771. [*ecquando* is an old emendation for *et quando* (cf. *Pha.* 673, where *ecquando* is a Renaissance conjecture); *ecquando* seems to fit better in a series of impassioned questions, cf. Livy 3.67.10 *qui finis erit discordiarum? ecquando unam urbem habere, ecquando communem hanc esse patriam licebit?* (*ecquando* is here a 16th-century correction for *et quando*), Nepos fr. 54 Marshall *denique quae pausa erit? ecquando desinet familia nostra insanire? ecquando modus ei rei haberi poterit?*]

60 spument aena: *aena* are bronze cauldrons (the plural perhaps for magnifying effect, cf. Ovid *Met.* 6.645 *pars . . . cavis exsultat aenis*, and contrast 767 *candente aeno*); cf. Verg. *Aen.* 1.213 *litore aena locant alii flammasque ministrant.* (The previous line in Vergil, *pars in frusta secant veribusque trementia figunt*, is echoed in Atreus' dismemberment of the children, cf. 760, 765, 1060 below.)

spument: the water in the cauldron foams when heated, a graphic detail perhaps suggested by Ovid's description of Medea's magical practices, cf. *Met.* 7.261–62 *posito medicamen aeno / fervet et exsultat spumisque tumentibus albet*, 282.

60–61 membra . . . eant / discerpta: translators (Miller, Thomann) understand *eant* as "go into the cauldron," but the absence of a connective or directional word seems very harsh.

per partes: "by pieces," *per* specifying the unit of division (*OLD* s.v. #8c), cf. Manilius 3.405 *per tris id divide partis.*

61 patrios polluat sanguis focos: Atreus pointedly inverts this view when recounting his actions at 1058–59 *caede votiva focos / placavi* (and note his careful travesty of sacrificial protocol at 689–95 *servatur omnis ordo*, etc.). [Some Mss read *patruos* for *patrios*, making the reference more specific (to Atreus, the *patruus* of 57), but less well suited to the Fury's purposes: *patrius* in the sense of "ancestral" (cf. Cic. *Phil.* 2.72 *contra deos patrios arasque et focos*) carries forward the pervasive theme of family guilt.]

62 epulae instruantur: the final clause in the Fury's vision is deliberately unemotional in wording; it draws its impact from the audience's awareness of what the *epulae* in question involve. (*Ag.* 11 *hic epulis locus* acts in a similar way.) After this climactic *sententia* the Fury turns back to Tantalus.

non novi sceleris tibi: "a crime that is not unfamiliar to you" (*tibi* with *novus* perhaps colloquial, cf. Cic. *Verr.* 2.24 *nova tibi sunt haec?*). In Senecan rhetoric anything done once can be described as "not new" or "customary," cf. *Med.* 447 *fugimus, Iason, fugimus—hoc non est novum, / mutare sedes*, Tro. 248–49 (Pyrrhus to Agamemnon) *at tuam natam parens / Helenae immolasti; solita iam et facta expeto*, *Ag.* 177 *iam tum* (n), Leo *Obs. crit.* 149–52.

62–63 sceleris . . . conviva: a striking phrase, in which *scelus* denotes the company Tantalus will join, on the analogy of *conviva deorum* in Hor. *C.* 1.28.7 (of Tantalus; see Nisbet-Hubbard for other examples) and of *conviva fratris* in Livy 40.10.7. Some translators take *scelus* as a substitute for *cena* or *epulae*, but the genitive with *conviva* does not appear to be so used.

63 Tantalus has been given a day's holiday (*liberum . . . diem*) from his torment to be present at Atreus' banquet (*ad istas . . . mensas* expressing purpose, see on 15). The Fury ironically suggests that this sight will allow Tantalus to satisfy his hunger (*ieiunia exple*), but she knows that his true reaction will be one of disgust (*dapes / quas ipse fugeres*).

64 tuamque . . . solvimus . . . famem: Ovid has *ieiunia virgo / solverat* in *Met.* 5.534–35 (cf. *F.* 4.607), but Seneca creates a stronger effect by having the Fury loosen

Tantalus' *fames*, as though hunger were a bond or tether.

65 mixtus in Bacchum cruor: Atreus employs just this method of concealing from Thyestes the fact that he is drinking his children's blood (cf. 914–16).

Bacchum: = *vinum* by metonymy, cf. 915, 983, 987, Lucr. 2.655–57 *si quis . . . Bacchi nomine abuti / mavult quam laticis proprium proferre vocamen.*

66 spectante te: the Fury will not in fact insist on Tantalus' presence at the banquet, apparently judging it sufficient for him to infect the house with his touch (101–105); the thought of compelling him to watch the atrocity may be meant to heighten the resemblance between the Fury and Atreus, who does require Thyestes to look on the results of his crime, cf. 895 *videat pater.*

66–67 inveni . . . fugeres: "I have discovered a feast that even you would run from"; pride in invention and the claim to have surpassed previous limits of crime (both foreshadowed in 4–5 *peius inventum est . . . aliquid?*) again link the Fury to Atreus, cf. 274–75 *maius hoc aliquid dolor / inveniat.* The stress on invention can also be seen in Oedipus' search for a punishment suited to his crimes, cf. 977 *inventa thalamis digna nox tandem meis* (and note 947 *utere ingenio, miser*). [These passages may owe something to Ovid's account of Jupiter's passion for Ganymede, *Met.* 10.156–57 *inventum est aliquid quod Iuppiter esse, / quam quod erat, mallet.* The Fury's words have some of the same cleverness; only a thin line separates this jibe from the overt humor of Martial 3.45 *fugerit an Phoebus mensas cenamque Thyestae / ignoro; fugimus nos, Ligurine, tuam.*]

68–83 These anguished lines elaborate the thought that Tantalus would prefer to endure any torment in the underworld rather than witness the approaching crime of Atreus. The speech recalls the opening of the play, but the tone has become even more agitated, with wishes and objurgations in place of questions. Tantalus' frustrated longing for escape also anticipates Thyestes' reaction at the thought of meeting Atreus (412–14).

68–69 Ad . . . fugas: answers the question *quo . . . ruis?*, with *ruo* to be understood. The incomplete syntax together with the polysyndeton *et . . . et . . .-que* and the synonyms *stagna-amnes-aquas* create a feeling of almost frenzied eagerness. (Contrast the lifeless *libet reverti* with which the same idea is introduced in *Ag.* 12.)

69 labrisque . . . fugas: a scene described in greater detail in 162–168 below, and pointedly re-enacted when Thyestes lifts the cup containing the blood of his children, *admotus ipsis Bacchus a labris fugit* (987). For emphatic *ipsis* ("from my very lips") compare the common *limine in ipso*, Lucr. 6.1157, Verg. *Ecl.* 8.92, *Aen.* 2.242, etc.

70–71 atrum . . . cubile: probably "gloomy lair" rather than "black couch" (Miller), which sounds too comfortable for this context; for *cubile* cf. *Pha.* 522–23 *non in recessu furta et obscuro improbus / quaerit cubili*, Plin. *Pan.* 49.1 *arcana illa cubilia saevique secessus*, Stat. *S.* 2.3.44, perhaps Verg. *Aen.* 6.273–74 *primis . . . in faucibus Orci / Luctus et ultrices posuere cubilia Curae* (note *habitant* in 275). Seneca seems to picture Tantalus as confined to a cell when not at his usual place of punishment.

atrum: a conventional epithet for the underworld, cf. Lucr. 3.966 *in Tartara atra*, Verg. *G.* 1.243 *Styx atra*, Stat. *S.* 2.1.227 *ab atro limine.*

carceris . . . mei: the possessive sounds almost affectionate.

72 mutare ripas: *ripa* almost = *flumen*. Tantalus offers to exchange the stream in which he normally stands for the fiery Phlegethon, a more gruelling punishment for which there seems to be no precedent (Phlegethon elsewhere surrounds the region where the damned are confined, cf. Verg. *Aen.* 6.551, *Pha.* 1227 *Phlegethon nocentes igneo* *cingens vado).* Tantalus' wish is taken up in stronger form by Thyestes, cf. 1016–19.

alveo medius tuo: for *medius* with the ablative cf. Prop. 1.10.8 *mediis caelo luna ruberet equis*, Ovid *Am.* 2.16.13 *si medius Polluce et Castore ponar.*

73 freto: properly applied to narrows of the sea, *fretum* for Seneca can be little more than a grander synonym for *amnis*, cf. 1018 below, *HF* 763 (also of underworld waters); this looser usage is foreshadowed by such passages as Ovid *Met.* 6.77 (a saltwater spring) and Sen. *Contr.* 5. *exc.* 5 (domestic fishponds).

74–83 Tantalus' tone becomes solemn and impassioned as he calls upon the other sufferers in Hades; the generalizing invocations (*quicumque* 74, *quisquis* 75, 77, 79) and the preliminary commands *vocem excipe* 80 and *credite* 81 generate a tension which is released in a paradoxical *sententia* (*amate poenas*). Then Tantalus breaks off with a moving cry of despair, *quando . . . superos?*
The figures addressed in these lines are not the famous sinners of 6–12 above; they are in general modeled on the inhabitants of Vergil's Tartarus in *Aen.* 6.548–627, but several of the details are original.

74 poenas lege fatorum datas: a grandiose expression, not conventional in accounts of punishment in the afterlife; cf. Cic. *Tim.* 43 *leges fatales ac necessarias*, Verg. *Aen.* 12.819 *illud . . . nulla fati quod lege tenetur*, Sen. *NQ* 1 *pr.* 3 *licet illi* (sc. *deo*) *hodieque decernere et ex lege fatorum aliquid derogare*, and *Ciris* 199, with Lyne's note.

75–77 quisquis . . . ruinam: based on Verg. *Aen.* 6.602–603 *quos super atra silex iam iam lapsura cadentique / imminet adsimilis* (a punishment often ascribed to Tantalus himself, see above. p. 39).

exeso . . . sub antro: perhaps derived from Verg. *Aen* 8.418–19 *Cyclopum exesa caminis / antra* (and cf. Luc. 9.468 *exesis . . . cavernis*); *exesus* (from *exedo*) is more usually applied to the mass in which a cavity has been made, cf., e.g., Verg. *G.* 4.418–19 *est specus ingens / exesi latere in montis* and *Pho.* 359 *latebo rupis exesae cavo. sub antro* (with *sub* nearly = "in") is frequent in Vergil, cf. *G.* 4.152, *Aen.* 3.431, 8.217, etc.

76 iam . . . venturi: a less vivid adaptation of Vergil's *iam iam lapsura cadentique . . . adsimilis*; here *venturus* is "about to arrive" and so "approaching," "coming near," cf. Verg. *G.* 4.156 *venturaeque hiemis memores.*

77–78 avidorum feros / rictus leonum: lions play no part in other ancient accounts of the underworld; Seneca may have elaborated the terrors of the afterlife with a scene from the amphitheater (see on 1033 *an beluis scinduntur*). Lions do, however, figure prominently in Roman funerary art "as a symbol of the ravening power of death" (J.M.C. Toynbee, *Animals in Roman Life and Art* [Ithaca, 1973], 65–69).

avidorum feros / rictus: a cluster of thematically significant terms: for *avidus* see on 2 above; *ferus* appears several times of various Tantalids, especially Atreus (cf. 85–86, 136, 150 *dapibus feris* of Tantalus, 546, 721); and of the three further occurrences of *rictus* in the play two are in similes comparing Atreus to a tiger (710) and a lion (734), while the last describes Thyestes drinking from the bloody cup (988). There might be a suggestion that hell's worst terrors are matched on earth by the savagery of Tantalus' descendants.

78 dira Furiarum agmina: the Furies are the jailers in Verg. *Aen.* 6.572 *agmina saeva sororum*, 605–606 *Furiarum maxima iuxta / accubat.*

79 implicitus: with typical Senecan abstractness the sinner is described as "entwined" or "entangled," but the instrument is not specified (a net, perhaps, or else the chains heard by Aeneas at *Aen.* 6.558 *stridor ferri tractaeque catenae*); the lack of detail throws greater emphasis onto the victim's helpless dread (*horres*).

79–80 quisquis . . . abigis: "all you who, half-charred, try to push away the torches thrust toward you" (*immissas*, cf. Verg. *Aen.* 8.246 *trepident immisso lumine Manes*, Ovid *Met.* 12.330 *lancea . . . costis immissa Petraei*). The picture may owe something to Ovid *Ibis* 632 *membra feras Stygiae semicremata neci*.

semiustus: a gruesome detail; the torches have left the victim partially burnt, cf. *HO* 1737 of Hercules on his pyre. [Here *semi-* carries its full value, and nothing prevents *semusta tecta* of *Tro.* 1085 from being read in the same way (I differ with Fantham here); only in *Ag.* 761 *semustas faces* (of the Furies) does the prefix seem to lack any force.]

81 credite experto: a Vergilian phrase, cf. *Aen.* 11.283.

82–83 quando continget . . . superos?: *contingo* of a hoped-for outcome, "when will it be my lot to escape the upper world?" For *superi* of those who live in the world above cf. Prop. 2.1.37 *Theseus infernis, superis testatur Achilles*, *Ag.* 4 *fugio Thyestes inferos*, *superos fugo*, *Tro.* 179. In the end, though, it is the gods (the *superi* in another sense) who are driven to flight by the events of the play, cf. 776, 893 *fugientes deos*, 995 *fugit omne sidus*, 1021 *fugere superi*.

83–86 The Fury insists that first (*ante*) Tantalus must inflame the house with a lust for strife (*ferri . . . amorem, insano . . . tumultu*). These lines produce no change in the situation, but by renewing the pressure on Tantalus they build toward the climax of the scene.

Tantalus' last lines contain an unusually high proportion of resolved long syllables, a means of underlining the excitement in his words (*implicitus horres* 79, *semiustus abigis* 80, *properantis*, 81, *effugere superos* 83); by contrast the almost complete absence of resolution in the Fury's reply (except for *regibus* 85) points up her implacable single-mindedness.

84–85 ferri malum . . . amorem: compare Verg. *Aen.* 7.460–62 (Allecto's effect on Turnus), *arma amens fremit . . . / saevit amor ferri et scelerata insania belli, / ira super*.

regibus: Atreus and Thyestes, as at 34 above.

85–86 concute . . . pectus: this might refer collectively to the hearts of Tantalus' descendants, but *concutere* is used in related contexts of stirring up one's own potential for disorder; cf. Verg. *Aen.* 7.338 (Juno to Allecto) *fecundum concute pectus*, *HF* 105 (Juno to the Furies) *concutite pectus*.

86–100 Tantalus' last speech is also his most remarkable. He rebels against the Fury's demands and attempts to prevent the coming atrocity (95 *stabo et arcebo scelus*); then he finds himself overpowered by the Fury and finally submits to her will. The lines exploit the dramatic tension in Tantalus' threat to obstruct the action of the play, depict the immensity of Atreus' crime through the terror it inspires in a sinner such as Tantalus (compare *Tro.* 926 *quantum est Helena quod lacrimat malum*, 1099, 1154), and prefigure the futile resistance of Thyestes.

86–87 Me . . . poenam: there is a strangely impressive dignity in Tantalus' refusal to bring disaster on his kin. The appeal to *quod decet* carries considerable weight in Roman moral thinking, cf. Livy 3.62.2 *qualem liberi populi exercitum decuit esse, talis fuit*, 7.35.8 *fameque et siti moriendum sit, si plus quam viros ac Romanos decet ferrum timeamus*.

87–88 dirus vapor / tellure rupta: "a deadly exhalation from a fissure in the earth," such as those described in *NQ* 6.28.1 *pluribus Italiae locis per quaedam foramina pestilens exhalatur vapor, quem non homini ducere, non ferae tutum est*. The comparison closely resembles that in *Ben.* 7.20.4, where enormous evil is likened to *hiatus terrae et e cavernis maris ignium eruptio*.

tellure rupta: appropriate for Tantalus, since figures from the underworld often emerged through a rupture of the earth's surface (cf. *Tro.* 179–80 *hiatus Erebi pervium ad superos iter / tellure fracta praebet*); the phrase also implies the violation of boundaries and the confusion of realms normally distinct, a result longed for by Thyestes at the end of the play, 1007–1019.

88 populis: "nations" (cf. on 648 below); the action of the play is frequently projected onto a global scale.

89 sparsura: "destined to scatter," cf. *Ag.* 43 *daturus coniugi iugulum suae* (n).

90 avus nepotes: see on *natum parens*, 40–41.

90–95 As at 74–82, Tantalus leads up to the high point of his speech through an extended apostrophe; here too this is followed by a surprising twist, the change of addressee from Jupiter (*magne divorum parens* 90) to Tantalus' descendants (*moneo . . . aras*, 93–95).

91 nosterque, quamvis pudeat: "my parent too (though the fact may cause you shame)"; perhaps echoed (and revised) by Thyestes in the final scene, 1035 *hoc est deos quod puduit*.

91–93 Seneca alludes here to another version of Tantalus' original offence, that he revealed the secrets of the gods to men (ps-Apoll. *Epit.* 2.1, Ovid *Am.* 3.7.51 *taciti vulgator*); this background explains the force of *nec hoc* in 93—"I shall not keep silent about *this* either."

91–92 ingenti licet . . . loquax: *licet* is concessive, "even though my tongue be condemned to severe punishment and tortured for speaking."

taxata: *taxo* is a technical term of the criminal code, referring to the assessment of actions in relation to their punishments; the verb is first attested in Seneca, who uses it several times, cf., e.g., *HF* 746–47 *scelera taxantur modo / maiore vestra* (addressed to rulers), *Cons. Marc.* 19.1.

ingenti . . . poena: ablative of penalty (AG 353.1), cf. ps-Quint. *Decl. min.* 331 *quod lex capite taxavit*.

92 linqua crucietur: *cruciare* of a part of the body is quite rare (Pl. *Curc.* 237 *cruciatur iecur* is comic hyperbole); the closest parallel is Val. Max. 7.8.8 in a metaphor for psychological anguish, *quasi tortore aliquo mentem intus cruciante*. The notion is a product of the almost obscene interest in torture-scenes shown by declamation, cf., e.g., Sen. *Contr.* 2.5.1–9, esp. 6 *instabat tyrannus; 'torque; illa pars etiam potest; subice ignes; illa parte iam exaruit cruor; seca, verbera, lancina oculos'* etc.

93 moneo: the absolute use (instead of, e.g., *moneo ne . . . violetis*) conveys a sense of urgency; compare *Ag.* 731 *timete reges, moneo, furtivum genus*, Ovid *Ars* 1.459 (in a parody of solemn advice) *disce bonas artes, moneo, Romana iuventus*. Seneca may have had in mind the warning given by Vergil's Phlegyas in Tartarus (*Aen.* 6.618–20): *miserrimus omnis / admonet et magna testatur voce per umbras: / 'discite iustitiam moniti et non temnere divos.'*

93–95 ne . . . violate . . . neve . . . aspergite: the plural verbs and the absence of a specific vocative suggest that Tantalus is addressing his descendants generally, not just Atreus. (The terms used might also fit Agamemnon's ritual murder of Iphigenia.) Tantalus' emphasis on ritual purity corresponds to Atreus' insistence on just this aspect of his crime (cf. 689–95, 1058–59, and 61 above).

sacra . . . caede: "accursed slaughter," i.e., rendering the agent *sacer* or liable to divine punishment, cf. Hor. *Epod.* 7.20 *sacer nepotibus cruor, Phoen.* 277–78.

94 furiali malo: the unusual phrase comes from Verg. *Aen.* 7.375 (Allecto infecting Amata); in both passages *furialis* retains its connection with the Furies (so too, perhaps, in its only other appearance in the plays, *Med.* 158 *siste furialem impetum*, cf. 958–66).

95 stabo: "I shall stand my ground," like a soldier maintaining a position against the enemy, cf. Livy 22.5.1 *stare ac pugnare iubet*, Luc. 6.155–56 *non ira saltem, iuvenes, . . . stabitis?*

arcebo: echoed (with irony) in 132.

96–100 The Fury's overpowering of Tantalus recalls Allecto's overpowering of Turnus, cf. *Aen.* 7.450–51 *geminos erexit crinibus anguis / verberaque insonuit . . .* and 456–57 *facem iuveni coniecit et atro / lumine fumantis fixit sub pectore taedas.* It may be significant that Vergil portrays the enemy of the future Rome as driven by hellish powers, while Seneca shows these same forces polluting a royal house described in strongly Roman terms (see on 641–49 and 659–64 below, where Seneca again makes his point through a revision of Vergil).

On one level the Fury overcomes Tantalus' resistance by stirring up his perennial hunger and thirst; on another, however, Tantalus' *fames* and *sitis* may represent an appetite for evil that he has failed to eradicate; lines 62–63 could point in this direction, and see on 102–103 below.

96–97 tortos . . . angues: "entwined snakes" (suggesting the intertwined strands of a whip), cf. *Med.* 961–62 *ingens anguis excusso sonat / tortus flagello*; the snake-whips of the Furies appear also in *Ag.* 761 *anguinea . . . verbera* (n).

97 minaris angues: for the instrument as obj. of *minari* (instead of the more common result, as in, e.g., Quint. 11.3.117 *minari verbera*) cf. Livy 5.36.5 *arma*, Prop. 4.6.49 *saxa*, Sen. *Contr.* 7.4.1 *catenas*, 290 below *fulmen*, 603 *equitem*.

97–98 quid famem . . . agitas medullis?: Tantalus' hunger is boldly spoken of as an object that can be manipulated within him; *agitas* might suggest a goad, cf. Verg. *Aen.* 1.337 *stimulis . . . agitabat amaris*, Ovid *F.* 2.779 *stimulis agitatus amoris.* Cf. *Epist.* 94.6 *fixam . . . medullis famem detrahe*, and see on 64 for a comparable treatment of *fames*.

98–99 flagrat . . . micat: *flagrare* and *incendere* were common metaphors for strong desires, and each had been applied to hunger or fever (cf. Lucr. 6.1168–69 *intima pars hominum vero flagrabat ad ossa, / flagrabat stomacho flamma ut fornacibus intus*, Ovid *Met.* 8.828–29 *furit ardor edendi / perque avidas fauces incensaque* [Heinsius: *immensaque* codd.] *viscera regnat*). To surpass such earlier passages Seneca piles on even more fire-imagery, some of it with unfortunate results (e.g., *micat* of an invisible flame). [Phaedra's account of her feelings for Hippolytus is even more elaborate: *pectus insanum vapor / amorque torret. intimis saevit ferus / [penitus medullas atque per venas meat] / visceribus ignis mersus et venas latens / ut agilis altas flamma percurrit trabes* (640–44; on the text see Zwierlein, *Philologus* 113 [1969], 259–261).]

flagrat . . . cor: since the heart does not literally feel thirst, the wording may imply that this *sitis* represents Tantalus' evil desires (a symbolism made explicit by the Fury's next lines, see on 101). Seneca makes similar use of *cor* in *NQ* 4B.13.11, after denouncing the affectation of cooling drinks with ice: *sitim istam esse putas? febris est, et quidem eo acrior quod non tactu venarum . . . deprehenditur, sed cor ipsum excoquit.*

100 sequor: it is not unusual for Seneca to place a climax near the beginning of a line (see on 23 above), but incomplete lines are rare: the other examples are *Pho.* 319—at the end of a scene—, *Tro.* 1103, and perhaps *Pha.* 605. The text has been suspected, but there seems no reason to doubt that the isolated *sequor* is genuine and depicts Tantalus' complete subservience to the Fury. Willingness to follow another's lead is another link between Tantalus and Thyestes, cf. *sequor* 489.

101–21 The Fury exploits Tantalus' submission, forcing him to pollute the house with his touch (101–104); she then orders him to leave the upper world and catalogues the dismal effects of his continued presence (105–121).

101 hunc furorem: i.e., the madness stirred up in Tantalus by hunger and thirst. The term *furor* suggests the metaphorical significance Seneca draws from Tantalus' traditional attributes; *suum . . . sitiant cruorem* (102–103) makes this shift even clearer.

divide in totam domum: "share it out among the whole house," as though Tantalus' *furor* were a sort of patrimony (which, in a sense, it is).

101–102 Hunc, hunc . . . sic, sic: W. M. Calder III has suggested (*CP* 79 [1984], 225–26) that these repeated words accompany lashes of the Fury's whip; he cites as a precedent Verg. *Aen.* 4.660 *sic, sic iuvat ire sub umbras*, where some ancient readers thought that *sic, sic* represented Dido's suicidal sword-thrusts (see Pease *ad loc.*). The Fury's lines are certainly spoken as she forces Tantalus toward the house, but in itself the repetition might only signal her excitement, cf. *Med.* 13, *nunc, nunc adeste*, 911 *iuvat, iuvat*, 980 *huc, huc*, *Pha.* 83 *hac, hac*, 1268 *hic, hic.*

102 ferantur: "let them (i.e., the inhabitants of the *domus*) be borne along," cf. 36, 109.

102–103 suum . . . cruorem: a wish fulfilled by Thyestes, cf. 917 *mixtum suorum genitor bibat.*

103 introitus: "entrance" rather than "near approach" (Miller), as noted by Calder (see on 101–102); cf. Cic. *Caec.* 39 *non introitu, sed omnino aditu prohibere*, Sen. *Ben.* 6.34.1 *magno aestimare introitum ac tactum sui liminis.* (Touching the *limen* is perhaps what Seneca's audience is meant to imagine Tantalus doing, cf. 104 *contactu.*)

103–104 sentit . . . domus . . . nefando tota contactu horruit: an adaptation of Ovid *Met.* 6.601–602 *ut sensit tetigisse domum Philomela nefandam, / horruit infelix totoque expalluit ore.* Seneca repeats several of Ovid's words but places them in new syntactical positions (*sensit-sensit, tetigisse-contactu, domum-domus, nefandam-nefando, horruit, toto-tota*, perhaps *expalluit-pallescit* 110); *infelix* is pointedly absent, since the Fury lacks the compassion of Ovid's narrator. Ovid's action is also inverted: the house becomes the victim, not the source, of horror.

105 actum est abunde. gradere: the influence of *Aeneid* 7 can again be felt: Juno commands Allecto (552) *terrorum et fraudis abunde est . . .* and (558) *cede locis.* The use of *abunde* is yet another link between the Fury and Atreus (cf. 279, 889).

106–107 iam . . . gravantur: "the lands are already revolting at your touch" (i.e., at the contact of Tantalus' feet with the earth); *gravor* is here used in a middle sense and governs a direct object (*OLD* s.v. #4b), cf. Lucan 7.284–85 *dominosque gravantur / quos* *novere magis.* [The A MSS give *tuo . . . pede* for *tuum . . . pedem*, a clear example of interpolation to replace an unfamiliar construction with one more common.]

106-119 The reaction of the house to Tantalus' presence (103-104) is now enacted on a larger scale, reproducing on earth a version of Tantalus' customary punishment, as all moisture (and fruit, cf. 110-11) retreats from his vicinity. The passage also foreshadows the far more violent and cosmic recoil that attends Thyestes' crime (789-884).

107 cernis ut: *cernis (cernitis)* is used at *HF* 1017 and *Tro.* 684 of persons visible (or imagined as visible) on stage, in *Tro.* 893-95 of objects supposedly nearby (*cernis hos tumulos ducum / et nuda totis ossa quae passim iacent / inhumata campis?*). Here, though, the Fury's vision extends far beyond the immediate setting, taking in Corinth and Thebes (111-14, 117) as well as Argos. No description of off-stage action in pre-Senecan drama (cf., e.g., Aesch. *Suppl.* 713-25, Eur. *Phoen.* 101-82, Pl. *Rud.* 160-77) approaches this passage in its range, and the closest Senecan parallels are in *Phoenissae* (394-400, 427-42); cf. *HSCP* 82 (1978), 251-54, and for other connections between *Thyestes* and *Phoenissae*, see above, p. 11.

108 introrsus actus: "driven within (the earth)," i.e., the water rushes back to its source.

ripae vacent: based on Ovid's account of the Nile during Phaethon's disastrous ride in the sun's chariot, *Met.* 2.255-56 *ostia septem / pulverulenta vacant, septem sine flumine valles.*

109 ventus . . . ferat: there are few clouds in the sky (*raras . . . nubes*) because the heat of the wind has caused nearly all moisture in the air to evaporate; the fire of Tantalus' hunger and thirst (98-99) has projected itself onto the outside world.

110 pallescit omnis arbor: *pallescere* functions in both a literal and figurative sense: the trees literally lose color because of the unusual heat (cf. Pliny *NH* 19.176 *ocimum sub Canis ortu pallescit*), but as personified entities they "grow pale" in fear at Tantalus' proximity (cf. Ovid *Met.* 8.759-60 *pariter frondes, pariter pallescere glandes / coepere*, of the oak fearing Erysicthon's axe-blows).

stetit: a good example of the "perfect of instantaneous result," used of an action which takes place so quickly that it has been completed before it can be described; cf. Verg. *G.* 1.330 *terra tremit, fugere ferae*, *Aen.* 1.82-84 *venti . . . perflant. / incubuere mari . . .*, *Ag.* 891 (n).

111-14 The first of four references to the Isthmus of Corinth (cf. also 124-25, 181-82, 628-29). Latin poets from Ovid onward were inordinately fond of the Isthmus (*Ag.* 563 [n]), but here Seneca employs it for a telling, though unobtrusive, effect: the contrasting perspectives of the Chorus, Atreus, and the Messenger are deftly suggested by the terms in which each refers, nearly on entrance, to this already familiar feature of the dramatic landscape. Here the Isthmus reflects the disturbance of natural order caused by Tantalus' presence: normally a slender strip of land dividing two bodies of water (*vicina gracili dividens terra vada*) the Isthmus has become broad (*latus*) as the waters on either side have retreated, so that instead of seething with nearby waves (*fluctibus . . . propinquis . . . fremit*), it now catches the far-off sound of distant tides (*longe remotos . . . exaudit sonos*). [The text of 114 has been suspected, and if it is sound the writing could be called somewhat vague, but no defense of E's *litus* for *latus* and no conjecture made so far is at all persuasive.]

113 vicina . . . vada: on the word-order see on 10 above; here the interlocking arrangement reflects the geographical facts, as in what was until recently the only surviving line of Cornelius Gallus, *uno tellures dividit amne duas* (of the Hypanis in Scythia).

gracili dividens terra: echoed by Lucan 1.101 *geminum gracilis mare separat Isthmos.*

114 exaudit: *exaudire* sometimes denotes hearing distant or indistinct sounds, a shade of meaning appropriate here; cf. Pl. *Merc.* 707 *quae loquatur exaudire hinc non queo,* Cic. *Att.* 4.8a.1 *dic clarius; vix enim mihi exaudisse videor,* Verg. *Aen.* 4.460–61, 6.557–58, 7.15, Ovid *Met.* 7.645.

115 Lerna: a marsh and stream near Argos, most famous for harboring the Hydra.

115–116 Phoronides . . . venae: a remarkably high-flown expression for the river Inachus. Phoroneus was the river-god's son, and the epithet *Phoronis* was used by Ovid of his daughter Io, cf. *Met.* 1.668, 2.524 (Ovid may have found it in Calvus' lost "epyllion" *Io*, but proof is lacking); *Phoroneus* appears later in Statius (*Th.* 12.465, *S.* 3.2.101) as a learned substitute for *Argivus* (cf. Theoc. 25.200).

venae: properly specifying a flowing stream of water (cf. Livy 44.33.2 *occultos latices, quorum venae in mare permanantes undae miscerentur,* Ovid *F.* 3.298, *Tr.* 3.7.16 *vena aquae,* Sen. *Epist.* 89.21 *aquarum calentium venae*), *vena* becomes an elegant post-Augustan equivalent for *aqua* or *fons,* as here, cf. Stat. *S.* 2.2.86, Mart. 10.30.10 *in Lucrina . . . vena.*

116–117 nec . . . undas: Alpheos is an important river of the Peloponnesus (cf. Ovid *Met.* 2.250, 5.576); in Accius' *Oenomaus* it identifies the inhabitants of Argos, 509 R^2 *omnes qui arcem Alpheumque accolunt* (for this association see also 130–31 below).

[**sacer / Alpheos**: the Mss read *sacras* (with *undas*), which seems to lack point—unlike, e.g., Ovid *Met.* 2.464 *nec sacros pollue fontes,* of the spring where Diana has bathed. On the other hand, Gronovius' emendation *sacer* is supported by *Med.* 81 *Alpheos . . . sacer* and Ovid *Her.* 2.114 *sacer Hebrus,* and gives a more satisfying arrangement of words, cf. Zwierlein, *Gnomon* 40 (1968), 768. (Costa on *Med.* 81 cites Milton's "divine Alpheus" [*Arcades* 30], and—although Senecan influence is doubtful—one thinks also of "Alph, the sacred river" in Coleridge's *Kubla Khan*.)]

117–118 Cithaeronis . . . nive: "the ridges of Cithaeron stand nowhere white, the snow having been put off" (*parte nulla* abl. of place; *cana* neuter pl. nom. in agreement with *iuga*; *deposita nive* abl. absolute). The phrasing is highly artificial, perhaps because Seneca was straining for an inverted allusion to Horace's snow-covered Soracte, *C.* 1.9.1–2 *vides ut alta stet nive candidum / Soracte*; Seneca's *nive deposita,* comparing the snow to a burden that has been laid down (cf. Livy 6.3.5 *sarcina . . . deponi iubet,* Verg. *Aen.* 12.707 *armaque deposuere umeris*), might be the equivalent of *nec iam sustineant onus* in Horace. Cithaeron, the mountain near Thebes, is not primarily known for its snowy ridges, but cf. *Oed.* 808 *nivoso sub Cithaeronis iugo*; see also on 126 below.

119 nobiles . . . Argi: the city rather than the inhabitants.

veterem . . . sitim: the legendary "primeval thirst" of Argos, before Danaus brought water to the city by digging wells, cf. Hes. *fr.* 128 M–W, Pliny *NH* 7.195. The somewhat obscure allusion permits a concluding reference to the central idea of thirst.

120–121 en . . . diem: the prologue ends with an anticipation of the sun's retreat at the sight of the banquet (a pointed use of the convention that the action of tragedy began at dawn, see on 49–50). Lucan begins his account of the day of Pharsalus with a similar but more elaborate description of the sun's reluctance to rise (7.1–6). Seneca's language stresses compulsion (*iubeat sequi, cogat . . . ire*), creating a cosmic parallel to the vain resistance of Tantalus (96–100).

sequi: apparently "to proceed" (on its course), a sense for which I have not yet found a parallel.

121 periturum diem: "a day destined to perish" (i.e., before its natural end); for this use of the future participle compare 89 *sparsura*. A suitably resonant and ill-omened concluding phrase.

CHORUS I

The first choral ode opens a broader perspective on the situation set out in the prologue, as the citizens of Argos[1] brood over the grim history of their royal house and beg the gods to prevent the cycle of evil from repeating itself in the present generation. By recalling the crimes of Pelops and Tantalus, the Chorus gives more definite shape to the concept of inherited wickedness that obsesses all the characters in the play; by singling out Pelops' treachery (139–43) and Tantalus' inhuman savagery (144–48), it unwittingly anticipates the even more dreadful actions of Atreus and Thyestes. The tone of the ode is involved and fervent (note, for example, the heartfelt cry *peccatum satis est*, 138), with no trace of the detached generalizing of many Senecan choral lyrics. Like all the odes in this play, it portrays with powerful empathy the feelings of subjects whose lives are ruinously affected by events they are helpless to control.

The ode falls into three sections: a plea to the gods for assistance (122–37), recollection of the offenses of Pelops and Tantalus (138–51), and an imagined contemplation of Tantalus in the underworld (152–75). Many choral songs of Greek and Senecan tragedy consist of prayers to the gods for help; the type of invocation seen here, in which the gods of a city are appealed to at a time of crisis, is found, for example, in the *parodos* (entrance-song) of Aeschylus' *Septem* (87–180) and Sophocles' *Oedipus Tyrannus* (158–215). What is unusual about this chorus is the abstractness of its references to the gods: no deity is named—one might have expected an appeal to Argive Juno—, and the prayers are couched in conditional sentences (122, 124, 126, implied in 130), making them sound tentative and uncertain. The contrast between these vague and subdued allusions to the gods and the sharply detailed images of the Argive landscape with which they are interwoven creates an impression—to be confirmed as the play proceeds—that the gods cannot be counted on to ward off the dangers that threaten the Chorus's world. Faith in a benign providence is further shaken, for the audience, by recollections of the prologue, which at several points anticipates and nullifies the Chorus's hopes (see on 126–29, 132–33, 133–35, 138).

The closing section of the ode has a more complex relation to its surroundings. There is irony in the implied assumption that Tantalus' hunger and thirst represent the ultimate in misery, since the prologue has shown Tantalus longing for these familiar torments rather than witness the evil that is to be enacted (68–83). But these lines also underscore a central motif of the play: the extraordinary description of Tantalus resisting his hunger but at last succumbing to intolerable temptation (158–68) recapitulates the climax of the prologue, when Tantalus defies the Fury but is in the end reduced to submission (90–100); it also foreshadows the struggle and ultimate failure of Thyestes to hold out against the attractions of wealth and position (440–90, 530–43).

The final lines, with Tantalus once more deprived of the food and drink he craves,

---

[1] Nothing in the Chorus's language marks it as old or young, male or female. Seneca is often less clear about the identity of his choruses than Greek dramatists (see my note on *Ag.* 57–101 [p. 181]), but here the lack of a specific persona may help the Chorus's statements bear a wider relevance; see above, p. 45.

recall the opening of the prologue, where Tantalus finds himself abruptly displaced from that customary state. For a moment the play seems to have come full circle; this temporary sense of closure heightens the effect of Atreus' first words, which violently propel the action forward again.

Meter: First asclepiads (see above, p. 31).

122-126 si quis . . . si quis . . . si quis: the repeated conditions balance the questions at the start of the prologue (*quis* 1, 3), and also betray uncertainty—more justified than the Chorus can know—whether any god does in fact care for Argos.

122 Argos . . . Achaicum: *Achaicus* is not a conventional epithet in Latin poetry (Seneca uses it only here); the conjunction with *Argos* may recall Homeric practice (cf. *Il.* 9.141, *Od.* 3.251). In Greek "Achaea" strictly refers to the northern Peloponnese or southern Thessaly, but looser applications are not uncommon; see Denniston on Eur. *El.* 1285. In Roman terms "Achaean Argos" denotes a familiar concept, since Argos lay inside the Roman province of Achaea.

de superis: qualifies *si quis* ("if anyone from among the gods"); *de* is partitive, generally a prose usage, cf. Caes. *BG* 1.15.2 *pauci de nostris cadunt*, Livy 22.59.9, Petr. 44.10.

123 Pisaeasque domos curribus inclitas: the area of Pisa in Elis was identified by Latin poets with Olympia and spoken of as the site of the Olympic races; cf. Verg. *G.* 3.180–81 *Alphea rotis praelabi flumine Pisae / et Iovis in luco currus agitare volantis,* *Tro.* 849–50, *Ag.* 938 (where Seneca again anachronistically projects the games back into heroic times), Juv. 13.99 *Pisaeae ramus olivae.* The identification may have been assisted by the fact that Pisa was the setting of the famous chariot-race in which Pelops defeated Oenomaus through the treachery of Oenomaus' charioteer Myrtilus, cf. Acc. 196 R² (from the *Atreus*), *simul et Pisaea praemia arrepta a socru possedit suo,* 500 R² (from *Oenomaus*); above, p. 39. The story will soon be explicitly recalled (139–43), but *curribus inclitas* already sounds an ironic note, since the "renown" of Pisa was not straightforwardly positive. (See also on 131.)

124 Isthmi . . . regna: the Isthmus reappears (see 111–14 above), here atypically described in the language of dominion, perhaps to establish the outlook of the Chorus as subjects in a *regnum*. Note also that the sea divided by the Isthmus is *dissidens* (125), often a term of political strife, cf. Phaedrus 1.30.1 *humiles laborant ubi potentes dissident,* Sen. *De ira* 3.2.4 *dissidit plebs tota cum patribus,* Florus 2.5 *sic urbe in una quasi in binis castris dissidebatur;* are the conflicts of the rulers being projected onto the Chorus's view of the realm?

125 portus geminos: a verbal link with the next mention of the Isthmus at 181 *geminum mare.*

126-29 The lines on the snows of Taygetus are the counterpart to the Fury's description of Cithaeron in 117–18; the Chorus evokes a regular and stable alternation of seasons, but belief in the natural order has been undermined by the prologue's depiction of a disjointed world. [Cithaeron and Taygetus are similarly paired in the proem to the third *Georgic*, 43–44 *vocat ingenti clamore Cithaeron / Taygetique canes.*]

127-28 Sarmaticus . . . Boreas: Boreas is traditionally associated with Thrace (cf. Hes. *Op.* 507, Verg. *Aen.* 12.365, Ovid *Ars* 2.431); here Seneca places it farther north, probably under the influence of Ovid's exile poetry, which brought the epithet *Sarmaticus* into Latin verse. Ovid has no example of *Sarmaticus Boreas*, but note *Pont.* 4.10.38 *mare Sarmaticum* and 41 *hinc oritur Boreas.*

129 veliferis . . . Etesiis: a conspicuously *recherché* phrase—neither the wind nor the adjective belongs to the common stock of Latin poetic diction. The *venti Etesii* are an apt choice to express opposition of summer and winter, since they were thought of as the estival counterparts of *aquilo* (cf. Lucr. 5.742 *Etesia flabra aquilonum*, 6.716, 730, Pliny *NH* 18.335). Poets generally showed little interest in them, and Seneca's knowledge may owe something to his research on winds for the *Naturales Quaestiones*; note in particular *NQ* 5.10.2–11.1, where the rising of the *Etesii* is linked with the melting of winter snows (and compare *composuit* in 128 with *nives et ponuntur et durant* in *N.Q.* 5.10.2).

veliferis: *velifer* is attested in a mere handful of places, and in all but one refers to "sail-carrying" ships or their masts (*carina*, Prop. 3.9.35, Ovid *Met.* 15.719, *Pont.* 3.2.67; *malus*, Lucan 1.500, Val. Fl. 1.126, Stat. *S.* 5.1.244). Seneca extends the force of *-fer* to denote the wind that propels ("bears") the sails, which stand by synecdoche for the entire ships. [Much later (ca. A.D. 300) Porphyrius Optatianus used *velifer pontus* (18.13) in a similar sense, probably as a variation on Vergil's *mare velivolum* in *Aen.* 1.244.]

130–32 quem tangit . . . advertat placidum numen: the subject of *advertat* and antecedent of *quem* has to be supplied: "let <that god> [*ille deus* or the like] who is moved by the Alpheos . . . turn hither a calming power."

tangit: "touch" emotionally, cf. *Pho.* 301–302 *non patris illos tangit afflicti pudor, / non patria*; often used as the premise of an appeal, cf. Verg. *Aen.* 12.932–33 *miseri te si qua parentis / tangere cura potest*, Ovid *Met.* 2.293–94, *F.* 5.489.

130 gelido flumine lucidus: the cool beauty of the river is suggested through the interplay of liquid sounds and the lulling repetition of *lu* in *flumine lucidus*. The clarity of the Alpheos is highlighted in Ovid's description at *Met.* 5.587–88 *aquas . . . perspicuas ad humum*, a passage echoed by Seneca in *Cons. Marc.* 17.3 (of the *fons Arethusa*) *nitidissimi ac perlucidi ad imum stagni, gelidissimas aquas profundentem*.

131 Alpheos . . . Olympico: for the connection cf. Verg. *G.* 3.180–81 quoted above on 123, also 3.19 where Alpheos itself stands for the Olympic games. The reference to the racing-track rounds off the section begun at 123 (*domos curribus inclitas*). For Thyestes too the *stadium* is one of Argos' strongest associations, cf. 409–10.

132 placidum: prayers often include the wish that the god addressed will be *placidus* ("gentle," "well-disposed"), cf. Verg. *Aen.* 3.265–66 *di talem avertite casum / et placidi servate pios*, 4.578, Ovid *F.* 4.161–62. The combination *placidum numen* is not conventional; here *placidus* may have active meaning ("calming"), as in *placidis dictis, placido ore* (Verg. *Aen.* 11.251, Ovid *Met.* 1.390, 4.652, etc.); compare Vergil's picture of Neptune rising to calm the storm in *Aen.* 1.126–27 *alto / prospiciens summa placidum caput extulit unda* (with Austin's note).

132–33 arceat . . . vices: *arceat* surely recalls *arcebo* in 95: the intervention that the Chorus hopes for has already been attempted, and has failed.

arceat . . . ne: *arcere* with an object clause is not common, but cf. Livy 27.48.8 *collis oppositus arcebat ne . . . adgrederentur*, with *quin* 26.44.9, later Amm. Marc. 17.12.12, Claudian *Bell. Goth.* 100–103.

133–35 These lines ironically echo the prologue, *alternae scelerum . . . vices* matching *alterna vice* in 25 and *succedat avo deterior nepos* blending *subit . . . turba* (18–19), *rabies parentum . . . eat in nepotes* (28–29), and *ducam in horrendum nefas / avus nepotes* (89–90). The parallels remind the audience that the cycle of crime has already renewed itself, with imminent consequences far more virulent than any the Chorus can imagine; their neatly balanced phrases (*nec . . . minoribus*) sound almost mild after the Fury's tirade.

134 succedat . . . nepos: in addition to the internal references noted above, the phrase might recall a famous earlier description of moral decline, Hor. *C*. 3.6.46–48 (the end of the "Roman Odes") *aetas parentum peior avis / tulit nos nequiores, mox daturos / progeniem vitiosiorem.*

136–37 tandem . . . Tantali: the Chorus's tone now becomes more fervent, with *tandem* expressing wearied exasperation and with an accumulation of emotionally charged adjectives (*lassa, feros, sicci, impia*).

136 lassa: cf. 152 *lassus*; both Tantalus and his descendants are fatigued by the consequences of his crimes. Here *lassa* is causal, implying that exhaustion, if not virtue, should prompt the Tantalids to abandon their wickedness; one of Seneca's sharpest epigrams redefined the "clemency" of the elderly Augustus as mere "exhausted cruelty" (*Clem.* 1.11.2 *ego vero non voco clementiam lassam crudelitatem*), cf. also *Epist.* 63.12 *est in homine prudente remedium maeroris lassitudo maerendi.* The Chorus's hopes are explicitly negated by Atreus' later actions, cf. 736 *dente iam lasso impiger.*

feros . . . impetus: *impetus* is a favorite Senecan term for the irrational impulses of *ira* or other passions (it is the standard Latin equivalent for the ὁρμή of Stoic psychology and ethics), and his plays abound in futile calls for their restraint, cf. *Ag.* 203 (n), *Med.* 381 *resiste et iras comprime et retine impetum*, *Pha.* 255 *moderare, alumna, mentis effrenae impetus.* Here the *impetus* are *feri* (the closest parallels are *feroces impetus* in *Tro.* 496, *Ag.* 127), a coloring which adds to the portrayal of the Tantalids as creatures of subhuman savagery (cf. p. 47).

exuat impetus: an apparently unique combination, which may suggest that these *impetus* are a habitual way of life rather than a momentary aberrration; for *exuere* of "putting off" a customary outlook or manner cf. Verg. *G*. 2.49–51 *haec quoque . . . exuerint silvestrem animum*, Ovid *Am*. 3.4.43–44 *vultusque severos / exue*, *F*. 3.281 *exuitur feritas.* It may be significant that the verb appears only once more in the play, when Atreus invites Thyestes to put off the filthy clothes he has worn in exile and accept the raiment of a king (524–26).

137 sicci: "parched," usually of the tongue, throat, etc. (so, e.g., Petr. *Sat.* 82.5 *sicco . . . ore* of Tantalus); but for the extended use cf. Ovid *F*. 3.304 *relevant multo pectora sicci mero.*

138 peccatum satis est: a sentiment contradicted by the Fury (note especially 28 *rabies parentum duret*, 29–30 *nec vacet cuiquam vetus / odisse crimen*) and later overturned entirely by Atreus, for whom no crime is ever fully sufficient, cf. 256, 890, 1053.

138–39 fas valuit nihil / aut commune nefas: "respect for right has had no effect [i.e., in restraining the Tantalids from crime], nor has shared wickedness." (For *aut* joining the subjects of a negatived verb, cf. Cic. *Tusc.* 1.30 *nec vero id collocutio aut consessus effecit*, *Sall. C.* 26.2 *neque illi . . . dolus aut astutiae deerant*, K-S 2.103). The second part of this phrase has been variously explained or emended; I take it to mean that not even the fact that depravity is common to the whole family has prevented one member from committing crimes against another (as detailed earlier, 25–48). [Thomann and Watling understand *commune nefas* as "common (i.e., normal) ideas of the limits of crime"; the sense is apt, but it strains the meaning of *communis*, which, even when it comes close to "ordinary" (as in, e.g., *HO* 177 *nullum querimur commune malum*), still primarily denotes what is shared with others. (In combination with *nefas, culpa, vitium*, etc., *communis* consistently describes a wrong that affects or is practiced by all the members of a stated group, cf. *Ira*. 3.26.7, Ovid *Ars* 1.395, *Met*. 13.304, *Pont*. 2.3.22, Livy 5.11.8, 8.14.9, 25.26.7, Luc. 1.6, etc.) Ascensius took *nefas commune* to mean "nihil valuit, quia impunitum mansit," which also seems not to do justice to *commune*. The medieval variant *at* for *aut* is palaeographically neat, but linguistically doubtful, while *sed*, which would give a tolerable opposition to *fas valuit nihil*, fails to account for the corruption to *aut*. The most ingenious suggestion made so far is Bothe's *ad*, giving the sense "right was powerless to treat the common depravity"; for *valere ad* in this medical sense (a variety of the use of *ad* to express purpose), cf. Pliny *NH* 28.105 *fimum . . . arefactum ad dysintericos valere*, *OLD* s.v. *valeo* #4b, s.v. *ad* #44b. The rarity of the usage is no objection (and would even help explain the change to *aut*), but the resulting positions of *fas* and *nefas* are rhetorically implausible: as Otto Zwierlein points out to me, these terms are more likely to be placed on the same footing, as in *Ira* 2.9.2 *ad fas nefasque miscendum*, Ovid *Ars* 1.739 *mixtum fas omne nefasque*, *Met.* 6.585–86.]

139–50 The Chorus recalls two incidents from the previous history of the house, Pelops' murder of Myrtilus and Tantalus' attempt to serve Pelops to the gods. (See Introduction, p. 39.) The narrative follows an ascending order of emotional intensity: the stress on Myrtilus' disloyalty to Oenomaus (*deceptor domini, fide / vectus qua tulerat*) makes his downfall seem almost just, and there is little indignation in the summing-up *notior / nulla est Ioniis fabula navibus*; by contrast the attack on Pelops is recounted in a highly involved manner, with pathetic details (*parvulus, dum . . . osculum*) and indignant glosses (*gladio . . . impio, immatura . . . victima*) culminating in an outraged apostrophe (147). Once the Chorus has reached this level of emotion in contemplating Tantalus' crime, it is then natural for it to reflect at length on the justness of his punishment (152–75).

139–40 proditus . . . deceptor: deceit is a recurrent theme of the first part of the play, cf. 47–48 *fides . . . pereat*, 159 *deceptus*, 223–24 *furto . . . fraude*, 235 *perfidus*, 312 *fraudis . . . vias*, 318 *dolos*, 320–21 *fallere . . . falles*, 473 *dolus*, 482 *fraudem*, 486 *decipi . . . times*.

deceptor: perhaps a Senecan coinage; it occurs only here in extant Latin poetry.

140–41 fide / vectus qua tulerat: "transported [i.e., by Pelops] with the loyalty with which he had carried [i.e., Oenomaus]." For *ferre* of conveying a passenger by ship, cf. *Cons. Liv.* 428, Sen. *Ben.* 6.19.1; I have not seen it used of a charioteer.

141 nobile: "notorious," cf. *Ag.* 566 *scelere Lemnon nobilem* (n). For this explanation of the name of the *mare Myrtoum*, which lies just east of the Argolid, cf. ps-Apoll. *Epit.* 2.8, Ovid (?) *Her.* 16.209–10 *nec Priamo pater est soceri de caede cruentus / et qui Myrtoas crimine signat aquas*.

142–43 notior . . . navibus: reminiscent of Ovid *Am.* 1.9.40 *notior in caelo fabula nulla fuit*, *Met.* 4.188–89 *diuque / haec fuit in toto notissima fabula caelo*, but perhaps with a different emphasis, i.e., the story is familiar to sailors because that stretch of the Aegean was particularly dangerous (cf. Hor. *C.* 1.1.14 *Myrtoum pavidus nauta secet mare*), and the ominous origins of its name were often recalled to account for the sea's treacherous character. (Seneca may have been thinking of places in Ovid where a metamorphosis produces a natural object avoided henceforth by sailors, cf. *Met.* 9.228 *scopulus quem quasi sensurum nautae calcare verentur*, 14.74.)

143 Ioniis: "Ionian" here refers to the *mare Ionium*, the part of the Mediterranean immediately to the east of Greece, cf. *Ag.* 565 where the Isthmus of Corinth divides the *mare Phrixeum* from the *mare Ionium*, also *Epist.* 80.7, quoting a line of earlier Latin tragedy: *en impero Argis . . . qua ponto ab Helles atque ab Ionio mari / urgetur Isthmus*.

144 exceptus: bitterly ironic, since *excipere* often means to receive someone with kindness or affection, cf. Ovid (?) *Her.* 18.101 *excipis amplexu feliciaque oscula iungis*, Verg.

Aen. 3.210–11, 5.41 *excipit ac fessos opibus solatur amicis.* The pointed use may have been suggested by Verg. *Aen.* 10.386–87 *incautum crudeli morte sodalis / excipit atque ensem tumido in pulmone recondit,* 3.332.

parvulus: the pathetic diminutive heightens the brutality of the crime, cf. *Tro.* 456, 1089–90 *incedit Ithacus parvulum dextra trahens / Priami nepotem, Oed.* 806.

145 dum . . . osculum: the murder of Itys in Ovid is preceded by a similar show of filial affection (*Met.* 6.624–26 *ut tamen accessit natus matrique salutem / attulit . . . mixtaque blanditiis puerilibus oscula iunxit*); Ovid's Procne, however, is at least temporarily softened by the sight, and Seneca's language is designed to make Tantalus appear utterly heartless (compare *Met.* 6.640–41 '*mater, mater*' *clamantem et colla petentem / ense ferit Procne*).

146 immatura . . . victima concidit: the slaughter of Pelops is described in a novel way, as a travesty of sacrificial ritual; this motif reappears in a more developed form in Atreus' "sacrifice" of Thyestes' sons (689–775).

focis: suggesting both "hearth" and "altar," cf. 767–68, *Ag.* 168 (sacrifice of Iphigenia).

immatura . . . victima: the sacrifice even on its own twisted terms is tainted, since the offering had not attained the requisite age. I have not found a parallel for *immaturus* in this sense, but sacrificial regulations strictly specified the qualities required in a victim, sometimes calling for an animal in its second year, cf. the Vergilian formula *mactant lectas de more bidentis* (*Aen.* 4.57 with Servius' note, *bidentes autem dictae sunt quasi biennes, quia neque minores neque maiores licebat hostias dare*; see Pease *ad loc.*).

147 divisus: echoed in Atreus' preparation of the feast at 760–61 *ipse divisum secat / in membra corpus.* (The instances of *dividere* in 101 and 1023 may also relate to this motif, part of the theme of "sundering," see above, p. 46.) The word *divisus* of a whole person is less graphic than *divisum corpus* in 760–61 (or such expressions as *divisum . . . caput* in *Ag.* 45–46 or *divisa . . . membra* in Ovid *Met.* 13.865), but the absence of detail may produce a grimmer effect, cf. *Med.* 132 *comes divisus ense.*

148 mensas ut strueres: *mensam struere* (or *instruere, exstruere*) is often "to set/deck a table (with food)," cf. Pl. *Men.* 101 *Cerialis cenas dat, ita mensas exstruit,* with addition of *dapes* or *epulae* Ovid *Met.* 8.572, 11.119–20, etc.; here, though, *mensas* probably = *cenam, cibos* (for which cf. Ovid *F.* 6.131–32 *avidae volucres, non quae Phineia mensis / guttura fraudabant, TLL* 8.741.56–742.76); note the close parallel with 61 *epulae instruantur* and 1106–1107 *fuerat hic animus tibi, / instruere similes inscio fratri cibos,* and for *mensa* so used see also 273, 899, 916.

149–51 hos . . . decentior: the repeated *hos* and *aeterna* may underscore the inexorability of the punishment; the symmetrical sound-pattern of 151 (*dēc-/po-/poe-/dēc-*) may suggest its suitability to the offense.

149 persequitur: remarkable in referring to the punishment rather than the punishing agent (as in, e.g., Tib. 1.8.28 *persequitur poenis tristia facta Venus*), and also in implying that Tantalus' punishment is in some sense still in the future (cf. Cic. *Verr.* 1.50 *vitam mehercule mihi prius quam vim perseverantiamque ad illam improbitatem persequendam defuturam*). The result—perhaps aided by the echo of *persequitur* in *sequi* 174—is to cast Tantalus and his punishment in complementary roles of eternal frustration: Tantalus can never escape retribution, but neither can that retribution ever exact its full claim.

152-75 The ode concludes with the most elaborate extant description of Tantalus in the underworld. Its length and prominence suit its thematic importance (see above, p. 106); in particular Tantalus' struggle to resist his hunger—an unconventional touch with clear symbolic overtones—is described with an Ovidian abundance of realistic detail (especially 160-61: narrowed eyes, pursed lips, gritted teeth). As a whole, though, the writing is remarkable for its avoidance of naturalism: metaphor and figurative language systematically distort normal perspective. Several unusual or unprecedented conjunctions of nouns and adjectives produce a sense of stylistic disorientation (*vacuum guttur* 152, *praeda fugax* 154, *folia languida* 164, *silva mobilis* 168, *profugus latex* 172, *sterile vadum* 173). The scale of the scene is fantastically inflated as the tree (*arbor* 157) becomes a grove (*nemus* 162) and at last a forest (*silva* 168, note also *totus . . . autumnus* 167-68). The final lines defy analysis, verging on the surreal with their mingled images of flight and vacuity (see on 172-73). The most complete inversion of normal categories surrounds Tantalus and the fruit and water he longs for. Throughout the passage, nature, represented by the tree and stream, is seen in strongly human terms: it threatens (*incubat* 155), teases (*insultant* 164), and affects a languorous heaviness (*languida* 164); it is capable of motion (*fugacior, mobilis, profugus*), fertile (*gravidis, fetibus* 155-56), wealthy (*divitias* 162), and ultimately barren (*sterili* 173). With Tantalus, on the other hand, the repeated emphasis on parts of his body (*vacuo gutture* 152, *capiti . . . noxio* 153, *patulis . . . hiatibus* 157, *oculos . . . ora . . . dentibus* 160-61, *irritas . . . manus* 165-66, *sanguis* 170, *ore* 172) makes him appear less than fully human, nearly equating him with the physical instruments of his appetites. The deliberate cultivation of unnatural perspectives in passages such as this gives point to the currently popular description of Seneca's style as "mannerist" (cf. Jo-Ann Shelton in *Poetica* 11 [1979], 38-82).

The passage has a carefully planned bipartite structure. In the first section (152-61), verbs of motion are exclusively applied to the fruit that tempts Tantalus (153 *impendet*, 155 *incubat*, 156 *tremens*, 157 *alludit*), while he remains frozen in static resistance (152 *stat*, 159 *neglegit*, 160 *obliquat . . . oculos, comprimit*, 161 *alligat*). Then, as his defenses are breached, movement becomes reciprocal and intertwined: 163-64 *demittit . . . insultant*, 166 *exercere, protulit*, 168 *rapitur*, 169 *instat*, 171-72 *stat . . . petens* (cf. 152 *stat*), 173 *avertit*, 174 *conantem sequi deserit*.

152 stat: balanced by *stat* in 171 (and perhaps an ironic echo of *stabo* in 95).

lassus: cf. 136, and note the chiastic repetition: *lassa feros* (136)—*feris* (150) . . . *lassus* (152).

vacuo gutture: a unique combination; the closest resemblances are in *Cons. Liv.* 422 *arida guttura*, *Culex* 242 (of Tantalus) *gutturis arenti . . . sensu*. Seneca may be inverting *plenum guttur*, for which cf. Ovid *RA* 536, *F.* 6.138, *Met.* 12.325; he may also have had in mind Ovid's description of Erysicthon (*Met.* 8.826): *exercetque* [cf. 166 below] *cibo delusum* [v.l. *desuetum*] *guttur inani*). The choice of *vacuus* links the phrase to the motif of fullness and emptiness; see on 22 *complebo*.

153 impendet: suggests a looming, threatening object, probably recalling the rock that hangs over Tantalus in the other main version of his punishment, cf. Lucr. 3.980-81 *nec miser impendens magnum timet aere saxum / Tantalus*, Cic. *Fin.* 1.60, *Tusc.* 4.35 *poetae impendere apud inferos saxum Tantalo faciunt*.

154 Phineis avibus praeda fugacior: "a prey more elusive than the birds that tormented Phineus" (i.e., the Harpies). The conjunction of *praeda* with a word denoting flight (*fugax*) could have been suggested by Vergil *Aen.* 3.243-44 *celerique fuga sub sidera lapsae / semesam praedam et vestigia foeda relinquunt*, but Seneca has boldly transferred the idea of flight from the birds to the food they carry off; a *fugax praeda* is a reversal of the norm, since *praeda* usually describes a passive recipient of action, cf. Ovid *Her.* 10.96 *destituor rapidis praeda cibusque feris*, *Met.* 7.31. The effect recalls *fugaces . . . cibos* in 2, or *poma fugacia captat / Tantalus* in Ovid *Am.* 2.2.43–44, but is considerably stronger than either.

The use of the Harpies as a point of comparison may be connected with their appearance in *HF* (759) as a literal part of Tantalus' underworld surroundings.

Phineis avibus: Vergil and Ovid use *Phine(i)us* only of things actually belonging to Phineus, e.g., *domus* (*Aen.* 3.212–13), *guttura* (*F.* 6.130–31): the extended use here—typical of "Silver" Latin style—is close to that in Petr. *Sat.* 136.6 (a parody of high poetry) *cum Phineo maduere veneno / fallaces epulae.*

155 incubat: like *impendet* in 153, *incubat* suggests that the tree menacingly "hangs over" Tantalus; cf. *imminere* in Verg. *Aen.* 6.603, Ovid *Met.* 4.459 *quaeque imminet effugit arbor.* This appears to be the first time the word in this sense describes a natural object (later of a tree in Stat. *S.* 2.3.55, of a mountain ridge Pliny *NH* 6.53, cf. *TLL* 7.1.1062.57–63); its ominous connotations, though, are clear in such earlier passages as Verg. *Aen.* 1.89 *ponto nox incubat atra*, cf. *Oed.* 47 *ater incubat terris vapor.* The occurrences of *incubare* later in the play (401, 571, 733, 909) predominantly exploit its overtones of threat and anxiety; in *Phaedra*, the other play in which the verb appears often (99, 259, 268, 1280), its leading associations are of weight and oppression.

156 curvata suis fetibus: Ovid uses *curvare* of trees "bent over" by their fruit (cf. *Ars* 3.705, *RA* 175, *Met.* 10.94), once of a tree in childbirth, so to speak (*Met.* 10.518–19 *nitenti tamen est similis curvataque crebros / dat gemitus arbor*). The word *fetus* is a common term for fruit or crops in high poetry (cf., e.g., Verg. *G.* 2.56, 4.231); with *gravidis frondibus* ("teeming" branches, cf. Verg. *G.* 1.111 *ne gravidis procumbat culmus aristis*), it establishes an image of fertility countered by *sterili* in 173.

tremens: *tremere* can simply denote rapid motion ("flickering" or "quivering") as in, e.g., Prop. 4.6.26, Martial 4.30.9; in particular it is used by Ovid of tree-tops or marsh reeds agitated by winds, cf. *Ars.* 1.554, 3.694, *F.* 2.439, etc., similarly *Oed.* 50–51 *altis flava cum spicis tremat . . . seges.* In this context, however, it seems hard to exclude the word's emotional force.

157 alludit: in *Oed.* 267, the only other appearance of *alludere* in Seneca, it means "play up against" and governs a dative, *nostro geminus alludis solo*; that meaning would also fit this passage. Seneca may have deliberately chosen a verb with suggestions of water (cf. also Cic. *N.D.* 2.100 *mare . . . litoribus alludit* [v.l. *eludit*]), since it is more often water than food that plays around Tantalus' mouth (cf., e.g., *HF* 753 *alluit mentum latex*).

patulis . . . hiatibus: a grotesque phrase, which makes Tantalus appear for a moment as nothing but a pair of straining jaws. (The plural adds to the effect by suggesting Tantalus' mouth gaping repeatedly.) By itself *hiatus* denotes an abnormally wide opening of the mouth or other orifice; so, for example, of people gasping for air in Prop. 3.7.52, Ovid *Met.* 7.557, Val. Fl. 4.277. The addition of *patulus* might imply a subhuman contortion, as it consistently does in Ovid, cf. *Met.* 6.378 *patulos . . . rictus* (frogs), 11.60 *patulos . . . hiatus* (a snake), 15.513 *patulo . . . ore* (the monstrous sea-bull that destroys Hippolytus); on the other hand, the phrase had clearly lost much of its force by the time of Silius, who uses *patulo . . . hiatu* (2.119) to mean "with wide-open mouth."

159–61 deceptus . . . alligat: the pictorial vividness of these lines is enhanced by a complex pattern of repeated hard consonants (d-t-g, c-qu).

159 deceptus totiens: cf. *HF* 754 *saepe decepto*, *Ag.* 20 *ore decepto* (the same phrase is applied to Thyestes in 988 below).

neglegit: "shows no concern (to)," almost "refrains (from)," with a clear suggestion of choice, cf. Cic. *Or.* 77 *verba etiam verbis coagmentare neglegat*, Val. Max. 4.5. ext. 3 *Athenienses quid sit rectum sciunt, sed id facere neglegunt*, without infinitive in Juv. 9.92.

160 obliquat . . . oculos: lit., "turns his eyes aslant" (i.e., "looks askance"), a reaction combining fear and suspicion (cf. *Oed.* 339, Ovid *Met.* 7.412 of Cerberus turning away from unaccustomed daylight); to look at a person or thing *obliquo oculo*, etc., connotes hostility, cf. Hor. *Epist.* 1.14.37, Ovid *Met.* 2.787 (*Invidia*), 706 of Atreus *torvum et obliquum intuens*.

ora . . . comprimit: the indefinite *ora* produces a more elevated phrase than, e.g., Plautus' *comprimere dentes* (*Ps.* 787) or Horace's *compressis labris* (*S.* 1.4.138), but the language, like the gesture it describes, remains homely.

161 inclusisque . . . alligat: for the metaphor of binding compare the inverse *solvimus . . . famen* in 64 above, with note. Seneca is fond of *alligare* in this transferred sense, cf. *HF* 710 (*locus*) *quem . . . umbris spissa caligo alligat*, 1079, *Oed.* 182; the other instances, though, are not as striking as this one.

inclusisque famem dentibus: the enclosing word-order matches the confinement described; for *includere* nearly = *claudere* ("with teeth tightly shut"), cf. *Ira* 3.19.3 *os inserta spongia includi*.

162 divitias: *dives* and *divitiae* of Nature's abundance are not uncommon, cf. Ovid *Met.* 15.80–81 *prodiga divitias alimentaque mitia tellus / suggerit*, Sen. *Apoc.* 2.1 *honores divitis autumni*; it is surely significant, though, that Tantalus is finally overcome by a display of "riches," just as Thyestes will be (430–89, 536–43).

omne nemus: a magnifying phrase; Tantalus is now tempted by the wealth of an entire grove.

164 insultant: the verb essentially describes a repeated up-and-down motion (e.g., of ships on waves in Ovid *Met.* 1.134 *fluctibus ignotis insultavere carinae* [v.l. *exsultavere*]), but it is normally used of actions far more violent than the bobbing of fruit on tree-branches; it is difficult not to feel the verb's suggestions of taunting and abuse, cf. Verg. *Aen.* 6.570–71 of the punishment of sinners in the underworld, *sontis ultrix . . . / Tisiphone quatit insultans*.

foliis . . . languidis: either dative with *insultant* (so apparently *OLD* s.v. #1) or, perhaps better, ablative of description ("the ripe fruit with its drooping leaves").

languidis: flaccid leaves usually denote withered or diseased plants (cf. Ovid *Am.* 3.7.65–66 *iacuere . . . membra / . . . hesterna languidiora rosa*, *F.* 5.317–18); the exception is the lily, cf. *Pha.* 768 *languescunt folio lilia pallido*, Pliny *NH* 21.23. Here *languidus* probably suggests the heaviness of the foliage when the fruit is at its most luscious, and also a drowsy, slow motion, lulling Tantalus into the belief that this time the fruit will not escape him.

165 accenduntque famem: for the metaphor see 97–99 above.

166 exercere: "to busy/agitate"; perhaps a reminiscence of Ovid *Met.* 8.826, quoted on 152 *vacuo gutture*.

167 et falli libuit: a striking phrase, for which I can offer only distant analogues in Ovid (e.g., *Met.* 7.832 *sperat . . . miserrima falli*). The stress on Tantalus' acquiescence is certainly deliberate (contrast *HF* 754 *fidemque cum iam saepe decepto dedit*, where the emphasis is on the faithlessness of the water); it deepens the symbolic meaning of the scene, in which Tantalus' surrender prefigures that of Thyestes (cf. especially 542).

167–68 totus . . . autumnus: for *autumnus* by metonymy for the produce of harvest-time cf. Verg. *G.* 2.5–6, Ovid *Met.* 14.660; the combination *totus autumnus* recalls *Met.* 9.91–92 *totum . . . tulit praedivite cornu / autumnum et mensas, felicia poma, secundas.*

in arduum: "into the air," an idiom usually found in prose.

168 silva . . . mobilis: a startling phrase (imitated in Statius' description of Tantalus in *Th.* 6.281 (*qui*) *refugae sterilem* [cf. 173 below] *rapit aera silvae*); to modern readers it inevitably suggests Birnam Wood (and might even be the inspiration for Shakespeare's "moving grove," *Macbeth* 5.5.37). After this arresting image, which functions as a *sententia*, there is a new start (*deinde* 169); the language of the next few lines is relatively straightforward (as far as *petens* 172), forming a lead-in to the dense and pointed phrasing of the final lines.

171 obvios: stronger than "put in his way" (*OLD* s.v. #6), since there is an idea of motion toward Tantalus; better "approaching" or "oncoming," as in Ovid *Met.* 1.528 *obviaque adversas vibrabant flamina vestes.*

172–75 fluctus . . . gurgite: here and in *HF* 752–55 Seneca piles up several near-synonyms for water (*fluctus . . . latex . . . vado . . . gurgite*); perhaps a way of mirroring Tantalus' sensation of water all around him, but never within his reach.

172–73 quos . . . vado: two images seem conflated, one of water suddenly swerving away from Tantalus' lips (*profugus, avertit*), the other of a stream drying up and leaving behind a dusty bed (*sterili deficiens vado*, 175 *altum . . . pulverem*). Each of these pictures parallels an aspect of the action to come: the flight of the water foreshadows that of the Sun (789–93, note *vertis iter* 791) and the gods (893, 1021), while the passage from fertile abundance (155–56) to sterility and emptiness looks ahead to the annihilation of Thyestes' offspring. Seneca has refrained from harmonizing the two conceptions, creating a juxtaposition whose coherence is emotive rather than logical.

fluctus . . . quos . . . latex / avertit: narrowly skirting self-contradiction, since *fluctus* and *latex* refer essentially to the same object; there may be a hint that the water possesses a will that overrules its natural course (somewhat as Thyestes finds his body disobeying his commands, cf. 419–20, 436–37). The water's change of direction is re-enacted when Thyestes lifts the cup with his children's blood (987–88).

173 sterili . . . vado: "with barren channel"; cf. *Oed.* 43 *nuda . . . vada*, and for *sterilis* of parched soil cf. Verg. *G.* 1.70 *sterilem exiguus ne deseret umor harenam.* Here the connotations of infertility are thematically important, cf. 156 *curvata suis fetibus.*

174 deserit: used of Tantalus by Tibullus (1.3.78) in the sense "let down," "leave in the lurch" (*iam iam poturi deserit unda sitim*); here with a stronger sense of departure and abandonment, underlined by *conantem sequi* (cf. Ovid *Met.* 11.327 *conantemque loqui cum sanguine vita reliquit*). The sense-pause after *deserit* comes in an unusual position, halfway through the second metron (contrast 138, 150, 166); the jarring rhythm reflects the abruptness of Tantalus' deception.

sequi: of Tantalus in Ovid (?) *Her.* 18.182 *spem . . . suo refugi fluminis ore sequi.* There may be a significant echo of *sequor* 100, as well as of *persequitur* 149.

175 altum . . . pulverem: the separation of adjective and noun and the postponement of *pulverem* to last position verbally portray Tantalus' last-minute frustration.

de rapido gurgite: *de* has a quasi-partitive sense: the thick dust is all that remains from a rushing stream, cf. Prop. 1.5.26 *quam cito de tanto nomine rumor eris*, *Tro.* 544 *igne de magno cinis*, *Ag.* 413 *exiguas . . . de classe rates*.

ACT II (176–335)

In the three plays of Seneca with prologues spoken by other-worldly figures (*Thyestes*, *HF*, and *Agamemnon*), the action proper begins in the second act. The audience has already experienced Atreus' imminent crime in the prologue, through the terrified anticipation of Tantalus; now Seneca offers a closer view of the same event, as the form of his revenge gradually takes shape in Atreus' mind. The scene is dominated by four long speeches of Atreus (177–204, 220–44, 267–86, 321–33); this arrangement, which is not found in other Senecan scenes of this type, reflects Atreus' unwavering control of the situation. (The fragments of Accius' *Atreus* show that it contained a comparable scene, a bravura display of tyrannical savagery by the title character. See above, p. 42.)

After an opening monologue, the bulk of the scene comprises an unequal dialogue between Atreus and an unnamed servant. The encounter between an impassioned protagonist and a confidant who vainly counsels restraint is one of Seneca's favorite dramatic situations; other examples occur in *Medea* 115–78, 382–430, *Phaedra* 85–273, and *Agamemnon* 108–225. The ultimate inspiration for these scenes may have been Euripides' *Medea* and *Hippolytus*, where Nurses play a somewhat comparable role. (Sophocles' way of contrasting the strength of will shown by Antigone and Electra with the caution advised by their sisters is also to a degree similar.) Seneca's handling of these supporting characters, however, owes little to Greek tragedy. Seneca's confidant(e)s are never developed into fully-formed characters (although the Nurse of *Phaedra* comes closest); their essential function is that of reacting to the evil contemplated by the protagonist. By reducing the interest of the supporting role, Seneca heightens the concentration on the leading character; instead of the interplay of two complex personalities (as, for example, in Euripides' *Hippolytus*), he depicts individuals in self-conscious isolation. This tendency reaches an extreme form in this scene. In a sense its only real conflict is within Atreus himself, as he methodically extirpates every trace of moral scruple or restraint (cf. 192–95, 241–43, 249–54, 283–84, 324–30). The servant not only fails to sway Atreus, but even finds himself compelled to abet his plans (cf. 245, 286–88, 334–35); this decline from pious protest to timid complicity is the play's second portrait of evil victorious over feeble resistance.

176-204 Each of Seneca's protagonist-confidant scenes begins with a major speech by the protagonist (cf. *Med.* 116–49, *Pha.* 85–128, *Ag.* 108–24). These speeches are essentially soliloquies, in which no notice is taken of the subordinate character. In all of them the speakers review their intolerable situations and rouse themselves to action. Atreus' speech provides no formal exposition; as in the prologue, earlier events are alluded to in emotionally charged language (178–79, 197–202) but are not narrated. The function of the monologue is to display Atreus' insane desire for revenge, and only later in the scene (222–41) does Seneca relax the tension for a short passage of narrative.

176-78 Ignave . . . inulte: the scene begins with an explosion of verbal energy that is also a masterful depiction of Atreus' restless and turbulent character. The opening sequence of epithets, all associated with inactivity or lack of will, leads to a surprising climax in *inulte*: in Atreus' scheme of values, only vengeance is proof of *virtus*. The sounds of these lines echo their sense, with snarling assonance of *ign-/in-/en-* . . . */in-* and taunting repetition of *-ner-* in *iners, enervis*. (See also above, p. 44.)

176 enervis: roughly "gutless," a popular term in post-Augustan criticisms of Roman *mores*, cf. Val. Max. 2.7.15, Sen. *Contr.* 1 *pr.* 9, Petr. *Sat.* 119.25.

176–77 quod . . . reor: the parenthesis increases expectation of the last element in the series and so heightens the impact of the pointed *inulte*. The phrasing recalls Accius' Atreus (206–208 R²), *quod re in summa summum esse arbitror / periclum, matres conquinari regias, / contaminari stirpem ac misceri genus*, but Seneca's character thinks above all not of the practical dangers of confused descent (see on 240), but of the mere fact of being unavenged.

177 tyranno: Atreus makes no apology for being a dictator, and appeals several times to the "rules" of tyrannical behavior, cf. 205–218, 247–48, 312–13. Other Senecan *tyranni*, such as Lycus (*HF* 511–13) and Aegisthus (*Ag.* 995), are similarly open about their status and methods.

rebus in summis: "in dangerous circumstances" or "in a crisis."

178–79 post . . . ruptum: the inflated description of Thyestes' crimes recalls the words of the Fury (47–48), *et fas et fides / iusque omne pereat*, and of the Chorus (138), *fas valuit nihil*.

179 ruptum: the notion of sundering what is normally whole runs through the play, cf. 88, 552–53, 777 (see note), 862, 956, 1008, 1039. Its last appearance gives the figurative rupture of *fas* a horribly literal form in the broken remains of Thyestes' children (*rupta . . . vestigia* 1039).

179–83 [The text as printed is based on the E-branch of the tradition; in its place the A manuscripts have: *questibus vanis agis / iras? at Argos fremere iam totum tuis / debebat armis, omnis et geminum mare / innare classis, iam tuis flammis agros / lucere et urbes decuit.* The E-version contains two difficult, but almost certainly authentic expressions, *agis* without an object and the apparent hyperbole of *totus . . . orbis*; the simpler A-text is probably an ancient interpolation designed to eliminate these features.]

179 questibus vanis agis: "do you take action with futile complaints?" (i.e., rather than with the forces at your command), cf. *lege agere* "to take legal action" (Livy 26.15.9, etc.), Verg. *Aen.* 7.523–24 *non iam certamine agresti / stipitibus duris agitur*, Sen. *Epist.* 95.34 *decretis agendum est*. Compare also Ovid's Procne (who has clearly influenced Seneca's portrayal of Atreus), *Met.* 6.611 '*non est lacrimis hoc' inquit 'agendum.*'

180 iratus Atreus: it is typically Senecan frankly to admit one's *ira*, cf. *Med.* 135–36 *nullum scelus / irata feci* (implying that Medea is now *irata*), *Oed.* 519 *quid arma possint regis irati scies*, *Ag.* 970 '*iustae parenti satis*' '—at iratae parum' (text uncertain). Atreus, though, goes a step further in combining *iratus* with a self-conscious use of his own name (cf. 53 *Tantalo*): for "Atreus" to stop at mere complaints would be shameful, but for "Atreus angered" to do so is unthinkable.

180–91 These lines assume that Thyestes is hiding somewhere in Argos. None of the activity mentioned actually occurs, though, since Atreus soon hits on the plan of luring Thyestes with an offer of joint rule (297–99). The passage thus serves mainly to exhibit Atreus' ruthless energy and the pleasure he derives from this imagined display of his power.

180–81 totus . . . orbis: if taken in the usual sense, "the whole world," the phrase would be badly out of line with the rest of this section, which is clearly centered on Argos. [Perhaps for this reason the A-text has *at Argos* instead of *Atreus* and omits *orbis*, making the geography consistent.] But *orbis* can also mean "area of control" (cf. *OLD* s.v., #13, and note especially Ovid *Met.* 8.100 *Creten, qui meus est orbis*, Sen. *NQ* 5.18.10 *parum est intra orbem suum furere*), so that the meaning is actually "my whole kingdom." This "globalizing" language is characteristic of Atreus, cf. *tot* 178, *omne* 179, *undique* 183, *tota* 184, *totus* 187, *quisquis* 188.

181–82 geminum . . . agere: "your fleets should have been stirring up the twin seas from either side," i.e., from either side of the Isthmus (see on 111–14). For *agere mare* cf. *Med.* 755 *egique ad imum maria*, Ovid(?) *Her.* 12.124 *quis freta ventus agat*. [Instead of *agere* the A-text reads *innare*, which is more choice and more vivid, but which normally describes swimming or floating rather than vigorous sailing.]

geminum . . . utrimque: for the pleonasm cf. Verg. *G.* 3.33 *bisque triumphatas utroque ab litore gentes*, which refers to two triumphs rather than four.

182 flammis: i.e., of torches held by the search-parties.

183–84 strictum . . . ferrum: Atreus fulfills part of the Fury's exhortation, *stringatur ensis* 26.

184 micare: the "flashing" sword is often a sort of synecdoche for battle, cf. Livy 1.25.4, 7.5.6, 33.10, etc.; for its usual emotional coloring note, e.g., Sen. *Const.* 6.2 *inter micantis ubique gladios et militarem in rapina tumultum, inter flammas et sanguinem stragemque impulsae civitatis. . . .*

184–85 sub nostro . . . equite: kings in Greek tragedy do not normally call up troops of cavalry; this is the first of several indications of a Roman coloring to Atreus' rule. The collective singular *eques* is common in Roman military contexts, cf. *OLD* s.v., #2b. The Chorus thinks in similar terms, cf. 381, 554, 603.

186 hostem: Atreus avoids naming his brother until 259, where the mention of "Thyestes" carries particular force. Not naming one's opponent is a rhetorical device— technically, *antonomasia* or *pronominatio*—that expresses contempt, cf. *Ad Her.* 4.42, Quint. 8.6.30, Dido in *Aeneid IV* (421, 497–98, 613, 640, 661–62), S. *Ag.* 165 (n).

186–87 altis . . . arces: another detail with possible Roman associations, since towns perched on hilltops were (and are) a distinctive feature of the Italian landscape, cf. Verg. *G.* 2.156 *tot congesta manu praeruptis oppida saxis*.

187 bellicum . . . canat: a technical term for giving the signal to initiate hostilities. There is a clear echo in 553 *cecinit . . . bellum*.

188 invisum caput: *caput* by synecdoche for "person" is usually a term of address, but for its use here and in 244 as a substitute for Thyestes' name cf. Verg. *Aen.* 4.612–13 *si tangere portus / infandum caput ac terris adnare necesse est*, 640 *Dardanii . . . rogum capitis*.

190–91 haec . . . fratrem ruat: Atreus imagines that his search for Thyestes might lead to the palace itself, and acccepts the consequences of pulling it down on both of them (*vel* in 191 = "even"). Willingness to die while destroying one's enemy is typical of characters bent on revenge, such as Sophocles' Electra (1078–81); neglect of one's own safety was more generally attributed to *irati*, cf. Hor. *C.* 1.16.9–12 with Nisbet-Hubbard's note, Sen. *Ira* 1.1.1 [*adfectus*] *dum alteri noceat sui neglegens, in ipsa inruens tela et ultionis secum ultorem tracturae avidus*. Seneca's Medea expresses a related idea: *trahere, cum pereas, libet* 427 (and cf. Costa *ad loc.*).

190 pollens . . . Pelopis domus: the phrasing may have Roman overtones, cf. Pl. *Capt.* 278 *quod genus illi est unum pollens atque honoratissumum*, Sall. *Jug.* 30.4 *ea tempestate Romae Memmi facundia clara pollensque fuit*.

incliti: Seneca is inordinately fond of this high-sounding epithet (he uses it nearly twenty times in the tragedies, twice as often as Vergil and Ovid combined); applied to Pelops, however, the word must have ironic force, cf. *domos . . . curribus inclitas* 123.

192–204 The rhetorical rhythm of the speech now quickens, and it ends with no fewer than seven *sententiae* on the theme of revenge. The only respite from the epigrammatic style comes in the middle lines (196–99 *et quod . . . quietem*) and here a trio of questions maintains the emotional drive. The rhythm literally changes as well: 192 begins with a rush of four short syllables, and the section as a whole is unusually rich in resolutions, conveying a sense of almost breathless eagerness.

192–93 age . . . taceat: Seneca's Medea also aims for undying renown in crime, cf. 432–33 *faciet, hic faciet dies / quod nullus umquam taceat*, but the sardonic opposition of *probet* and *taceat* gives Atreus' lines a sharper point, cf. *Tro.* 1128 *odit scelus spectatque*. Atreus' wish is recalled in the words of the Messenger, 753–54 *o nullo scelus / credibile in aevo quodque posteritas neget*.

192 anime: the standard term of self-address in Senecan drama, corresponding to θυμέ in Euripides (e.g., *Med.* 1056); it often appears in exhortations to action (i.e., to crime), cf. *Med.* 895, *Pha.* 592, *Ag.* 108 (n). Although *anime* was similarly used by earlier Latin tragedians (cf. Pacuvius 284 R², Accius 489 R²), it is particularly prominent in Seneca, perhaps because of his philosophical belief that voluntary acts require the assent of the rational faculty, cf. *Ira.* 2.1.4 *nobis placet nihil illam* [sc. *iram*] *per se audere, sed animo adprobante*. This style of self-address is not common in later drama, but note, e.g., Othello's "it is the cause, it is the cause, my soul" (5.2.1).

193–95 aliquod . . . mallet: Atreus improves on the conventional adjectives *atrox* and *cruentum* by finding a more pointed description of the revenge he must devise—one that Thyestes could wish he had taken on him. For a similar twist see 16–18.

195–96 ulcisceris . . . vincis: the second person verbs are addressed to no single listener, but are instead "gnomic" (as in "you can't take it with you"), cf. *HF* 343–44, *Oed.* 25–26.

196 vincis: "outdo," as in 19 (*turba*) *quae suum vincat genus*. The echo shows that Atreus belongs to the *turba* foreseen by Tantalus; note also 20 *inausa audeat* and 193 *audendum*. Atreus returns to this point at 1052–53 *sceleri modus debetur ubi facias scelus, / non ubi reponas*. In this, as in other respects, Atreus' outlook is a complete inversion of traditional morality, cf. *Ira* 2.32.1 *non enim ut in beneficiis honestum est merita meritis rependere, ita iniurias iniuriis. illic vinci turpe est, hic vincere*, also Sall. *Jug.* 42.5 *sed bono vinci satius est quam malo more iniuriam ulcisci*.

198–99 numquid . . . quietem?: "does he accept any limit in prosperity, or retirement in adversity?" That is, Thyestes was not content to enjoy prosperity within limits as Atreus' brother but schemed to gain power for himself; once defeated, he is not willing to live obscurely but plots another attempt on the throne. By claiming that Thyestes cannot endure *modus* and *quies*, Atreus nimbly assumes a position of moral superiority *vis-à-vis* his victim. [Seneca himself described Cicero in remarkably similar terms, *BV* 5.1 *nec secundis rebus quietus nec adversarum patiens*.]

rebus . . . fessis: *res fessae*, "adverse conditions," is a Vergilian expression (*Aen.* 3.145, 11.335) which later became part of high style in both prose and verse.

199 quietem: under the Principate *quies* often denotes avoidance of political involvement, cf. *OLD* s.v., #6b; *quies* is what Seneca asked of Nero in A.D. 62, cf. Tac. *Ann.* 14.54.5, 14.56.3, above, p. 7.

viri: *vir* is often a substitute for the oblique cases of *is*, which are generally avoided in poetry, cf. Verg. *Aen.* 4.423 *sola viri mollis aditus et tempora noras* (where, as here, *viri* has an edge of hostility or at least distance). In prose as well, *viri* can take the place of *eius*, cf. Sall. *Cat.* 51.16 *eos mores eamque modestiam viri cognovi*.

200 indocile: a surprisingly mild word; Seneca does not want to overshadow the following *sententia*.

flecti . . . potest: other Senecan characters lament the difficulty of bending a proud or obdurate spirit, cf. *Med.* 202, *Pha.* 137, 229; Atreus characteristically concludes that stronger measures are needed. The combination of *flectere* and *frangere* appears (with the opposite inference drawn) in Livy 2.23.15 *concitatos animos flecti quam frangi putabat cum tutius cum facilius esse*; Livy 42.48.3 links *flectere* and *docere* (cf. *indocile*), *non eis animis audiebantur qui aut doceri aut flecti possent*.

non potest . . . potest: for other *sententiae* based on this opposition cf. Sen. *Prov.* 3.1 *potest . . . miser dici, non potest esse*, *Ira* 3.26.1 *quis . . . iniuriam non potest ferre qui potest iram?*, *Pho.* 66 *perire sine me non potes, mecum potes*.

202 petatur . . . petat: "let him be attacked first, so that he may not attack me when I am off guard." Atreus is obsessed by the suspicion—which the next scene shows to be groundless—that Thyestes may even now be plotting against him, cf. 270 *occupa*, 314–16, 1104–1110. His counterparts in Accius and Varius also portray themselves as acting in self-defense, but it is not clear if they resembled Seneca's character in paranoia, cf. Acc. 199–202 R² *iterum Thyestes Atreum adtractatum advenit, / iterum iam adgreditur me et quietum exsuscitat; / maior mihi moles, maius miscendumst malum, / qui illius acerbum cor contundam et comprimam*, Varius 1 R² *iam fero infandissima, / iam facere cogor*.

203 aut perdet aut peribit: the last of a series of symmetrical phrases, cf. 192–93 *nulla . . . probet, / sed nulla taceat*, 195–96 *non ulcisceris / nisi vincis*, 198–99 *secundis . . . rebus modum, / fessis quietem*, 200 *flecti non potest, frangi potest*, 202 *petatur . . . ne . . . petat*. If this fondness for balanced expressions is meant to characterize Atreus, one might interpret it as a form of verbal assertiveness, a drive to impose order on language, and so on reality.

203–204 in medio . . . positum: the crime is "set between" the opponents like a prize, cf. Ter. *Phorm.* 16–17 *in medio omnibus / palmam esse positam*, Livy 26.32.3 *praemium victoris in medio positam urbem*.

204 occupanti: "for the one who gets there first"; *occupare* in the sense "anticipate," "pre-empt"; cf. Sen. *Epist.* 29.5 *omnia quae dicturus sum occupabit*, *Tro.* 998, *Ag.* 193 (n). Fear of being anticipated is strong in Atreus, cf. 270, 274, perhaps 716.

For the device of breaking off a speech early in a trimeter see on 23 above, also 286, 690, 716, 1021, 1068, 1076.

204–219 The first section of dialogue illustrates several traits of Senecan stichomythia as contrasted with its Greek counterparts. It is competitive, concerned to win a point rather than to impart information or plan action. It avoids extended one-line exchanges in favor of less symmetrical forms, with lines frequently divided between speakers (*antilabe*). It is verbally intricate, developing ideas through a complex interplay of echo and revision (as with *laus* and *laudare*, *cogere* and *velle/nolle* in these lines). Finally, it is highly gnomic; in this case, lines 205b to 218 consist entirely of general statements. (Similar, but shorter gnomic exchanges occur at, e.g., *HF* 463–64, *Tro.* 332–36, *Med.* 159–63, 504–505, *Oed.* 699–706, *Ag.* 150–54.) The combination of these features gives passages such as this a keen sense of intellectual excitement, as irreconcilable positions are set against one another in the starkest possible form.

The subject of debate, the relation of ruler and ruled, is also a common one in Senecan drama, cf., e.g., *Oed.* 699–706, *Tro.* 332–36, *Med.* 195–96. This treatment is remarkable for its depiction of tyranny at its most cynical and arbitrary. The arguments Atreus brushes away coincide at several points with Seneca's advice to Nero in *De clementia*; the author of *Octavia* drew both on this play and on the treatise for the scene in which Seneca vainly urges restraint on Nero (440–62).

205–207 Maximum . . . laudare: Seneca's Atreus takes a step further the notorious dictum of his predecessor in Accius (203–204 R²), *oderint, dum metuant*: his subjects are to be coerced, not merely into acquiescence, but into praise. Atreus here gives the tyrant's view of a phenomenon noted by several writers of the Principate, the corruption of free speech through constant *adulatio* of the emperor, cf. Tac. *Ann.* 1.1.2, 2.32.2 (and see Goodyear *ad loc.*), Plin. *Pan.* 2–3, R. Syme, *Tacitus* (Oxford, 1958), 573–74, 580–81.

205 Maximum . . . bonum: *maximus* often acts as a lead-in to a pointed definition, cf. 175–77, 293, *Oed.* 629–30 *maximum Thebis scelus / maternus amor est*; *Tro.* 311–12, 422–23 *hic mihi malorum maximum fructum abstulit, / nihil timere*, *Ag.* 271–72 *id esse regni maximum pignus putant, / si quidquid aliis non licet solis licet*, *Pha.* 1119–20.

207 tam ferre quam laudare: "to praise as well as to endure." The word-order is inverted to give full weight to *laudare*; for similar inversions of logical sequence cf. *HF* 622 *o nate, certa at sera Thebarum salus*, *Clem.* 1.3.3 *illius demum magnitudo stabilis fundataque est, quem omnes tam supra se quam pro se sciunt*.

207–208 Quos . . . inimicos metus: the idea occurs often in discussions of tyranny, cf. Sen. *Epist.* 105.4 *qui timetur timet; nemo potuit terribilis esse secure*, *Oed.* 705–706, *Ag.* 72 (n).

209 favoris gloriam veri: the ideal of "true glory" is explicitly described by Cicero, *Off.* 2.43 *quod si qui simulatione et inani ostentatione et ficto non modo sermone sed etiam vultu stabilem se gloriam consequi posse rentur, vehementer errant. vera gloria radices agit atque etiam propagatur, ficta omnia celeriter tamquam flosculi decidunt, nec simulatum potest quidquam esse diuturnum*, *Tusc.* 3.3.

211–12 Laus . . . falsa: Atreus perversely welcomes feigned praise as a measure of his power, since there is no reason to flatter the lowly. Seneca's Eteocles develops a similar paradox, that a ruler's power is increased by the hatred of his people (*Pho.* 654–58).

211 et humili . . . viro: *et* underlines *humili*, "even to the man of low position," cf. Ovid *Tr.* 1.2.101 *quod licet et minimis*, "what is permitted even to the humblest."

212 quod nolunt velint: "let them (i.e., my subjects) will what they do not wish." Atreus does not merely demand flattery, but sadistically aims at inflicting mental pain. His wish is fulfilled by Thyestes, 420 *moveo nolentem gradum*, 965–66 *nolo infelix, sed vagus intra / terror oberrat*. [The radical conflict of will and reluctance is also felt by Phaedra, cf. 604–605 *vos testor omnes, caelites, hoc quod volo / me nolle*.]

213 Rex . . . volet: pursuing the theme of volition, the attendant pictures an ideal harmony of king and subjects (*velit . . . volet* in contrast to *nolunt velint*). The assumptions made here are explicit in *De clementia* 1.3.5–4.1, where Seneca calls the ruler the unifying bond and animating spirit of the state.

214–15 Ubicumque . . . regnatur: the demand for total license is typical of Senecan tyrant-figures, cf. *Med.* 195 *aequum atque iniquum regis imperium feras*, *Tro.* 335 *quodcumque libuit facere victori licet*, *Oct.* 451 (Nero) *fortuna nostra cuncta permittit* *mihi*, *Ag.* 271–72 (quoted on 205 *maximum*; see note *ad loc.* for other examples). In *De clementia* 1.8.2 Seneca argues that Nero's position in fact deprives him of the freedom enjoyed by his people: *quam multa tibi non licent quae nobis beneficio tuo licent.*

214 tantum: adverbial with *honesta*, "only what is right."

215 precario regnatur: "one reigns on sufferance" (that is, one's power depends on the consent of others); *regnatur* is impersonal passive. Suetonius recorded it as a sign of Claudius' unassertive manner that he obtained the Senate's consent (*precario exegit*) for the decisions of his magistrates (*Claud.* 12).

215–17 Ubi . . . est: this is the attendant's most forceful intervention (note the asyndetic series *cura iuris sanctitas pietas fides*, cf. 52 above); the point is the same as in *Tro.* 258–59 *violenta nemo imperia continuit diu, / moderata durant* or *Med.* 196 *iniqua numquam regna perpetuo manent*, but the expression is much more vigorous. The dialogue is approaching its climax.

217–18 Sanctitas . . . sunt: rather than responding to the attendant's point, Atreus repeats some of his words in a dismissive tone. (It is easy to imagine an actor sarcastically mimicking the attendant's impassioned delivery. This is one of many passages where Seneca's rhetoric has a strong theatrical flavor.)

218 qua iuvat reges eant: not an argument, but the overt statement of a thought implicit at 214, that kings may act as they please. The way Atreus breaks off debate with this arbitrary assertion encapsulates the leading idea of the dialogue, the futility of reasoning with tyrants.

qua iuvat . . . eant: "going one's own way" is a colloquialism for being able to do as one wishes, cf. Petr. *Sat.* 18.6 *hoc amo, quod possum qua libet ire via.*

219 Nefas . . . puta: the attendant shifts his ground: Atreus should regard it as wrong to harm a brother, even a wicked one (*vel* as in 191). [E reads *puto*, making the line an opinion rather than an exhortation. This seems weak, and for *puta* used in argument, cf. *Pho.* 616, *HO* 448.]

220–44 A listener might expect the point made in 219 to touch off a new round of stichomythia, and Atreus' first line does indeed sound like a self-contained reply. Atreus now goes on, however, to recall Thyestes' offenses against him and to urge himself even more insistently to take vengeance. The speech sweeps aside the attendant's scruples, and when dialogue resumes at 245 the question is no longer whether to retaliate, but how.

220 Fas . . . nefas: Atreus objects that Thyestes has never shown the restraint advocated by the attendant; the response is emotionally plausible, if not logically cogent.

in illo . . . in fratre: *in* here means "in the case of," cf. OLD s.v., #42, Ovid *F.* 6.576 *caeca . . . in hoc uno non fuit illa* [sc. *Fortuna*] *viro.*

222–24 coniugem . . . domum: Atreus again displays the tendency toward balanced phrasing noted earlier (see on 203, and add 220): *abstulit* neatly couples the literal abduction of Atreus' wife with the figurative theft of power, and the two charges made in 222–23 *coniugem . . . furto* are then repeated in chiastic order in 223–24 *specimen . . . domum*, with *fraude . . . fraude* playing a similar linking role. Accius' Atreus is much more diffuse, cf. 205 R² *qui non sat habuit coniugem inlexe* [= *inlexisse*] *in stuprum*, 209–212 R² *adde huc quod . . . agnum inter pecudes aurea clarum coma / quondam Thyestem clepere ausum esse e regia.*

223 specimen . . . imperi: "the outward sign of rule," cf. Verg. *Aen.* 12.162 *solis avi* *specimen* ("the sign of his descent from the Sun"); in Accius (210 R²) the ram is called *regni stabilimen mei.*

225–41 Atreus now settles down to the only passage of exposition in the play. The description of the ram with golden fleece is far more detailed than the corresponding lines in Accius (209–213 R², partially quoted above on 222–24), and might ultimately be based on a prologue-speech in a Greek treatment of the story. The elevated diction and leisurely pace of these lines offer a welcome contrast to the foregoing succession of clipped *sententiae.*

225 est: *est* marks the start of a descriptive passage giving the background for the main part of a narrative; the story usually resumes with a demonstrative word, in this case *hunc* (234). See further on 641–82.

Pelopis . . . pecus: = *est nobile* ("renowned") *pecus in stabulis altis Pelopis.* The artificial word order is a mark of high style.

225 altis . . . in stabulis: *stabula alta* is virtually a formula of Latin epic, cf. Verg. *Aen.* 6.179, 9.388, Ovid *Met.* 5.627, 6.521, 8.554.

pecus: the neuter noun is rarely used of a single animal, cf. perhaps Ovid *Ibis* 453, Gratt. *Cyn.* 265; less certain are Ovid *Met.* 11.248 *pecoris fibris*, Sen. *Ag.* 806 *pecore votivo*, since more than one animal might be offered in sacrifice. Euripides has ποίμνα (normally "herd") of this ram in *El.* 725. *Pecus* (fem.) describes the animal with golden fleece sought by the Argonauts, cf. Ovid. *F.* 4.903, Sen. *Med.* 983.

226 arcanus aries: not merely "secret" or "hidden," but "mysterious," "with magic powers," a sense not common before Seneca (cf. Prop. 4.7.37 *arcanas . . . salivas*) but frequent in Flavian poetry, cf. Val. Fl. 4.15, Sil. 2.426, 13.420, Stat. *S.* 3.4.92.

ductor . . . gregis: *ductor* was originally a loftier word than *dux* (cf. *Ag.* 39 [n]), but in referring to the bull loved by Pasiphae Seneca uses *pecoris . . . ducem* (*Pha.* 116) and *ductor . . . gregis* (118) interchangeably; *dux gregis* is an Ovidian phrase, cf. *Ars* 1.326, *Met.* 5.327, 7.311, and *ductor* was applied by Vergil to stags (*Aen.* 1.189) and bees (*G.* 4.88).

opulenti gregis: *opulentus* of a herd of animals is remarkable; Seneca elsewhere uses it of fabulously rich places (the garden of the Hesperides, *HF* 239, the Pactolus, *Pho.* 604) or of the possessions of kings and other magnates (*HF* 332, *Tro.* 1021, *Pho.* 54, *Oed.* 691). It seems appropriate that the symbol of Tantalid rule should suggest lavish wealth; see also on 344–47, 645–47.

227–29 huius . . . gerunt: "a fleece of gold hangs down all over its body, and new kings in succession to Tantalus bear scepters adorned with gold from its back."

[*Effuso* is the reading of E, *infuso* of A; *infuso* would imply that the fleece was smeared with gold, as hair might be with nard, cf. Lucan 1.166, while *effuso* describes a secretion of the ram itself, cf. *Tro.* 410 *effuso . . . fletu*, *Oed.* 624 *sanguine effuso*.]

228 e tergo: lit., "from the covering of its back"; *tergum*, usually applied to ox-hide, is here a virtual synonym for *coma*. Ovid has *tergum* of the original Golden Fleece, cf. *Am.* 1.15.22, *Her.* 6.104.

231–33 tuta . . . tegens: these lines are wrought to a high level of verbal artistry—another instance of Atreus' linguistic virtuosity. Nouns and adjectives are elegantly intertwined: *tuta seposita . . . in parte . . . prata* (= abBA), *fatale saxeo pascuum muro* (= abAB). The sound-patterns are equally intricate: 232 plays delicate variations on *p, a, r, t* (*parte carpit prata*), while 232 and 233 both set repeated *a*'s at the start of the line against darker vowels in the fifth foot (*cludit, muro*). The diction is mannered: *lapis* as a collective singular is quite rare (cf. *Pha.* 1095 *ora durus pulchra populatur lapis, Ciris* 108 *saepe lapis recrepat Cyllenia murmura pulsus*—perhaps with neoteric precedent?), and in 233 *saxeo* is to be scanned as a disyllable by synizesis (i.e., *eo* form a single syllable), an artificial license adopted by Latin poets in imitation of Greek practice, cf., e.g., Verg. *Aen.* 6.412, 7.33 *alveo*, and Norden on *Aen.* 6.280. Atreus seems to let his imagination linger over the picture of the ram safe in its enclosure before passing on to its removal by Thyestes (234).

233 fatale: "fateful," since it determines the *fata* of the kingdom of Argos, cf. Ovid *Met.* 8.85–86 *fatali nata parentem / crine suum spoliat*, Sen. *Ag.* 730–31 *fatalis . . . pastor* (Paris).

234–35 hunc . . . avehit: another artfully arranged set of lines. The object and verb are at opposite ends of the sentence, enclosing three emotionally charged subordinate elements (*facinus ingens ausus, perfidus, assumpta . . . thalami*). The separation of *hunc* and *avehit* lets the audience "see" Thyestes devising his scheme before it is put into effect, while the position of *perfidus* between *nostri* and *thalami* mirrors his disruption of Atreus' marriage.

236 hinc: "from this cause."

cladis mutuae: "disaster inflicted by each of us upon the other" (the strict meaning of "mutual").

237 per . . . mea: deposed for a time, Atreus was an outcast in what he still regarded as his own kingdom.

238 pars nulla . . . vacat: the phrasing is Ovidian, cf. *Pont.* 4.15.6 *a meritis eius pars* [sc. *vitae*] *mihi nulla vacat*, but *vacat* also looks back to the prologue (see on 22 *complebo*).

239–40 corrupta . . . sanguis est: after three relatively straightforward and slow-paced lines (236–38), the pace now quickens and the sounds become harsher (*corrupta coniunx . . . quassa; domus . . . dubius; dubius sanguis est*) as Atreus heads into the climactic *sententia*.

240 dubius sanguis: Atreus here first touches on an important point, the suspicion that Agamemnon and Menelaus may really have been fathered by Thyestes, cf. 327–30, 1098–1102.

240–41 certi . . . hostis: for similar pointed expressions cf. *Epist.* 99.9 *rerum humanarum nihil cuiquam nisi mors certum est*, 88.45 *si Protagorae credo, nihil in rerum natura est nisi dubium, si Nausiphani, hoc unum certum est, nihil esse certi.*

certi: partitive gen. with *nihil*.

241 quid stupes?: despite the absence of *anime* or a similar vocative (as at, e.g., *Pha.* 719), these words must be addressed to Atreus himself (*profare* 244 marks the return to dialogue). Seneca's protagonists are concerned with their own feelings, not with those of their confidants, and the reference to Tantalus and Pelops has force only if Atreus is invoking his own ancestors.

242 animos . . . sume: probably double-edged: *tollere animos* or *sumere animum* means "lift up one's spirits/courage," cf. Verg. *G.* 2.350, Ovid *F.* 1.147, Sen. *Ben.* 3.36.3, *Epist.* 107.7, etc., but *animi* are often violent feelings (cf. Pl. *Truc.* 603 *nunc ego meos* *animos violentos meamque iram ex pectore iam promam*, perhaps a parody of tragedy), and in Ovid *RA* 518 *sumere animos* means "to become angry." There may be a similar play on the two ideas in Ovid *Met.* 3.544–45 (Pentheus to the Thebans) *illius . . . animos, qui multos perdidit unus, / sumite animos.*

aspice: "consider," a rhetorical way of introducing a striking example, cf. Ovid *Am.* 1.13.43, *RA* 175–78, Sen. *Pha.* 575, *Ira* 1.2.2 *aspice nobilissimarum civitatum fundamenta vix notabilia; has ira deiecit. aspice solitudines per multa milia sine habitatore desertas; has ira exhausit.* Its use by Thyestes in 416 is not exactly parallel.

243 ad . . . meae: "my deeds must be in accordance with *these* models" (*haec* in emphatic position). For *manus meae* by metonymy for "the work of my hands" cf. 1096 below, *Med.* 977 *approba populo manum.*

ad haec . . . exempla: like *secundum haec exempla*, "in conformity with these models," cf. Cic. *De or.* 3.190 *ad legem*, *Att.* 4.18.2 *ad naturam.* Atreus looks to his ancestors as models of behavior, a traditional Roman attitude (cf., e.g., Verg. *Aen.* 12.439–40). In the house of Tantalus, however, family tradition inspires crime rather than virtue (similarly among the descendants of Oedipus, *Pho.* 331, 479); the inversion is explicitly stated by Ovid's Procne (*Met.* 6.635–36): *cui sis nupta vide . . . marito; / degeneras! scelus est pietas in coniuge Terei.*

244 profare . . . via: in the previous lines (236–43) Atreus' thoughts moved gradually inward, from measured exposition to excited self-address; now he turns again to the attendant, marking the change with a shift back to high poetic style.

profare: the word is virtually confined to epic and tragedy, cf. Pac. 145 R^2 *piget paternum nomen profari* (the sort of phrase parodied in Hor. *S.* 1.6.57 *namque pudor prohibebat plura profari*), *HF* 1176, *Pha.* 358.

dirum . . . caput: see on 188.

qua . . . via: the expression (for which cf., e.g., Ter. *Hec.* 73, 569) would probably have sounded old-fashioned in Seneca's time; it occurs only here in his writing (*Oed.* 949 *quaeratur via, qua . . .* is not quite the same).

mactem: *mactare* is a technical term for killing a sacrificial victim (cf., e.g., Verg. *G.* 3.489), and its ritual overtones often remain present when it is used to mean "murder" or "destroy," cf. Cic. *Pis.* 16 *in Catilinae busto vobis ducibus mactatus essem*, Sen. *Ag.* 219 (n), 713–14 below.

245 Ferro . . . expuat: the answer is couched in the same formal diction as the question (perhaps a way of depicting the attendant's wish to conform with Atreus' plans): *peremptus* is more elevated than, for example, *caesus* or *occisus*, and the closest parallels for *spiritum expuere* (also in *Pho.* 44) are in Terence (*Eun.* 406) and Lucretius (2.1041), both times in the milder form *aliquid ex animo expuere.*

246 De . . . volo: Atreus rejects the attendant's suggestion as much by the form of his reply as by its content: he deflates the high rhetoric of the previous exchange by answering in the plainest language possible. Atreus' insistence on a drawn-out punishment reappears at 907 *miserum videre nolo, sed dum fit miser.* (Hamlet shows something of the Atrean spirit when he declines to kill Claudius while he is praying, on the grounds that "this is hire and salary, not revenge" [3.3.79].)

247–48 in . . . impetratur: that is, for Atreus death is not a punishment but a favor to be begged for. Seneca's other *tyranni* expound the same view, cf. *HF* 511–12, *Ag.* 995 *rudis est tyrannus mortem qui poenam exigit* (n). Roman listeners might have been reminded of Tiberius or Gaius, cf. Suet. *Tib.* 61.5 *mori volentibus vis adhibita vivendi. nam mortem . . . leve supplicium putabat,* Sen. *NQ* 4A *pr.* 17 *sciebam olim sub illo* [sc. Gaio] *in eum statum res humanas decidisse ut inter misericordiae opera haberetur occidi.*

248 Nulla . . . pietas: *nulla* is an adj. modifying *pietas,* but with some adverbial force ("does *pietas* not move you at all?"), cf. 396 *nullis nota Quiritibus,* Ovid *Met.* 4.529 *nullo tardata timore.*

249-50 Excede . . . fuisti: Atreus has no personal struggle with *pietas* and is simply confirming its absence by a formal announcement; in contrast, the similar wish of Medea, *fas omne cedat, abeat expulsus pudor* (900) arises from a painfully divided spirit (cf. 943-44 *ira pietatem fugat / iramque pietas*).

249 si modo: "if in fact," an expression usually found in prose, cf. *OLD* s.v. *modo,* #3a.

250-54 dira . . . monstro: in calling on hellish spirits of vengeance to augment the violence of his own heart, Atreus resembles the Juno of *HF* (86-112). Atreus' case is more complex, however, since his appeal inevitably recalls the first scene, where it has been, so to speak, fulfilled in advance; note in particular 253-54 *impleri iuvat / . . . monstro* and 53 *imple Tantalo . . . domum,* 252-54 *non . . . monstro* and 85-86 *concute . . . tumultu,* and see above, p. 85. Other visions of the Furies in Seneca (*Med.* 958-66, *Ag.* 759-64) are clearly projections of the characters' own hopes or fears. (Both Atreus and Juno have influenced Shakespeare's Lady Macbeth, cf. 1.5.38-41 "come, you spirits / that tend on mortal [i.e., murderous] thoughts, unsex me here / and fill me from the crown to the toe top-full / of direst cruelty" etc.)

252-53 non satis magno . . . furore: the first appearance of a central element in Atreus' thinking, the constantly thwarted drive toward a truly sufficient revenge, cf. 256, 267-68, 273-75, 279-80, 889-90, 1056-68. Here the idea is connected with the "fullness" motif (cf. 12 *plenum recenti pabulum monstro*). Atreus' inability to find lasting satisfaction marks him as a true descendant of Tantalus.

254 rabidus: "maddened," normally an abusive epithet (cf. *HF* 397), is here offered and apparently accepted as a simple statement of fact. Atreus is again fulfilling the Fury's wish: *rabies parentum duret* (28).

struis: *struere* is often used of devising a plot or deceit, cf. *OLD* s.v., #6a, Ovid *Met.* 1.198 *struxerit insidias notus feritate Lycaon.* An earlier Latin tragedian (perhaps Accius) applied it to the revenge of Procne and Philomela, *struunt sorores Atticae dirum nefas* (*inc. inc. fab.* 240 R²).

255 Nil . . . modum: "nothing that accepts the normal limit of suffering"; that is, Atreus' revenge must exceed all customary limits. Medea similarly exhorts herself *quaere poenarum genus / haud usitatum* (898-99). The fascination with what lies beyond the norm is a trait these characters share with their creator (see also on 272-77 below).

doloris . . . assueti modum: an example of "transferred epithet" or hypallage, since *assuetus* seems logically to be as closely connected to *modus* as to *dolor.* It is often helpful to see such expressions as the product of condensation rather than mere transference, so that *doloris assueti modus* implies *doloris assueti modus assuetus;* see Bell, 315-29.

capiat . . . modum: "that accepts/puts up with a limit," cf. 496 *vix dolor frenos capit,* ps-Ovid *Nux* 4 *lentam non capit ira moram, OLD* s.v. *capio,* #28. [Madvig conjectured *modus* for *modum,* which would alter the sense to "nothing that the accustomed limit of pain could encompass." This is quite acceptable, and could be paralleled by passages like Ovid *Met.* 6.609–10 *iram / non capit ipsa suam*, Sen. *Ag.* 489 *non capit sese mare* (n), etc., but it does not seem decisively superior to the transmitted reading, and I have therefore not adopted it.]

256 nullum relinquam facinus: "I shall overlook no crime." Atreus may be mischievously playing on the positive overtones *relinquere* in this sense usually carries, cf. Verg. *Aen.* 6.509 *nihil o, tibi, amice, relictum*, Sen. *Cons. Pol.* 16.3 *sic . . . adfectum meum rexi ut nec relinquerem quidquam quod exigi deberet a bono fratre.*

257 The division of a trimeter into four short speeches (cf. also *Med.* 171) has only one precedent in surviving Greek tragedy (Soph. *Phil.* 753), but is not rare in the more loosely structured dialogue of New Comedy (cf. Men. *Dysc.* 85, *Samia* 409, etc.). Seneca uses this division to quicken the pace of a dialogue when the emotions of the protagonist reach a high point of intensity. Here the accelerated tempo leads into the heart of the scene, Atreus' plan to serve Thyestes the bodies of his children (first hinted at in 259 *ipso Thyeste*).

Ferrum . . . ignis: this combination derives from the use of surgery and cauterization in treating wounds, but—like "fire and sword" in English—is often a metaphor for extreme measures of any kind, cf. Prop. 1.1.27 *fortiter et ferrum saevos patiemur et ignes*, Sen. *Ag.* 152 (n), Otto s.v. *ignis*, #1. Here *ferrum* and *ignis* stand for the "normal" means of violent action, scorned by Atreus as inadequate. Atreus (and Seneca) may be "outdoing" Ovid's Procne, who rejected only *ferrum* (*Met.* 6.612–14): '*non est lacrimis hoc' inquit 'agendum, / sed ferro, sed si quid habes quod vincere ferrum / possit.*'

259 Ipso Thyeste: the audience knows the full significance of these words, but for Atreus they mean only that Thyestes will in some way be the agent of his own punishment. Juno in *HF* reaches a similar conclusion (84–85): *quaeris Alcidae parem? / nemo est nisi ipse; bella iam secum gerat.* (Compare *Antony and Cleopatra* 4.15.16–17 "so it should be, that none but Antony / should conquer Antony.")

Maius . . . malum: "this is an evil greater than the wrath that provokes it" (*ira* is abl. of comparison); less a protest than a stunned response to the enormity of the act being devised.

260 Fateor: not a sign of regret or guilt (as, for example, at *Tro.* 266), but a near equivalent of "yes," spoken with grim satisfaction. The single word is typical of the broken rhythm of this section, in which short, unsubordinated phrases suggest Atreus' mounting excitement.

attonitus: "frenzied"; for *attonitus* in Seneca see Fantham on *Tro.* 442, and cf. especially *HF* 1219–20 *nondum tumultu pectus attonito carens / mutavit iras.*

261 penitusque volvit: "and it agitates my heart deep within me." For *penitus* cf. *Oed.* 516–17 *terra se retro dedit / gemuitque penitus.* This use of *volvere* is quite unusual; the idea of being set in motion is developed in *rapior.*

261 rapior: *rapere* is frequently used of divine possession, cf. Hor. *C.* 3.25.1 *quo me, Bacche, rapis . . . ?*, Sen. *Ag.* 720–22 *quid me . . . sacra Parnasi iuga, / rapitis?* (n); perhaps Atreus is being "inspired" by the family spirit of evil. His vagueness about the force that is possessing him is appropriate, since it ultimately proceeds from within him (compare Ovid's Althaea, *Met.* 8.481 *quo rapior?*).

quo nescio: adverbial, "I know not where," usually seen in the form *nescio quo* (or better *nescioquo*).

262-65 These unnatural signs might be thought to exist only in Atreus' mind, but such a psychological reading is not clearly correct. In Senecan drama a dislocation of the moral order can set off correspondingly violent reactions in the physical world, and in no other play does evil make its presence seen and felt as pervasively as in *Thyestes*: cf. 103-121, 700-702, 789-826, 990-95, and, most interestingly, 668-79 (see note *ad loc.*). (The motif is not uniquely Senecan, although his use of it is distinctive. Belief in portents was widespread even among sophisticated Greeks and Romans, and some of the signs in this passage resemble those traditionally observed before the deaths of rulers, cf. on 263, 264-65.)

262 imo . . . solum: the earth is often said to groan at the emergence of figures from the underworld (i.e., at a violation of the usual boundaries of the upper and lower worlds), cf. *Tro.* 171-72, *Oed.* 173, 576-77, Verg. *Aen.* 4.490 with Pease's note. The sound of these words suits their meaning, with repeated *m*'s and prominent dark vowels.

263 tonat dies serenus: thunder in a clear sky was conventionally treated as an ominous portent, cf. Cic. *Div.* 1.18, Verg. *G.* 1.487-88 (of the omens preceding the death of Julius Caesar), Hor. *C.* 1.34.5-16.

263-64 totis . . . crepuit: lit., "the palace, as if shattered (*ut fracta*), has given a crash in all its buildings." The change from present (*mugit, tonat*) to perfect (*crepuit, vertere*) accelerates the pace: the latter portents happen so quickly that Atreus can only describe them after the fact (see on *stetit*, 110 above). The palace reacts similarly to the touch of Tantalus, cf. 103-104.

264-65 moti . . . vultum: compare Lucan's account of Rome on the eve of civil war (1.556-57): *Indigetes flevisse deos Vrbisque laborem / testatus sudore Lares*, also the similar phenomena preceding the assassination of Caesar, cf. Verg. *G.* 1.480, Ovid *Met.* 15.792. Statues were usually thought to show horror by tears or sweat (cf. 702 below and Cic. *Div.* 1.98); the averted gaze of the *Lares* here prefigures the reaction of the Sun to Atreus' banquet, cf. 791 *quo vertis iter*.

264 moti: "disturbed" (but perhaps with a hint of physical motion as well).

Lares: Seneca often (14 times) uses *lar* as an equivalent for *domus* (sometimes more specifically of a house as a place of refuge, cf. *Med.* 224, *Oed.* 258), but this is one of the few passages that clearly refers to the *Lares* as household gods (cf. also *HF* 917, *Pho.* 344, *Ag.* 392a); another touch of explicitly Roman coloring in the account of the Tantalids.

265 hoc . . . nefas: *hoc* is emphatic, "let *this* crime be done which you fear, o gods." For the excited repetition of *fiat* compare *Med.* 423-24 *faciet hic faciet dies / quod nullus umquam taceat*.

266 tandem: here expressing impatient curiosity (almost like "what *are* you planning?"), cf. *OLD* s.v., #1b.

267-86 The speech in which Atreus defines the punishment he will inflict on his brother is among Seneca's most remarkable depictions of a mind in the grip of *ira*. Atreus' commitment to revenge is never in doubt, but his attitude to the specific act that reveals itself to him is constantly shifting. Within the space of a few lines he greets it with eager delight (270-72 *ita sit . . . mensas*), rejects it as "already done" (*occupatum* 274), and finally embraces it with renewed enthusiasm (279-80, but see on *tantisper*). At one moment he is gloating in anticipation of Thyestes' agony (281-83 *patris*), at the next he is shuddering at the product of his own imagination (283-84). These mercurial changes of mood are clear symptoms of *ira*, a passion that, Seneca says elsewhere, has no solid or permanent basis but is volatile and insubstantial (*Ira* 1.20.2 *non ex firmo mansuroque oritur, sed ventosa et inanis est*).

267-69 Nescioquid . . . manibus: "my mind swells with something greater, larger than normal, and beyond the bounds of human custom, and (it) presses insistently upon my sluggish hands." Atreus describes his indistinct thought in three phrases of increasing size—*maius, solito amplius, supra . . . fines moris humani*—a *tricolon abundans* corresponding verbally to the "swelling" of the plan within him.

268 supra . . . humani: Atreus' ambition to exceed human limits is even clearer after the banquet, cf. 885 *aequalis astris gradior*. Such *folie de grandeur* is, for Seneca, another typical manifestation of *ira*, cf. *Ira* 1.20.2 *omnes quos vecors animus supra cogitationes extollit humanas altum quiddam et sublime spirare se credunt; ceterum nil solidi subest* etc.

tumet: Atreus practically diagnoses himself as an *iratus* in Stoic terms by speaking of his swollen *animus*, cf. 519-20, *Pho.* 352 *tumet animus ira*, Cic. *Tusc.* 3.19 *sapientis . . . animus semper vacat vitiis, numquam turgescit, numquam tumet; at irati animus eiusmodi est*. See on 361-62 below.

269 pigris manibus: Atreus' hands appear inactive to him because they are slow to execute the plan he has begun to conceive; compare the Fury's impatient question *dextra cur patrui vacat?* (57).

269-70 haud . . . est: here, as in this whole passage, Seneca is clearly thinking of Ovid's Procne, cf. *Met.* 6.618-19 *magnum quodcumque paravi; / quid sit adhuc dubito.* (Atreus' phrases are in the opposite order, placing greater stress on the positive claim *grande quiddam est.*) Atreus' words in their turn almost certainly lie behind the outburst of Lear (2.4.77-81): "No, you unnatural hags, / I will have such revenges on you both, / that all the world shall—I shall do such things— / what they are yet I know not, but they shall be / the terrors of the earth." Shakespeare turns Atreus' hyperbole to a new dramatic purpose by making it expose the powerlessness of Lear's fury.

The wish to perform some unspecified great deed is a traditional mark of a heroic spirit, cf. *Il.* 22.304-305 (Hector), Verg. *Aen.* 9.186-87 (Nisus) *aut pugnam aut aliquid iamdudum invadere magnum / mens agitat mihi*. It was probably applied to a revenge-plot in Ovid's lost *Medea*, to judge from the imitation (as I regard it) in *Her.* 12.212 *nescioquid certe mens mea maius agit*.

270 ita sit: a first sign of recognition.

occupa: here not so much "anticipate" (as in 204, 274) as "take possession of," cf. Sen. *Ag.* 567-68 *arcem occupat / Palamedis . . . genitor.*

271 dignum: Seneca's characters have an acute, if twisted, sense of their *dignitas*, and insist on committing only those crimes appropriate to it, cf. *HF* 111-12 *facere si quidquam apparo / dignum noverca*, *Med.* 50 *maiora iam me scelera post partus decent*, *Ag.* 124 (n). Atreus pays Thyestes the inverted compliment of treating him as an equal in this respect.

272 uterque faciat: Atreus' fear that Thyestes may be plotting against him finds an outlet in wit: the crime he is considering is one that both of them can—and must—commit, since Thyestes himself will play an essential part in it. [The point is blunted if one reads with E *quod uterque faciat*. E at times inserts syntactical glosses into the text, and *quod* might be one of these, cf. *Ag.* 458 *id* E *iam* A, 970 *dixi* E *iustae* A, perhaps *Med.* 991 *et invitam* E *invitam* A, my edition of *Agamemnon*, pp. 61-62.]

272-77 Like the Fury (56-57 *Thracium fiat nefas / maiore numero*), Atreus sees the legend of Procne, Tereus, and Itys as a precedent for his own situation. Atreus' feelings toward the earlier story are divided: it is both a source of inspiration (275 *animum Daulis* *inspira parens*) and a threat to his originality (273–74 *immane est scelus, / sed occupatum*). In the end Atreus overcomes his reluctance to follow an established model, apparently because he sees a way to improve on his exemplar (see note on 277–78).

It is not unusual for mythical characters in ancient literature to be aware of stories other than their own: Ovid's Byblis can cite *exempla* to justify her passion for her brother (*Met.* 9.507–508), and Vergil's Dido, in her lurid fantasies of killing Ascanius, draws on what seem like half-conscious memories of Medea and Procne (*Aen.* 4.600–602). Atreus, though, goes further: in his overt awareness of the Procne-Tereus story, and particularly in his desire to surpass it, he resembles Seneca himself in his relationship to Ovid. The challenge and anxiety of *imitatio* are shared by author and character.

273 Odrysia: = "Thracian," first found in Ovid (of Tereus, *Met.* 6.490).

fateor: concessive and impatient ("yes, of course"), cf. *Med.* 936.

274 hoc: abl. of comparison with *maius.*

275–76 Daulis . . . parens / sororque: the "Daulian parent" is Procne, mother of Itys, and her sister is Philomela. In some versions of the story Tereus rules at Daulis in Phocis rather than in Thrace, cf. Thuc. 2.29.3, perhaps Catullus 65.14, *Ciris* 199–200. For several Latin poets after Ovid, however, *Daulis* or *Daulias* is simply a *recherché* epithet that can be freely conflated with the usual Thracian setting, cf. *Cons. Liv.* 106 *deflet Threicium Daulias ales Ityn*, ps-Ovid *Epist. Sapph.* 154, *HO* 192–93. The ostentatious adjective is in keeping with the artifice of invoking the absent Procne. [The vocative in *-is*, common in early Latin, is used instead of *-i*, the standard Augustan form, for metrical convenience; cf. Housman on Luc. 8.251.]

276 causa: "my justification"; Atreus claims to be avenging Thyestes' seduction of his wife, and so can compare himself to Procne, who avenged her sister's rape by Tereus.

assiste: "stand by my side," as a supporter (conceivably as a supervisor?, cf. Quint. 1.2.12 *neque enim scribenti ediscenti cogitanti praeceptor adsistit*).

277–78 avidus . . . gaudensque: the adjectives are emphatic, since it is essential to Atreus' ideal revenge that Thyestes should not only eat his children, but do so greedily and with enjoyment. This hope is in large part fulfilled (909–913), though not to Atreus' complete satisfaction (1067–68).

279 bene est, abunde est: Atreus' momentary exuberance leads him to use an unpoetic, perhaps colloquial expression, which recurs in his first moments of triumph, 889 (note also *actum est abunde* 105); this is a variant of the fullness/satiety motif, cf. on 12 above, also p. 46.

modus: here "form" or "means," not "limit."

280 tantisper: "for the moment," "in the meanwhile" (rare in poetry after Plautus). Atreus qualifies his pleasure almost before he has expressed it, as again in 889–90 *iam sat est etiam mihi. / sed cur satis sit?* [Miller's Loeb text punctuates *modus. / Tantisper ubinam est?*, and the line was read this way by Nicholas Trevet in the fourteenth century, but the use of *tantisper* in a question is unexampled, and ending a sentence with a point early in the line is very much in Seneca's manner, cf. on 23, 204 above.]

280–81 tam . . . Atreus?: close in tone to the Fury's words at 57 *dextra cur patrui vacat?*, but with greater force generated by Atreus' sense of his own character—an "innocent Atreus" is for him almost a contradiction in terms.

281–82 tota . . . errat: perhaps based on Ovid's description of Procne (*Met.* 6.586) *poenae . . . in imagine tota est*, but more vividly expressed. The unusual metaphor in *errat* is significantly repeated in two lines of Thyestes, 473 *errat hic aliquis dolus* and 965–66 *vagus intra / terror oberrat*. Atreus' revenge "wanders" elusively until it lodges itself, literally and figuratively, inside Thyestes. (Atreus' vision faintly resembles Macbeth's "Is this a dagger which I see before me . . . ?" 2.1.33–49.)

282–83 ingesta . . . patris: a shocking phrase, which makes even Atreus recoil, if only for a moment. Two senses of *ingero* and *os* are at work: the words can mean "the father's childlessness (*orbitas* = the bodies of his children, whose death makes him *orbus*) thrust in his face," cf. *Med.* 132 *funus ingestum patri* (with Costa's note), but another meaning, "thrust into his mouth," also seems to be intended. Seneca again plays on these meanings of *ingero* in *NQ* 1.16.3, describing a notorious libertine who surrounded his bedroom with mirrors *ut . . . quae secreta quoque conscientiam premunt . . . non in os tantum sed in oculos suos ingereret*.

283–84 anime . . . subsidis?: impassioned characters in Seneca often find that their emotions need periodic reinforcement, and are apt to fail before the crucial moment, cf. *Pha.* 592–99, *Med.* 895, 927–28, 988–89, *Ag.* 228–29. These sudden losses of nerve illustrate the principle *affectus cito cadit, aequalis est ratio* (*Ira* 1.17.4).

284 ante rem: "before the event," i.e., as distinct from merely thinking or speaking about it.

285 quod . . . nefas: a lead-in phrase, with *praecipuus* in the role played elsewhere by *maximus* (see note on 205).

286 ipse faciet: Atreus has now fully realized the implications of *ipso Thyeste* in 259.

286–88: The attendant yields still more ground. From this point onward he questions only the means by which Thyestes can be lured into Atreus' trap.

287 dabit . . . in laqueos pedem: "place his foot in the snare," not a common idiom, for which the closest parallel I have found is Tib. 1.4.16 *sub iuga colla dabit*. (On periphrastic expressions with *dare* see 1057 below.) Atreus elaborates the hunting metaphor at his next appearance (491, 497–503).

288–89 Non . . . vellet: Atreus' image of Thyestes is distorted and self-serving, but not without foundation, cf. especially 920–46.

288 poterat: the imperfect indicative is often used in poetry instead of the subjunctive in contrary-to-fact conditional sentences, AG 517c.

290–93 Atreus lists three conventional instances of extreme danger, then caps them with a novel climax (*fratem videbit*). The technique is the same as in Oedipus' words at *Pho.* 313–19 *hic Oedipus Aegaea transnabit freta / iubente te . . . iubente te praebebit alitibus iecur, / iubente te vel vivet* (the repeated *iubente te* corresponds to *hac spe* here); see also on 16–18 above, *Med.* 19–20 with Costa's note. It is characteristic of such twists that the pointed conclusion is verbally plainer than the phrases which precede it. Atreus exploits the device to the full, spinning out the introductory phrases with a verve that suggests conscious enjoyment. Later in the play (476–82) Thyestes reacts to the idea *amat Thyesten frater* in equally exaggerated terms, but with no trace of wit. [I have adopted the order of lines in some late MSS, which departs from the traditional order in placing the reference to Jupiter (290) after that to the sea and the Syrtes (291–92). This gives a smoother progression of thought—Jupiter's thunderbolt is more frightening than dangers of navigation—and also a better alternation of simple and elaborate clauses.]

291 subibit . . . minas: the terrors of the sea also figure among the threats that cannot intimidate the true king (360–62).

tumidi: swollen by storm-winds, cf. *Ag.* 469 *agitata ventis unda venturis tumet* (n).

292 dubium . . . fretum: the Syrtes were a pair of large sandbanks off the northern coast of Africa; the hazard they posed to navigation made the area a byword for a dangerous stretch of water, cf. Pease on Verg. *Aen.* 4.41, Nisbet-Hubbard on Hor. *C.* 1.22.5. Readiness to face the perils of the sea and the Syrtes is a typical sign of steadfastness, cf. Ovid *Am.* 2.16.21-22 *cum domina Libycas ausim perrumpere Syrtes / et dare non aequis vela ferenda Notis.*

dubium: "unpredictable," "unreliable," cf. Ovid *Am.* 1.9.29 *Mars dubius, nec certa Venus, Pont.* 4.10.10 (*Ulixes*) *iactatus dubio per duo lustra mari.*

290 minanti fulmen occurret Iovi: "he will confront Jupiter as he threatens his thunderbolt" (*fulmen* obj. of *minanti*). This picture of foolhardy daring should be set against the ideal of the true king in the following chorus: *quem non concutiet cadens / obliqui via fulminis* (358-59), *qui . . . occurrit . . . suo libens / fato* (365-67).

293 quod . . . malum: the delaying-clause is very similar to that in 176-77; see also on 205.

294 fidem pacis: "a guarantee of peace," cf. 327 *prolis incertae fides.*

dabit: i.e., to Thyestes.

295 cui tanta credet?: "whose word will he take on such a matter?" The idiom seems to be a conflation of *credere alicui*, "to trust someone," and *credere aliquid*, "to believe something"; it appears several times in Plautus, and may be colloquial, cf. Pl. *Aul.* 306 *haec mihi te, ut tibi med, aequom est, credo, credere,* Ovid *Met.* 1.753–54 *matri . . . omnia . . . / credis* ("you believe everything your mother tells you"), *TLL* 4.1144.41–80.

Credula est spes improba: Thyestes unwittingly echoes Atreus' language at 962–63 *credula praesta / pectora fratri.*

Credula: "too ready to believe," "gullible," the word's normal meaning in Seneca (cf., e.g., *Pha.* 634 *o spes amantum credula*); at 962 (just quoted) Thyestes uses it to mean simply "trusting," but the context ironically supplies the more common sense.

296 tamen: i.e., even though Atreus claims that Thyestes' hopes of power will make him eager to believe whatever favors them, he will *nevertheless* entrust the offer to the most persuasive messengers, his sons Agamemnon and Menelaus.

297-99 relictis . . . dominus: the *ut*-clause contains the substance of the *mandata* and is syntactically dependent on the idea of ordering in the word (as if Atreus had said *mandabimus ut . . .*).

298 regno ut miserias mutet: "that he exchange his misfortunes for a kingdom" (*regno* abl.), cf. Hor. *C.* 1.16.25-26 *nunc ego mitibus / mutare quaero tristia.* Atreus' words are double-edged, since by accepting his offer Thyestes falls into even greater *miseriae,* cf. 896-97 *discutiam tibi / tenebras, miseriae sub quibus latitant tuae.*

299 ex parte dominus: "as a part-master"; the wording may have a legal flavor (as "part-owner" would in English), cf. Tac. *Ann.* 2.48 *quamquam ipse heres in parte legeretur.*

300 [liberos eius rudes: *eius* is generally avoided in high poetry, and this is its only transmitted occurrence in the tragedies. Heinsius suggested replacing it with *aevi* (defining gen. with *rudes*, as in *integer aevi*), but the case for emendation is not conclusive. A usage can be unique without becoming suspect—*eius* appears only once in Ovid's *Metamorphoses* (8.16), where it looks perfectly sound—and in this context, where Atreus has just spoken of his own children, the defining force of *eius* serves a useful function. Also, Heinsius' *aevi rudes*, although elegant, would itself be a rare construction; the closest parallel I have found is Val. Fl. 1.771 *aevi rudis altera proles*.]

rudes: "inexperienced" or "unskilled," cf. *Med.* 915 *ad omne facinus non rudem dextram afferes*.

302 praecommovebunt: "they (i.e., the *preces* of 299) will move Thyestes' children first," that is, Thyestes' children will be easier to sway than their father, and their influence will in turn help to overcome his resistance—as in fact it does, cf. 429–90. [This is the reading of A; E gives *prece commovebo*, which will not scan. Several conjectures have been based on E's text, among them *prece commovebunt* (L. Müller) and *preces movebunt (recc.)*, but they all require a rhetorically pointless repetition of *preces* in some form. There is admittedly no other recorded instance of *praecommovere*, but this in itself may speak in its favor, since an interpolator is less likely to have shown such bold invention. Seneca was not reluctant to coin words, among them *praedomare* (*Epist.* 113.27), and Ovid had formed several new compounds with *prae-*, e.g., *F.* 6.634 *praecompositus*, *Met.* 7.489 *praeconsumere*, *Met.* 11.731 *praedelassare*.]

regni furor: "the insane desire for rule" (*regni* obj. gen.), cf. *Pha.* 540 *impius lucri furor*. Atreus' description of this desire as "long-standing" (*vetus*) is meant to apply only to Thyestes, but perhaps carries a wider relevance, cf. 339 *quis vos exagitat furor?*

303–304 egestas . . . durus labor . . . subigent virum: the verb and its object are held off until the end, mirroring the gradual failure of Thyestes' defenses; see on 234–35 for similarly artful word-order. Atreus may be slyly echoing a well-known passage of the *Georgics* (1.145–46), *labor omnia vicit / improbus et duris urgens in rebus egestas* (note also *subigere* in the sense "subdue," "bring to submission," at 1.125 *ante Iovem nulli subigebant arva coloni*). [Cf. *Tro.* 907, where Helen speaks of herself as *graviora passa* (i.e., than the Trojans), taking over Aeneas' address to his Trojan followers, *o passi graviora*, in *Aen.* 1.199.]

304 quamvis rigentem . . . malis: "even though he has been hardened by so many misfortunes"; compare Andromache in *Tro.* 417–18 *quodcumque accidit / torpens malis rigensque sine sensu fero*. Ovid took the metaphor literally in his account of Niobe: *deriguit . . . malis* (*Met.* 6.303). See also on 634 below.

virum: see on 199.

305 Iam: "by now."

tempus . . . leves: "time heals all wounds" was as much a commonplace in ancient as in modern thinking, cf. Sen. *Epist.* 63.12 *scio pertritum iam hoc esse . . . finem dolendi etiam qui consilio non fecerat tempore invenit*, Otto s.v. *dies*, #6. It is characteristic of the conventionally-minded attendant to offer such a saw as an argument, and of Atreus summarily to reject it.

aerumnas: Seneca is fond of this word, which probably sounded august and somewhat archaic to his contemporaries (cf. *Ag.* 305 [n]), but in *Thyestes* it appears only here and in 426–27, where Thyestes unconsciously echoes the attendant's argument: *aerumnas fugis / bene collocatas?* (and note *iam* meaning "by this time" in 427).

306 malorum sensus: "the awareness of misfortunes," cf. *OLD* s.v. *sensus*, #5b.

die: "with the passage of time," cf. *OLD* s.v., #10. [Menedemus in Terence's *HT* questions the truth of the saying in similar language, but his bemused tone is far removed from Atreus' dogmatic certainty: *aut ego profecto ingenio egregio ad miserias / natus sum, aut illud falsum est quod vulgo audio / dici, diem adimere aegritudinem hominibus; / nam mihi quidem cotidie augescit magis / de filio aegritudo* etc. (420–24).]

307 leve . . . grave: "it is easy to endure suffering [i.e., for a short time], hard to keep on enduring it." Atreus is not content to disagree with the attendant, but presents his own view as a universal truth. This line was parodied by Martial in a delightful poem about a schoolmaster whose early morning lectures kept him from sleeping (9.68.10): *nam vigilare leve est, pervigilare grave est.*

308 The attendant backs off again, and merely questions Atreus' proposal to use his own sons as intermediaries.

tristis: "grim" or "savage," cf. Livy 25.6.2 *etsi non iniquum, certe triste senatus consultum.*

309 Peiora . . . praecepta: Latin uses *melior* and *peior* where English would prefer "good" and "evil," cf. Ovid *Met.* 7.20–21 *video meliora proboque / deteriora sequor*; here *peiora praecepta* are therefore "wicked instructions." Atreus is not arguing that children are naturally inclined to evil, but that their inexperience makes them readier to obey immoral guidance.

310 In patre . . . in patruo: "in the case of their father/uncle"; see on 220 above.

311 saepe . . . sua: the attendant briefly emulates Atreus' assertiveness with a generalization of his own. The thought is, as might be expected, a commonplace, cf., e.g., Ovid *Am.* 1.4.45–46 *multa miser timeo, quia feci multa proterve, / exemplique metu torqueor ipse mei*, Smith on Tib. 1.6.10.

redierunt: "gnomic" perfect, cf. Verg. *G.* 1.84 *saepe etiam sterilis incendere profuit agros*, AG 475.

312–16 Atreus commandingly "tops" the attendant's rather pallid *gnome* with three brilliant *sententiae*. These are not logically connected—in fact, the first and second point in different directions—and never directly address the attendant's objection. Atreus carries his point by sheer verbal intimidation.

312 Ut: concessive, "even if," cf. AG 527, *OLD* s.v., #35.

313 regnum: almost = "power." The statement gains in force from being made by a ruler; Lucan similarly places the advice *exeat aula, / qui vult esse pius* (8.493–94) in the mouth of the courtier Pothinus. The corrupting effect of rule is a leading theme of *Phoenissae*, cf. 582–84 *tam ferus durum geris / saevumque in iras pectus? et nondum imperas! / quid sceptra facient?*

313–14 ne . . . nascuntur: "are you afraid they may become wicked? They are born (that way)"; the unstated assumption is that any child of Atreus must be evil. Moral evaluations of the "like father, like son" type are usually directed at others (e.g., at Agamemnon and Menelaus in Cic. *Tusc.* 4.77 *ut facile appareat Atrei filios esse*), but Seneca's characters are apt to recognize in themselves an inherited attraction to vice, cf. *Pha.* 113 *fatale miserae matris agnosco malum, Pho.* 334–38.

fiant . . . nascuntur: for this opposition cf. *Ira* 2.10.6 *scit neminem nasci sapientem, sed fieri, Epist.* 12.23.

314 saevum asperum: this kind of asyndeton can serve to raise the emotional temperature, cf. *Med.* 191 *monstrum . . . saevum horribile iamdudum avehe*, *Pha.* 1221 *exitia machinatus insolita effera*. In Atreus' mouth, though, the effect is ironically deflating: the melodramatic language makes the attendant's scruples sound overdone.

316 illic: "on the other side" (i.e., perhaps the same crime is being planned by Thyestes with his own children).

316–35 The attendant makes no further attempt to restrain Atreus, confining himself to questions and an assurance of loyalty.

317 Tacita . . . fides: i.e., reliability that takes the form of keeping silent, discretion that can be counted on (almost a poetic inversion of *fidelis taciturnitas*), cf. *Oed.* 799 *praestare tacitam regibus soleo fidem*.

tam: to be taken with *rudibus . . . annis*, "in such tender years" (by metonymy for "in those so young").

319 discitur: impersonal passive (cf. 214 *regnatur*): "one learns to keep silent through bitter experience." Perhaps a distorted echo of the words of another ruler, Dido in *Aen.* 1.630 *non ignara mali miseris succurrere disco*. Atreus again clinches his point with a general assertion.

321 Ut . . . vacent: the purpose clause depends on an understood assent to the attendant's question ("Yes, I *shall* deceive them, so that . . ."). For the elliptical syntax, a feature of informal speech at home in lively or excited dialogue, cf., e.g., *Med.* 496 (Jason) *Medea amores obicit?* (Medea) *et caedem et dolos*, *Tro.* 663–64 (Ulysses) *funditus busta eruam.* / (Andromache) *quae vendidistis?*, 68–69 above, 1101 below.

321–33 Atreus' last extended speech displays the same rapid changes of direction as the one before it (267–86). He starts to argue for sparing his sons from involvement in his plan (321–23), but he quickly catches himself in what he regards as a dangerous concession and chooses instead to make their participation a test of their paternity (324–30); then at the last moment he doubts their skills in deception and decides to keep them in ignorance. The speech does not advance the action, but fills out the portrait of Atreus by showing him rooting out the last vestiges of respect for goodness.

321 crimine et culpa vacent: compare Medea's description of her children, *crimine et culpa carent* (935, in another scene where the claims of morality are overcome); here, though, *crimine et culpa* may be a hendiadys for *criminis culpa* ("so that they may be without blame for the crime").

323 per nos: i.e., Atreus and Thyestes.

odia . . . explicent: "let our enmities resolve themselves," cf. *Oed* 832 *ipsa se fata explicent*.

324 male agis: in much the same way, Seneca's Ulysses brings himself up short when he is about to believe Andromache's story that Astyanax has died: *quid agis, Ulixe? Danaidae credent tibi, / tu cui? parenti?* (*Tro.* 607–608).

324–25 si . . . illis: since both sets of children are equally innocent, both must either be spared or sacrificed. Medea, too, faces this objection: *sunt innocentes; fateor, et frater fuit* (936).

parcis . . . parces: the balanced phrasing recalls 310 *in patre . . . in patruo*. Like the attendant, Atreus recognizes the need to act consistently, but the inference he draws is the reverse of the one urged on him.

325-27 consili . . . adsit: a solemn pronouncement, the only time in the play when Agamemnon and Menelaus are mentioned by name. Agamemnon is given greater prominence as the older brother (he is *maior Atrides* in Ovid, e.g., *Met.* 13.359, *Ars* 3.12).

326 sciens . . . sciens: a variant of the figure called κύκλος, where a phrase begins and ends with a form of the same word. Seneca sometimes uses it to heighten a *sententia* (cf., e.g., *Ag.* 527 *vehit ista Danaos classis? et Troas vehit*), but here the repetition adds to the formality of Atreus' decision, cf. *HF* 638–39 *differ amplexus, precor, / coniunxque differ*.

326-27 fratri sciens . . . adsit: "let Menelaus knowingly second his brother"; *adesse* + dat. often means to lend support to another by one's presence, particularly in a crisis or difficulty, cf. Ovid *Pont.* 2.3.45 *adfuit insano iuvenis Phoceus Orestae*. [*fratri sciens* is Bentley's correction of the manuscript readings *patri sciens* (E) and *patri/patris cliens* (A). E's reading is not impossible, but since Atreus will not be present at this encounter, *fratri* fits *adsit* better than *patri*.]

327 prolis incertae fides: "a proof of my doubtful paternity" (lit. "offspring"). Atreus is not certain whether Agamemnon and Menelaus are really his children or Thyestes' (cf. 240); since he assumes that any child of his must be evil (313–14), he will take reluctance on their part as proof of bastardy.

329 gerere . . . odia: *odia gerere* can mean "to bear ill-will," cf. Livy 28.22.3 *extra necessitates belli praecipuum in Romanos gerebant odium*, but here (and perhaps also at *HF* 362) it seems to carry a stronger sense, "to wage/conduct enmities," on the analogy of the common *bellum gerere* (*bella* in 328 helps make the connection).

330 eatur: "let them be on their way" (lit., "let it be gone," impersonal passive), cf. *Med.* 460, Ter. *HT* 743, Cic. *Att.* 13.42.3. The expression may belong to colloquial speech rather than high poetry (although Costa *ad loc.* thinks otherwise). It is perhaps too patently symmetrical that Thyestes should use just this word when he gives in to his son's arguments (488).

330-32 multa . . . produnt: Atreus justifies his change of plan with two *gnomai*, turning on himself the style of argument he had earlier used against the attendant.

330-31 multa . . . vultus: an often-expressed thought, cf. Ovid *Met.* 2.447 *heu quam difficile est crimen non prodere vultu*, Curt. 8.6.22 *vultus haud sane securi animi index*, Sen. *Ag.* 128 (n).

331 quoque: to be taken with *nolentem*: "momentous plans give one away even against one's will." For the thought cf. Sen. *Contr.* 2.5.2 *sive isti aliquid excidit, sive magna consilia non bene vultus texit*.

332 quantae rei: obj. gen. with *ministri* (cf. *consili . . . minister* 325–26).

333 nostra . . . occule: Atreus' last words sound almost like an afterthought; one can imagine an actor delivering them as he exits, with hardly a glance in the attendant's direction. The harsh staccato sound of the *t*'s and *c*'s matches the baldness of the syntax. [E's *occules* is adopted by many editors. The imperative, however, seems more idiomatic, and *tu* might have prompted the scribe of E or an ancestor to expect a finite verb. For *tu* adding emphasis to an imperative—"as for you" or "for your part"—cf. Verg. *Aen.* 3.388 *signa tibi dicam, tu condita mente teneto*, 4.50 *tu modo posce deos veniam*.]

334-35 ista . . . fides: the attendant effusively answers the plain *occule* with the grandiloquent *in pectore . . . claudet* (cf. Sall. *Cat.* 10.4 *aliud clausum in pectore, aliud in lingua promptum habere*). This eagerness to please, along with the quite unbelievable claim that loyalty weighs more heavily with him than fear, rounds off a grimly humorous, but also pathetic, portrait of total submission.

CHORUS II

A meditation on kingship that is both an interlude in the surrounding action and an implicit commentary on it. The Chorus registers the report of a settlement between Atreus and Thyestes (336–38), then reflects on the mad lust for power that drives them to mutual destruction (339–43). Against this misguided pursuit of dominion the Chorus sets its own definition of a king: free from fear and the other passions (344–48), as impervious to the attractions of glory and riches (350–57) as to the threat of violence (358–64), safe above all circumstances, meeting fate gladly and accepting death without complaint (365–68). Kings may band together from the far corners of the earth, but reason's rule is secure (369–80); it needs no arms to defend it, for it lies within the gift of each individual (381–90). The ode ends with the Chorus's wish for an untroubled, retiring existence (391–403).

Although the Chorus is ignorant of the true state of affairs between Atreus and Thyestes, its reflections still provide a background against which the action of the play is to be understood. The portrait of the true king stands between scenes dominated by Atreus and Thyestes, and its implications extend both backwards and forwards.[1] This dual reference is underlined by the ode's arrangement: the generalizing central section (344–90) is preceded by thoughts of revenge and reciprocal crime that recall the scene just past (339–44) and followed by an ideal of tranquil withdrawal (391–403) that closely matches Thyestes' sentiments in the scene to come. The ode is thus both a subtle bridge-passage and a stable criterion for judging the remoteness of both Atreus and Thyestes from true kingship.

The relevance of the ode extends beyond its dramatic setting; the apostrophe to those who long for rule (cupidi arcium 342) has a meaning for Romans as well as Argives. Indeed much of the ode is overtly Roman in outlook, from the use of Quirites (396) to represent the political dimension of a community to the vision of distant lands and peoples as they would strike the imagination of a Roman in the mid-first century A.D. (368–79). Roman coloring of this extent can hardly be the result of accident or inadvertence; it leaves no doubt that the ode's utter rejection of the striving for power is meant to apply to Seneca's own world.

The notion of the sapiens as the only true king is a familiar article of Stoic belief,[2] but much of the imagery with which Seneca here elaborates that thesis has its origins in Augustan poetry. The trappings of wealth, for example, are described in terms that strongly recall Horace's Odes,[3] and Horace is also the source for the colorful procession of foreign opponents who cannot threaten the true king's composure (369–79).[4] The most important Roman antecedent of Seneca's ideal king, however, is the figure praised by Vergil in a famous passage of the Georgics:

> felix qui potuit rerum cognoscere causas
> atque metus omnis et inexorabile fatum
> subiecit pedibus strepitumque Acherontis avari. . . .
> illum non populi fasces, non purpura regum

[1] Specific connections between the ode and other parts of the play are suggested in the notes on 338, 343, 345, 346, 347, 348–49, 358–62, 361–62, 365, 366, 367–68, 381, 390, 393, 394, 401, 402–403.

[2] See on 344.

[3] See notes on 347, 350–57, 360–62, 369–79, 381–87. On Horatian echoes in the choral odes of other plays see Fantham on Tro. 1020–21, my note on Ag. 91–107, J. Spika (cited above, p. 17 n. 83).

[4] Seneca has, however, fundamentally changed the import of Horace's lines; see note ad loc.

> flexit et infidos agitans discordia fratres,
> aut coniurato descendens Dacus ab Histro,
> non res Romanae perituraque regna. . . . (*G.* 2.490–92, 495–98)

The germ of a considerable part of the ode can be seen here,[5] but some of Seneca's revisions of Vergil are at least equally significant. The focus has been redefined: for Vergil "dominions that will pass away" are only one among the world's allurements, but Seneca makes *regnum* the central issue. How is a mere individual to retain a measure of control in this vast world? His response mutes the Vergilian tone of triumph: fear and passion are not decisively "ground underfoot" (*subiecit pedibus*), but "put off" or "laid aside" (*posuit* 348), suggesting a burden or encumbrance gratefully escaped. Most revealing of all, fate (i.e., death) is not overcome but willingly met (367 *occurrit . . . libens*). Seneca's final answer to the question of kingship is a characteristic paradox that owes nothing to Vergil: true dominion lies in the acceptance of powerlessness, in the readiness to die.[6]

The style of the ode is in keeping with its mood, sober and grave. The short glyconic lines, mostly end-stopped, convey a feeling of pensive calm; there is none of the linguistic virtuosity of the first chorus, and in particular the basic statements of principle are nearly devoid of verbal adornment (cf. 348–49, 365–68, 380, 390). Against this subdued background, the shift to the first person singular in the coda (391–403) brings a welcome infusion of warmth. Discreetly sensual imagery portrays *otium* and *quies* as appealing, even pleasurable (*me dulcis saturet quies* 393, *leni perfruar otio* 394), while a finely judged control of rhythm gives the passage a gentle, even flow that perfectly matches its content. This is the play's closest approach to a positive statement of values; the course of the action will overshadow the Chorus's hope for tranquil peace, but the beauty with which these lines evoke that ideal remains deeply satisfying.[7]

Meter: Glyconics (see above, p. 31).

336–38 The Chorus shows no awareness of the plot that the audience has just heard Atreus devise; it reacts only to the "public" report that Atreus has invited Thyestes to return from exile and be reconciled with him. [Seneca often treats his Chorus as "absent" between odes, an aspect of dramatic technique on which he differs markedly from the practice of fifth-century Greek tragedy, cf. *HSCP* 82 (1978), 223–28.]

336 regia: on the prominence given to the "house" throughout the play, see above, 45.

337 antiqui . . . Inachi: Inachus was an Argive river-god and legendary first king of Argos. (The river is a poetic equivalent for "Argos" at *HO* 139.) The allusion may owe something to Horace, for whom Inachus is a proverbially ancient figure, cf. *C.* 2.3.21 *prisco natus ab Inacho*, 3.19.1.

338 composuit: the sense intended by the Chorus is "has settled," on the analogy of *componere litem* or *bellum*; to the audience, though, *componere* might also suggest "place in opposition," as in *NQ* 5.18.6 *quae nos dementia exagitat* [cf. 339] *et in mutuum componit exitium?* The uses of *componere* in 433 and 694 are clearly double-edged.

339–43 The Chorus turns from the immediate situation (as it misconceives it) to brood

---

[5] In addition to the obvious points of contact, Vergil's juxtaposition of kingly purple and fraternal strife (*purpura regum, infidos agitans Discordia fratres* 495–96) may have influenced the opening lines of the ode (339–47).

[6] The point is made explicitly in *Ag.* 604–10, a passage itself indebted to these lines of the *Georgics*: cf. 607–608 *qui vultus Acherontis atri, / qui Styga tristem non tristis videt.*

[7] The ode was highly regarded by poets and critics of the sixteenth and seventeenth centuries, cf. C. J. Herington in *CHLL*, 527.

on the habitual aggression of the Tantalids. The shift is marked by the change to the present tense in *exagitat* 339. The present also points to the ironic sense of the lines, since this *furor* is in fact at work even now.

[Lines 336–38 were bracketed by Richter as an interpolation, on the grounds that they are inconsistent with 339–43 and anticipate the Chorus's reaction to the apparent reconciliation at 546–59. The first point is countered by the interpretation sketched above: 336–38 refer to the latest development, 339–43 to a recurring pattern of behavior. Nor do 336–38 conflict with 546–59; here the Chorus speaks in vague terms of a settling of hostilities, while in the later passage it responds specifically to the scene it has just witnessed. On the other hand, without 336–38 a listener could easily assume that 339–43 refer to Atreus' scheme, and so be surprised by the Chorus's ready acceptance of the false reconciliation. There is also a structural argument for retaining 336–38, although it cannot be pressed very hard: with the lines in place, but with 388–89 bracketed, the ode falls into two main sections of 33 lines, each of which ends with a form of *morior* (336–68 *nec queritur mori*, 369–403 *ignotus moritur sibi*). The lines were also defended by Zwierlein, *Rezitationsdramen* 79, but he admits more incoherence in Seneca's technique than I think is necessary.]

339 vos: in the first instance Atreus and Thyestes, the *fratres* of 338, but a broader application soon becomes obvious (see on 342).

340 alternis dare sanguinem: "to shed blood by turns." Since neither Atreus nor Thyestes has physically harmed the other, the Chorus is either thinking of earlier episodes in the family saga (as at 139–48) or using *dare sanguinem* in a generic sense, like *stringere ensem* in 26. (The Chorus's words could also apply ironically to events still in the future, for example, Aegisthus' murder of Agamemnon, cf. 43–44.)

alternis: adverbial, cf. Ovid *F.* 6.484, 486; a variation on, e.g., *alterna vice* 25, 133.

dare sanguinem: this sense of *dare* ("to cause to be emitted") may have been applied to blood on the analogy of *dare lacrimas*. The closest antecedents of Seneca's phrase are in Ovid, cf. *F.* 2.666 *quantum patriae sanguinis ille dedit*, *Met.* 15.423 (Troy) *per . . . decem potuit tantum dare sanguinis annos*. (On periphrases with *dare* see on 1057 below.)

342 nescitis: the Chorus may still be thinking of Atreus and Thyestes, but Seneca wishes to include all those who long for power.

arcium: the *arx* is the fortified citadel of a town, like the Acropolis in Athens or the Capitol in Rome. By the early Principate *arx* had become a standard term for a tyrant's "castle," cf. Sen. *Contr.* 1.7.16 *vidi filium unum in arce, alterum in adulterio*, Sen. *Ag.* 77–78 *quas non arces scelus alternum / dedit in praeceps* (n). The palace of the Tantalids is located *in arce summa* (641, see note).

343 quo iaceat loco: *quo . . . loco* raises a question to which the rest of the ode develops the answer; note *tuto positus loco* near the mid-point (365) and, specifically, *obscuro positus loco* (394) in the final section.

iaceat: *iacere*, like English "lie," can mean simply "to be situated" (cf. *OLD* s.v., #11b), but Seneca may be evoking as well a more restricted sense, "to lie low/in obscurity," cf. Ovid *Met.* 11.747 *tunc iacet unda maris*, Sen. *Brev. vit.* 9.1 *omnia quae ventura sunt in incerto iacent*. This sense is also implied in Thyestes' picture of carefree meals consumed *humi iacentem* (451). The contrast is with the *arx*, literally as well as figuratively elevated, cf. 392 *aulae culmine lubrico*, Clem. 1.19.6 *in altum editas arces*.

344 regem: using the concept "king" to symbolize ultimate control and felicity, the Stoics claimed that only the *sapiens* was truly a king, Cic. *Acad.* 2.136, Hor. *S.* 1.3.125, *Epist.* 1.1.107, Sen. *Ag.* 610 *par ille regi, par superis erit, Epist.* 108.13 *ipse* (sc. Attalus the Stoic) *regem se esse dicebat.*

344–47 The general statement that riches (*opes*) do not make a king is illustrated by three examples, each of which relates to the action of the play. The trappings of high position are listed in studiously neutral language, perhaps to show that they exercise no appeal for the true king; contrast the highly colored images of luxury elaborated by Thyestes in 455–69.

345 vestis Tyriae color: hypallage for *vestis* (gen.) *Tyrius color* (= *purpura*). Purple garments were a universal mark of royal status in the ancient world, cf. Pease on Verg. *Aen.* 4.134. (The close connection makes possible Horace's vivid *purpurei . . . tyranni, C.* 1.35.12.) Thyestes later accepts Atreus' invitation to put on clothing appropriate to a king (525–26), and at his fateful meal he reclines on coverlets of purple and gold (909).

346 frontis nota regia: i.e., the diadem, originally an Eastern emblem of kingship, which became a sign of royalty for Greeks and Romans after Alexander, cf. Nisbet-Hubbard on Hor. *C.* 2.2.21. In Roman eyes the diadem was an odious symbol of despotism; even Julius Caesar felt compelled to decline it on the famous occasion when Mark Antony "thrice presented him a kingly crown, / which he did thrice refuse" (*Julius Caesar* 3.2.96–97). Thyestes' ambition is not made of such stern stuff; he refuses Atreus once (531–32), but accepts when the offer is pressed (544). [The MSS of Seneca unanimously read *regiae*, and *regia* is found only in a citation of 342–52 by Lactantius Placidus, a late antique commentator on Statius. Since Seneca is insisting on the irrelevance of external emblems to genuine kingliness, *regia nota* seems much more apt than *regia frons*; cf. also 701 below *regium capiti decus, Ag.* 8, etc.]

347 auro nitidae trabes: gilded roof-beams, a sign of conspicuous wealth frequently denounced by Roman moralists, cf. Prop. 3.2.12 *nec camera auratas inter eburna trabes*, Sen. *Pha.* 497–98 *nec trabes multo insolens / suffigit auro.* The detail recurs in the description of the *domus Pelopia*, cf. 646–47. [E reads *fores* for *trabes* in A and Lactantius. The reading is not impossible, cf. Verg. *G.* 2.461 *foribus domus alta superbis*, but it is not as well paralleled as *trabes* and lacks a telling connection with the later action (901–902 *fores / templi relaxa* would be the closest link).]

348–68 This section begins and ends with positive statements (348–49, 365–68), which frame a triad of negative examples (350–57 attractions of high status, 358–62 natural forces, 363–64 military threats). Each of these negative segments is further subdivided (3-2-2 respectively), and each adopts a different temporal perspective (*movet* 352, *concutiet* 358, *domuit* 364). The opening and closing lines are themselves linked and contrasted (*posuit* 348, *positus* 365; *posuit* vs. *videt . . . occurrit . . . queritur*); the conclusion details the lasting results of the action named at the outset.

348–49 rex . . . pectoris: freedom from fear is a cardinal point in Stoic-Epicurean moralizing, cf. Verg. *G.* 2.490–92 *felix qui . . . metus omnis et inexorabile fatum / subiecit pedibus*, Sen. *Const.* 9.2 *sapiens . . . nescit nec in spem nec in metum vivere.* At first 348 sounds like a statement of this view, but the next line makes an unexpected addition: "the evils of a dreadful heart" seems too strong a description for the other emotions from which the *sapiens* ought to be free (hope, joy, and sadness, cf. Verg. *Aen.* 6.733 with Austin's note), and seems instead to imply the sort of furious drive for revenge seen in Atreus. (Both *pectus* and *dirus* have already figured in references to his passion, cf. 250, 253–54, 260–61.) That connection suggests a possible second meaning for 348, "a king is one who has laid aside terror," that is, who does not, like Atreus, use fear as a basis for governing (cf. 207–208, and for *metus* = "intimidation" cf. *OLD* s.v., #1e).

posuit: "put off" or "lay down," cf. 519 *ponatur omnis ira.*

350–57 The first and third items appear together in Hor. *C.* 1.1.7–10: *hunc* (sc. *iuvat*) *si mobilium turba Quiritium / certat tergeminis tollere honoribus; / illum, si proprio condidit horreo / quidquid de Libycis verritur areis.* Horace's poem has influenced this ode at several points, cf. 360–62, 393, 396.

350 impotens: "uncontrolled," usually of persons or their *animus*, but also of, e.g., *fortuna* (*Ag.* 247, 593) and *furor* (*Ag.* 801, *Med.* 851).

351–52 numquam stabilis favor / vulgi praecipitis: *praeceps* ("rushing headlong") is a characteristic "Silver" heightening of an earlier epithet, i.e., *mobilis* as applied to the fickle populace, cf. Horace's *mobilium turba Quiritium* (*C.* 1.1.7), Livy 24.31.14 *experti . . . quam vana aut levi aura mobile vulgus esset,* Ovid *Tr.* 1.9.13 *mobile sic sequitur Fortunae lumina vulgus.* Seneca's wording suggests the violence of popular feeling as well as its mutability, cf. Phaedr. 5.1.3 *ut mos est vulgi, passim et certatim ruit.* Other versions of the theme in *HF* 169–71, *Pha.* 488–89.

352 movet: "sway," "attract," cf. Ovid *Met.* 10.615 *non me movet ipse, sed aetas.*

353–55 The notion of "mineral wealth" is expressed in Roman terms: Spanish mines were Rome's main source of gold, cf. Fordyce on Catullus 29.19. Mining was often held up as a symptom of degenerate greed (cf. Ovid *Met.* 1.138–40), but here the focus is on the enormous quantity of gold produced (*quidquid*).

353 Occidens: by a bold personification "the West" is said to mine the earth; even Lucan substituted a milder form of words in imitating the line, *quidquid fodit Hiber* ["the Iberian"], *quidquid Tagus expulit auri* (7.755). The result is to present this wealth on the largest possible scale; compare Tac. *Agr.* 30.5 (a denunciation of Roman greed) *ambitiosi, quas non Oriens, non Occidens satiaverit.* (Similarly "All the perfumes of Arabia will not sweeten this little hand," *Macbeth* 5.1.50–51.)

354 Tagus: the modern Tejo, which passes through Toledo and empties into the Atlantic at Lisbon. Its gold deposits were a well-known item of geographical lore, especially popular with Spanish writers, cf. Mela 2.86, 3.8, Sen. *HF* 1325, Luc. 7.755 (quoted above), Mart. 7.88.7, 10.17.4, Juv. 3.55, 14.299, Otto s.v. *Tagus.* Seneca's wording is closest to Ovid *Met.* 2.251 *quod . . . suo Tagus amne vehit, fluit ignibus aurum;* he is in turn the model for Martial 6.86.5 *possideat Libycas messes Hermumque Tagumque.*

355 claro . . . alveo: the river-bed gleams with light reflected by the gold it contains; for this use of *clarus* cf. Acc. 211 R² *agnum inter pecudes aurea clarum coma,* Ovid *Met.* 13.704 *claram . . . auro gemmisque coronam.* The next section of the ode also describes light reflected by precious objects under water (371–73).

356–57 The coloring remains Roman: Libya supplied Rome with wheat as Spain did with gold. "All the grain harvested in Libya" is a hyperbole already used by Horace, cf. *C.* 1.1.9–10 (quoted on 350–57 above), cf. also *S.* 1.1.45–46 *milia frumenti tua triverit area centum; / non tuus hoc capiet venter plus ac meus.*

Libycis . . . messibus: apparently an abl. of time or circumstance, "at the Libyan harvests" or "when the wheat is harvested in Libya."

357 fervens: the threshing-floor may be "blazing" because it is in Libya (cf. Prop. 4.9.46 *Libyco sole perusta coma*), because the threshing takes place at mid-day (cf. Verg. *G.* 1.298 *medio aestu,* Varro *R.r.* 1.51.2), or because of the heated activity of the threshing itself (compare *fervidis . . . rotis* Hor. *C.* 1.1.4). The use of graphic language that does not resolve itself into clear images is a hallmark of Senecan style.

358–62 Horatian coloring is especially strong in these lines, cf. *C.* 3.1.25–28 *desiderantem quod satis est neque / tumultuosum sollicitat mare / nec saevus Arcturi cadentis / impetus aut orientis Haedi*, 3.3.1–6 *iustum et tenacem propositi virum / . . . non vultus instantis tyranni / mente quatit solida neque Auster, / dux inquieti turbidus Hadriae, / nec fulminantis magna manus Iovis.* Here this picture of *constantia* takes on an ironic dimension, since Atreus has used similar terms to depict Thyestes' fearless pursuit of power (290–92).

358–59 cadens / obliqui via fulminis: double hypallage for *fulmen cadens obliqua via*, cf. Verg. *Aen.* 6.268 *ibant obscuri sola sub nocte per umbram*, Bell 317–18. This wording produces a more vivid picture by focusing on the lightning's downward path; at the same time the repeated *c*'s in *concutiet cadens* may suggest the crash of thunder.

359 obliqui: "zigzag," of lightning in *Cons. Marc.* 18.3, Luc. 1.153–54.

360 Eurus: the proper name for particularizing effect; Eurus, strictly speaking the East wind, often represents a typically stormy wind, cf. Hor. *C.* 1.28.25–26 *quodcumque minabitur Eurus / fluctibus Hesperiis*, *Epod.* 16.54 *aquosus Eurus*, Ovid *Met.* 15.603 *ubi trux insibilat Eurus*.

rapiens: "violently taking hold of," cf. *Ag.* 475–76 *rapiunt . . . pelagus . . . adversus Euro Zephyrus et Boreae Notus*, *OLD* s.v., #14c, where fire is the active force.

361–62 saevo . . . Hadriae: the Adriatic fits more naturally in a Roman than in an Argive frame of reference; Horace made it a byword for destructive violence, cf. *C.* 1.33.15 *fretis acrior Hadriae*, 2.14.14, 3.9.23 *iracundior Hadria*, 3.27.18–19.
These lines are remarkable for their profusion of adjectives: *saevus, rabidus,* and *ventosus*, with *tumor Hadriae* suggesting *tumidus Hadria* (see note below). The prominent epithets might hint at a correlation between the terrors of nature and raging human passions: *rabidus* and *tumere* have already been applied to Atreus (255, 258), *saevus* is used several times of him or his projected crime (196, 314, 715, 726, 743), and *saevire* and *tumere* appear together at 737 *Atreus saevit atque ira tumet.* (All other uses of *tumere* and *tumidus* in the play are also clustered around these two points: of the sea in 291, 577, and 960, and of the "swollen faces" of kings in 609.)

361 [rabidus: E's *rabidus* seems preferable to A's *rapidus* both for the parallel with *rabidus* in 255 and also because *rapidus* would weakly repeat *rapiens* in 360. The words are regularly confused in manuscripts (see my note on *Ag.* 484).]

362 tumor Hadriae: nearly equivalent in sense to *tumidus Hadria*, but more forceful; the noun + gen. construction implies that the Adriatic can almost be defined by its *tumor*, cf. Cic. *Mil.* 3 *P. Clodi furor* (= *P. Clodius furiosus*), Verg. *Aen.* 4.88 *minae . . . murorum* (= *muri minantes*), 2.235–36 *rotarum . . . lapsus* (= *rotae labantes*), Bell 219.

363–64 non lancea militis / non strictus . . . chalybs: threats of war are symbolized by spear and sword. The *lancea* is usually wielded by the enemies of Rome (cf. [Caes.] *BG* 8.48.5, Verg. *Aen.* 12.375, Livy 10.26.11, 22.6.4, Tac. *Germ.* 6.1), but *militis* makes the picture more generic; similarly *chalybs* (= "steel"), originally connected with the Chalybes of Armenia (cf. Fordyce on Verg. *Aen.* 8.421), seems here only an elegant substitute for *ferrum = ensis*, cf. Luc. 7.517–18 *sceleris sed crimine nullo / externum maculant chalybem.*

365 tuto positus loco: unwittingly echoed by Atreus, who has a very different concept of safety: *iam tuto in loco / versantur odia* (493–94).

366 infra se videt omnia: the *sapiens* was traditionally said to look down on all human concerns, cf. Cic. *Rep.* 1.28, *Tusc.* 3.15 *res humanas despicere atque infra se positas arbitrari* (a state boldly appropriated by Seneca's Medea, *fortuna semper omnis infra me stetit*, 520).

367-68 occurritque . . . mori: the ultimate freedom from fear, and so the ultimate rule (cf. 348), consists in the readiness to die. This too is a tenet of Thyestes' professed belief, cf. 442 *'pater, potes regnare' 'cum possim mori.'*

occurrit . . . fato: the true *rex* goes to meet *fatum* as it approaches; for this use of *occurrere* (not attested before Seneca) cf. *Epist.* 76.20, Luc. 4.479–80 *nec gloria leti /* *inferior, iuvenes, admoto occurrere fato*, Stat. *Theb.* 1.640. [The same idea is more epigrammatically phrased at *Tro.* 1146, where Polyxena's *animus* is *leto obvius*; with less restraint, Oedipus' eyes are said to rush to meet their own blinding, *vulneri occurrunt suo* (*Oed.* 946).]

suo libens / fato: the spilling over of the phrase into the following line may reflect the eagerness with which the *rex* meets destiny.

libens: so Seneca describes Socrates drinking his hemlock, *venenum laetus et libens hauriet* (*Prov.* 3.13) or Priam receiving the death-blow from Pyrrhus, *penitus actum* [sc. *ferrum*] *cum recepisset libens* (*Tro.* 49). [So also perhaps Cassandra at *Ag.* 973 (n).] The word denotes ready acceptance of fate, not the longing for death that Seneca stigmatizes as *libido moriendi* (*Epist.* 24.25).

368 nec queritur mori: best taken literally ("who makes no complaint at dying") rather than as litotes for (e.g.) *gaudet mori*; compare *Ag.* 608 *qui Styga tristem non tristis videt*.

369-79 The geographical frame of reference is patently Roman: the names mentioned represent the northern and eastern limits of the empire at the time of Augustus. This "global" aspect of Seneca's writing has been stressed by Herington, "Senecan Tragedy," 437–38 (= 185–86), cf., e.g., *Pha.* 54–72, *Ag.* 64–70, *HF* 1323–29. It can be clearly grasped by comparing Ovid's account in *Met.* 7.220–33 of Medea gathering her magic herbs—a purely Thessalian landscape with one excursion as far as Anthedon in Boeotia— with the Senecan counterpart in *Med.* 705–30, where Medea harvests her crop from Sicily to the Caucasus and from Spain to the Danube.

Here the Roman coloring has a specific source, Hor. *C.* 4.15.21–24 *non qui profundum Danuvium bibunt / rumpent edicta Iulia, non Getae, / non Seres infidique Persi, / non Tanain prope flumen orti*. While echoing Horace's phrases, Seneca pointedly alters their application: in Horace Roman power, symbolized by the *edicta . . . Iulia* and the *custos rerum Caesar* (17), guarantees the *otium* of peoples, whereas for Seneca that security belongs exclusively to the isolated *sapiens*. (See above, p. 137.) This perspective has also influenced the treatment Seneca gives these far-off peoples: they are made to seem exotic rather than formidable, unable either to tempt or intimidate the true *rex*.

369 Reges: not a "true" king (as at 348), but those who in fact hold power (as in Ps. 2.2 "the kings of the earth rise up, and the rulers take counsel together").

conveniant: "band together" (*OLD* s.v., #1d). The subjunctive is jussive-concessive (AG 440); so too *certet* in 376.

370 qui . . . Dahas: "who rouse the scattered Dahae" (i.e., for warfare), cf. Verg. *Aen.* 10.71 *gentes agitare quietas*, Luc. 2.643–44. The Dahae are *sparsi* because they are nomadic, cf. Luc. 7.429 *vetitos errare Dahas*. The Romans knew them as mounted archers (cf. 603 below), and from Augustan times onward they represent the romantic lands at the fringe of the empire, cf. Verg. *Aen.* 8.728 *indomiti . . . Dahae*, Livy 35.48.5, 49.8, Luc. 2.296 *(Roma) motura Dahas . . . clade Getasque*.

agitant: perhaps a counterpart to *exagitat furor* in 339; throughout the ode tranquil inactivity is upheld against violent agitation.

371-73 qui . . . tenent: "who hold in their power the waters of the Indian Ocean and the sea stained red over a wide expanse by brightly-shining gems." Both clauses refer to the *Mare Rubrum*, first by simple periphrasis (*rubri vada litoris*), then by naming the precious stones for which it was famous (cf. Prop. 1.14.12, [Tib.] 4.2.19-20, Petr. *Sat.* 55.6.9). For this doubling technique cf., e.g., Ovid *Met.* 1.62 *vesper et occiduo quae litora sole tepescunt*; in such phrases the connective (*et*, as in 372) is "epexegetical," almost equivalent to "i.e."

371 rubri . . . litoris: the Indian Ocean stands for "the East" in Augustan writers, cf. Hor. *C.* 1.35.31–32 *examen Eois timendum / partibus Oceanoque rubro*, Verg. *Aen.* 8.686 *victor ab Aurorae populis et litore rubro*.

372 gemmis: a generic term for a precious stone (cf. Fedeli on Prop. 1.14.12), here probably not "pearls" (Miller) but "rubies" or other stones of reddish hue, whose reflection turns the sea blood-red. Seneca appears to be offering a "gloss" on the name *Mare Rubrum*.

373 sanguineum: here "stained red," elsewhere of the staining agent, cf. Verg. *Aen.* 12.67–68 *Indum sanguineo . . . violaverit ostro / si quis ebur*, Pliny *NH* 22.48 *manus . . . inficit sanguineo colore*.

374-75 aut . . . Sarmatis: "or who throw open the ridges of the Caspian to the bold Sarmatians," i.e., the rulers of Armenia, who rely on the Causacus mountain range for protection against the marauding Sarmatians to the north.

Caspia . . . iuga: cf. *HF* 1206 *rupes . . . Caspiae*, of the rocks in the Caucasus where Prometheus was chained. In *Tro.* 1105–1106 the Caspian region suggests barbarism (*quae Caspium tangens mare / gens iuris expers*), but here it seems only to represent the remote northeast, as at Verg. *Aen.* 6.798–99 *Caspia regna / responsas horrent divum et Maeotica tellus*.

375 Sarmatis: the Sarmatae (or Sauromatae) were nomads (*vagus Sarmata, Pha.* 71) who ranged through what is now Soviet Georgia and the Ukraine. Ovid frequently uses *Sarmaticus* and *Sarmatis* of his place of exile on the Black Sea, stretching fact considerably to increase pity for his hardships. Seneca's geography is more precise here and also at *HF* 539 where the Sarmatians are associated with Scythia (cf. ps-Sen. *HO* 157–58).

376 certet: continuing the thought begun with *conveniant* in 369 (see note); *certare* here = "contend in battle" (*OLD* s.v., #2).

376-77 Danuvii . . . ingredi: the Danube belongs to Seneca's Horatian model (*C.* 4.15.21), but the picture of foot-soldiers crossing the frozen river comes from Ovid's description of the Black Sea in *Pont.* 4.10.32 *hic freta vel pediti pervia reddit hiemps* (a poem which also mentions the Danube, 57–58). Latin poets were intrigued by the picturesque possibilities of frozen bodies of water, cf. Verg. *G.* 3.360–62, Sen. *HF* 533–41, Luc. 5.436–41. Val. Fl. 4.218–29.

378-79 et . . . nobiles: the catalogue ends with its most remote constituent. The Seres, inhabitants of the southwest part of modern China, were known to the Greeks and

Romans as traders, not as a military power. In the role of imagined opponents, the Chinese with their bolts of silk cut an odd, even droll figure. Seneca may be shifting the ground of argument from power to wealth, but he may also intend this section to end with a "threat" that seems almost insubstantial (*quocumque loco iacent*), implying the impotence of all forces opposing the rule of reason.

378 et: sc. *et certent.*

quocumque loco iacent: most obviously a reference to the remoteness of the Seres, but also perhaps an allusion to scholarly disagreement about their location. [On the "limited and speculative" information about the Seres transmitted by Greek and Roman geographers, cf. J. Ferguson, "China and Rome," *ANRW* 2.9.2 (1978), 582–85.]

379 vellere: the fleecy raw silk deposited by silkworms on the leaves of mulberry and other bushes, but thought by the Romans to be a natural plant product, cf. Verg. *G.* 2.121 *vellera . . . ut foliis depectat tenuia Seres*, Silius 6.4 *Seres lanigeris repetebant vellera lucis.*

Silk garments were often denounced by Roman moralists as extravagant or, because diaphanous, as indecent, cf. Smith on Tib. 2.3.53, Prop. 1.2.2, 4.8.23, Petr. *Sat.* 119.21, Sen. *Ben.* 7.9.5 *video sericas vestes, si vestes vocandae sunt, in quibus nihil est quo defendi aut corpus aut denique pudor possit*, Tac. *Ann.* 2.33.1 with Furneaux's note.

380 mens . . . possidet: the simple counterpart to the long concessive clause 369–79: kings may assemble, etc., (but) *mens bona* retains control of its dominion. (For *regnum* in this sense cf. Cic. *Rep.* 1.28.) The contrast requires a strong sense for *possidere* ("exercise control over"), for which cf. Ovid *Ars* 2.35 *possidet et terras et possidet aequora Minos*, Sen. *Ag.* 258 *maritam possidens paelex domum.*

mens . . . bona: "good sense," nearly equivalent to *ratio*, which Seneca uses only in dialogue sections: *mens bona* here signifies more than simply a "sound mind," as in the conventional wish for *bona mens, bona valetudo*, cf. Petr. *Sat.* 88.8, Juv. 10.356. There was a Roman cult of *Mens Bona*, cf. Prop. 3.24.19, Ovid *F.* 6.241–48, but Seneca is referring to a purely individual state of mind.

381–90 These lines address an implied question, e.g., "how is this *regnum* acquired?" Three forms of aggression are presented in increasingly elaborate terms (a type of *tricolon abundans*, see on 267–68), but are all rejected in favor of the plain answer *hoc regnum sibi quisque dat* 390. [On 388–89 see note *ad loc.*] The content and triadic structure of 381–87 recall Hor. *C.* 1.22.1–4 *integer vitae scelerisque purus / non eget Mauris iaculis neque arcu / nec venenatis gravida sagittis, / Fusce, pharetra.*

381 equis: as employed by Atreus as an instrument of terror, cf. 184–85, 554.

382–84 nil . . . fugas: the Parthian cavalry tactic of launching barrages of arrows while riding away from the enemy was devastatingly effective against the Romans at Carrhae in 53 B.C. (cf. Plut. *Crass.* 24.6); it also gave generations of Latin poets an occasion for wit and paradox. Ovid's entries are, not surprisingly, the most outrageous, cf. *Ars* 1.211, 3.786 *ut celer aversis utere Parthus equis* (i.e., in lovemaking), also (e.g.) Hor. *C.* 1.19.11–12, 2.13.17–18, Prop. 2.10.13–14, 3.9.54, Ovid *RA* 155, 224, Sen. *Oed.* 118–19, *Med.* 710. In keeping with the mood of this ode, Seneca treats the commonplace with conspicuous restraint.

382 inertibus: "unwarlike," because not wielded in face-to-face combat; *inertia tela* is an oxymoron for which my closest parallel is Ovid *Met.* 13.694 *demisso per inertia vulnera telo* (the wounds are *inertia* because inflicted by an unmilitary instrument, a weaving-shuttle).

385-87 admotis . . . rotantibus: "no need of siege machines drawn up to flatten walls, whirling boulders far and wide." The last image of violent assault is the most extended, set off by artful word-order (the framing hyperbaton *admotis . . . machinis*) and choice diction (see on *sternere*); line 387 is not needed for sense, but adds vivid detail.

385 admotis: a technical term for "bringing up" troops or machinery, cf. Livy 30.8.1 *Vticae oppugnandae intentum iamque machinas admoventem muris*, Cic. *Cluent.* 36.

386 sternere: inf. of purpose with *admotis*; the usage is archaic, revived in Augustan poetry, cf. Verg. *Aen.* 1.527-28 *non . . . Libycas populare penates / venimus* with Austin's note, Fedeli on Prop. 1.1.12.

machinis: the generic term is more elevated than, e.g., *balista* (Ovid *Met.* 11.509, Sen. *Pha.* 535).

387 longe: for magnifying effect, like *late* in 373.

saxa rotantibus: a verbal echo of Verg. *Aen.* 10.362-63 (of a river) *qua saxa rotantia late / intulerat torrens*, a passage also in Seneca's mind at *NQ* 3.27.7 *devolutus torrens altissimis montibus . . . saxa revolutis remissa compagibus rotat*.

388-89 [Line 389 is missing in the A manuscripts, and both lines were bracketed by Leo, supported by Zwierlein in *Gnomon* 38 (1966), 684—although Professor Zwierlein now informs me that he has accepted the lines; the best defense is by Seidensticker, 106 n. 76. The absence of 389 in A is not an argument against its authenticity: scribes were often puzzled by sets of similarly-worded lines, and many sound verses were omitted as a result, cf., e.g., Ovid *Met.* 1.326, 481. The case for deletion rests on language and relation to context. As transmitted the lines contain an inexplicable shift in tense from *metuit* to *cupiet*. The only plausible emendation is to read *metuet* for *metuit* (Bentley); the future tenses are justified as "gnomic" by Seidensticker, who compares, e.g., Hor. *Epist.* 1.16.65-66 *nam qui cupiet, metuet quoque; porro / qui metuens vivet, liber mihi non erit umquam*. But the combination of *est* with *metuet/cupiet* is still awkward; the inverse sequence would seem more natural, as at *Ag.* 608-10 *qui . . . audet . . . vitae ponere finem, / par ille regi, par superis erit*. Furthermore, the use of *nihil* in 388-89 seems rather flat after its effective repetition in the "tricolon abundans" of 381-87. Finally, 388-89 virtually repeat the point of 348-49 in a less interesting form. If interpolated, the lines might be the work of a reader who did not see that *hoc regnum* in 390 looks back to *regnum* in 380.]

390 sibi quisque dat: in implied contrast to the false *regnum* that the audience will see Thyestes accept from Atreus (529, 540-42). Seneca here adapts to the pervasive imagery of dominion a common idea of Roman moralizing, that virtue is within the reach of every individual, cf. Hor. *Epist.* 1.18.112 *(Iuppiter) det vitam, det opes; aequum mi animum ipse parabo*, Sen. *Epist.* 41.1 *bonam mentem quam stultum est optare cum possis a te impetrare*, Juv.(?) 10.363 *monstro quod ipse tibi possis dare*.

391-403 The Chorus now moves from the general to the highly personal. Although this section begins and ends with images of a life that is rejected (391-92, 401-403), the prevailing tone is positive for the first time in the ode; the only traces of the negative phrasing prominent earlier are *nullis nota Quiritibus* (396) and *nullo cum strepitu* (399), which denote welcome absences rather than imposing threats. The tranquillity that the Chorus longs for is reflected in the calm, measured pace of the lines; the progress from static *quies* and *otium* (393-95) through smoothly flowing years (397-99) to death in humble old age (400) is handled with masterful restraint.

391-93 The technique of prefacing one's own opinions or values with those of others is common in early Greek poetry and traditional in later periods; modern scholars have given it the name "priamel" (German for "preamble"), cf. Nisbet-Hubbard on Hor. *C.* 1.1 (pp. 2–3), W. H. Race, *The Classical Priamel from Homer to Boethius* (Leiden, 1982). Here it appears in abbreviated form, confined to the choice between power and its absence. The opening lines of Tibullus' first elegy are similar in form and to a degree in content: *divitias alius fulvo sibi congerat auro . . . me mea paupertas vita traducat inerti* (1.1.1–5).

392 aulae culmine lubrico: "on the slippery pinnacle of power"; *aulae* is appositional genitive (i.e., the *aula* is the *culmen*), cf. Caes. *B.G.* 1.60.5 *auxilia legionum*, AG 343d, K–S 1.418–19.

aulae: in Augustan poetry, e.g., Hor. *C.* 2.7.10, an *aula* is any grand (and so enviable) house, but here it specifically refers to the palace of a ruler or powerful figure, cf. *Ag.* 81 (n).

lubrico: cf. Sen. *Epist.* 94.73 *cogitat enim varios casus et in sublimi maxime lubricos*, Luc. 5.249–51.

393 me: emphatic ("for my part"); at the end of a priamel, cf. Sappho 16.3 LP ἔγω δέ, Hor. *C.* 1.1.29, 1.7.10.
As a rule, personal statements by Senecan choruses are in the plural, cf. 621, 875–81 below, *Oed.* 124–25, 980–84, *Tro.* 378–79, etc. Of the exceptions two seem to carry no particular weight (*Ag.* 332 *velim*, *Pha.* 355 *quid plura canam?*) and a third is difficult to assess (in *Ag.* 656 *vidi* probably represents a heightening of emotion after *vidimus* 612, 627 and *duximus* 628); in the other three instances, though, there is an unmistakable sense of strong personal feeling, cf. *HF* 192–201, *Oed.* 882–91. It can hardly be accidental that the subject of all three passages is the longing for a peaceful, inconspicuous existence.

dulcis: with *saturet*, *dulcis* retains its full sensual meaning: *quies* is satisfying in the same way as fresh water (Ovid *Pont.* 2.7.73) or succulent fruit (Ovid *F.* 2.256).

saturet: Seneca could have written, e.g., *placeat*, but *saturet* makes the Chorus's wish a contrast to the Tantalid appetites for power and revenge (see on 2 *avido*, 26 *modus*, 256 *nullum est satis*). Thyestes, who abandons *quies* for the *aula*, experiences a hideous perversion of *satietas*, cf. 913 *satur est*, and see on 955–56 *saturas . . . vestes*.

quies: especially in conjunction with *otium* (395), *quies* suggests lack of engagement in political life, cf. Cic. *De or.* 3.56, see also on 198 above. The preference for *quies* has Epicurean overtones, cf. Lucr. 5.1129–30 *ut satius multo iam sit parere quietum / quam regere imperio res velle et regna tenere*.

394 obscuro . . . loco: "in an unobtrusive station"; compare Thyestes' similar wish, *liceat in media mihi / latere turba* (533–34), and the combination *obscura quies* at *Pha.* 1126.

395 perfruar: *per-* strengthens the basic sense, suggesting "to enjoy completely/ thoroughly," cf. Cic. *Att.* 3.17.3 *tantum velim fortuna det nobis potestatem ut incolumes amore nostro perfruamur*.

396 nullis nota Quiritibus: an overt rejection of Roman political ambitions, cf. Verg. *G.* 2.498 *res Romanae* (see above, p. 138), Hor. *C.* 1.1.7 (see on 350–57). *Quirites* appears only here in the tragedies.

397 aetas per tacitum fluat: a remarkable adaptation of Verg. *Aen.* 9.30–32 *ceu altus / per tacitum Ganges . . . / cum refluit*. Seneca combines Vergil's *per tacitum* with the metaphor of time as "an ever-rolling stream" (see Nisbet-Hubbard on Hor. *C.* 2.14.2), and gives a commonplace a new meaning: instead of the imperceptible slipping away of years (compare, e.g., Ovid *Tr.* 4.10.27 *tacito passu labentibus annis*), the emphasis here is on the tranquillity of life as actually lived; *per tacitum* denotes the medium through which time flows as well as the manner of its passage.

398–99 cum . . . dies: the absence of even a slight sense-pause at the end of 398 momentarily quickens the tempo, as the focus shifts to the end of life (*cum trans-ierint . . . dies*).

399 nullo cum strepitu: perhaps based on Ovid *Tr.* 3.7.35–36 *damnosa senectus / quae strepitus passu non faciente venit*, but with *strepitu* continuing the water-metaphor of 397, cf. Verg. *G.* 2.492 *strepitum . . . Acherontis avari*, Ovid *Met.* 3.568–69 *torrentem . . . modico strepitu decurrere vidi*.

400 plebeius: emphatic, suggesting "even in my old age let me remain a man of the people"; *plebeius* meaning "common," "ordinary" (*OLD* s.v., #2b) is often a term of approval with moralists, cf. Lucr. 2.36, Sen. *Pha.* 1139, Petr. *Sat.* 119.8, sometimes linked with *privatus*, as in Cic. *Sest.* 77, Luc. 5.538–39.

401 mors gravis incubat: "death weighs heavily," i.e., is an oppressive prospect; the metaphor inverts the traditional wish for the dead, *sit tibi terra levis*, cf. *Pha.* 1280 *gravis . . . tellus impio capiti incubet*. For *incubare* see on 155, *Epist.* 95.74 *gravior ipsis felicitas incubat*.

402 notus nimis: "all too well known," cf. Verg. *Aen.* 9.471–72 *ora virum praefixa movebant / nota nimis miseris*.

402–403 omnibus . . . sibi: for the phrasing cf. *Med.* 654 *omnibus verax, sibi falsus uni* (sc. Mopsus).

403 ignotus . . . sibi: a memorable phrase, not attested earlier; Ovid has the positive equivalent, *Ars* 2.501 *qui sibi notus erit*, and Seneca ascribes *ignoratio sui* to the inebriated (*Epist.* 83.21) and the feeble-minded (*VB* 5.2).

Several choral odes in Seneca end with a *sententia*, cf. *Pha.* 354–57, *HF* 590–91, 1134–37, *Ag.* 865–66, *Oed.* 992–94. Here, as in *Tro.* 407–408, the element of cleverness is kept in balance, and the verbal twist clinches rather than breaks the mood of the ending.

The man who is "all too well-known to others, but unknown to himself" is an ironically apt description of Thyestes, not yet aware of the susceptibility to power and wealth which Atreus has seen only too clearly (cf. 288–91). When Thyestes discovers the truth about himself and his brother, the words *illi mors gravis incubat* take on a gruesomely literal appropriateness (cf. 1000, 1051 *premor . . . natis*).

ACT III (404–545)

This act comprises two scenes (404–90, 491–545), with the focus in each on the character of Thyestes. Thyestes presents himself as a proponent of the simple life, reluctant to exchange the peace of obscurity for the anxieties of power and deeply suspicious of Atreus' intentions in the proposed reconciliation. (Accius may also have portrayed Thyestes as a figure with pretentions to wisdom; see above, p. 42.) From the outset, however, Seneca hints that Thyestes may be less than fully committed to the ideals he professes (see note on 404), and as the first scene progresses his attraction to the life of wealth and influence is more and more openly suggested (see on 446–70). Throughout this act Seneca surrounds Thyestes' language with ironic second meanings, creating a masterful portrait of a man who literally does not know his own mind (cf. 403). The clearest impression Thyestes makes, though, is of a fatal weakness of will; he twice allows his judgment to be overruled, first when his son Tantalus (perhaps significantly named) persuades him to go ahead with the planned meeting with Atreus, and then when, after a brief resistance, he accepts Atreus' offer of a share in the kingdom. At the end of the act Thyestes is obviously in Atreus' power; Atreus' final words, a double-edged reference to sacrificial offerings (545), look forward to the mock-ritual executions of the following act.

The movement of both scenes, in which good intentions are ultimately overcome, closely parallels that of the prologue (cf. in particular 90–105), while the beginning of each scene contrasts the energy of Atreus with Thyestes' passivity and lack of control. Thyestes' opening soliloquy leads to no firm resolution, as Atreus' does, but only to a bemused conflict of mind and body (419–20); the intervention of young Tantalus is needed to get the scene moving again. In the second scene the dramatic initiative passes even more clearly to Atreus: Thyestes is held in suspension while Atreus calmly observes his intended victim and thinks himself into his assumed role of the forgiving brother (491–507).

404–20 Thyestes rejoices at the sight of his native land, but his mood changes suddenly when he recalls that he will have to see Atreus again (412). The speech is far removed from the conventional remarks of homecoming travelers in drama (on which cf. *Ag.* 392a–394a [nn]); it depicts in miniature the conflicting impulses in Thyestes' character. In two sections of nearly equal length, Thyestes first expresses delight at returning to "wealthy Argos" (*Argolicas opes* 404) and then renewed longing for "escape to the woods" (*silvestres fugas* 412). At the exact center of the speech stands Atreus (412, midway through the 9th line in a speech of 17 lines), whose image thwarts Thyestes' hopes and makes him turn back toward the safety of exile.

404 Optata: Thyestes' first word reveals that he is not a true *sapiens*, since he is still subject to hope. (For the link between hope and fear in Seneca's thinking cf. *Epist.* 5.7; it is precisely Thyestes' lingering hopes that make him susceptible to anxiety.)

Argolicas opes: Thyestes consciously means only "wealthy Argos" (*opes Argolicae = Argos opulentum*, cf. Prop. 3.9.25 *hostes Medorum = Medi hostiles*), but the audience comes gradually to see that the literal sense "longed-for wealth of Argos" (with *optatas* supplied from *optata*) more accurately represents Thyestes' feelings.

405 miseris . . . bonum: Atreus also uses a lead-in phrase with *maximus* in his opening words (176–77). The differences in style and content are telling; see above, p. 44.

miseris: modifies *exulibus*.

406 tractum soli natalis: *natale solum* is Ovidian, cf. *Met.* 7.52, perhaps 8.184, *Pont.* 1.3.35; the combination with *tractus* ("region," "district") is apparently new and seems cumbersome, perhaps deliberately so.

patrios deos: i.e., the statues or images of the gods greeted by entering characters in ancient drama, cf. Pl. *Bacch.* 172–73, Sen. *Ag.* 392a–94a *delubra et aras caelitum et patrios lares . . . supplex adoro* (n).

407 si sunt tamen di: "if there actually *are* gods," a remarkably skeptical statement for an opening speech; the closest parallel in Seneca is Jason's *cri de coeur* at the end of *Medea* (1027) *testare nullos esse qua veheris deos* (and see Costa *ad loc.*). In Stoic terms Thyestes' lack of faith could be linked to his failure to abide by his principles, cf., e.g., *Epist.* 73.16 *deus ad homines venit, immo . . . in homines venit; nulla sine deo mens bona est.* Paradoxically, Thyestes' last words in the play profess belief in divine vengeance (1110–11 *vindices aderunt dei* etc.)—a claim that rings hollow in its dramatic context, and that may be further weakened by the memory of Thyestes' original agnosticism.

si . . . tamen: introduces a proviso, cf. Ovid *Pont.* 3.4.3–4 *ut . . . suo faveas mandat, Rufine, Triumpho, / in vestras venit si tamen ille manus.*

407–408 Cyclopum . . . decus: i.e., the walls of Mycenae, built of enormous blocks of stone and therefore said to have been the work of the Cyclopes, cf. Bond on Eur. *Her.* 15, Roscher s.v. "Kyklops" 1687–89. The motif is rare in Latin; besides this passage I know only of *HF* 997–98. The conflation of Argos and Mycenae has precedent in Greek tragedy, see again Bond on *Her.* 15, my edition of *Agamemnon*, pp. 160–61.

408 labore . . . humano: "the work of human hands" (abl. of comparison with *maius*), with *labor* standing by synecdoche for the product of effort, cf. *OLD* s.v., #4, Verg. *Aen.* 7.248 *Iliadum . . . labor vestes.* Thyestes' bland reference to "greater than human effort" makes an interesting counterpart to the lines in the previous act (267–68) where Atreus' own *animus* produces a crime *supra . . . fines moris humani.*

decus: here a "source of distinction" (*OLD* s.v., #2); of a city's walls, cf. Livy 26.48.5 *praecipuum muralis coronae decus*, Sen. *Tro.* 15 *alta muri decora.*

409 celebrata iuveni stadia: "the racing-track thronged by the young men"; *iuveni* is collective singular, cf. Luc. 7.37–38 *te mixto flesset luctu iuvenisque senexque / iniussusque puer*, Silius 4.220.

409–10 nobilis . . . tuli: a clear echo of Hor. *C.* 1.1.3–6 *sunt quos curriculo pulverem Olympico / collegisse iuvat . . . palmaque nobilis / terrarum dominos evehit ad deos.* Thyestes prides himself on the victory that Horace declined to pursue; the reversal of attitude will not have escaped an audience that has just heard the Chorus subscribe to the Horatian viewpoint and even echo the next lines of the same ode (see on 350–57).

nobilis: "renowned," in pointed opposition to the Chorus's wish *plebeius moriar senex* (400).

paterno . . . curru: the allusion to Pelops recalls the conditions under which *his* victory was won (cf. 139–43), casting an even darker shadow over these lines; see also on 660–62.

411 occurret . . . occurret: the repetition suggests excitement, as Thyestes warms to his fantasy of a triumphant reception.

populus occurret frequens: Thyestes thinks the people will greet him as a benefactor or even a ruler, cf. Pacuvius 187 R² *ibo et edicam frequentes ut eant gratatum hospiti*, Verg. *G.* 4.216 (the bees around their *rex*) *circumstant fremitu denso stipantque frequentes.*

populus . . . frequens: in a Roman context the words would denote a large citizen assembly, cf. Cic. *Phil.* 1.32, Sall. *Jug.* 73.7, Livy 7.6.7.

412 sed nempe et Atreus: "yes, but so will Atreus." With *nempe* Thyestes reminds himself of an obvious fact that he has allowed to escape his notice; compare *Tro.* 743–44 *spiritus genitor facit? / sed nempe tractus*, in dialogue *Tro.* 325, 340, ps-Sen. *HO* 437.

repete silvestres fugas: this urge to flee clearly recalls the prologue (68–82); like Tantalus, Thyestes longs for a state that would normally be considered unbearable (cf. 417 *quae putant cuncti aspera*).

silvestres: not just descriptive ("in the forests"), but implying a life of deprivation, cf. *Pha.* 461 (the ascetic Hippolytus) *truculentus et silvester.*

fugas: "places of refuge/exile" (= *perfugia*), cf. Prop. 2.16.40, Ovid *Pont.* 1.2.128 *ut* *propior patriae sit fuga nostra roga.*

413–14 mixtam . . . vitam: "an existence shared with wild beasts [*OLD* s.v. *misceo*, #9] and like theirs in style." Thyestes is thinking not just of the hardships of animal life but also of the innocence sometimes attributed to it, cf. *Pha.* 913–14, *Epist.* 95.31 *non pudet homines . . . gaudere sanguine alterno et bella gerere cum inter se etiam mutis ac feris pax sit*, probably Verg. *Aen.* 4.550–51 *sine crimine vitam / degere more ferae*, Mayor on Juv. 15.159. Here too Thyestes speaks more truly than he knows: the life he has returned to is also both "shared with wild beasts" (i.e., Atreus, cf. 546, 721) and "like theirs," in that Thyestes himself is hunted like an animal by Atreus, cf. 286–87, 491–503.

414–15 clarus . . . auferat: "there is no reason why [*non est quod*] this bright gleam of power should dazzle my eyes with its deceptive radiance." Thyestes speaks of power as if it were a precious stone (cf., e.g., Ovid *Pont.* 3.4.23 *nitor argenti . . . et auri*), perhaps an indication of the luxury it implies for him (cf. 455–69).

non est quod: a prosy, perhaps colloquial expression (often in the form *nihil est quod*), of which Seneca is noticeably fond (six uses in *De brevitate vitae* alone), cf. *OLD* s.v. *sum*, #6d.

fulgore: *fulgor* stands for the "flashiness" of a luxurious life in *Epist.* 94.74 *tunc laudant otium lene et sui iuris, odio est fulgor et fuga a rebus adhuc stantibus quaeritur*. (The whole passage is relevant to Thyestes' situation.)

auferat: "carry off for itself" and hence "captivate" (*OLD* s.v., #4b), but with a strong suggestion of "mislead" (*ibid.*, #13), cf. *Epist.* 94.74 *secunda rectum auferunt*; the subjunctive is characterizing, cf. AG 535a, K-S 2.278. The combination *auferre oculos* first appears in a mannered line of Ovid (?), *Her.* 12.36 *abstulerant oculi lumina nostra tui*. The idea of being "carried off" (suggesting Thyestes' basic passivity) returns in *abductus* 437.

416 cum . . . aspice: i.e., while power has its specious attraction, concentration on the hateful figure of Atreus (*dantem*) should keep Thyestes from accepting his offer. This attempt at firmness finds expression in a *sententia*, with symmetrically balanced nouns and verbs—*quod datur-dantem, spectabis-aspice*: neat enough, but no match for the rhetorical power of Atreus. (In fact it is Atreus who looks carefully at Thyestes, cf. 505 *aspice*.)

417–20 As often after a *sententia*, the thought moves in a new direction. Here the effect is especially telling: the confidence that Thyestes has tried to summon (414–16) vanishes, and he faces his dilemma in movingly direct and simple terms.

417 modŏ: temporal, "a short while ago" or "just now."

417–18 inter . . . laetusque: a paradox stated again in 446–49 with the terms reversed.

418 fortis . . . laetusque: "resolute and cheerful," a favorite Senecan description of the *sapiens*, cf. *Epist.* 30.3 *hoc philosophia praestat, in conspectu mortis hilarem <esse> et in quocumque corporis habitu fortem laetumque*, 54.3, *Prov.* 5.8. The terms are causally linked, since the confidence of an undivided mind brings with it a general sense of well-being, cf. *Tranq.* 16.3 *dicamus 'tanto fortior, tanto felicior.'*

419 revolvor: probably middle ("I return"), cf. Ovid *Met.* 10.335 *quid in ista revolvor?*, but Thyestes' alienation from himself could justify taking it as a true passive.

haeret: "is stuck" (i.e., in perplexity), cf. *Med.* 309, *OLD* s.v., #9. The combination *animus haeret* is not simply more elevated than *haereo*, but also stresses the sense of detachment from self that several of Seneca's emotionally divided characters experience, cf., e.g., *Tro.* 642–44, *Med.* 926–28, 939–44, *Ag.* 132–40 (n).

420 moveo nolentem gradum: this conflict resembles the state that Atreus wishes to impose on all his subjects, *quod nolunt velint* (212); Thyestes fittingly encounters it as soon as he has returned to Argos and so placed himself under Atreus' jurisdiction. (Thyestes will again suffer his body's resistance when he is about to drink the blood of his sons, 985–86.) See also above, p. 47.

421–28 Thyestes has been communing with himself, and his sons have not heard any of the previous speech. One of them now remarks on their father's strange behavior. Thyestes' next words (423–28) are also addressed to himself, and not until 429 does a true dialogue begin. This combination of soliloquy with comments on the soliloquizing character by others on stage is alien to Greek tragedy, although there is something approaching it in Euripides' *Hecuba* 726–51, where Hecuba soliloquizes while Agamemnon vainly tries to get her attention. More exact analogies are found in New Comedy, cf., e.g., Pl. *Trin.* 843–69 or Ter. *Ad.* 299–320, where Sostrata and Canthara comment on the agitated manner of their slave Geta, but do not overhear his monologue. Compare in particular 421 *pigro (quid hoc est?) genitor incessu stupet* and *Ad.* 305 *me miseram, quidnam est quod sic video timidum et properantem Getam?* (See further *HSCP* 82 [1978], 238–39.) The closest parallel of all, however, is in *Macbeth* 1.3.142, where, after Macbeth's soliloquy beginning "Two truths are told . . ." Banquo says to the other lords on stage "look how our partner's rapt." Both Macbeth and Thyestes become oblivious to their surroundings because of their troubled fascination with the prospect of rule.

As Atreus had foreseen (300–302), Thyestes' children are easily gulled by the offer of reconciliation. Seneca portrays young Tantalus as frankly attracted by power (440–44) and naively convinced that it can be accepted without risk; his misguided certainty makes him the perfect foil for his wiser, but weaker, father.

421 Pigro . . . incessu: perhaps a counterpart to the *pigrae manus* that Atreus reproaches in himself (268).

422 vultum . . . versat: "turns his face this way and that," cf. Ovid *Tr.* 3.9.21 *dum quid agat quaerit, dum versat in omnia vultus*; perhaps referring specifically to opposite sides of the stage, representing Argos and the forests.

se . . . tenet: *se tenere* stresses volition; it is not "to be uncertain," but "to keep oneself in uncertainty," "to remain uncertain," like *se tenere intra silentium*, "to remain silent," Pliny *Epist.* 4.17.8, or *se tenere in servitio*, "to keep oneself in subjection," Livy 4.35.6.

423 anime: the usual indication of a soliloquy in Seneca, see on 192.

423–24 consilium . . . facile: it may be significant that the audience cannot at first tell which *consilium* is meant; is the "simple [*facile*] course of action" returning to exile or accepting Atreus' offer? Only Thyestes' further questions show that the former is intended.

424 torques: "twist," i.e., by subjecting it to close scrutiny, cf. *Ben.* 4.11.5, Tac. *Hist.* 1.85.3 *versare sententias et huc atque huc torquere*; compare also Sen. *Brev.* 12.4, *Epist.* 100.2, where *torquere* refers to excessive complexity in speech, etc.

424–27 Thyestes' language becomes unusually pointed as he tries to argue himself into doing what he knows is right: each segment of the question *credis . . . metuis . . . fugis* contains a striking conjunction of noun and adjective (*res incertissimae-frater*; *mala-mansueta*; *aerumnas-bene collocatas*), and this elaborate structure is then "capped" with the paradox *esse iam miserum iuvat*.

425 fratri atque regno: the uncertainty of power is a commonplace (cf., e.g., *Tro.* 1–4, *Ag.* 57–76), but only a Tantalid would place brothers on the same level (cf. 40 *fratrem expavescat frater*).

426 mansueta: "tamed," perhaps suggesting a wild beast that has been subdued (*victa*) and made gentle; *malum mansuetum* is attested only here and in Livy 3.16.4; compare also Ovid *Tr.* 3.6.23 *mansuetior ira*.

426–27 aerumnas . . . bene collocatas: "well spent misfortunes," an oxymoron (cf. *VB* 7.6 *honestas miserias*) suggesting that Thyestes' time in exile, though unpleasant, was profitable in that it taught him a true appreciation of external riches. For *bene/male collocare* = "to make good/bad use of" (perhaps a metaphor drawn from investing money), cf. Sen. *Epist.* 93.5, Martial 1.113.3.

427 iam: "by now," as in 305 (which this line recalls).

428 teque eripe: reminiscent of Hector's warning to Aeneas in Verg. *Aen.* 2.289 'teque his' ait 'eripe flammis.' The echo might imply the gravity of the danger that Thyestes is confronting.

430 visa: with causal force (i.e., Thyestes turns back "at the sight of" his homeland), cf. Ovid *Met.* 1.490 *Phoebus amat visaeque cupit conubia Daphnes.* There may be a significant echo of *male . . . visas domos* in 3.

430–31 sinum / subducis: a graphic (and very Roman) image of rejecting good fortune. The *sinus* is the upper part of the toga, the folds of which were often used for carrying or hiding small objects, cf. Hor. *C.* 2.18.27, Suet. *Cal.* 46, Quint. 7.1.30, Tac. *Ann.* 1.40; in *VB* 23.3 Seneca describes the small-minded man hiding the gifts of fortune "as though keeping a prized possession safely in his pocket" (*intra sinum*). Here the implied image is of someone pulling his toga closely about him so as not to receive the *bona* being showered upon him by Fortune; compare the more explicit picture in *Epist.* 74.6 *nam qui aliquid virtute melius putat aut ullum praeter illam bonum, ad haec quae a Fortuna sparguntur sinum expandit et sollicitus missilia eius expectat.* (The *missilia* are small gifts thrown to the crowds by the emperor, cf. Suet. *Cal.* 18.2, *Nero* 11.2.)

431 frater . . . redit: Atreus is returning to normal brotherly affection; the "brother" in him is again dominant. (Seneca's Medea speaks of herself in similar terms [927–28], *ira discessit loco / materque tota coniuge expulsa redit*.)

431–32 redit . . . reddit: probably deliberate sound-play, cf. Verg. *Aen.* 4.271 *qua spe Libycis teris otia terris*, Juv. 3.127–28 *si curat nocte togatus / currere*.

432–33 lacerae . . . artus: a densely-packed and ominous phrase: *componere* here has a medical sense of "setting" broken bones (cf. Celsus 8.10.2), but it both looks back to the Chorus's belief that the brothers have "composed" their differences (338) and forward to the moment when Atreus carefully "arranges" the children before killing them (694); *lacerae domus* is also bitterly ironic, foreshadowing the dismemberment of Thyestes' sons (cf. 60–61) and their "rending" by their father (cf. 277–78).

433 te . . . restituit tibi: Tantalus means only that Atreus will restore Thyestes to his own kingdom, but his words imply an identification between Thyestes and power that is close to being true. In its immediate context the statement is ironic in a different way: the thought of seeing Atreus has had just the opposite of the effect Tantalus speaks of, dividing Thyestes from himself, cf. 419–20, 436–37.

434 Causam . . . ignoro: here Thyestes closely resembles the figure spoken of by the Chorus, *nimis notus omnibus . . . ignotus sibi* (402–403).

ipse: with *ignoro*.

436 membra . . . labant: epic phrasing, used by Vergil of an exhausted fighter (*Aen.* 5.432) and of Turnus made weak-kneed by terror (*Aen.* 12.905).

437 alio . . . quam quo nitor: *alio* and *quo* are adverbial, "in another direction than the one in which I am struggling (to go)."

abductus feror: the theme of futile resistance (above, p. 47) in an extreme form; Thyestes speaks like a helpless victim, perhaps from a wish to see his actions as forced on him rather than chosen (cf. 488–89, 542 *regni . . . impositi*).

438–39 sic . . . refert: word-order and phrasing precisely reflect the struggle between Thyestes' rational determination to flee and his equally strong desire to be rich and powerful again; Phaedra uses comparable terms of her efforts to resist passion (181–83), but presents the battle as already lost. (For other sea-similes of this kind cf. Ovid *Met.* 8.470–72, Sen. *Med.* 939–42, *Ag.* 139–40 [n].)

438 concitatam: "spurred," with an implied metaphor from horse-riding, cf. Livy 30.25.8, 37.11.10, Curtius 4.3.2.

remige et velo: to use both oars *and* sails is to make a supreme effort, as Aeneas' men do when escaping Charybdis (*Aen.* 3.563); cf. also Cic. *Fam.* 12.25.3 *ventis remis in patriam omni festinatione properavi*, Ovid *Met.* 3.663, Otto s.v. *remus*. The wording here is closest to Ovid *Met.* 6.445 *veloque et remige portus / Cecropios intrat*.

440 Evince quidquid obstat: "overcoming all obstacles" is the act of a courageous hero (cf. *HF* 558 *evincas utinam iura ferae Stygis*), but Tantalus, with unconscious irony, applies it to suppressing one's better judgment.

441 reducem: modifying *te* understood.

vide: the counterpart of Thyestes' charge to himself in 416 *dantem aspice*.

442–44 The divided lines present the opposing viewpoints in the most highly concentrated form possible. (On stichomythia see above on 204–19; on this passage cf. Seidensticker, 104–109.) The exchange shows that Thyestes has a clear grasp of the principles he will soon betray.

442 pater: the vocative lends urgency to this phase of the dialogue.

Cum possim mori: "(yes,) since I have the ability to die." Thyestes here sees *regnum* in the same terms as the Chorus, cf. 365–68.

443 Nulla . . . nihil: Thyestes interrupts his son and finishes the sentence on his own terms, a sign of firm control, cf. *Med.* 171 '*Medea*'—'*Fiam.*' This thought too is an echo of the previous ode, cf. 342–49.

Nulla: "of no importance/value," cf. *OLD* s.v., #1f, Livy 6.18.8 *vindex vester . . . nullus repente fui*.

444 Natis . . . duos: i.e., leaving his kingdom to his children would bring no benefit, since power cannot be shared and would only provoke strife between the heirs. Thyestes' decisiveness here contrasts with his failure in the next scene to dispute Atreus' claim *recipit hoc regnum duos* (i.e., himself and Thyestes).

Non . . . duos: a virtual axiom in ancient views of absolute power, cf. *Ag.* 259 *nec regna socium ferre nec taedae sciunt* (n); Seneca himself was cited as a rare exception, see above, p. 5 and n. 24.

445 Miser . . . potest: "does anyone who can be happy prefer being wretched?" Tantalus has not heard 425–28 and so invites his father to explain what seems a perverse preference for "misery" (cf. 427) over good fortune.

446–70 Thyestes' fullest exposition of his beliefs and also Seneca's most subtle depiction of this divided character. The speech may appear at first a mere string of commonplaces, a eulogy of the simple life such as can be found in nearly every Latin writer from Lucretius to Juvenal; its arrangement and style, however, suggest a more complex attitude. Tantalus' original question is fully answered in the opening section, which culminates in 454 *malam bonae praeferre fortunam licet*. Both logically and rhetorically this line has the force of a conclusion, and it should perhaps seem surprising that Thyestes then launches into a long description of the *bona fortuna* he has rejected. The progress of thought in this section—"I may not have A or B or C, but I *do* enjoy X and Y and Z"—is traditional (see on 455–69), but the negative and positive sides of the picture are grossly unbalanced, and there is also a clear difference in style between them: what Thyestes says about the advantages of poverty, both at 449–52 and 468–69, sounds vague and pallid when compared to the vivid detail he lavishes on the life of luxury. The gusto with which Thyestes enumerates the trappings of wealth seems a clear sign that he does not find this existence as distasteful as he claims.

Denunciation of wealth was a standard theme of Hellenistic popular philosophy, enthusiastically adopted by Roman poets from the late Republic onward, cf. Nisbet-Hubbard on Hor. *C.* 2.18 (pp. 288–89). This was also a set topic in schools of declamation, cf. S. F. Bonner, *Roman Declamation* (Berkeley, 1949), 61; J. de Decker, *Iuvenalis declamans* (Ghent, 1912), 144–51. Its treatment by Seneca's teacher Papirius Fabianus is preserved in Sen. *Contr.* 2.1.11–13, and is close to Thyestes' speech in several details. Elsewhere in Seneca cf. *Pha.* 483–525, *Epist.* 122.5–9.

446 Mihi crede: Thyestes strikes a superior tone of wisdom earned by experience (like the *praeceptor* of Ovid's *Ars Amatoria*, cf., e.g., 1.66, 2.259).

446–47 magna . . . dura: neuter pls. as substantives, "great things" (= the state of being prominent, etc.) and "harsh conditions"; cf. Verg. *G.* 4.176 *si parva licet componere magnis*.

446 falsis . . . nominibus: i.e., if the terms '*magna*' and '*dura*' were scrutinized, it would be clear that they were being misapplied; for this type of argument by redefinition cf. *Oed.* 1034–36 *iacet ferro meus / coniunx—quid illum nomine haud vero vocas? / socer est*, Ovid *Met.* 5.524–26 *si modo nomina rebus / addere vera placet, non hoc iniuria factum, / sed amor est*. In his prose works Seneca often attacks what he regards as misconceptions based on faulty definition—*falsa nomina* or *falsae opiniones*—, cf. *Ben.* 1.5.5, *Epist.* 90.34, 94.6, 33, 110.8, 119.12.

447 excelsus: of "lofty" position cf. *Ag.* 58–59 *in praecipiti / dubioque locas nimis excelsos* (n, and pp. 182–83 for the commonplace that those in high places lead anxious lives). By contrast, Atreus in his triumph glories in being *caelitum excelsissimus* (911).

448–49 ipsum . . . lateris: "the sword I carried at my own side"; that is, the means needed for safety were themselves causes for worry. The detail is balanced by 468, *tuta sine telo est domus*.

450 obstare nulli: "to get in nobody's way" (i.e., because the lowly have no ambitions that might conflict with those of others).

capere securas dapes: the stress (here and in 452) on not worrying about what one eats has, of course, an ironic appropriateness for Thyestes.

451 humi iacentem: i.e., rather than reclining on high couches (as Thyestes himself does later, cf. 909); compare Lucretius' beautiful picture of simple refreshment enjoyed *prostrati in gramine molli* (2.39). The phrase also works metaphorically, opposing those at "ground level" to the "heights" of luxury (*excelsus*), cf. on 343 *iaceat*, 456 *humilis*.

scelera . . . casas: the *casa* is a humble dwelling; the sentiment is the same as in Juvenal's memorable phrase *rarus venit in cenacula miles* (10.18).

452 mensa . . . angusta: probably an echo of Hor. *C.* 2.16.13–16 *vivitur parvo bene, cui paternum / splendet in mensa tenui salinum, / nec levis somnos timor aut cupido / sordidus aufert*. Seneca is characteristically more extreme in his categories: Horace's *tenuis* implies "simplicity rather than indigence" (Nisbet-Hubbard *ad loc.*), whereas *angustus* can suggest actual poverty, as in Hor. *C.* 3.2.1 *angustam . . . pauperiem pati*, Juv. 3.164–65 *haud facile emergunt quorum virtutibus obstat / res angusta domi* ("slow rises worth, by poverty oppressed" Johnson).

scyphus: strictly defined as a two-handled vessel of large capacity, *scyphus* is a generic term for a drinking-cup as early as Cicero, cf. *Fam.* 7.22, *Tusc.* 1.97. At *Pha.* 208 a *vilis scyphus* stands for plain living (corresponding to *mensa . . . angusta*), but here the emphasis is signaled by *tutus*, marking the contrast of carefree poverty and anxious wealth. [In both places *scyphus* is a conjecture for *cibus*; here the change seems justified to avoid repetition with 450 *capere . . . dapes* and to obtain a closer antithesis to the drinking in 453.]

453 in auro: *aurum* stands by metonymy for *pocula ex auro facta*, and golden goblets are a standard emblem of luxury, cf. *Ag.* 878 (n), *Pha.* 518–19 *sollicito bibunt / auro superbi*. Thyestes' next words (*expertus loquor*) are cruelly ironic, since he is shortly to drink something more dreadful than poison from a silver goblet (913).

454 licet: "one may," i.e, there are reasonable grounds for this choice. [Heinsius' *libet* would make the statement more personal, but Thyestes, although using himself as an example, is arguing a universal proposition.]

455–69 In stating a preference for the simple life, it was customary first to list the comforts one thereby lacked, then the blessings that outweighed these losses (a type of "priamel," on which see 344–47 and note *ad loc.*); cf. Lucr. 2.24–33, Verg. *G.* 2.461–74, Hor. *C.* 2.18.1–4, Sen. *Epist.* 86.9–10, *Tranq.* 1.5–7, *Culex* 58–97. In all these passages there is either a close balance of negative and positive statements or else a clear weighting toward the positive. (The passage from *De tranquillitate animi*, too long to cite in full, is especially worth consulting on this point.) Thyestes' speech is therefore conspicuous for the length of its catalogue of absent pleasures, which makes the two lines on the benefits of poverty seem perfunctory. [There is a similar imbalance in Ovid's account of the Golden Age in *Met.* 1.89–100, perhaps meant to imply the unreality of that idealized state.]

Many of the items in Thyestes' list are staples of the Roman iconography of excess, but one or two carry more specific associations. For example, not even the most abandoned hedonist in declamation oratory competed with Jupiter for divine honors (463–64); here at least the life Thyestes is describing must suggest that of a Roman emperor. (It may be relevant that the same paragraph in Suetonius' life of "Caligula" [22] records his enormous extension of the imperial palace [cf. 455–56] and the institution of his own divine cult.)

456 imminentem: "overhanging" (i.e., *civitati*), with clear connotations of menace and oppression, cf. *Tro.* 1085, *Oed.* 228 (and note 642–43 below, especially *urbem premit*). [This is Bentley's correction of the transmitted *eminentem*, which adds little to the previous phrase (*vertice alti montis impositam*) and which fails to account for the fear felt by the city below.]

456 humilis: the town is "low-lying" in relation to the *palazzo* on the hill-top, but also "humble" in status; it trembles at the house on the hill because of its inordinate size. The whole picture is strikingly similar to the account of the *domus Pelopia* in 641–45, a resemblance that suggests Thyestes is drawing on his own experience in sketching the life of the powerful.

457 altis . . . tectis: "on the lofty ceilings" (abl. of place); the reference is to ivory inlay on the *lacunaria*, or ornamental panel-work, cf. Hor. *C.* 2.18.1–2 *non ebur neque aureum / mea renidet in domo lacunar*, Sen. *NQ* 1 pr. 8 *lacunaria ebore fulgentia*.

458 excubitor: the highly specific word might make a Roman audience think of the imperial palace, cf. Suet. *Claud.* 42.1, *Nero* 8.

459 non classibus piscamur: i.e., I do not employ a fleet to catch fish for my dinner—an original (and delightfully hyperbolic) addition to the commonplace.

et: connects *piscamur* and *fugamus*, both governed by *non* (see on 774 below).

459-60 retro . . . mole: i.e., by driving piles into the sea-bed to serve as foundations for building, a practice often decried by moralists as unnatural, cf. Hor. *C.* 3.1.33–34, Sen. *Contr.* 2.1.13 (Fabianus) *litoribus quoque moles iniungunt congestisque in altum terris exaggerant sinus*, Sen. *Epist.* 89.21 *nec contenti solo nisi quod manu feceritis, mare agetis introrsus*, 122.8, Nisbet-Hubbard on Hor. *C.* 2.18.21.

460-61 nec . . . gentium: the reference is to the gourmet's fondness for imported delicacies, but *tributum gentium* recalls the tax levied by Rome on its provinces and thus implies the misuse of public wealth. Seneca is almost certainly echoing a phrase of the declaimer Argentarius quoted in his father's collection of *Suasoriae* (6.7): *popina tributo gentium instruitur*, referring to the lavish dinners of the "Second Triumvirate." In *Cons. Helv.* 10.5 Seneca applied the point to the gluttonous "Caligula," who despite great effort *vix tamen invenit quomodo trium provinciarum tributum una cena fieret*.

460 improbum: "remorseless," unsparing in its demands, cf. Austin on Verg. *Aen.* 4.386. Seneca may be refashioning Vergil's comparison (at *Aen.* 2.356–57) of the Trojans to ravenous wolves, *quos improba ventris / exegit caecos rabies*; by having *improbus* modify *venter* Seneca makes the organ seem to exert a will of its own. (Compare Fabianus *ap.* Sen. *Contr.* 2.1.11 *an, ne quid ventri negetur libidinique, orbis servitium expetendum est?*)

461 gentium: "whole nations," like *populi* in 648 below; cf. *Clem.* 1.8.5 (Seneca to Nero) *loqui non potes nisi ut vocem tuam quae ubique sunt gentes excipiant*.

mihi: "for my benefit," "to feed me."

462 ultra Getas . . . et Parthos: Roman terms for "at the ends of the earth"; for the frame of reference, cf. 369–79, 383–84.

463-64 non ture . . . arae: aspiring to divine honors is a form of megalomania found in myth, e.g., in Ovid's story of Niobe, which has influenced Seneca's wording (cf. *Met.* 6.171-72 *cur colitur Latona per aras, / numen adhuc sine ture meum est?*). But Roman audiences would surely have thought as well of their own emperors, most notably Gaius, who had replaced the head of a statue of Jupiter with his own likeness (cf. *excluso Iove*) and had styled himself *Iuppiter Latiaris* (Suet. *Cal.* 22).

464-65 nulla . . . silva: roof-top gardens are mentioned as early as Cicero (*frag. F.* 5.78), but were more common—or at least more often denounced—in the early Principate, cf. Sen. *Contr.* 5.5 *in summis culminibus mentita nemora*, Sen. *Epist.* 122.8 *non vivunt contra naturam qui pomaria in summis turribus serunt?*, with Summers's note.

465 nutat: *nutare* of swaying tree-tops can describe a placid (Verg. *Aen.* 9.682) or an ominous motion (*Aen.* 2.629). Here Thyestes pictures trees moving in a gentle breeze, but the darker meanings predominate in the Messenger's description of the palace grove (654–55). Cf. also Sen. *Epist.* 122.8 *silvae in tectis domuum ac fastigiis nutant*.

465–66 nec fumant . . . stagna: "nor do I have smoking pools, heated by many hands." Since water could only be heated by manual labor, an abundant supply of hot water was an advertisement of wealth, cf. Sen. *Epist.* 86.9 (of baths in simpler times) *non suffundebatur aqua nec recens semper velut ex calido fonte currebat*.

manu . . . multa: collective singular, cf. Hor. *C.* 1.5.1 *multa . . . in rosa*, Luc. 2.454 *multo milite*, K-S 1.67–70.

466 stagna: *stagnum* of a bathing-pool or basin is not attested before Seneca, and may imply enormous size; the *calentia stagna* of *Epist.* 122.8 are large enough for simulated sea-storms. (In Tac. *Ann.* 15.64.4 Seneca commits suicide by entering a *stagnum calidae aquae*.)

466–67 nec somno . . . datur: the perversity of drinking by night and sleeping by day is the subject of *Epist.* 122. The topic was usually handled with sardonic wit (cf. Mayor on Juv. 8.11, Sen. *Contr.* 3.1), but Thyestes' language is noticeably free of mockery or invective. Thyestes himself, of course, will invert day and night by over-indulgence in food and drink; the irony may explain why this item ends the catalogue of luxuries.

467 Baccho: by metonymy for "drinking," cf. 973 *satias . . . me . . . Bacchi tenet*.

iungenda: predicative with *datur*: "night is given to drinking to be joined to it," cf. *gestandus . . . venit* 7; *iungere* suggests that the union is not a natural one, cf. *Oed.* 54 *iuvenes . . . senibus iungit* (sc. *pestis*), a subtlety missing from the otherwise close parallel in Just. *Epit.* 12.13.7 *cum diei noctem perviligem iunxisset*.

468 non timemur: not being feared (and therefore hated) is one of the advantages of low status, cf. *Epist.* 105.4. Thyestes means the plural as generalizing ("we lowly people"), but an audience could see irony in its application to Thyestes himself, who is very much feared by his brother (cf. 40, 289–93, 314–16).

469 rebus . . . quies: another statement whose relevance to Thyestes is open to dispute: Atreus denies that his brother can accept *quies* (199).

[**magna**: this is E's reading; A has *alta*, which has good Senecan parallels (cf. *Ag.* 596 *pax alta*, *Clem.* 1.1.8 *securitas alta*), but which is for that reason more likely to be the result of interpolation (to which A is more prone than E). The banal antithesis *parvis-magna* suits the level of Thyestes' rhetoric. See also Leo, *Obs.*, 39.]

470 immane . . . pati: "to be able to do without a kingdom is itself an enormous kingdom." This attempt at a ringing *sententia* falls short of conviction. The choice of *pati* is revealing, a sort of "Freudian slip": by saying that he can "manage" or "get along" without a kingdom, Thyestes shows that he—unlike the Chorus, cf. 343, 380, 390—regards power as a positive good. For this sense of *pati* cf. *OLD* s.v., #6; in the other examples cited (Sen. *Contr.* 2.2.4, Sen. *NQ* 3 *pr.* 6) the things done without are clearly of great worth, a *vir* and a *patria*. [Lucan gives the idiom a characteristically sharp point: at 5.314 he urges Caesar *disce sine armis / posse pati*—"learn how to get along without warfare," implying that in Caesar's warped view war is a desirable thing.]

471–90 From this point on Thyestes gradually gives ground. His replies lack the firmness he showed earlier (442–44): he does not, e.g., dispute any of his son's gnomic assertions, however dubious (cf. 474–75, 487, 489–90), nor does he question Tantalus' faith in the gods (471, 489–90), even though it conflicts with his own skepticism (407). It is as though his long speech has weakened rather than strengthened his resolve, by reminding him of the comforts he has lacked in exile.

471–72 Nec abnuendum . . . nec appetendum est: the balanced phrases strike a judicious tone, cf. Cic. *Sen.* 72 *illud breve vitae reliquum nec avide appetendum senibus nec sine causa deserendum.* Both manner and content resemble Seneca's defence of his own wealth, cf. *VB* 23.2 *patrimonio per honesta quaesito nec gloriabitur nec erubescet,* 3 *magnas opes, munus fortunae* [cf. 430–31] *fructumque virtutis, non repudiabit nec excludet.*

473 errat . . . dolus: see on 282 above.

474–75 Redire . . . amor: Tantalus keeps up the knowing, gnomic tone. His appeal to the claims of kinship is plausible in general terms (cf. 549–59), but in this context it is clearly false: Atreus has formally banished *Pietas,* cf. 249–50 *excede, Pietas, si modo in nostra domo / umquam fuisti.*

476–82 Thyestes reacts incredulously to the suggestion that there could be love between himself and Atreus. It was common to lend emphasis to an assertion by claiming either that it will remain true as long as the universe obeys its laws or else that the operations of nature will cease before it is invalidated. (For examples see Smith on Tib. 1.4.65–66, Nisbet-Hubbard on Hor. *C.* 1.29.10.) The device is found here in an appropriately abnormal form: instead of supporting an assurance of undying love, or fame, or gratitude—cf., e.g., Prop. 1.15.29–30, 2.15.31–34, Verg. *Ecl.* 1.60–64, *Aen.* 1.607–10, Ovid *Pont.* 4.5.41–44—, Thyestes uses it to bolster a conviction of perennial hatred (similarly *Med.* 401–407). The cosmic scale of the impossible events (*adynata*) traditionally invoked also takes on a new significance: nature's laws *will* be overturned before the play is over, precisely because of an ostensible *foedus* between Atreus and Thyestes.

Thyestes lists two groups of *adynata,* first a miscellaneous set of unnatural phenomena (476–80 *terris*), then a trio of unthinkable unions (480–82 fire-water, death-life, sea-wind). It may be oversubtle to suggest that Thyestes is meant to sound long-winded, but these lines certainly lack the power of Medea's thrilling speech beginning *dum terra caelum media libratum feret* (401–407).

476–77 aetherias . . . pontus: the circumpolar constellations Ursa Major and Minor (= the two "bears" or *Arcti*) were never "drenched by the sea"; compare *Med.* 405 *dum siccas polus / versabit Arctos,* where *siccas* corresponds to *aetherias.* The Chorus foresees this *adynaton* coming to pass in 867–74 below.

477 Arctos: fem. pl.

477–78 Siculi . . . unda: "the ravaging waves of the stormy Sicilian sea." The strait between Italy and Sicily at Messina was notoriously dangerous, cf. 577–87 below, *Epist.* 14.8. For *Siculus aestus* cf. Stat. *S.* 1.3.97–98 *si . . . Siculos . . . per aestus / sit via, Th.* 10.623 *repercussum Libyco mare . . . ab aestu.* The somewhat vague combination *unda aestus* (gen.) is, to my knowledge, without parallel, but Ovid (?) *Her.* 21.41–42 [*navem*] *quam . . . Boreas propellit, aestus et unda refert* comes close, especially if *aestus et unda* is taken as a hendiadys. [I owe special thanks to Otto Zwierlein for help with this note.]

480 ante: carries on the construction begun with *prius* (476).

cum flammis aquae: an especially popular *adynaton,* cf. Otto s.v. *aqua* 1, Luck on Ovid *Tr.* 1.8.4.

481–82 fidem / foedusque: Thyestes' certainty that Atreus is incapable of *fides* and *foedus* is proven true in the final scene, cf. 1024 *hoc foedus? haec est gratia? haec fratris fides?*

482 Quam . . . times?: Tantalus challenges his father to define the danger he fears: *fraus* is here a specific act of deception (*OLD* s.v., #5), and *tamen* alludes to the shift in the argument ("granted that Atreus may hate you, what precisely are you afraid of?").

483 timori . . . modum: for other denials of *modus*, cf. 26, 255, 1051–52.

484 tantum . . . odit: "his potential (i.e., for harm) is as great as his hatred"—implying that neither has any limit. (An interesting extension of a common experience, that of being able to do something normally beyond one's powers when driven by a strong emotion. Ovid had invoked it to explain miraculous feats of agility, cf. *Met.* 4.528 *vires insania fecit*, 11.731, but Seneca goes further: Atreus' boundless *ira* and *odium* free him from all normal human restraints, and so in a perverse way he becomes omnipotent. See also on 885.)

485–86 vos . . . timendum: Thyestes' concern for his children may be quite genuine (cf. 975, 996), but by shifting the ground of his resistance from himself to them he also makes it easier to follow Tantalus' advice (488). By contrast, Atreus refuses to let concern for his own children deflect him from his purpose, 321–30.

486 cautus: emphatic, introducing Tantalus' new point ("are you afraid of being taken in, seeing that you are on your guard?"). [All Mss read *captus*, and *cautus* is a conjecture of Madvig. *Decipi captus times?* can only mean "are you afraid of being deceived, having been caught already?"; this would in fact describe Thyestes' situation, but there is no way for Tantalus to utter this sentiment. Madvig's emendation removes the problem and gives *cavendi* in 487 a needed point of reference.]

487 Serum . . . malis: to parry Tantalus' stress on wariness (*cautus*), Thyestes points out that prudence comes too late for one who has gone as far as he has. The thought is impeccably commonplace (cf. Publ. Syr. 684 *sero in periclis est consilium quaerere*), but the conclusion Thyestes draws is the opposite of that implied by conventional morality: he sees the contradictions of his position but uses them as a pretext for abandoning the fight. (See again at 964.) [Line 487 is given to Thyestes by S[2] and several late Mss, to Tantalus by E PCS[1]. The attribution to Thyestes has been supported by Zwierlein, *Philologus* 113 (1969), 264–65, who well states the arguments in its favor: 487 does not suit the confident Tantalus, and the echo *cautus-cavendi* should accompany a change of speaker, as consistently in this dialogue, cf. 472–73 *rogat / rogat*, 475–76 *amor / amat*, 482–83 *times / timori*, 484 *potest / potest*, 484–85 *in te / pro me*.]

488 eatur: see on 330 (and for the abruptness of Thyestes' announcement, cf. 542, *HF* 1295).

testor: "I declare" (by some public word or action, here by saying so openly).

489 vos sequor, non duco: a pathetic attempt to salve his conscience, which convicts him of failure to fulfill a parent's role as guide and model. Thyestes' willingness to "follow" links him with Tantalus as seen in the prologue, cf. 100 *sequor* (Tantalus' last word). [For "leading" and "following" as metaphors for a proper set of moral priorities, cf. *Ben.* 6.43.3.]

Respiciet: "will regard with favor," cf. *Ag.* 407 (n).

490 bene cogitata: "what has been well devised," by which Tantalus means the course of action he has urged on Thyestes, but which surely makes an audience think of Atreus' "well-devised" plot (cf. 320 *cogitas*, the only other appearance of the verb in the play).

perge: Tantalus re-enacts the exhortation of the Fury to his namesake (23).

non dubio gradu: reversing *nolentem gradum* in 420.

491–511 Atreus enters, catches sight of Thyestes and his sons, and delivers a long aside before addressing Thyestes in 508. The speech is a brilliantly original crossing of two dramatic conventions, the entrance-monologue of late Euripides and New Comedy (see on 404–20) and the "eavesdropping aside" of New Comedy, in which a character makes unnoticed remarks about his own intended actions or about the behavior of other characters on stage before a dialogue begins (cf., e.g., Men. *Dysc.* 149–52, Ter. *Ad.* 450–53). Seneca reverses the usual pattern of having a character already on stage comment aside on a new arrival and extends the aside to a length unparalleled even in Plautus. The result may be "untheatrical" by certain standards, but it is undeniably effective, displaying both Atreus' absolute control of the situation and his keen enjoyment of his power over Thyestes. The speech is also a pointed counterpart to Thyestes' opening monologue: while Thyestes' internal conflict withdrew him from his surroundings, Atreus remains intensely aware of every detail in the scene he is manipulating, from the pounding excitement of his own heart to the matted tangle of Thyestes' beard. [On asides in New Comedy, cf. D. Bain, *Actors and Audience* (Oxford, 1977), 105–34; in Seneca, Zwierlein, *Rezitationsdramen*, 63–67, also *HSCP* 82 (1978), 241–46.]

491 Plagis . . . fera: the hunting metaphor has been foreshadowed at 286–87.

tenetur: "is caught," cf. *Tro.* 630, *Med.* 550 (also in an aside); see on 973.

492 una: adverbial, "together."

generis invisi indolem: "the promise of this hateful race"; *indoles* often denotes an individual's "potential" or "capacity" (cf. *indoles virtutis* in Cic. *Cael.* 39 etc., *pro indole* "as a sign of promise," Quint. 12.6.3), and so *indoles generis* refers to the children who represent the race's potential for continued existence, cf. *Pha.* 869 *per . . . natorum indolem* ("by the promise of our children"). The language shows Atreus' characteristic skill and invention: the abstract (*indoles*) for the concrete (*liberi*) singles out the aspect of the children that most concerns him (see on *tumor Hadriae* 362); while *invisi* clashes with the normal positive overtones of *indoles* to produce an effective oxymoron (as one might speak of the "healthy growth" of a noxious weed).

493 cerno: points the parallel with Thyestes' first speech, cf. *cerno* 407.

tuto in loco: perhaps meant to be contrasted with *tuto positus loco* in 365.

494 versantur odia: *versari* here seems to mean "live/dwell/pass one's time" (*OLD* s.v., #10), cf. 280–81 *tam diu cur innocens / versatur Atreus?*, Ovid *Pont.* 1.2.15 *hostibus in mediis interque pericula versor*. Its use with *odia* is a remarkably strong personification, a sign of the way Senecan characters regard their emotions almost as living things; see on 496, 1056, *Med.* 953 *ira, qua ducis, sequor*. The echo of 280–81 might even suggest that Atreus thinks of his *odia* as nearly synonymous with himself, a notion taken up later, cf. 713.

494–95 venit . . . venit: this form of emphatic repetition (called *anadiplosis* or *epanalepsis*) conveys particularly strong emotion: savage joy, as here and *Ag.* 1011 *iam iam iuvat vixisse post Troiam, iuvat*, or deep bitterness, as in Andromache's ironic command at *Tro.* 901–902 *celebrate Pyrrhi, Troades, conubia, / celebrate digne* (with *digne* a pointed addition like *totus* here). Other examples in Canter, 157–58.

495 et totus quidem: "yes, and all of him," referring to the children; for Atreus "Thyestes" includes his offspring (note *iunctam parenti* 493, implying an inseparable bond). For *totus* compare *Tro.* 613–14 *nunc advoca astus, anime, nunc fraudes, dolos, / nunc totum Ulixem.*

496 vix . . . vix: Atreus' eagerness recalls Ovidian descriptions of characters scarcely able to contain erotic feelings, cf. *Met.* 2.862 (Jupiter) *vix iam, vix cetera differt*, 4.350 (Salmacis) *vix . . . moram patitur, vix iam sua gaudia differt*. The prospect of bloodshed gives Atreus the intense pleasure usually derived from sex.

vix tempero animo: "I can scarcely restrain my *animus*," a remarkable expression. In this sense *temperare* is most often combined with a reflexive pronoun (*mihi, sibi*, etc.) or a word denoting a part of the body (*linguae, manibus, oculis*, etc.). In the only other instance of *temperare animo* I have found, Curt. 5.9.9 *haud mirum est Dareum non temperasse animo, animus* means something like "temper" or "anger"; the closest parallel of all is perhaps Livy 5.45.7 *vix temperavisse animis quin extemplo impetum facerent*, where *temperare animis* is "to restrain oneself" (so too Vell. Pat. 2.34.2). This could be its meaning here, but there might be some point in taking *animo* as analogous to *manibus* or *linguae*, i.e., as naming the part of Atreus that is barely under control (cf. 267–68).

vix dolor frenos capit: the image of "reining in" emotions is common, cf. *Ag.* 207 (n), but here the metaphor takes on an unexpected life: having cast his *dolor* in the form of a hunting dog straining at the leash, Atreus elaborates the idea in a formal simile.

capit: "endures," "accepts," cf. 255.

497–503 The most striking instance of a typical feature of Senecan tragedy, the use of "epic" similes in dramatic speech; for other examples cf. *Ag.* 138–40, *Pha.* 181–83, *Med.* 382–84, 940–42, *Tro.* 572–76, 794–98. These similes, especially those in which characters describe their own feelings, have often been criticized as far-fetched or unnatural (cf., e.g., Zwierlein, *Rezitationsdramen*, 118 n. 17, Fantham on *Tro.* 672–76), but none is without dramatic point, and the most successful are well adapted to the character who delivers them. With Atreus, the length and detail of the simile reflect the control of language he shows throughout; one might suggest that the heaping up of descriptive phrases (*longo . . . loro, presso . . . ore, lento . . odore, tacito . . . rostro, cervice tota*) demonstrates the conscious pleasure he takes in imagining the scene. (At another level it is apt for Atreus to liken himself to an animal, since he is later compared to a ravenous tiger and lion, cf. 707–11, 732–36.)

Seneca may have derived some touches from the well-known similes of hunting dogs in Verg. *Aen.* 12.749–57 and Ovid *Met.* 1.533–38, but his simile is closer to a passage of Ennius' *Annales* (340–42 V[2]) in which an army impatient to meet the enemy is compared to a dog that has scented its prey: *veluti si quando vinclis venatica velox / apta solet si forte feras ex nare sagaci / sensit, voce sua nictit ululatque ibi acute*.

497 sagax: "keen-scented," as in Ennius; cf. also Silius 3.295–96 *Umber . . . sagax*.

498 Umber: perhaps suggested by Vergil's *vividus Umber* in *Aen.* 12.753. Umbrian dogs were renowned for their scent but were not given to attacking animals larger than themselves (cf. Grattius *Cyn.* 171–73); hence this dog barks for its master when it smells the prey close at hand. [In a simile influenced by these lines, Lucan speaks of dogs who do not bark even when the prey is found, but who signal by silently tugging on their leashes, 4.437–44.]

499 scrutatur: "probes"; Seneca is fond of this strongly graphic word, cf. *Tro.* 812 with Fantham's note.

dum: "as long as," with generalizing indicatives *sentit, pererrat*; it is balanced by *cum* 501.

499–500 lento . . . odore: "by its lingering smell"; *lentus* of things slow to fade or cease, cf. Ovid *Her.* 2.9 *spes quoque lenta fuit*, Sen. *NQ* 4B.4.3 *bruma lentas pluvias habet et tenues*.

500 pāret: "it obeys" (i.e., it does not try to get free of the leash).

501 pererrat: the verb suggests diligently traversing an area, cf. Verg. *Aen.* 5.441, 11.766, Ovid *Met.* 3.6, 9.645.

fuit: either generalizing perfect ("when the prey is closer") or an example of *esse* as a verb of motion, almost = *venire* ("when the prey has come nearer"), cf. Lewis and Short s.v. *sum* I.B.6; in this case *propior* would be the equivalent of, e.g., *in amicitiam* or *in conspectum* in Cic. *Caec.* 66, Suet. *Aug.* 16.

502 cervice tota: i.e., with all the strength in its neck.

503 morantem: seen from the animal's perspective.

seque retinenti eripit: perhaps an adaptation of Ovid *Met.* 1.537–38 *ipsis / morsibus eripitur* (a hare plucking itself from a hound's mouth).

retinenti: abl. of separation ("from the one holding it back"), cf. Livy 29.32.5 *sequentibus se eripuit*.

504 cum sperat ira sanguinem: just as the imagery of *vix dolor frenos capit* (496) anticipates the hunting-simile, so *sperat sanguinem* carries that language back into the actual situation.

nescit: *nescire* often denotes an absolute impossibility, cf. Hor. *AP* 390 *nescit vox missa reverti*, Sen. *Ag.* 113 *qui redire nescit cum periit pudor*. Atreus relishes the difficulty of the role he is about to assume.

505 aspice, ut: "just look at how . . ."; the construction is found in elevated poetry (cf., e.g., Verg. *Ecl.* 4.52), but here the tone of amused disgust gives it a colloquial flavor, cf. Pl. *Most.* 855 *quin tu illam aspice ut placide accubat*, Ovid *Ars* 1.315 *aspice ut ante ipsum teneris exsultet in herbis* (also illustrating exasperated address to a purely imaginary listener).

505–506 ut multo . . . coma: i.e., *ut coma, gravis multo squalore, obruat maestos vultus*. A small masterpiece of parody: the droll hyperbole in *obruat* and the arch symmetry of the word order reveal Atreus' scorn for the moral pretensions symbolized by Thyestes' hirsute appearance. (The closest parallel is in Seneca's warning to Lucilius in *Epist.* 5.2 against pseudo-philosophers who parade their ascetic habits: *asperum cultum et intonsum caput et neglegentiorem barbam et indictum argento odium et cubile humi positum* [cf. 451] *et quidquid aliud ambitionem perversa via sequitur evita*.)

505 gravis: perhaps an anticipation of the more sinister "heaviness" that afflicts Thyestes later, cf. 781, 910, etc.

506 squalore . . . coma: almost a "Golden Line" (abCBA, with *squalore* relating to *coma* through *gravis*), see on 10 above.

obruat: Thyestes' hair "obliterates" his features, cf. Lucilius 597 *squalitate summa ac scabie . . . obrutam*; similar hyperbole is popular in rhetorical prose, cf. Sen. *Contr.* 1.1.18 *obrutus sordibus*, Sen. *Epist.* 14.13 *obrutus sputis*, ps-Quint. *Decl.* 6.18 *aures impexis obrutae comis*.

maestos: "gloomy" or "woebegone," from ethical rigor or (more probably) lack of decent food; compare Marcus Aper's caricature of the orators of the past in Tac. *Dial.* 23.3 *maesti et inculti illam ipsam quam iactant sanitatem non firmitate sed ieiunio consequuntur*.

507 iaceat: Thyestes' beard "droops" rather than being neatly combed; compare *iacere* of unkempt hair, *Pha.* 804, ps-Ovid *Her.* 15.73.

praestetur fides: *praestare fidem* usually means "be true to one's word," "fulfill one's promises" (cf. *Pha.* 1142–43 *nec ulli praestat velox / Fortuna fidem*), and refers to the reconciliation that Atreus must now seem to go through with; but Atreus also means to say "let a show of *fides* be made, let a believable performance be given" (*fides* = "believ-ability," cf. Cic. *De or.* 2.156 *imminuit . . . et oratoris auctoritatem et orationis fidem*). It is a signal that his next words will be spoken "in his part" of the devoted brother.

508–11 Atreus' change of "voice" as he turns to Thyestes is reflected in his language, which becomes studiously plain. He is making a considerable effort to say only the "right" things, but even so he cannot resist the temptation to indulge in *double entendre*.

509 expetitos: "eagerly sought," in two senses.

510 sanguis ac pietas: a sort of hendiadys, "respect for the claims of blood" (for *sanguis* = "kinship" cf. Ovid *Met.* 9.466 *nomina sanguinis odit*, Val. Max. 2.1.7 *tantum religionis sanguini et adfinitati . . . tributum*). Atreus appears to be acting just as young Tantalus had predicted (cf. 474–75), but *sanguis* inevitably recalls 504 *sperat ira sanguinem*. The sacral overtones of *colatur* ("be worshiped") may also carry ironic force, since Atreus will in fact turn his bloodshed into a ritual act, cf. 689, etc.

512–21 Thyestes is completely taken in by Atreus' show of good will; he abandons all attempts to defend his past actions, and abjectly begs for Atreus' forgiveness. Seneca's character-portrayal is here very acute: Thyestes' uneasy awareness of his past crimes makes him particularly susceptible to Atreus' ploy, and blunts the suspicions he had expressed shortly before (473).

512 Diluere . . . fores: "if you were not as you are, I would be able to explain away everything." Thyestes has come prepared to rebut Atreus' charges against him. The lan-guage recalls the courtroom: *diluere crimen* is to "dilute" the force of an accusation (*OLD* s.v., #4), and is one of the many legalisms introduced into poetry by Ovid, cf. *Am.* 2.2.37, *RA* 695 *nec peccata refer, ne diluat*. See also on *causa* 514, *pedibus intactae manus* 518.

cuncta: like *omnia* in 513, the sweeping term conveys Thyestes' effusive tone.

513 admisi: "committed" (with an implied notion of wrongdoing), cf. Ovid *Pont.* 4.14.23 *sed nihil admisi* ("I've done nothing wrong").

514 causam: in the legal sense, "my case," cf. *OLD* s.v., #4, Ovid *Met.* 13.190 *difficilem tenui sub iniquo iudice causam*.

515 hodierna pietas: Thyestes means "the *pietas* you have shown today," but an audi-ence might take the words as suggesting "this *pietas* that lasts only for today."

515–16 est . . . nocens / . . . est nocens: Thyestes sums up his feelings of guilt in a somewhat ponderous *gnome*. For the figure of speech—*conversio*—in which the same word ends successive lines, cf. 207–208 *quos cogit metus / laudare, eosdem reddit inimicos metus*, Canter 158–59.

517 lacrimis agendum est: "tears are called for," surely a pointed contrast to Atreus' earlier rebuke to himself *questibus vanis agis?* (179).

518 pedibus intactae manus: Thyestes' hands are "untouched by feet" because he has never been a suppliant before, cf. Andromache in *Tro.* 691–93 *quam . . . nullius pedes / novere dextram pedibus admoveo tuis*.

At Roman trials friends of the accused sometimes prostrated themselves before the jury (Asconius *in Scaur.* p. 28 C, cited by Fantham on *Tro.* 691). Thyestes' gesture might recall this practice, but it conforms even more closely to another Roman ritual, the obeisance shown to emperors by client kings, cf. Suet. *Nero* 13.2 on Nero's reception of Tiridates in 66: *primo ad genua admisit adlevatumque dextra exosculatus est* (see also on 521–22, 599). Thyestes' next line strengthens this association, since client kings often sent their sons to Rome as pledges of loyalty, as in the case of Phraates IV of Parthia, who entrusted his four sons to Augustus, cf. Josephus *AJ* 18.42.

519 omnis ira . . . tumor: these words are similarly coupled in Verg. *Aen.* 8.40–41 *tumor omnis et irae / concessere deum.*

ponatur: = *deponatur,* cf. 348 *posuit,* Ovid *Met.* 8.474 *in . . . vices ponit positamque resuscitat iram.*

519-20 ex animo tumor . . . abeat: an unwitting inversion of Atreus' real state of mind, cf. 267–70 *nescioquid . . . animus . . . tumet . . . hoc, anime, occupa.*

520 erasus: properly used of scraping or paring away excess growth, but here apparently a synonym for *deletus* or *sublatus,* cf. *Epist.* 104.20 *omnem ex animo erade nequitiam.* (Applied to *tumor,* however, *eradere* might retain some of its basic meaning, cf. Celsus 8.10.7 *ut, si quid pingue est, eradatur.*)

obsides fidei: "pledges of my good faith," cf. Cic. *Fam.* 10.17.3 *Apellam . . . quo obside fidei illius et societatis in re publica administranda uterer.*

[**fidei accipe**: scanned *fĭdĕī͜ āccĭpĕ*; for *fidei* (always an anapestic fifth foot) see also 764, *HF* 370.]

521 frater: the simple vocative at the end of the speech is a sign of Thyestes' guileless trust.

521-22 A . . . pete: Atreus makes the gracious response that also signifies his acceptance of Thyestes' plea, cf. Hom. *Il.* 24.515, Suet. *Nero* 13.2 (see on 518).

523 senum praesidia: if the *senes* are himself and Thyestes, Atreus is imagining a harmonious future in which Thyestes' children will look after both of them. This seems to have more point than taking *senum praesidia* as an implied generalization ("young men are the protectors of the old").

tot iuvenes: Atreus lingers for a moment over the number of Thyestes' children, savoring his revenge in advance.

524-26 squalidam . . . meis: changes of clothing often portend disaster in tragedy, especially when the new garments are rich or exotic, cf. Eur. *Ba.* 912–76, Sen. *Tro.* 883 *depone cultus squalidos, festos cape,* Ag. 881–83. (The "tapestry-scene" in Aesch. *Ag.* 908–74 presents a variant of this motif.) Here the proffered regalia symbolize the temptation to power that Thyestes cannot in the end resist.

525 oculis . . . nostris parce: "show some consideration for my eyes"; Atreus wryly suggests that Thyestes in his present state is painful to look at. (Seneca similarly uses *auribus parcere* of avoiding offensive or rebarbative language, cf. *Ben.* 2.11.6, *NQ* 2.2.4.)

525-26 ornatus . . . pares meis: "adornments equal to my own" (*ornatus* acc. pl.); *ornatus* appears only here in the tragedies, *ornare* three times in *Thyestes,* always with negative overtones (54, 464, 684).

526 laetus: inoffensive in its context, but perhaps paralleling 277–78 *liberos . . . /*

gaudens . . . laceret; Atreus' revenge is not complete unless Thyestes actively participates in it, cf. 285–86, 1065–68.

imperi: the syncopated form of the genitive singular (*-i* for *-ii*), which had fallen out of common use by the end of the Augustan age, is used thereafter for metrical convenience, cf. *Ag*. 155 *coniugi*.

527 capesse: more than a high-flown synonym for *cape*, since *imperi capesse partem* must recall *rem publicam capessere*, "to enter public life" (cf. *OLD* s.v. *capesso*, #8b, Cic. *Sest*. 23 *rem publicam capessere hominem bene sanum non oportere*). Thyestes' situation evokes that of a Stoic or Epicurean deciding whether to embark on a public career.

laus: "praiseworthy action," "grounds for praise," cf. Ovid *Pont*. 4.8.89 *unde tuas possim laudes celebrare recentes*.

528 paternum . . . decus: probably not just "ancestral dignity" (Miller) or "royal birthright" (Watling), but the ancestral diadem, the *regium capiti decus* of 701, cf. *HF* 257, Ovid *Met*. 9.690 *regale decus*. Atreus here extends the diadem, which remains suspended between the brothers until Thyestes accepts it at 542.

529 habere . . . dare: a plausible facsimile of a Senecan *gnome*, comparable to his advice to Nero that granting life is superior to taking it (*Clem*. 1.5.6 *vita enim etiam superiori eripitur, numquam nisi inferiori datur*); the distinction between *casus* and *virtus* is also authentically Senecan, cf. *VB* 24.1 (*consilium* vs. *casus* and *impetus*), *Epist*. 29.3 (*casus* vs. *ars*). Atreus' glib dictum is undermined, however, by the earlier passages it recalls: 36 *fluctu . . . regnum casus assiduo ferat*, which places all external *regnum* in the control of chance, and 390 *hoc regnum sibi quisque dat*, which makes it impossible for anyone to receive true *regnum* at another's hands.

530–31 Di . . . rependant: another irony that remains hidden from Thyestes: his last words in the play will invoke divine punishment on Atreus for his crimes, 1110–11.

531–33 Thyestes gives two reasons for declining Atreus' offer: that the poverty of his chosen way of living (*squalor . . . noster*) is incompatible with royal status, and that the guilt of his past actions (*manus infausta*) makes him unsuited to rule. These are noticeably less forceful arguments than the ones Thyestes used earlier with his son, 442–44.

531 regiam capitis notam: cf. 346.

532 squalor: a preference for *squalor* is among the ascetic practices criticized in *Epist*. 5.4 *hoc contra naturam est, torquere corpus suum et faciles odisse munditias et squalorem adpetere et cibis non tantum vilibus uti sed taetris et horridis*.

532–33 manus . . . refugit: Thyestes again speaks of his body as if it were independent of himself (cf. 419–20), perhaps because he does not wholeheartedly shun the prospect of rule.

533 infausta: probably thinking of his adultery with Aerope, Thyestes claims that he would bring evil fortune on the sceptre by accepting it.

533–34 liceat . . . turba: "allow me to be lost in the crowd" (*media turba* = the common people), cf. *Clem*. 1.8.1 *condicio eorum qui in turba . . . latent*, *Ag*. 103–104 *felix mediae quisquis turbae / sorte quietus* (n).

534 Recipit . . . duos: a flat contradiction of Thyestes' own conviction (444) and of all ancient thinking on the subject; it is astonishing (and revealing) that Thyestes allows it to pass.

535 Meum . . . tuum: Thyestes means that he does not need to share formally in governing the kingdom, since his closeness to Atreus gives him all he could desire; the underlying principle is that of the proverbial κοινὰ τὰ τῶν φίλων. (For a similar argument cf. Creon in *Oed.* 687–93.) Considering the prior relations between the brothers, though, the remark is a serious blunder: Atreus is bound to interpret it as meaning "I regard the kingdom you now rule as belonging to me," cf. 289 *regna nunc sperat mea*.

536 Quis . . . abnuit?: Atreus uses in a crisper form the same arguments as young Tantalus (cf. 430–31, 445, 471).

influentis: transferred from *dona* (hypallage, see on 255 above). In *Epist.* 50.5 Seneca denies that *mens bona* can "pour in" by chance, *illud desperandum est, posse nobis casu tantum bonum influere*.

537 Expertus . . . effluant: since Thyestes clearly meets the specified condition (*expertus*, cf. 453 *expertus loquor*), the universal form of his statement exerts added pressure on him to abide by its terms.

538 gloria: ostensibly the renown won by a generous act, but Atreus is thinking ahead to a different sort of glory, cf. 1097 *nunc parta vera est palma*.

539 Tua . . . mea: Thyestes means that, by offering a share of power, Atreus has already earned his praise (*peracta est* = "is complete"), but that his own praise is still to be won (*restat*), that is, the praise that will follow his resolute indifference to wealth and power. Once again, though, Thyestes unwittingly incriminates himself: Atreus can understand him to mean "your glory is finished, but mine is still to come," with *gloria* standing for the position of king, and *peragere* in the sense "complete the tenure of," like *peragere consulatum* (*OLD* s.v. *peragere*, #5b).

540 respuere . . . mihi: this line has all the appearances of a decisive statement. The language is forceful (*respuere, certum est*), and by departing from the stichomythic pattern Thyestes seems to imply that there is nothing more to be said. To dramatize Thyestes' fundamental lack of strength, Seneca makes his change of mind seem an instantaneous abandonment of a deeply-felt conviction.

respuere: of scornful rejection, *Epist.* 13.12 *robore animi evidentem quoque metum respue*, *Ag.* 390 (n).

certum: "fixed," "unalterable," cf. Ovid *Met.* 9.684 *certa sua est Ligdo sententia*.

541 Why does Atreus' threat to resign his own share of power affect Thyestes so strongly? The answer is perhaps suggested by 535: Thyestes hopes for the comforts of high status without its responsibilities, and so he is shaken by the prospect of having to resume a life of poverty.

Meam . . . tuam partem: perhaps a mocking echo of Thyestes' words, cf. 535 *meum . . . tuum*, 539 *tua . . . gloria . . . mea*.

542 regni nomen: "the title of dominion," rather than the thing itself (*OLD* s.v. *nomen*, #16), an ironic echo of Thyestes' assertion that high position only attracts through *falsa nomina* (446).

impositi: with *feram*, *impositi* suggests a burden Thyestes has agreed to shoulder, cf. Ovid *Met.* 15.820 *impositum feret unus onus*, of Augustus assuming responsibility for the Roman empire.

543 iura . . . servient . . . tibi: Thyestes means that "the laws will be under your command" (cf. Ovid *Met.* 15.831 *pontus quoque serviet illi*, again of Augustus), but one cannot help recalling that for Atreus *cura iuris* is a mere *privatum bonum* (216–18) and that the ultimate effect of his rule is to be the extinction of all law (*ius . . . omne pereat* 48).

mecum: i.e., *et ego tibi serviam*, another statement that carries a meaning not evident to Thyestes.

544 vincla: *vinc(u)lum* can be used of headgear, cf. Ovid *F.* 4.870 (a garland), Sen. *Pho.* 471 (a helmet), *Tro.* 273 (a diadem). Atreus, however, is well aware of the *double entendre* in his words (*gerere vinc(u)la* = "to be bound by chains," cf. Ovid *Met.* 4.681) and knows that by getting Thyestes to accept the diadem he has made him helplessly captive.

545 ego . . . dabo: a final specimen of Atrean wit. The exit to perform a sacrifice is common in Senecan drama (cf. *HF* 514–15, *Med.* 299–300, *Ag.* 583–85, 802–807), and Atreus seems to be mimicking the prescribed formula while giving it a gruesome new meaning: the "sacrifice" he means to offer will have Thyestes' sons as its victims, cf. 685–95, 712–16, etc. (Similarly loaded phrasing in *HF* 899, *Med.* 39.)

destinatas victimas: "designated offerings"; *destinare* of a sacrificial victim, cf. Verg. *Aen.* 2.129 *me destinat arae* (Sinon on his fictitious escape from the Greeks).

superis dabo: not merely a deception: the victims will be offered to Atreus' *ira* and Atreus himself, cf. 712–13, but their deaths make Atreus think he has attained the status of a god, see on 885, 911.

CHORUS III

The ode begins with astonished relief at the apparent reconciliation of the brothers. Comparing the city's sudden calm with its recent state of near-panic, the Chorus is led to reflect on the mutability of human affairs; its closing words urge restraint on kings and detachment from the moment on all of humanity.

The Chorus's deluded optimism, playing against the edgy ironies of the previous scene, heightens the suspense preceding the Messenger's grisly report. In this function it resembles several choral odes in Sophocles which express a hope that is immediately crushed by news of catastrophe (cf. *Ajax* 693–717, *Trach.* 633–62, *Ant.* 1115–54, *OT* 1086–1109).[1] Seneca's handling of the ode differs from Sophocles' in an important respect. Both dramatists exploit the ironic potential of the situation,[2] but Sophocles' Choruses maintain their cheerfulness to the end, thus increasing the shock of the following reversal, while the mood of this ode grows progressively darker as the grim past gives place to the unknown future, until at last the Messenger's report seems a natural extension of the Chorus's own thoughts.[3]

At no point, in fact, does Seneca's Chorus abandon itself entirely to happiness; words denoting "fear" and "dread" recur with almost obsessive regularity throughout, suggesting

---

[1] This type of stasimon is virtually unique to Sophocles (cf. R. W. B. Burton, *The Chorus of Sophoclean Tragedy* [Oxford, 1980], 31), and appears only here in Seneca (although *Ag.* 310–404 is remotely similar); there may have been an ode of this sort in Sophocles' *Thyestes*.

[2] For Sophocles cf., e.g., *OT* 1094–95, and for Seneca see notes on, e.g., 546 *credat hoc quisquam?*, 559 *negantes*, 614.

[3] This link has its verbal equivalent in the Messenger's echoing of the Chorus's last words: *res deus nostras celeri citatas / turbine versat—quis me per auras turbo praecipitem vehet?* (621–23).

that anxiety has been suppressed rather than allayed.[4] Even in the opening sections, memories of danger outweigh the celebration of deliverance (552-57 vs. 558–59, 561b–71 vs. 560–61a, 573–76), and the long sea-simile also gives more prominence to the raging storm than to the calm that succeeds it (577–87 vs. 588–95).[5] By these unbalanced proportions the Chorus nicely illustrates its own maxim: *dolor ac voluptas / invicem cedunt; brevior voluptas* (596–97).

In its thoughts on change and unpredictability the Chorus seems markedly less confident than in its previous ode. There it dwelt on the security conferred by *mens bona* (380), but the picture of human life in the closing lines of this ode (607–22) implicitly rules out seclusion and self-sufficiency. If "every kingdom is under the sway of a more oppressive power" (612), can the dominion of the *sapiens* (390) be exempt? The question is answered by the unobtrusive yet climactic *nostras* (621): we are all caught up in the whirlwind, and only by renouncing attachment to the present can we hope to withstand its blast.

The ode is more interesting for the complexity of its movement and the intricacy of its design than for the power of its poetry. The unvarying hendecasyllables do not escape monotony,[6] there are several inert adjectives,[7] and the elaborate storm-simile, though justified by its structural importance, seems to lose focus and to decline into preciousness.[8] The ode's best things are its sharply observed details: a wife's alarm at the sight of her husband transformed into a soldier (564), the night guard nervously crouching at his post on the ramparts (570–71), and—perhaps most memorable—counting the fish that swim in the clear water beneath one's idling boat (593).

Meter: Sapphic hendecasyllables (see above, p. 32).

546-48 The Chorus is reacting to Atreus' aside in 491–507; not having overheard his words, the Chorus attributes his long "silence" to amazement at the sight of his brother.

546 Credat: potential subjunctive (AG 447.3), with implied condition ("would anyone believe this [without having seen it]?"). The irony may seem too blatant to be effective, but the question reminds the audience that Thyestes *has* accepted this "unbelievable" show of *pietas*; it may also suggest that even the Chorus finds it difficult to give it full credence (cf. 640).

ferus: a stong term of condemnation, cf. *Ben.* 7.19.5 *non tantum malus sed ferus, sed immanis.* It is apt for Atreus, who is several times described in bestial images, cf. 497–503, 707–11, 732–36.

---

[4] Cf. 562 *pallidae*, 563 *timuit*, 570 *pavidus*, 571 *anxiae*, 572 *timor* (but see note *ad loc.*), 573 *minae*, 580 *timuere*, 582 *metuit*, 587 *tremente*, 590 *timuit*, 595 *timuere*, 600 *tremuere*, 603 *minanti*, 604 *anxius*, 605 *metuit*, 610 *expavescit*, 611 *minatur*.

[5] The respective lengths of the simile's components are even more lopsided than they at first appear, since in the "calm" section 588–95 four of the eight lines actually look back to the storm (590–91, 594–95).

[6] Note, for example, the eleven instances of the *-ere* form of the perfect, all at the same point in the line: 554, 562, 563, 573, 577, 580, 588, 592, 595, 600, 601.

[7] Cf., e.g., 552 *magnis . . . causis*, 573 *saevi . . . ferri*, 608 *ius . . . magnum.*

[8] See notes on 582–85, 586–87. Extended similes in Senecan lyrics often seem to wander from their subject, cf. *Ag.* 64–72 (n. on 57ff.), *Pha.* 764–72.

547 nec potens mentis: "unable to control his mind" (*mentis* obj. gen.), cf. *Ag.* 126 *consili impotens* (n), Livy 9.14.5 *suarum impotens rerum*. The description ironically fits Thyestes better than the calculating Atreus, cf. especially 919 *nec satis menti imperat*.

548 haesit: "stopped dead" (*OLD* s.v., #10); perhaps an echo of Verg. *Aen.* 3.597 *paulum aspectu conterritus haesit*.

549-59 The power of *pietas* is first stated in general terms (549–51), then illustrated by Mycenae's recent escape from civil war (552–59); the key term neatly frames the section, occupying the same metrical position in its first and last lines. The signs of imminent conflict correspond closely to the measures ordered by Atreus in his opening speech (180–90). From the Chorus's perspective, however, they sound much more real than they did earlier; in fact the ode seems to presuppose that Mycenae was poised to repel an armed attack by Thyestes and his supporters.

550 externis: "in the case of strangers," "where strangers are concerned," dat. of reference (AG 376). In Roman terms *externus* could suggest wars against foreign opponents as distinct from civil war (cf. Cic. *Leg. agr.* 2.90 *domesticis externisque bellis*, Ovid *Am.* 1.8.41–42 *nunc Mars externis animos exercet in armis / et Venus Aeneae regnat in urbe sui*); Roman associations are overt later, cf. on 560–61, 565–66.

551 quos . . . tenebit: the thought is similar to that in 474–75, but the implicit metaphor in *tenere* ("hold fast") sounds like an ironic echo of 491 *plagis tenetur . . . fera*.

552 cum: generalizing *cum* in a temporal clause with the verb in the indicative (AG 547).

magnis . . . causis: compare Atreus' statement of his grievances (178–79): *post tot scelera, post fratris dolos / fasque omne ruptum*.

553 gratiam rupit: *gratia* here almost = *amicitia* (*OLD* s.v., #2). The metaphor in *rupit* (for which cf. Hor. *Epist.* 1.3.31–32 *an male sarta / gratia nequiquam coit et rescinditur?*) echoes *fas . . . ruptum* in 179 (see note *ad loc.*).

cecinitque bellum: cf. 187 *bellicum . . . canat*.

554 leves . . . turmae: cf. 184–85 *sub nostro sonet / Argolica tellus equite*; *turma* is a technical term for a squadron of cavalry (used by Vergil for Roman coloring at *Aen.* 11.599).

leves: "fleet," cf. *Pho.* 545 *equitatu levi*.

frenis sonuere: a variation on *frenos sonantes* or *frena sonantia* in Augustan writers (cf. Verg. *G.* 3.184, Ovid *Met.* 2.121), with a characteristic displacement of the graphic term (*sonare*).

555 hinc illinc: "on this side and that," cf. *undique* 183.

agitatus ensis: "brandished," cf. 183–84 *strictum . . . micare ferrum*.

556-57 quem . . . recentem: a conventional picture of Mars, cf., e.g., Verg. *Aen.* 12. 332–33 *sanguineus Mavors clipeo increpat . . . bella movens* (and note 713 *crebros ictus*).

557 sanguinem . . . recentem: "fresh bloodshed," implying that Mars' appetite needs to be constantly assuaged with new victims.

558 manibus . . . iunctis: *Pietas* links the kinsmen's hands in friendship, cf. Luc. 1.117 *armatas manus* (of Caesar and Pompey) *excusso iungere ferro*. The phrase may ironically foreshadow Atreus' real actions, cf. 685 *post terga iuvenum nobiles revocat manus*.

559 ducit ad pacem: the wording implies a procession with *pax* at its end-point, as if it were an altar or temple, cf. Verg. *G.* 2.146–48 *albi . . . greges . . . Romanos ad templa deum duxere triumphos.*

negantes: concessive, "even though they withheld their consent." The Chorus credits *Pietas* with the power to overcome the combatants' own wills, but its words unwittingly correspond to the true situation, in which Atreus rejects the claims of *Pietas* while going through the motions of reconciliation.

560–76 Mycenae's recent danger and sudden rescue.

560–61 Otium . . . fecit?: a clear echo of Verg. *Ecl.* 1.6 *deus nobis haec otia fecit*; by opposing *otium* to the *arma civilis . . . belli*, Seneca makes explicit a connection that remains below the surface of Vergil's poem. Vergil's confident assertion has become a question, another instance of uncertainty about the gods' activities or even existence, cf. 127–32, 407.

562 crepuere: "rattled," "clattered," cf. Verg. *G.* 2.540 *impositos duris crepitare incudibus enses*, Ovid *Met.* 1.143 *crepitantia concutit arma* [sc. *bellum*]. (Both passages refer, directly or by allusion, to civil war at Rome.)

563 pallidae . . . matres: an obvious reworking, in plainer language, of Verg. *Aen.* 7.518 *trepidae matres pressere ad pectora natos* (as war breaks out between the Trojans and Latins).

564 armato: emphatic; the wife does not normally see her husband in armor (cf. Juv. 6.154 *armatis . . . nautis* of the Argonauts), and so fears for his safety.

marito: "on behalf of her husband," dat. of advantage (AG 376), cf. Verg. *Aen.* 2.729 *me . . . pariter comitique onerique timentem.*

565–66 cum . . . quietae: the sword is "unwilling" because the rust that has dulled its edge makes it hard to grasp; it does not "follow" the hand in the sense of fitting itself neatly to the hand's grip. (This sense of *sequi* is not common, but cf. Verg. *G.* 3.564–65 *olentia sudor / membra sequebatur*, where it means "follow the course of.") The personification is unusual and striking; in this play even inanimate objects are forced to act against their will. (See on 100 *sequor*, above, p. 47).

566 vitio: "through the harmful effects of," cf. *Epist.* 109.7 *sunt . . . quidam quibus morbi vitio mel amarum videatur.* Rusting weapons are normally seen as welcome signs of peace, cf. Verg. *G.* 1.493–95, Tib. 1.10.49–50, but the overtones of *vitio* suggest instead the view of a soldier for whom warfare is the norm.

567–71 In 565–66 the focus shifts from the fearful onlookers to the male citizen-soldiers, whose preparations for attack are sketched in four brief scenes. The three infinitives at the same point in successive lines (*stabilire, renovare, cohibere*) deftly suggest concurrent activities directed to a common goal. [This picture of bustling effort may owe something to Aeneas' first view of Carthage in *Aen.* 1.423–28 *pars ducere muros / molirique arcem et manibus subvolvere saxa, / pars optare locum tecto et concludere sulco . . . hic portus alii effodiunt, hic lata theatris / fundamenta petunt*, etc.]

567–68 labentes . . . situ quassas: like its defenders' weapons, Mycenae's walls and watchtowers have been allowed to fall into decrepitude; this emphasis makes the struggle to restore them sound plausibly urgent, but it jars slightly with the impression given earlier (cf., e.g., 339–42) of a city long accustomed to strife.

568 situ quassas: almost a paradox, since *quatere* usually denotes violent battering (e.g., of ships by storm-winds, Verg. *Aen.* 1.552, Ovid *Tr.* 5.11.13), whereas *situs* implies slow decay and is more naturally coupled with, e.g., *labi* (Columella 12.3.5, Sen. *Oed.* 817–18). The juxtaposition suggests imperceptibly gradual decline ending in sudden collapse; a good example of "Silver" compression.

569 claustris: the iron bolts that secure the doors, cf. Verg. *Aen.* 7.185 *portarum ingentia claustra.* Seneca's wording recalls Hor. *Epist.* 2.1.155 *claustra . . . custodem pacis cohibentia Ianum,* but with an inversion of sense, since bolting the doors of Janus' temple was a sign that Rome was at peace.

570 certabat: "was struggling/striving," apparently without the usual sense of competition, cf. Ovid *F.* 1.213 *quaerere ut absumant, absumpta requirere certant.*

pinnis: sc. *murorum,* the parapets on top of the ramparts; *pinna* in this sense belongs to Roman military language (cf. Caes. *BG* 5.40.6, Livy 40.45.3, etc.) and was used by Vergil for its Roman associations at *Aen.* 7.158–59 *primas . . . in litore sedes / castrorum in morem pinnis atque aggere cingit;* cf. also *Tro.* 1070.

pinnis: dat. with *incubabat,* cf. Ovid *Met.* 6.431–32 *tecto . . . profanus / incubuit bubo.*

571 noctis vigil: a poetic equivalent for *vigil nocturnus* (for which cf. Pl. *Am.* 350, Pliny *NH* 10.46), on the analogy of *vigil castrorum* ([Caes.] *BG* 8.35.4) or *vigil urbis* (*Eleg. in Maec.* 1.14).

incubabat: like the watchman who delivers the prologue to Aeschylus' *Agamemnon,* this guard crouches on the roof-top but does not dare fall asleep.

[**noctis**: the manuscripts divide between *noctis* (E) and *nocti* (A); *nocti* would be governed by *incubabat* in a different sense ("was brooding over the night"), and *pinnis* would then be abl. of place. The objection to *nocti* is that it does not cohere well with *incubabat;* as the examples in *OLD* s.v. *incubare* #5 show, the verb in this sense implies either jealous possessiveness or threatening hostility (cf. also 733 below), neither of which applies to the fretful watchman.]

572 [I have bracketed this line, which appears in all the manuscripts, because it seems intrusive. A *gnome* at this point breaks the close focus of the section, which is concerned with the recent dangers of Mycenae, and also loosens the link between 567–71 and 573–76 by creating a premature sense of closure. (This structural damage can be seen in editions that begin a new section at 573 instead of the correct place, 577.) For other intruded gnomic statements cf. 388–89 above, *Tro.* 1143–44, *Oed.* 100, *Ag.* 934.]

timor ipse: logically *ipse* seems to cohere with *bello* rather than *timor* ("fear of war is worse than war itself," cf. *HF* 706 *ipsa . . . morte peior est mortis locus*); for a similar displacement, cf. Ovid (?) *Her.* 12.61 *hinc amor hinc timor est; ipsum timor auget amorem.*

573–76 The counterpart to the previous scenes of anxious exertion and an elaboration of the *otium* mentioned in 560.

iam: balances *modo* 561.

minae: cf. 338 *fratrum . . . minas.*

574–75 iam . . . strepentis: an inverted echo of Hor. *C.* 2.1.17–18 *iam nunc minaci murmure cornuum / perstringit auris, iam litui strepunt.* (Horace's stanza also contains a triple *iam,* as in 573–75.)

classicorum . . . litui: Roman poets often pair military musical instruments, cf. Hor. *C.* 1.1.23–24 *lituo tubae / permixtus sonitus,* 2.1.17–18 (just quoted), Ovid *Met.* 1.98 *non tuba derecti, non aeris cornua flexi.* With typical exuberance Lucan describes a complete brass ensemble: *stridor lituum clangorque tubarum / non pia concinuit cum rauco classica cornu* (1.237–38, cf. 7.476–77).

576 revocata: perhaps suggesting an exile invited to return (cf. *OLD* s.v., #3b); the personification of *pax* would then balance its "concretizing" in 559 (see note).

577–95 Despite its great length, this simile is fairly simple in thought: when the Sicilian sea grows stormy, Scylla roars and sailors fear Charybdis, the Cyclopes fear for their forges, and Laertes thinks Ithaca might be submerged; but when the winds fall, the sea lies open for sport and leisure. The primary interest of the passage (and also its main weakness) lies in its fullness of detail.

577 ex alto: "from their depths," cf. Sen. *NQ* 6.24.3 *terram ex alto moveri,* perhaps Caes. *BG* 3.12.1 *cum ex alto se aestus incitavisset.*

578 Bruttium . . . pontum: Bruttium is the ancient name of the southernmost region of Italy (modern Calabria); *pontus Bruttius* is an (apparently unique) equivalent for *mare Siculum* (see note on 477–78).

Coro: the northwest wind, a favorite in Senecan storm-scenes, cf. *Ag.* 484 (n).

579–81 Scylla . . . Charybdis: the proper names neatly frame this brief section, and the verbs they govern also form a matched pair (*resonat, revomit*).

579 Scylla . . . cavernis: based on Verg. *Aen.* 3.431–32 *vasto vidisse sub antro / Scyllam et caeruleis canibus resonantia saxa.* Seneca's changes heighten an already harrowing image of frenzy: Scylla herself, rather than the dogs that teem around her, produces a roaring noise, in furious protest at the battering of her cave by the winds (*pulsatis . . . cavernis*).

580 in portu: either the sailors remain in harbor rather than face the sea churned up by Charybdis, or else Charybdis makes even the water in the harbor violent enough to cause fear. [Instead of *in portu* the A manuscripts read *in tutum,* which makes no sense. I have considered *inflatum,* describing the sea swollen when Charybdis spews forth the water it has sucked in; cf. Verg. *Aen.* 3.422 *fluctus rursus . . . sub auras / erigit alternos et sidera verberat unda,* and for *inflare* of water swelled by additional water cf. Livy 23.19.4, 40.33.2. The change would produce a more vivid image, and would also introduce an effective link between this section and the later line *ponite inflatos tumidosque vultus* 609. (Some later Mss. read *intortum,* which conveys a similar sense and is even closer to the A reading.) Emendation is not, however, clearly required, and the parallel between the sailors cowering in harbor and the citizens of Mycenae inside their walls might favor retaining *in portu.*]

timuere: generalizing perfect, cf. also 592 *patuere.*

581 rapax: cf. on 360 *rapiens;* the epithet is applied to Scylla in Ovid *Met.* 7.63.

haustum revomit: the metaphor recalls Ovid *Met.* 13.731 *vorat haec raptas revomitque carinas, RA* 740 *hic vomit epotas dira Charybdis aquas,* but it may carry added point in a Thyestean context; *haurio* appears twice in the last act in connection with Thyestes' feast, cf. 985, 1105.

582–85 The emotional coherence of the scene begins to waver; the image of the Cyclopes concerned for their blast-furnaces is droll rather than moving or awe-inspiring, and the diction displays its artifice so openly as to rule out empathy.

582 parentem: Homer's Cyclopes were children of Poseidon (cf. *Od*. 1.30–33, 9.412, also, e.g., Eur. *Cycl*. 21, Gell. 15.21) and *Neptunus* often = *mare* (*OLD* s.v., #2a), so "the Cyclops fears his parent" is a mannered way of saying that he fears the turbulent sea. Such expressions are often playful, as when Ovid describes Diana as *fraternis languida flammis* in *Met*. 2.454 (*frater* = Apollo, often identified with the Sun-god), but here the child's fear of its parent is another instance, though a remote one, of the distortion of family ties (cf. 40–41 *expavescat . . . natus . . . patrem*). [To make this point Seneca conflates Homer's sheep-tending Cyclopes, descended from Poseidon, with the forge-workers of Hephaestus/Vulcan who appear first in Hesiod, *Theog*. 139–40.]

583 in: with *rupe* (= *residens in rupe ferventis Aetnae*); the wide displacement is another sign of mannered writing.

rupe . . . residens: an echo, perhaps unconscious, of a very different scene involving the Cyclops Polyphemus, cf. Ovid *Met*. 13.786–87 (Galatea speaking) *latitans ego rupe meique / Acidis in gremio residens*.

ferventis: "blazing," because of the fires within the mountain.

584 ne . . . violetur: dependant on *metuit* in 582; "he fears his parent, (afraid) that," etc.

violetur: a strong word, suggesting that it would be a profanation for the fire to be put out, as if Vulcan's fire were a sacred trust, like the flame guarded by the Vestal Virgins at Rome. (These associations might be strengthened by *aeternis* in 585, since the fire sacred to Vesta was called an *ignis aeternus*, cf. Livy 5.52.7, 26.27.14, Verg. *Aen*. 2.296–97.)

585 aeternis: probably "ever-burning," on the analogy of *aeternus* used of ever-flowing streams (Ovid *Met*. 15.551, *Am*. 3.6.20) or ever-falling snows (Manil. 3.358).

586–87 The scale of the imagined storm suddenly becomes vastly greater, and its effects are said to be felt on Ithaca, at the other side of the Ionian sea. (Perhaps an anticipation of the universal destruction envisaged in the final chorus; compare *mergi . . . posse* 586 with the stronger assertion *merget condens omnia gurges* 868.)

sua . . . regna: explained by *Ithaca tremente*; the small island is the whole of Laertes' "kingdom" (the ironic force of *regna* was probably suggested by Verg. *Aen*. 3.272 *effugimus scopulos Ithacae, Laertia regna*).

586 pauper: Laertes is "poor" because Ithaca lacks the land and fertile soil needed to support large-scale farming or animal husbandry, cf. Hor. *Epist*. 1.7.41–42.

587 Laertes: father of Odysseus, in advanced old age when Odysseus returns home after his twenty-year absence at Troy and elsewhere (*Od*. 24.233); since the Trojan War is at least a decade in the future at the time of this play, Seneca's chronology is here unexceptionable.

Ithaca tremente: circumstantial abl. with causal force, balancing *Coro feriente pontum* in 578.

588–89 si . . . pelagus: a reminiscence of Hor. *C*. 1.12.30–32 *concidunt venti fugiuntque nubes / et minax, quod sic voluere* [sc. Castor and Pollux] *ponto / unda recumbit*. Seneca typically makes Horace's language less graphic (*pelagus recumbit* for *ponto / unda recumbit*), but he enlivens the scene with the hyperbolic *mitius stagno*, based on Verg. *Aen*. 8.89 (of the Tiber) *mitis . . . in morem stagni placidaeque paludis*. He omits Horace's reference to divine causation and (perhaps pointedly) notes that the winds' own (*suae*) powers have failed; nothing in the simile lends itself to any view of divine providence or anger.

588 ventis: dat. of reference (AG 377), producing a more elevated phrase than, e.g., Livy 26.39.8 *venti vis omnis cecidit*.

589 recumbit: the image of relaxed reclining forms a neat contrast to the earlier scenes of anxious watchers perched on high places, 570–71 *pinnis . . . incubabat*, 583 *rupe . . . residens in Aetnae*.

590–92 The essential distinction is between the *navis . . . fusis speciosa velis* and the *ludens cumba*: seas that were once too rough even for large sail-driven ships now lie open to small pleasure-craft. Compare *Med.* 365–67 *non . . . quaeritur Argo; / quaelibet altum cumba pererrat*. [Other modern texts place the comma after *secare* in 590 and make *speciosa* modify *alta*; *fusis speciosa velis* would then describe the sea "studded with bellying sails, a beauteous sight" (Miller). This arrangement produces an awkward disproportion: *navis* is unqualified while *alta* is given two descriptive phrases that do not fully cohere with each other. (If the waters are *strata* and safe even for small rowboats, there is probably not enough wind to make sailing practical; note also *mitius stagno* in 589.) The punctuation given here is that of most editions before Leo, restored to prominence by Zwierlein in *Gnomon* 41 (1969), 768.]

590 secare: originally a metaphor from ploughing, *secare aequor*, etc., is often simply an elegant term for sea-travel, cf. *Ag.* 430 (n).

591 fusis . . . velis: "with sails unfurled," cf. Sil. 2.25 *fundentem vela carinam*. [If *speciosa* is taken with *alta*, *fusis . . . velis* will mean "with scattered sails," i.e., sailing ships scattered across the surface of the sea, cf. Manil. 4.382 *fusas . . . per aequora terras* (i.e., islands).]

speciosa: "splendid," "impressive," an apt description of a large sailing-ship, cf. Ovid *Met.* 3.20–21 *speciosam cornibus altis / . . . frontem*.

592 strata: "made smooth" (*sterno*), cf. Verg. *Aen.* 8.87–89 *ita substitit unda . . . ut . . . sterneret aequor aquis*, Hor. *C.* 1.9.10.

ludenti . . . cumbae: the *cumba* as a pleasure-craft was usually found on secluded lakes, cf. Ovid *Tr.* 2.329–30 *non ideo debet pelago se credere, si qua / audet in exiguo ludere cumba lacu*, Sen. *Epist.* 51.12 (of Baiae, the elegant resort-town on the Bay of Naples) *tot genera cumbarum variis coloribus picta et fluitantem toto lacu rosam*, Juv. 12.80–81 *interiora petit Baiarum pervia cumbae / tuti stagna sinus*. For the open sea to be accessible to a *cumba* is an effective hyperbole.

593 vacat . . . pisces: a charming detail, implying both the clarity of the unruffled water and the leisure of the boatman who does not have to watch the sea for storms. (Cf. Cic. *Att.* 2.6.1 *fluctus numero*, in an account of complete *otium*.)

vacat: "there is time to," cf. Ovid *Met.* 5.333–34 'sed forsitan otia non sint, / nec nostris praebere vacat tibi cantibus aures?'

mersos . . . pisces: cf. Ovid *Met.* 5.587–89 *aquas . . . perspicuas ad humum, per quas numerabilis alte / calculus omnis erat*.

mersos: balances *mergi* in 586; the storm no longer threatens to engulf the land, and only the sea's natural inhabitants are covered by its water.

595 Cyclades . . . motae: the Cyclades were proverbially stormy (cf. Hor. *C.* 1.14.20 with Nisbet-Hubbard *ad loc.*), and so *motae* suggests "shaken," "disturbed" (see on 264 *moti Lares*). But Seneca is almost certainly alluding as well to the legend that Delos, the chief island of the group, had no fixed position in the sea until Leto gave birth there to Apollo and Diana, cf. Ovid *Met.* 6.189–91, Sen. *Ag.* 384–91 (n); there is probably a similar allusion in Verg. *Aen.* 8.691–92 *pelago credas innare revulsas / Cycladas.* The Cyclades would therefore have particular reason to fear stormy seas, since in the past they had literally been "moved" by them; *motae*, coming last in its clause, has a pointed causal force. This is the only striking *sententia* in the ode; it has been carefully placed to create the sense of an ending before the most important transition.

596–606 Until now the Chorus has opposed present relief to the threats of the recent past. Now both past and present are seen as phases in a continuing cycle, and immediate happiness begins to seem only a prelude to renewed misfortune. The shift is signaled in 596–98, whose short phrases contrast sharply with the elaborately detailed scenes that precede; at this distance the anxieties and pleasures that recently filled the mind appear simply as *dolor* and *voluptas*, mere specks in the vast expanse of time.

597 brevior voluptas: these stark words have the ring of a hard-won truth; the absence of verbal ornament only adds to their authority.

598 ima . . . summis: a more conventional statement, with time (*hora*) in a role usually played by Fortuna, cf. Hor. *C.* 1.34.12–13 *valet ima summis / mutare*, Tac. *H.* 4.47.3 *instabilis fortunae summaque et ima miscentis.*

permutat: probably suggested by Hor. *Epist.* 2.2.171–73 *tamquam / sit proprium quidquam puncto quod mobilis* [= *levis*] *horae / . . . permutet dominos.*

599–601 The king who serves as an exemplar of unstable felicity bears a strong resemblance to a Roman emperor; compare the words Seneca puts in the mouth of Nero at the start of *De clementia* (1.1.2): '*Egone ex omnibus mortalibus placui electusque sum, qui in terris deorum vice fungerer?* [cf. 607] *Ego vitae necisque gentibus arbiter*; [cf. 608] *. . . ex nostro responso laetitiae causas populi urbesque concipiunt*; [cf. 600] *. . . haec tot milia gladiorum, quae pax mea comprimit, ad nutum meum stringentur*; [cf. 601] *. . . quos reges mancipia fieri quorumque capiti regium circumdari decus oporteat*, [cf. 599] *quae ruant urbes, quae oriantur, mea iuris dictio est.*

599 qui . . . fronti: "who bestows a diadem on another's brow," as Roman emperors did with client kings (and as Atreus has just done with Thyestes), cf. *Clem.* 1.1.2 above, Suet. *Nero* 13.2 (quoted on 518).

600 genu . . . gentes: a generalized form of the obeisance made by client kings, cf. Suet. *Nero* 13.2 *primo . . . admisit ad genua.*

601 cuius ad nutum: "at whose beck," cf. Cic. *Or.* 24 *ad eorum arbitria et nutum totos se fingunt*, Hor. *Epist.* 2.2.6, Sen. *Clem.* 1.1.2 above.

posuere: "lay aside" (gnomic perfect), cf. 348, 609. In *Clem.* 1.1.2 Seneca gives Nero the opposite claim, that he can unleash warfare on a vast scale (*haec tot milia gladiorum . . . stringentur*).

602–603 Medus . . . Indus . . . Dahae Parthis: the geographical frame of reference— thoroughly Roman and imperial—recalls that of the previous ode, especially 369–84: 370 (*Dahae*), 371–73 (*Indi*), 374–75 (*Medi*), 383–84 (*Parthi*).

602 Phoebi propioris Indus: *Phoebi propioris* is gen. of quality (AG 345); by metonymy (cause for effect), it denotes the Indian's dark skin, thought to be caused by his nearness to the sun. The connection is explicit at *Oed.* 122–23 *Phoebus . . . flamma propiore nudos / inficit Indos.* (This explanation was traditionally applied to the Ethiopians, cf. [Aesch.] *PV*

808–809, but the Indians and Ethiopians were regarded as neighbors, and Ovid speaks of the Indians as *positi sub ignibus, Met.* 1.778 with Bömer's note.) *Phoebi propioris Indus* is thus a precious equivalent for, e.g., *decolor Indus* in Ovid *Ars* 3.130, Sen. *Pho.* 345, etc.

603 Dahae . . . minati: "the Dahae who threaten the Parthians with cavalry"; the same construction in 611 *hoc vobis dominus minatur.*

equitem: collective singular, as in 185 above.

604–606 This thought, crystallized in Shakespeare's "uneasy lies the head that wears a crown," is a specific form of the common ancient belief that the powerful and successful have most to fear from fortune's changes (cf. Fantham on *Tro.* 253, my edition of *Agamemnon*, p. 182 and nn. on 71–76). Sometimes only vicious rulers are said to suffer from this anxiety (cf. [Aesch.] *PV* 224–25, Sen. *Clem.* 1.7.3 *crudele regnum turbidum tenebrisque obscurum est . . . ne eo quidem qui omnia perturbat, inconcusso*), but that is not this Chorus's point; the king only feels with particular keenness the uncertainty that attends all human affairs.

604–605 moventes / cuncta: *cuncta* is obj. of *moventes*, which modifies *casus* and *tempus* ("chance and time, which keep everything in motion").

605 divinat metuitque: "foresees and fears," a hendiadys for "nervously anticipates"; Seneca may have been recalling Ovid *Met.* 11.694 *hoc erat hoc, animo quod divinante timebam.*

605–606 casus / mobiles rerum: "swiftly changing fortunes/outcomes of events"; for *casus* cf. *OLD* s.v., #4b, Cic. *Tusc.* 1.91 *propter incertos casus*, Livy 30.30.11 *incerta casuum.*

606 mobiles: cf. *Pha.* 1141–42 *volat ambiguis mobilis alis / hora.* There is a distinction between *moventes* (604) and *mobiles*: the *casus* are themselves restlessly changing and also the cause of change in all things.

dubium: "unreliable," cf. 292.

607–22 The Chorus moves from reflection to exhortation, addressed first to kings (607–14) and finally to all human beings (615–16 *nemo*, 618 *omne fatum*).

607–608 Vos . . . vitae: Roman coloring is here very strong, since by Seneca's time it was a tenet of imperial ideology that the emperor was chosen by the gods and specifically by Jupiter; cf. *Clem.* 1.1.2 (quoted above on 599–601), J. Rufus Fears, *Princeps a dis electus* (Rome, 1977).

maris atque terrae / . . . necis atque vitae: the resounding parallel phrases may echo (with a touch of irony) the grandiose claims made by rulers.

607 rector maris atque terrae: not a traditional epithet for Jupiter, who is usually called *rector* of the sky (*r. caeli* 1077 below, *r. Olympi HF* 205, Ovid *Met.* 2.60) or of gods (and men), cf. Verg. *Aen.* 8.572, Ovid *Met.* 2.848, Sen. *HF* 517, *Pha.* 880. The polar expression *maris atque terrae* suggests the entire world, with a possible glance at the sea-imagery of 577–95.

609 ponite . . . vultus: an interesting metaphor, which treats the *vultus* as an artificial covering (like a mask) that can be removed at will. Its opposite is *induere vultus*, "putting on" an appearance other than one's own, cf. Ovid *Met.* 2.425, 8.854, *Am.* 3.14.27, Sen. *Ag.* 707. There may be an echo of 519–20 *ponatur omnis ira et . . . tumor / erasus abeat* and 348 *rex est qui posuit metus.* (Elsewhere cf. *Tro.* 399 *spem ponant avidi, solliciti metum.*)

inflatos tumidosque: each word in itself describes the arrogance brought about by success (*tumidus*, e.g., *Tro.* 301, *HF* 384; *inflatus*, Cic. *Off.* 1.91, Livy 6.11.6); the combination is conspicuously orotund, matching the state described. (Similar parodic intent is evident in *Ag.* 247–48 *superba et impotens flatu nimis / fortuna magno spiritus tumidos daret.*)

610–14 It is impossible not to hear these lines as an unconscious comment on the situation of Atreus, yet nothing in the play supports belief in a higher power that will oppress him as he does others. (Certainly Thyestes' appeals to the gods for vengeance in the final scene do not carry much weight, see on 1110.) Seneca surely meant this passage to have an impact beyond its immediate context, as an appeal for restraint addressed to rulers everywhere (especially Rome). But the failure of the Chorus's view to account for what the audience is about to experience is also important: it suggests that the evil generated by Atreus' passions is so great that it exceeds the limits of what, in a well-ordered universe, ought to be possible.

610 a vobis: "at your hands," cf. Cic. *Phil.* 2.116 *quae est . . . vita dies et noctes timere a suis?*

minor: substantive, "a subordinate/inferior," cf. *Pha.* 543 *factus praeda maiori minor.*

expavescit: perhaps an echo of 40 *fratrem expavescat frater.*

611 hoc vobis . . . minatur: for the syntax see on 603.

612 omne . . . est: a bleaker version of the view stated by Horace in *C.* 3.1.5–6 *regum timendorum in proprios greges, / reges in ipsos imperium est Iovis.*

graviore: "more oppressive," cf. Prop. 1.5.19 *grave servitium*, Tac. *Ann.* 1.10.5 *Livia gravis in rem publicam mater, gravis domui Caesarum noverca.*

613–14 quem . . . iacentem. an adaptation of an old commonplace, that good fortune can be wiped out in a single day (cf. *Ag.* 626 [n]), but the stress on the day's arrival and flight (*fugiens*), along with the change from plural (*vos, vobis*) to singular (*quem, hunc*), makes one suspect an unintentional allusion to Thyestes. The wording of 614 at least permits this sense: this day *will* flee at the sight of Thyestes *iacens*, i.e., reclining at his horrid feast (cf. 909 *resupinus . . . incubat*).

614 iacentem: the primary meaning is "fallen," "prostrate" (generally "low" in contrast to *superbus*); see on 343, 451. For the possible ironic sense "reclining" (previous note), cf. *Ag.* 879 *sublimis iacet.*

615–16 Nemo . . . lassis: cf. *NQ* 3 pr. 7 *itaque secundis nemo confidat, adversis nemo deficiat; alternae sunt vices rerum.* A link with Thyestes is suggested by the reminiscence of Atreus' question *numquid secundis patitur in rebus modum, / fessis quietem?* (197–98).

615 secundis: sc. *rebus* (so too with *lassis* 616).

616 desperet meliora: "lose hope of better things," cf. Cic. *Att.* 7.20.1 *pacem . . . desperavi*, Sen. *Suas.* 2.12 *cenant . . . tamquam crastinum desperent.*

lassis: "unfortunate," "depressed," like *res fessae*, 198 above. [Several editors have printed *lapsis*, found in some late manuscripts, but there is no doubt that *lassis* is correct: *res lassae* is well attested both elsewhere in Seneca and in other authors, cf. *Cons. Pol.* 16.6, *Ben.* 6.25.4, Verg. *Aen.* 2.114 (where *lapsis* is an ancient variant), Ovid *Pont.* 2.2.49, 2.3.93, *Tr.* 5.2.41 with Luck's note. The change of *lassus* to *lapsus* is very common; manuscripts of Seneca attest *lapsus* even where sense rules it out, cf. *HF* 803, *Oed.* 593. The same arguments apply at 658 below.]

617-21 This view of human affairs makes no attempt at philosophical exactness; it is certainly alien to orthodox Stoicism, in which all that happens belongs to a providentially ordered "chain of causes" (cf. *Oed.* 980–92; F. H. Sandbach, *The Stoics* [London, 1975], 79–82). The Chorus is offering not so much an explanation of events as a response to their apparent unpredictability; the profusion of agents named (*Clotho, Fortuna, deus*) conveys a sense of helplessness before the forces that seem to control human lives.

617 miscet: a traditional pursuit of *Fortuna*, cf. Sall. *Cat.* 10.1 *saevire Fortuna ac miscere omnia coepit*, Sen. *NQ* 3 *pr.* 7 *nescit enim quiescere, gaudet laetis tristia substituere, utique miscere.*

haec illis: i.e., *lassa secundis.*

Clotho: one of the three Fates (the others being Atropos and Lachesis), mentioned in Plato *Rep.* 617c. In Sen. *Oed.* 986 Lachesis is the embodiment of the destined order of events, the Stoic *series rerum*. [The Greek names for the Fates do not appear in Latin before the late poetry of Ovid, cf. *F.* 6.757 (text uncertain), *Ibis* 241, 243, *Tr.* 5.10.45, then *Cons. Liv.* 239, Sen. *Apoc.* 4.1 and Flavian writers.]

617-18 prohibet . . . / stare: a variation on epithets of *Fortuna* like *levis* or *mobilis*, which attribute to the goddess the motion she symbolizes.

618 [Fortunam: it is often hard to be sure whether to write *Fortuna* or *fortuna* (i.e., whether or not a reference to a personified figure is intended). Here I have opted for the personal form because of the absence of a qualifying term (in contrast to *omne fatum*).]

rotat: like *miscet* in 617, an action often performed by *Fortuna* herself, cf. *Ag.* 72 (n); *rotare* implies a circular motion, perhaps alluding to the image of "Fortune's wheel," for which cf. Nisbet on Cic. *Pis.* 22, Smith on Tib. 1.5.70.

fatum: "individual destiny," cf. Verg. *Aen.* 6.759 *te tua fata docebo*, 7.294 *fatis contraria nostris / fata Phrygum*; at *Oed.* 980, on the other hand, *fatis agimur* means "we are driven by destiny."

619 tam: with *faventes.*

habuit: gnomic perfect ("no-one has ever had").

621-22 res . . . nostras . . . versat: the ode concludes with its only statement in the first person (*nostras*). When it sings of *res nostrae*, the Chorus is consciously thinking of all human beings (including, by implication, the audience), but the words apply with special point to the Chorus as citizens of Mycenae, who are about to learn that their world has indeed been turned upside down.

621 deus: for unspecific *deus* in statements of mutability cf. *Oed.* 989, Menander *Aspis* 417–18 (quoting the tragedian Carcinus) ἐν μιᾷ γὰρ ἡμέρᾳ / τὸν εὐτυχῆ τίθησι δυστυχῆ θεός.

celeri citatas: Seneca enjoys this pleonastic combination, cf. *Ag.* 913 *celeres concitus*, *Pho.* 403 *concita celerem gradum*, *Epist.* 99.7 *cogita brevitatem huius spatii per quod citatissimi currimus.*

622 turbine: the primary sense is probably "spindle," evoking the picture of the Fates weaving the threads of destiny, cf. Catullus 64.314 *tereti versabat turbine fusum*, *Cons. Liv.* 164 *celeri turbine Parca neat*. But there is also a play on *turbo* = "whirlwind," an image connected with rapid changes of fortune (cf. Luc. 2.243–44 *virtutis . . . fides quam turbine nullo / excutiet Fortuna tibi*, Sil. 5.54); this sense is echoed in the first words of the Messenger, *quis me . . . turbo praecipitem vehet?*

ACT IV (623-788)

A Messenger relates to the Chorus Atreus' murder and dismemberment of Thyestes' sons. The atrocity takes place in a mysterious grove deep within the palace, a region of infernal sights and sounds where the very laws of nature seem suspended (650–82). Atreus conducts the killings in a grotesquely exact travesty of sacrificial procedure, preparing the flesh of his victims as if for a ritual feast (684–772).[1] The sun turns back in horror at the sight, but by the end of the scene Thyestes has already gorged himself on the bodies of his children.

Despite traces of artificiality,[2] this is arguably Seneca's most interesting and accomplished messenger-scene, showing complete mastery of form and structure as well as the thematic density typical of Senecan narrative passages.[3] It is one of only two Senecan messenger-scenes situated in the penultimate episode[4] (the most common place for messenger-speeches in Greek tragedy), and admirably carries out its function as a link between the central act and the finale: the Messenger's account of Atreus' actions is so vivid that it maintains the immediacy of his presence, and the focus of his narrative shifts with superb fluidity from the exterior of the palace (as at 491–545) to its inner recesses and finally to the dining hall, leading directly into the action of the following scene.

Part of the scene's success results from its original handling of form and characterization. In the three Senecan plays which on other grounds seem to be early works—*Agamemnon*, *Oedipus*, and *Phaedra* (above, p. 11)—the Messenger delivers his report in a single enormous speech, preceded by short introductory dialogue (*Ag.* 392a–420, 421–578; *Oed.* 509–29, 530–658; *Pha.* 990–99, 1000–1114). The five remaining plays with messenger-figures show a more flexible treatment of the convention: the report is either broken up by questions or reactions from the listeners (in *HF*, *Troades* 1056–1164, and *Thyestes*) or is actually suppressed, the Messenger being discarded after a brief announcement of his news (*Phoenissae* 387–402, *Medea* 879–90). *Thyestes* goes further than any other play in the direction of dialogue,[5] and is unique in suggesting an evolution in the Messenger's attitude to his story. From an initial state of nearly speechless horror, the Messenger grows steadily more involved with his narrative, becoming at last almost buoyant in displaying his powers of description.[6] By the latter part of the scene he has absorbed Atreus' flair for the ironic retort,[7] and in his final lines he sounds as jubilantly confident as Atreus himself that the crime can no longer be suppressed. Even in the conventional figure of the Messenger, Seneca has dramatized the triumph of evil over all attempts to contain it.

623–40 The Messenger enters delirious with horror, and only embarks on the narrative after several increasingly agitated requests from the Chorus. Tragic messengers are traditionally reluctant to impart disastrous news (see my note on *Ag.* 416), but Seneca here

---

[1] On this motif see below on 687–90.

[2] We are not told (nor are we meant to ask) how the Messenger witnessed these events without attempting to prevent them, and the treatment of the Chorus as a speaking character (the only place in *Thyestes* where it so functions) is somewhat wooden.

[3] For phrases with links to recurring themes, see, e.g., on 628–29, 641–47, 659–64, 673, 699, 707–11, 760–61, 769, 777, 787 *gravis*.

[4] The other is *Pha.* 1000–1114, which does not fill as large a part of the dramatic structure. In other plays Seneca defers the main narrative section to the last act (*Troades*), promotes it to the third act (*Agamemnon*, *Oedipus*, *HF*), and even omits it entirely (*Medea*, *Phoenissae*; see below).

[5] See introductory note to prologue (above, p. 86).

[6] See on 723, 728–29, 749–51, 754, 759–60, 766, 771, 783, 784–87.

[7] See 717–18, 744–45, 746–47.

transcends the conventionality of such scenes as *Tro.* 1056–67, *Pha.* 991–99, and *Ag.* 406a–20; the Messenger's hyperbolic outcries are not dramaturgical formulae but a plausible reaction to an experience that beggars description.

623 Quis . . . vehet: an obvious rephrasing of the Chorus's last words (*res deus nostras celeri citatas / turbine versat*), but with a radical change of attitude: the Chorus finds the whirlwind of change alarming, but the Messenger feverishly hopes that it may sweep him far from the intolerable present. (Cf. Ovid *Met.* 6.310–11 of Niobe: *validi circumdata turbine venti / in patriam rapta est.*) These opening lines are similar to, though better motivated than, *Pho.* 420–21 *quis me procellae* [cf. 637] *turbine insano vehens / volucer per auras ventus aetherias aget?* (and note also 422–23 *atra nube subtexens diem / Stymphalis*).

624–25 ut . . . eripiat: "so that it might snatch"; on *eripere* see at 998 below.

625 domus: as with Tantalus (22), the Messenger's thoughts quickly turn to the house that figures so prominently throughout the play; cf. also 190–91, 901–902.

625–26 Pelopi . . . pudenda: "that would shame even (*quoque*) Pelops and Tantalus"; a fulfillment of Tantalus' foreboding in 19–20 *turba quae suum vincat genus / et me innocentem faciat.* Atreus invoked Pelops and Tantalus as his models (242–43), but he has far surpassed them in evil.

627–32 The Messenger cannot believe he is in a civilized part of the world (let alone one famed for fraternal loyalty); he wonders if he has come instead to some remote and barbarous country. This idea is usually expressed by those who hear of dreadful events rather than by those who relate them, cf. *Pha.* 906–907 and especially *Tro.* 1104–1109 (similarly with the cognate thought "you cannot have been born of human parents," cf. Hom. *Il.* 16.33–35, Cat. 64.154–56, Verg. *Aen.* 4.365–67); putting it in the Messenger's mouth adds to the impression of derangement he makes at his entrance.

627 ista: "this," virtually equivalent to *haec,* cf. *OLD* s.v., #4, Ovid *Her.* 10.85, *Met.* 9.144, Sen. *Med.* 971.

627–28 pios . . . fratres: Castor and Pollux, a legendary pair of devoted brothers, cf. Ovid *Tr.* 4.5.29–30 *diligat et semper socius de sanguinis illo, / quo pius affectu Castora frater amat,* Cons. *Liv.* 283 *Ledaeos, concordia sidera, fratres.* The most famous illustration of their *pietas* is Pollux' sharing of immortality with his mortal brother Castor, cf. "Apollodorus" *Bibl.* 3.11.2.

628 sortita: "having been allotted" (i.e., by fate), suggesting a blessing or adornment, cf. Mela 1.28 *regio ignobilis et vix quidquam inlustre sortita.*

628–29 maris . . . Corinthos: the Isthmus of Corinth appears for the fourth time in the play (cf. 111–14, 124–25, 181–82); here too the details are chosen to suit the mood of the scene (see next note).

premens / fauces: the *fauces* are the narrow outlets of water on either side of the Isthmus, and *premens* means "touching" or "bordering directly on"; a close parallel in *Pho.* 611 *fauces . . . Abydo Sestos oppositas premit.* The phrase, though, is unusual and suggests both oppression (*premens*) and the literal sense of *fauces* as in 782–83 *saepe praeclusae cibum / tenuere fauces.* The vision the Messenger cannot yet confront openly forces itself into his speech through this distorted view of a familiar landmark.

629–31 The regions representing savagery again evoke the fringes of the empire in Seneca's time, cf. 369–79, 601–603. For a similar list cf. *Pha.* 166–68, *Tro.* 1104–1106.

629–30 feris . . . Alanis: the Alans, a nomadic Sarmatian tribe, are mentioned here for the first time in extant Latin literature; their next appearances are in Lucan 8.223, 10.454, then Pliny the Elder *NH* 4.80, Val. Fl. 6.42, 656, Martial 7.30; cf. A. B. Bosworth, *HSCP* 81 (1977), 222. The present passage is unusual in placing them near the lower Danube rather than on the steppes of the Caucasus. This need not be the result of mere confusion (as Bosworth assumes); Seneca could be using *Alani* to refer to the Rhoxolani or "Red Alans" whom Plautius Silvanus encountered pressing against the northern borders of Moesia, cf. *ILS* 1.986; M. Hofmann in *RE* 21 (1951), 36–39; Chilver on Tac. *Hist.* 1.6.12, 79.1. The date of this engagement is disputed, but it cannot have been earlier than A.D. 57—a fact with possible consequences for dating the play (above, pp. 12–13).

fugam / praebens: i.e., the frozen river furnishes the Alans with a means of escape, cf. *HF* 541. The stress on "flight" may be significant, see p. 46 above.

631 Hyrcana tellus: Hyrcania (at the southeast end of the Caspian Sea, now northern Iran) was indelibly linked with inhuman cruelty for Roman readers by Dido's words in *Aen.* 4.366–67 *duris genuit te cautibus horrens / Caucasus Hyrcanaeque admorunt ubera tigres*; this is probably the region alluded to in *Tro.* 1105–1106 *quae Caspium tangens mare / gens iuris expers.* Hyrcania is not stereotypically cold, but Seneca may be endowing it with the attributes of the "frosty Caucasus" (*Richard II* 1.3.295). [Compare Luc. 3.265–67, perhaps influenced by this passage: *tinxere sagittas / errantes Scythiae populi, quos gurgite Bactros / includit gelido vastisque Hyrcania silvis.*]

vagi . . . Scythae: cf. *Tro.* 1104 *sedis incertae Scytha, Lear* 1.1.116–19 "the barbarous Scythian . . . shall to my bosom / be as well neighbor'd, pitied, and reliev'd, / as thou my sometime daughter."

632 conscius: i.e., as a witness, cf. Ovid *RA* 225–26 *fugito loca conscia vestri / concubitus, Met.* 2.438.

634 Si steterit animus: the protasis of a future conditional of which the apodosis is to be supplied: "(I shall do as you ask) once my *animus* has come to a standstill." For the elliptical syntax, cf. 321, 443, and for the sense of *stare* ("to come to rest after a disturbance") cf. Verg. *Ecl.* 2.26 *cum placidum ventis staret mare.*

metu corpus rigens: normally hair stands stiffly on end from fear (cf. Ovid *Met.* 3.100 *gelido . . . comae terrore rigebant*), but Seneca amplifies the emotion by extending its effect to the whole body.

635 remittet artus: "will let go of my limbs," an unusual expression that makes the Messenger's body seem independent of his control (a state several times experienced in the play, cf. 419–20, 985–86). The combination of his palpitating *animus* and his frozen body is strange, but effective.

haeret in vultu: "lingers before my face," a variation on passages like Verg. *Aen.* 4.4 *haerent infixi pectore vultus*, where a sight lingers in a person's heart or mind, cf. also Luc. 9.71 *imis haeret imago* (sc. *Pompei*) *visceribus.*

636–38 ferte . . . raptus: this wish recalls the Messenger's first words (623–24) and so rounds off the opening section of the scene. When he resumes, the Messenger shows no further signs of hysteria or reluctance.

637 illo . . . quo: adverbial, "to that place . . . where."

637–38 quo . . . raptus: meant in general terms, "where the day is borne when it is carried off from here" (i.e., to the ends of the earth, a stronger equivalent of *procul* 636), but foreshadowing the unnatural way *this* day will be "carried off," cf. 793 *rapis*).

638 gravius: with *tenes*, "you hold us more oppressively in suspense" (i.e., the uncertainty becomes harder to bear with each new delay).

640 uter: i.e., Atreus or Thyestes; a surprisingly sharp statement, suggesting that the Chorus never fully believed the ostensible reconciliation.

641–82 The narrative begins with an enormous *descriptio loci*, introduced in traditional style with *est* and concluding with a relative word where the narrative resumes (*quo* 682). The short *descriptiones loci* in Greek tragedy are meant only to sketch the scene of the following action (cf., e.g., Eur. *Hipp.* 1199–1200, *IT* 1450–52; Zwierlein, *Rezitationsdramen* 116). In Seneca the *descriptio* often defines not only the location but also the atmosphere of a scene, and even its significance; it is no mere lead-in, but a vital constituent of the narrative. (For other examples cf. *Tro.* 1068–74, *Oed.* 530–47, *Ag.* 558–66 [n].) This difference reflects the influence of declamation oratory, where an elaborate *descriptio* might be the high point of a declaimer's performance (cf. Bonner 58; the specimen in *Contr.* 2.1.10–13, by Seneca's teacher Papirius Fabianus, is especially instructive), and also of Augustan epic, which contains several *descriptiones* remarkable for their rich detail and thematic importance (cf., e.g., Verg. *Aen.* 1.159–69, 7.563–70, Ovid *Met.* 1.568–76). Here the link with Augustan poetry is particularly close, since this *descriptio* makes conscious and pointed allusion to Vergil's account of the palace-temple of Latinus in *Aen.* 7.170–91. The Vergilian passage was thought in antiquity to refer to the palace of Augustus on the Palatine (so Servius on 7.170); Seneca's lines are even more overtly Roman in coloring, but Seneca has replaced Vergil's evocation of imposing power with a picture of extravagant tyranny.

641 In arce summa: corresponding to *urbe . . . summa* in *Aen.* 7.171, but *arx* adds a hint of absolute power (cf. on 342 *cupidi arcium*, *Ag.* 77 [n], Luc. 7.593–94), and while Vergil's *templum* is at the highest point of the city, here the *domus* seems separate from the *urbs* and a threat to it (*premit* 643).

642 conversa ad Austros: "facing south," cf. Verg. *G.* 1.241 *devexus ad Austros*, Pliny *NH* 4.58 (but perhaps implying the vulnerability of high position, as in *Pha.* 1128–29 *admota aetheriis culmina sedibus / Euros excipiunt, excipiunt Notos*). The detail is oddly precise, and it may not be coincidental that the imperial residence on the Palatine extended to its south end, where it overlooks the Circus Maximus. [More specific connections may not be possible: both Gaius and Nero were notorious for grandiose expansions of the imperial palace, but Gaius' was directed toward the Capitol (Suet. *Cal.* 22) and Nero's toward the Esquiline (Suet. *Nero* 31). Nero's *Domus Aurea* resembles the Tantalid palace in several details, but that may simply be because it contained all the standard luxuries of the period.]

643 aequale monti: "as high as a mountain"; for the hyperbole cf. Verg. *Aen.* 2.15 *instar montis* (the Trojan Horse), Tac. *Ann.* 2.61 *instar montium eductae certamine et opibus regum* (the Pyramids). For *aequalis* see also on 885.

urbem premit: "dominates the city," i.e., by its size and position (cf. Luc. 7.594 *iuris . . . humani columen, quo cuncta premuntur*, Stat. *Theb.* 5.153–54 *insuper ingens / mons premit*), but with obvious implications of an oppressive weight.

644–45 contumacem . . . ictu: *contumacem . . . suis* probably describes a potential situation ("if [or "when"] the populace defies its kings, the palace has them within striking distance"); the phrase, though, could also function literally, depicting a constant state of defiance on one side and devastating retaliation on the other.

644 contumacem . . . populum: the Mycenaeans show the resistance to tyranny that was a recurring, though never dominant, strain of Roman political life under the Principate, cf. Tac. *Agr.* 42.3–4, *Ann.* 4.20 *dubitare cogor . . . an . . . liceat . . . inter* *abruptam contumaciam et deforme obsequium peragere iter ambitione ac periculis vacuum*. Seneca elsewhere prescribes an *animus fortis et contumax* in the face of disaster (*NQ* 3 pr. 13) and elicits admiration for Andromache's *contumacia* toward Ulysses in *Troades* (589), but he also admits that *contumacia* is a defect in a courtier (*Tranq.* 6.2). The present passage maintains an interestingly neutral tone.

645 sub ictu: literally "within range of a blow falling from above," figuratively in a state of complete subjection (cf. "under one's thumb"). In *Clem.* 1.26.4 Seneca imagines a tyrant whose cruelty cannot be satisfied *nisi eodem tempore grex miserorum sub ictu stetit*; for the *domus Pelopia* to have an entire *populus* in this position marks a truly advanced state of tyranny. Roman audiences might have thought of "Caligula," *qui optabat ut populus Romanus unam cervicem haberet, ut scelera sua tot locis ac temporibus diducta in unum ictum et unum diem cogeret* (*Ira* 3.19.5).

645-47 The palace's size and lavish decoration recall the life that Thyestes has professed to despise (455-57) and that the Chorus has distinguished from true kingship (344-47). In *Epist.* 90.25 Seneca denounces contemporary extravagance in similar terms: *quid loquar marmora quibus templa, quibus domus fulgent? quid lapideas moles in rotundum ac leve formatas quibus porticus et capacia populorum tecta suscipimus?*

647 variis columnae nobiles maculis: Vergil's *centum sublime columnis* (*Aen.* 7.170) has been revised to include a reference to multi-colored stone, a refinement often criticized in Neronian moralizing, cf. *Tranq.* 1.7, *Epist.* 115.8, Petr. *Sat.* 119.29.

maculis: "spots" of color, with an underlying suggestion of defilement, for which cf. Verg. *Aen.* 12.67-68 *Indum sanguineo veluti violaverit ostro / si quis ebur*.

648 post ista vulgo nota: a pointed transition: if these are the public areas of the palace, surely its inner precincts will contain even more rare and choice treasures. This expectation is fulfilled, with a typical inversion of normal values, in 659-64.

populi: "whole nations," suggesting the enormous size of the rooms, cf. Sen. *Contr.* 2.1.11 *ut convivia populis instruantur*, Sen. *Epist.* 90.25 *capacia populorum tecta*; *populi* also depicts Pelopid rule on an imperial scale, cf. Verg. *Aen.* 2.556 *Pergama tot quondam populis terrisque superbum / regnatorem Asiae*, 6.851 *tu regere imperio populos, Romane, memento*.

colunt: primarily referring to assiduous attendance or service, as in, e.g., Livy 7.32.16 *semper ego plebem Romanam . . . colo atque colui*, but perhaps with religious overtones as well, for which cf. Ovid *Met.* 11.578 *Iunonis templa colebat*. It would suit Tantalid pretensions for their palace to be treated as an object of cult; see on 902.

649 spatia: "areas" or "rooms," cf. Ovid *Met.* 7.670 *in interius spatium pulchrosque recessus* [cf. *secessu* 650] / *Cecropidas ducit*.

discedit: the unusual personification heightens the sense of the palace's vast size; the literal meaning of *discedere* may also be evoked, as the inhabited areas "disperse" and the listener confronts the mysterious region at its center. [Seneca might have been recalling Cat. 64.43 *quacumque opulenta recessit / regia*.]

650 arcana . . . secessu: = *arcana regio* (nom.) *in imo secessu*; for *secessus* of the innermost part of the Princeps' dwelling cf. Plin. *Pan.* 83.1 *magna fortuna . . . nihil tectum, nihil occultum esse patitur; principum vero non domus modo sed cubicula ipsa intimosque secessus recludit, omniaque arcana noscenda famae proponit atque explicat*.

651-56 The details of the grove closely resemble those in *Oed.* 530-47, describing the *lucus* where the spirit of Laius is raised from the underworld. By placing the grove at the center of the palace (contrast *Oed.* 530 *procul ab urbe lucus*), Seneca both symbolically equates the source of evil with the seat of power and also strengthens the Roman color of the scene: the grove is a perverted counterpart of the inner courtyard of a large Roman house, with its man-made lakes and forests, cf. Sen. *Contr.* 2.1.13 (Papirius Fabianus) *quin etiam montes silvasque in domibus marcidis et in umbra fumoque viridia aut maria amnesque imitantur*, 5.5, Suet. *Nero* 31.2 (the *Domus Aurea*) *stagnum maris instar, circumsaeptum aedificiis ad urbium specimen; rura insuper arvis atque vinetis et pascuis silvisque varia.* (In *Aen.* 7.172 Latinus' palace is *horrendum silvis*, but those trees surround the building rather than being enclosed by it.)

651 alta . . . nemus: groves and vales are a natural combination, cf. *Oed.* 530–31 *lucus . . . Dircaea circa vallis . . . loca*, Pho. 15–16 *per obscurum nemus / silvamque opacae vallis*, Ovid *F.* 3.263–66. Here, though, the *vallis* does not merely surround the grove but "confines" it (*compescens*); the image suggests checking a noxious growth, cf. Ovid *Met.* 14.629–30 *spatiantia passim / bracchia compescit.*

652 penetrale regni: the *penetralia*, or innermost parts of a palace, are often the setting for violent or mysterious events, cf. Verg. *Aen.* 2.484, 508 (Priam's murder), 4.504 (Dido's funeral pyre), 7.59 (the omens given to Latinus), Ovid *Met.* 6.646 (Procne's killing of Itys).

nulla: with *arbor* in 653, placed first for emphasis.

laetos: primarily "abundant" or "flourishing," cf. Verg. *G.* 1.1 *quid faciat laetas segetes*, Sen. *Cons. Helv.* 9.1 *non est haec terra frugiferarum aut laetarum arborum ferax*, but also implying "of good omen," cf. Ovid *Pont.* 3.1.19–20 *rara neque haec felix in apertis eminet arvis / arbor.*

653 aut ferro coli: *coli* (pass. inf. of *colere*) is parallel to *praebere* and dependent on *solet.* "Tending with iron" is a high-flown way of referring to pruning, a sign of normal care naturally absent here.

654 taxus . . . cupressus . . . ilice: unlike the Theban grove in *Oedipus*, made up of trees of all kinds (538–41, inspired by Ovid *Met.* 10.90–103), this wood is limited to trees of ill omen or gloomy appearance. The yew (*taxus*) was thought to be poisonous (cf. *Oed.* 555 *mortifera*) and therefore often appears in places linked to the underworld, e.g., Ovid *Met.* 4.432, Luc. 6.645, or in the underworld itself, as at *HF* 690–91. (It is still found in many English churchyards.) The cypress was associated with death and mourning, cf. Hor. *C.* 2.14.22–24 *neque harum quas colis arborum / te praeter invisas cupressos / ulla brevem dominum sequetur* (with Nisbet-Hubbard *ad loc.*). The holm-oak (*ilex nigra*) was not intrinsically unlucky (Ovid uses it for the avian Elysium of *Am.* 2.6.49), but its dense shade could easily evoke feelings of mystery and dread, cf. Ovid *F.* 2.165, 3.295.

655 nutat: see on 465; this "nodding wood" contrasts pointedly with Thyestes' idealized picture (and is perhaps the reality that underlies it).

655–56 quam . . . nemus: as in *Oed.* 542–44, the grove is dominated by a tall oak, but while the Theban oak stands watch over the trees beneath (544 *una defendit nemus*), the tree here looks down on them and "conquers" the grove (*vincit*)—even nature seems to share the Tantalid striving for dominion (cf. 339–42). [Seneca's oaks are probably inspired by Ovid's description of the grove of Ceres violated by Erysichthon in *Met.* 8.743–50; Ovid's *una nemus* in 744 may be the source of *una defendit nemus* in *Oed.* 544. Seneca might in turn have contributed to Lucan's famous comparison of Pompey to a tottering but still revered oak in 1.135–43.]

656 nemus: echoes *nemus* at the end of 651 and closes off this segment of the narrative.

657 hinc: "from this place" (linked to the idea of "beginning" in *auspicari*, see next note).

auspicari regna: "solemnly to begin their reigns," a clear echo of Verg. *Aen.* 7.173–74 *hic sceptra accipere et primos attollere fasces / regibus omen erat*, also applied to the Tantalids in *Ag.* 9–10 *hinc auspicari regium capiti decus / mos est Pelasgis*.

658 lassis: see on 616.

659–64 The grove is hung with votive offerings commemorating the triumphs of the ruling house. Seneca's revision of Vergil is here at its most pointed, cf. *Aen.* 7.183–92. Latinus' *captivi . . . currus* (184) are transformed into the chariot of Oenomaus, sabotaged for Pelops by Myrtilus (see on 139–43 above), and Vergil's portrait of Latinus' ancestor Picus as a proto-Roman is countered by the depiction of Pelops in blatantly oriental colors (662–63). If the Tantalids are meant to suggest Rome's own rulers, this passage implies a particularly bitter comment on imperial crime and hypocrisy.

659 dona: for spoils of war hung up in a sacred grove cf. *Med.* 483–86.

vocales tubae: in a normal triumphal setting *tubae* would be war-trumpets, but as the following words show, here they are the trumpets used to signal the start of a chariot-race, cf. Verg. *Aen.* 5.113, 139, Ovid *Met.* 10.652 with Bömer's note.

660 Myrtoi maris: a highly condensed allusion to Pelops' drowning of Myrtilus (see on 139–43).

662 omne gentis facinus: *facinus* can have a neutral or positive sense and in Roman military contexts often denotes a courageous "exploit," cf., e.g., Livy 3.12.5, 40.40.9 *Romanorum equitum tam memorabile facinus*. Here the unrevealing *omne* allows the audience to imagine what kind of *facinora* is meant.

662–63 Phrygius . . . tiaras Pelopis: Pelops was Phrygian by birth, since his father Tantalus had reigned in Sipylus, cf. Ovid *Tr.* 2.3.85–86 *non Tantalides . . . / Pisaeam Phrygiis vexit eburnus equis?* Pelops, however, did not himself rule in Phrygia, and by focusing on his "Phrygian tiara" Seneca is probably alluding to the Phrygian origins of the Romans; Vergil's Priam wore just such an oriental turban, cf. *Aen.* 7.247 with Fordyce's note.

664 de: "from," cf. 175 *de gurgite*; the *chlamys* is a remnant of the triumphal ceremony.

triumpho . . . barbarico: there is irony in the Phrygian Tantalids celebrating a victory over "barbarian" enemies, especially since Ennius and Vergil had used *barbaricus* to describe the Phrygian Trojans (cf. Enn. *Sc.* 94 V², Verg. *Aen.* 2.504 of Priam's palace, *barbarico postes auro spoliisque superbi*). The implied perspective is perhaps again Roman, reflecting the Roman view of Gallic or German opponents as *barbari* (while deflating Roman assumptions of superiority).

chlamys: i.e., an embroidered robe worn by a conquered foreign enemy in a triumph, such as those mentioned by Persius (6.46 *chlamydas regum*) as procured for Gaius' spurious German "triumph," cf. Suet. *Cal.* 47.

665–67 These lines complete the preliminary description of the grove, to which the sluggish stream serves as a kind of border, cf. *Oed.* 545–47 *tristis sub illa, lucis et Phoebi inscius, / restagnat umor frigore aeterno rigens; / limosa pigrum circumit fontem palus.*

665 stat: "stands immobile," i.e., rather than flowing naturally; cf. *haeret* 666.

665–66 nigra . . . palude: probably abl. of description ("sticks fast in a black pool").

666–67 talis . . . unda: for the comparison cf. *Ag.* 493–94 *dirae Stygis / inferna nox est*, Luc. 6.648–49 *non Taenariis sic faucibus aer / sedit iners*. Here the reference to Styx is more than figurative, since there is a real link between the grove and the lower world.

667 deformis: the meaning of *deformis* increases in strength from merely "unsightly" here to "disfiguring" in 775 and finally to "lacking [or "destroying"] all shape" in 832 *deforme chaos*.

quae . . . fidem: an oath that a god swore by the Styx could not be broken (cf. Hom. *Il.* 14.271, Verg. *Aen.* 6.324); Styx therefore "induces belief" in heaven (*fidem facere*, cf. *OLD* s.v. *fides*, #11). The Messenger casts, as it were, a glance upward to the gods of heaven, where *fides* still has some place, before plunging into the infernal heart of the grove.

668–79 The grove is a place where the lower world intrudes onto the world above, a confusion of realms that recalls the prologue (and that also looks forward to the final scene, where the dead and the living are perversely mingled in the body of Thyestes, cf. 1050–51, 1090–92). Compare *Oed.* 160–79, on Thebes at the height of the plague.

668–69 hinc . . . sonat: the groaning and noise of chains are reminiscent of Vergil's Tartarus, cf. *Aen.* 6.557–58 *hinc exaudiri gemitus et saeva sonare / verbera, tum stridor ferri tractaeque catenae*.

668 ferales deos: "the gods of the dead," an expression found only here and in *Med.* 740, and nearly equivalent to the common *di manes*, as *manes* in 670 implies; cf. *HF* 1146 *turba feralis*, "a throng of spirits."

669 catenis . . . excussis: more energetic than Vergil's *tractae . . . catenae* (see on 668–69); these ghosts vigorously shake their chains, perhaps in frustration, or else to cause fright. (There is no need to take *excussis* as "shaken off," cf. Ovid *Met.* 5.596 *excussa . . . bracchia iacto*, Sen. *Ag.* 5 *pavor membra excutit*.)

669–70 lucus excussis . . . ululantque: the *u* sounds suggest the eerie moaning of the shades.

670–71 quidquid . . . videtur: a progression upward in terror, from sound to sight; *quidquid* for emotive effect, cf. 5 *aliquid*, 15 *si quid*.

670 audire est metus: "it causes fear even to hear of"; cf. Ter. *Ph.* 482 *quantum metus est mihi videre . . . salvum . . . patruum*.

671–72 errat . . . turba: the dead normally rise from their tombs only in response to a great calamity, cf. Ovid *Met.* 15.796–98 (at the assassination of Julius Caesar) *inque foro circumque domos et templa deorum / nocturnos ululasse canes umbraeque silentum / erravisse ferunt*, similarly *Evang. Matth.* 27.52. In the courtyard of the Tantalid palace this seems an everyday occurrence.

671 errat: "walks abroad," of spirits usually confined beneath the earth, cf. Verg. *Aen.* 7.557–58 (Juno to Allecto) *et super aetherias errare licentius auras / haud pater ille velit*, Ovid *Met.* 15.798 (just cited), Sen. *Oed.* 172. (There may be a link with other uses of *errare*; see on 282.)

672 emissa: "released" from normal restraint, cf. Verg. *G.* 3.551–52 *in lucem Stygiis emissa tenebris / pallida Tisiphone*, Sen. *Ag.* 2 (n).

insultant loco: probably not "spring from the place" (Miller) but "leap in the place," in a ghostly travesty of a dance (cf. Enn. *Sc.* 127 V² *Bacchico insultans modo*); perhaps also with a suggestion of mockery, as in 164 above, cf. *Ag.* 839 (n).

673 maiora notis: the Tantalids, with their insatiable urge to surpass previous levels of crime (cf. 19–20, 255–56, 267–70), are fittingly haunted by apparitions "greater than what has been known."

673–75 A mysterious fire can often be seen, which burns but does not consume. Similar portents in Luc. 3.420 (a forest), Silius 8.626 (soldiers' weapons); the phenomenon may be related to the appearance of fire above or around a person's head, as in Verg. *Aen.* 2.682–86, 7.73–77; see Pease on Cic. *Div.* 1.121. This fire loosely parallels the flames of 767–70, which also behave unnaturally.

673 quin: "not only that, but," introducing a climax, cf. 990, *HF* 392, *Med.* 441, *Ag.* 410a, etc.

tota: with *silva*, abl. of place, cf. Ovid (?) *Her.* 18.152 *micat gelido . . . Ursa polo*. [Several unconvincing attempts have been made to replace *tota* with a more pointed adjective; for intensifying *totus* see 696 below, *Oed.* 570–71 *tota succusso solo / pulsata tellus*.]

674 trabes: probably not the roof-beams of the palace, as in 646, but the tree-trunks of the grove, cf. *Ben.* 3.29.5 *aspice trabes, sive proceritatem aestimes, altissimas, sive crassitudinem spatiumque ramorum, latissime fusas*.

675–76 saepe . . . saepe: the tempo accelerates as the Messenger nears the end of his description; sound and sight, presented in 668–70 and 671–76, now recur in shorter phrases (*latratu* vs. *simulacris*).

latratu . . . trino: "threefold barking" suggests Cerberus (cf. Verg. *Aen.* 6.417 *Cerberus haec ingens latratu regna trifauci / personat*), but here it is more likely to announce the presence of Hecate, as in the closely similar lines *Oed.* 569–70 *latravit Hecates turba; ter valles cavae / sonuere maestum* and *Med.* 840–41 *ter latratus / audax Hecate dedit*.

676 remugit: possibly a reminiscence of Vergil's Cumaean Sibyl, cf. *Aen.* 6.99 *horrendas canit ambages antroque remugit* (see on 681 below); *remugire* of a barking sound, though, is perhaps unfortunate.

676–77 simulacris . . . magnis: "enormous phantoms" (*simulacra* = *umbrae*, cf. Ovid *Met.* 4.434, 10.14); an ominous vagueness, as with *quidquid* 670. See also *Ag.* 765–68.

677–79 The Messenger elaborates the last element of the description, the blurring of day and night, in a sort of *tricolon abundans* (see on 267–69), each phrase more pointed and emphatic than the last. The theme clearly anticipates the reaction of the cosmos to Atreus' crimes, cf. 777, 789–92.

678 nox propria luco est: "the grove has a night all its own," i.e., the evil concentrated in it is so great that the succession of day and night does not operate—another inversion of the norm that will soon be felt in the outside world, cf. 813. The thought resembles that in *Oed.* 549 *praestitit noctem locus* (of the Theban grove), but the expression is more pointed.

678–79 superstitio . . . regnat: the violation of normal boundaries is especially clear here, cf. *HF* 56 *sacra dirae mortis in aperto iacent*.

678 superstitio: simply "dread," without implications of baselessness, cf. Verg. *Aen.* 12.817 *una superstitio superis quae reddita divis* ("the one thing which makes the gods feel dread"); *inferum* is obj. gen., "the dread produced by the lower world."

679–82 hinc . . . solvente: the oracular function of the grove has been alluded to earlier (658), but this detail does not figure in the rest of the narrative. Seneca may have placed it here to provide a religious context for Atreus' "sacrifice."

681 laxantur . . . fata: the *fata* (= "individual destinies," as in 618) are "released" in the sense of being made known, set free from obscurity (perhaps on the analogy of opening a door, cf. *HF* 962 *laxare fores*), or alternatively "disentangled," i.e., from the chain of causes (cf. *Oed.* 990 *quae nexa suis currunt causis*, and note *laxare* of untying knots, Livy 24.7.5, Luc. 4.632). The expression seems without parallel.

adyto: either "in the innermost recess" of the grove (abl. of place) or "from the innermost recess" (if the *fata* are confined there); for the latter cf. Ovid *Met.* 15.635–36 *cortina . . . reddidit imo / hanc adyto vocem.*

immugit specus: cf. Verg. *Aen.* 6.98–99 (quoted above on 672 *remugit*), 3.92 *mugire adytis cortina reclusis.*

682 quo: at last the narrative resumes (or, more precisely, begins); for *quo* in this function cf. Ovid *Met.* 2.19.

684 ornantur arae: the same phrase appears at 464, another correspondence between the grove and Thyestes' vision of exalted state (see on 655 *nutat*).

quis . . . eloqui?: in formal speech (lament, panegyric, description) it is common to begin by doubting one's ability to treat the subject adequately; the device is called "initial hesitation" by M. Alexiou, *The Ritual Lament in Greek Tradition* (Cambridge, 1974), 161, the "inexpressibility topos" by E. R. Curtius, *European Literature and the Latin Middle Ages* (New York, 1953), 159–60. A particular stylized version is seen in the Homeric "not even if I had ten tongues could I describe . . ." (*Il.* 2.488–89) and its Vergilian amplification *non mihi si linguae centum sint . . .* (*Aen.* 6.625, with Austin's note). By reducing the idea to a fleeting question, Seneca transforms a "rhetorical flourish" (Austin) into a harrowing cry of despair. (Contrast Thyestes' use of the motif in 1035–36.)

685 revocat: "draws/pulls back," cf. *Ag.* 296 (*Phoebum*) *frena revocantem sua, Oed.* 416–17 *spargere effusos sine lege crines, / rursus adducto revocare nodo.* The word may suggest a formal, even ceremonial action. [E's *religat* looks like either a simpler substitute or a mistaken anticipation of *ligat* in the line below.]

686 vittā . . . purpureā: the band of wool placed around the head of a sacrificial victim, cf. Verg. *G.* 3.486–87 *stans hostia ad aram / lanea dum nivea circumdatur infula vitta.* It adds a horrible sense of ritual correctness to scenes of human sacrifice, cf. Lucr. 1.87 (Iphigenia), Verg. *Aen.* 2.133 (Sinon), Ovid *Pont.* 3.2.74–75 (Orestes and Pylades). In this case the band is purple—Atreus' ironic tribute to his victims' royal status (see on 345).

687–90a Atreus directs the "sacrifice" with his customary energy, insisting on complete verisimilitude. (The reference to the children as *victimae* in 688 recalls Tantalus' attempted murder of Pelops, *immatura focis victima concidit* 146; perverting sacrificial ritual seems to be an inherited trait.) The depiction of the murders as a sacrifice is a traditional element of the story, found as early as Aeschylus (*Ag.* 1592); it also appears in other myths of cannibalism (e.g., that of Lycaon, cf. "Apollodorus" *Bibl.* 3.8.1), and may be a survival of actual cult practices of an earlier period, cf. W. Burkert, *Homo necans* (Eng. trans. [Berkeley, 1983]), 83–134. Seneca gives this motif a new significance: the sacrificial slaughter is a ritual by which Atreus affirms (or perhaps establishes) his status as a god, see on 544–45, 712–13, 885.

687-88 tura . . . Bacchi liquor . . . victimam: wine, incense, and a blood-victim constitute a traditional form of generous sacrifice, cf. Hor. *C.* 1.19.14-16 *tura . . . bimi cum patera meri . . . victima*, Ovid *Met.* 11.247-48 *vino . . . fuso / et pecoris fibris et fumo turis*. [Compare also *Ag.* 806-807 *pecore votivo libens / Arabumque donis supplici et fibra colam*, where the change of *pecore* to *latice* (suggested to me by C. P. Jones) both removes an awkward repetition (*pecore-fibra*) and introduces the third element of this common triad.]

687 sacer Bacchi liquor: for the high-flown periphrasis cf. Verg. *G.* 2.192 *laticis, qualem pateris libamus*, Sen. *Med.* 810 *sacrum laticem*.

688 tangens . . . mola: *mola salsa*, a mixture of salt and husked wheat, was sprinkled on the forehead of the victim, on the hearth, and on the sacrificial knife (so Servius on Verg. *Aen.* 2.133); it is a staple of Latin poetic accounts of sacrifice (some examples in Pease on Verg. *Aen.* 4.517), but this passage is unusual in specifying that the *culter* was used to daub the victims with the mixture, cf. Luc. 1.610, Juv. 12.84. The detail manifests Atreus' concern to follow approved procedure to the letter. (See on 1057-65.)

690 Quis . . . admovet?: the Chorus cannot imagine who would take part in this grotesque charade, and so asks who wielded the knife.

manum ferro admovet: "stretches out his hand to the blade," cf. *Tro.* 693 *dextram pedibus admoveo tuis*, 947 *admoveri crinibus patitur manus*. Miller's note calls *admovere manum* a technical term of sacrifice (for which cf. perhaps *Oed.* 336), but here it seems only a piece of normal high-poetic diction.

691-95 Atreus plays all the parts in his sacrificial drama. There is a faint foreshadowing of these lines in Vergil's account (*Aen.* 4.60-64) of the love-sick Dido, who herself (*ipsa* 60) prepares victims for sacrifice and plunges her hands into the still-quivering entrails.

691 funesta prece: a loose abl. of manner (AG 412), which defines the *carmen letale* of 692 as having the form of a prayer.

692 carmen: the prescribed formula uttered by the *pontifex* (*OLD* s.v., #1e), here a *carmen letale* (i.e., a formula to accompany murder) on the analogy of, e.g., *carmen exsecrabile* (a curse-formula) in Livy 31.17.9.

ore violento: Atreus' furious delivery (if that is what the phrase means) seems a slightly jarring touch, since ritual practice required the words of the prayer to be uttered without any distortion, cf. Sen. *Cons. Marc.* 13.1 (a *pontifex* who received news of his son's death as he was sacrificing) *ille exaudisse dissimulavit et sollemnia pontificii carminis verba concepit, gemitu non interrumpente precationem*.

694 contrectat: an unsettlingly precise detail: Atreus handles the children's bodies to make sure that they are unblemished, as required by sacrificial law (cf. Servius on Verg. *Aen.* 4.57 *moris . . . fuerat ut ad sacrificia eligerentur oves quibus nihil deessent*).

componit: "arranges" them in the order he wishes, the ironic fulfillment of young Tantalus' description of Atreus (432-33): *lacerae domus / componit artus*.

ferro parat: "readies them for the knife," *ferro* dat. of purpose (AG 382.2), cf. Ovid *Met.* 9.34 *pugnae membra paravi*. [*ferro parat* is a conjecture, produced independently by Otto Zwierlein and myself; all Mss read *ferro admovet*, which seems impossibly lame after 690 and which also gives the wrong picture: it is the sword that approaches the victim, as 721-23 show. The most elegant of earlier conjectures is Bentley's *atque arae admovet*, but no reference to the *ara* is needed after 693; all the actions of 694 are to be imagined as happening at the altar. The suggestion printed here is a refinement of Koetschau's *ferrum parat*; the change to *ferro* makes the children (*devotos neci*) the object of *parat*, as they are of *contrectat* and *componit*. If this proposal is correct, the error arose when a scribe copying 693 glanced instead at the *ferro* of 690 and went on with the next word in that line.]

695 attendit ipse: "he himself acts as observer," i.e., he watches for any ill-omened detail that might compromise the ritual; such a functionary is mentioned by Pliny (*NH* 28.11) in a reference to Roman state sacrifices conducted by the chief magistrates.

perit: i.e., is "lost" through neglect, cf. Ovid *Am.* 2.3.14 *indigna est pigro forma perire situ*. Atreus' solicitude for the "health" of his ritual contrasts with his attitude to the lives of his victims, a sign of his essential derangement.

696–702 A series of premonitory disturbances, as the outer world registers the imminent evil; see on 262–65, 985–95.

696 succusso solo: cf. 989, *Oed.* 570.

697 nutavit: a more violent form of the "nodding" image seen earlier in 455, 655.

697–98 dubia . . . similis: the mannerism of attributing hesitation to inanimate objects was made popular by Ovid (cf. *Met.* 8.472, *Tr.* 1.2.26 *nescit cui domino pareat unda maris*) and carried further by Seneca and Lucan, cf. *Ag.* 140 (n). Here, though, it is not merely decorative: the wavering of the *aula* is the physical counterpart of the shifting fortunes of the house, a specific instance of the condition set out by the Fury in the prologue: *dubia violentae domus / fortuna reges inter incertos labet* (33–34). (This dynastic aspect of Atreus' crime may explain why several of the portents named correspond to signs observed before the death of a ruler.)

698 fluctuanti similis: "seeming to waver"; *similis* with a present participle describes an action that only appears to be happening, cf. Verg. *Aen.* 6.602–603 *silex . . . cadenti . . . adsimilis*, 8.649–50 *illum indignanti similem similemque minanti / aspiceres*.

laevo: in Roman augury the left was the favorable side, but Roman poets freely adopted the Greek association of the left with ill omen, cf. Fordyce on Catullus 45.8, Pease on Cic. *Div.* 2.82. Context usually shows which sense is meant; here *atrum . . . limitem* specifies an unnatural portent.

699 sidus: a shooting star of the kind that fell to presage the assassination of Julius Caesar, cf. Verg. *G.* 1.488 *diri totiens arsere cometae*, Luc. 1.526–29. Seneca's wording, though, seems specifically to recall (and invert) the favorable omen of Roman rule in *Aeneid* 2.692–97, *subito . . . fragore / intonuit laevum* [cf. 698 *e laevo aethere*] *et de caelo lapsa per umbras / stella facem ducens multa cum luce cucurrit . . . tum longo limite sulcus / dat lucem*, etc. For the *limes* ("trail") of the comet cf. also Ovid *Met.* 15.849 *flammiferum . . . trahens spatioso limite crinem*.

700–701 libata . . . Baccho: for the portent cf. *Oed* 324 *libata Bacchi dona permutat cruor*. It has particular point here, since Atreus will in a sense transform wine into blood at Thyestes' feast, cf. 914–17, 984–88.

mutato fluunt / cruenta Baccho: *cruenta* is predicate adj. (compare "the rivers ran red"), and *mutato . . . Baccho* is an ablative absolute defining the means by which the change takes place, i.e., through a loss of the wine's essential character (symbolized by Bacchus). Normal syntax is pressed rather hard, perhaps suggesting the unnatural action being described; compare 172–73, also depicting a metamorphosis.

701 regium capiti decus: cf. 346, 531. The toppling diadem symbolizes the insecurity of Tantalid power, cf. 32–33 *superbis fratribus regna excidant*. (See also 947.)

702 bis terque lapsum: probably not to be taken literally, but like *ter quater*, i.e., "again and again," cf. Ovid *Met*. 4.517–18 *bis terque per auras / more rotat fundae*.

flevit . . . ebur: again recalling the portents of the death of Julius Caesar, cf. Verg. *G*. 1.480 *maestum inlacrimat templis ebur*, Ovid *Met*. 15.792 *mille locis lacrimavit ebur*; of omens preceding Caesar's invasion of Italy, Luc. 1.556–57 *indigetes flevisse deos Urbisque laborem / testatos sudasse Lares* (sc. *accipimus*). See also on 264–65.

703–704 movere . . . constat: after a quick glance at the terrified observers (*movere cunctos monstra*), Seneca focuses again on Atreus, alone in his mad resolution. This technique for isolating a crazed protagonist is found in Ovid's stories of Niobe (*Met*. 6.287 *qui praeter Nioben unam conterruit omnes*) and Erysicthon (*Met*. 8.765 *obstipuere omnes*).

sibi . . . constat: Atreus possesses the fixity of purpose that usually marks a *sapiens*, cf. Hor. *Epist*. 1.14.16 *me constare mihi scis*, Sen. *Ira* 3.27.1, *Epist*. 66.45 (of Epicurean *tranquillitas*) *animus constat sibi et placidus est*. Atreus' travesty of *constantia* is underscored by young Tantalus' true fortitude, cf. 720 *stetit sui securus*. (See also on 713 *sibi*.)

704–705 deos / terret minantes: Atreus reacts as he did to the earlier portents (cf. 265–66 *fiat hoc, fiat nefas / quod, di, timetis*), but with even greater vigor; *ultro* stresses his taking the initiative.

705–706 iamque . . . adsistit aris: the narrative resumes with a quickened tempo (*dimissa mora*) and a new "scene-setting" phrase, *adsistit aris* (renewing 693), for which cf. Ovid *Met*. 8.480 (Althaea) *ante sepulcrales infelix adstitit aris*. In Ovid this introduces a soliloquy, here a substantial simile.

706 torvum et obliquum intuens: the sidelong glance (*obliquum*) recalls Tantalus in the underworld (cf. 160 *obliquat . . . oculos*), but *torvum* defines the look as hostile (cf. Petr. *Sat*. 113.6 *obliquis trucibusque oculis*) and also anticipates the tenor of the simile, since *torvus* is often used of wild animals, e.g., the lioness of Verg. *Ecl*. 2.62.

torvum et obliquum: adverbial or "cognate" accs. (AG 390b).

707–11 Atreus' changing moods as the slaughter proceeds are reflected in a pair of comparisons, first to a tigress whose hunger is so fierce that it cannot decide which of the available victims to attack first, later (732–36) to a lion that goes on killing even when its hunger has been sated (734 *pulsa fame*). The simile in 497–503 plays a comparable role at an earlier stage of the action. In *Troades* a series of similes likening Astyanax to a young animal connects the views taken of him by Ulysses (537–40), Andromache (794–99), and the more objective Messenger (1093–96).

The tigress-simile is based on Ovid *Met*. 5.164–67, Perseus wondering which of two opponents to set upon: *tigris ut auditis diversa valle duorum / exstimulata fame mugitibus armentorum / nescit utro potius ruat et ruere ardet utroque, sic dubius Perseus, dextra laevane feratur*, etc. Seneca embellishes his adaptation with the exotic detail *silvis . . . in Gangeticis* (itself drawn from Ovid, *Met*. 6.636–37, of Procne: *traxit Ityn, veluti Gangetica cervae / lactentem fetum per silvas tigris opacas*). He also heightens the element of doubt (*incerta, famem dubiam tenet*) in keeping with the prominence of this theme elsewhere (see above, p. 46 n. 158), and introduces language linking the simile with the motifs of "wandering" (*erravit* 708, see on 282) and desire (*cupida* 709, see on *avido* 2).

708 erravit: generalizing perfect, see on 553, 580; the present tenses that follow (*ferat*, *flectit, reflectit, tenet*) describe the scene in closer focus.

709-10 quo . . . ferat . . . morsus: indirect question dependent on *incerta*, which is coordinate with *cupida*.

710-11 flectit . . . rictus . . . reflectit: the repeated *ct* sounds may suggest the gnashing of teeth.

hoc . . . illo: adverbs, "in this direction . . . in that direction," cf. *Ben.* 5.6.5, *NQ* 5.1.1. [On *hoc*, more often seen as *huc*, cf. my edition of *Agamemnon*, p. 366.]

711 dubiam: predicate adj. ("keeps his hunger in doubt").

712 capita devota: *capita* here = "lives" to be consumed in a *devotio* or ritual immolation, cf. Verg. *Aen.* 3.370-71 *vittas . . . resolvit / sacrati capitis*, Cic. *Dom.* 145 *me . . . atque meum caput . . . devovi*, Sen. *Ag.* 163 *lustrale classi Doricae . . . caput*, TLL 3.416.49-74.

712-13 impiae . . . irae: Atreus' *ira* is the "deity" to whom the children are to be offered, taking the place of the *Di Manes* who would normally receive a *devotio*, cf. Livy 8.9.8 *legiones . . . mecum Deis Manibus Tellurique devoveo*, Flor. *Epit.* 1.12 *Decius . . . devotum Dis Manibus obtulit caput*. Medea also sacrifices the lives of others to her emotions, cf. *Med.* 1019-20 *plura non habui, dolor, / quae tibi litarem*. From here it is a short step for Atreus to regard the murders as an offering to himself, as he does in 713.

713 speculatur: the word remains partially within the animal-simile, since *speculari* can describe the watchfulness of a predator stalking its prey, cf. *Ben.* 4.20.3 *ut aves . . . lassa morbo pecora et casura ex proximo speculantur*, Pliny *NH* 8.33. (See also note on 504 *sperat sanguinem*.)

mactet sibi: the dative with *mactare* regularly names the divinity to whom a victim is offered (*OLD* s.v., #3, 4); Atreus is here openly usurping the honors of a god (cf. also 545 above, 885, 911 below). He thus achieves the standing that Thyestes has claimed to reject (464-65); Tantalus, too, had aspired to mingle with the gods (148). Atreus' "apotheosis" suits his depiction as an inverse *sapiens* (see on 703-704), since the *sapiens* could claim equality with the gods, cf. *Ag.* 610 *par ille regi, par superis erit* (n).

715-16 nec interest . . . ordinare: a revealing aside; the assertion of control is so important to Atreus that he derives satisfaction from it even when nothing depends on the result.

716 tamen: "all the same" (i.e., despite this hesitation, Atreus must have started with *one* of the children).

ferro occupat: the usual sense of *occupare* with weapons is to "strike first" before an opponent can act (*OLD* s.v., #11b, cf. Verg. *Aen.* 12.299-300 *venienti Ebyso plagamque ferenti / occupat os flammis*), but this meaning hardly fits an attack on helpless, bound victims; *occupare* here may have the sense "carry off," "sieze" (with connotations of violence), as in *HF* 64 *regna ne summa occupet*, *Pho.* 247-48 *protinus quosdam editos / nox occupavit*. The verb has a special association with Atreus, see on 204, 274.

717 ne . . . putes: i.e., *pietas* dictates that Tantalus, as the namesake of his great-grandfather, should be given the "place of honor" (*primus locus*). This almost gleeful irony is worlds away from the gibbering incoherence of the Messenger's first lines; as he proceeds his control of the narrative becomes more and more overt, reaching at last a witty detachment equal to that of Atreus himself (cf. also 744-45, 746-47). [For sarcastic ascription of motive see *Ag.* 184-85 *ne . . . desertus foret / a paelice umquam . . . torus* (n).]

719-21 Young Tantalus dies with composure, like Astyanax in *Troades* (cf. 1091–1103). His bravery, though, unlike that of Astyanax, appears to have no larger thematic significance; it seems meant primarily to heighten revulsion at Atreus' savagery.

720 sui securus: "without care for himself" (i.e., for his own life), cf. *Ben.* 4.4.1 *deus . . . securus et neglegens nostri, aversus a mundo*, ps-Sen. *HO* 1693.

721 perire: "to be wasted," "to go for naught"; perhaps a deliberate counterpart to 695 *nulla pars sacri perit.* See also on 1097.

illi: dat. of reference (AG 376), identifying Tantalus as the recipient of the action—a good example of the so-called "dative of disadvantage."

ferus: Atreus was called *ferus* in 546–47 *ferus ille . . . Atreus,* but here the absence of his name (or any other noun) and the surrounding animal-similes make one wonder whether *ferus* might be a substantive ("the beast").

722-23 in vulnere . . . commisit: as often in Senecan descriptions of violent death, the emphasis is not on bloodshed but on more subtly disturbing images—the "hiding" (*abscondit*) of the sword in the wound, the unremitting pressure of the thrust (*penitus premens*), and finally the grotesque juxtaposition of Atreus' hand and Tantalus' throat (*iugulo manum commisit*). The last is especially striking: *committere* often denotes the joining of like with like, cf., e.g., Ovid *Am.* 1.4.43 *nec femori committe femur, Her.* 2.31 *fides ubi nunc, commissaque dextera dextrae?*, but in this play, just as what belongs together is sundered (see on 179), so things that have no natural connection are forced into bizarre unions. (See also on 998.)

723-24 educto . . . ferro: several scenes in Ovid's *Metamorphoses* describe a weapon being withdrawn from a wound (cf. 5.39, 6.252, 9.129, 12.421–22); instead of the usual spray of gore, Seneca depicts a macabre mime of hesitation, which recalls and caps the previous uses of this image at 697–98 and 709–15.

723 stetit: a mocking echo of Tantalus' resolute "stand" of a moment ago, *stetit sui securus* 720; another sign of the Messenger's absorption of Atreus' spirit.

724 cadaver: pointedly emphatic: what remained erect was a mere corpse. [In general *cadaver* is a more highly charged word than *corpus,* carrying a stronger sense of the physical realities of death, cf. Verg. *G.* 3.557 and Ovid *Met.* 7.602 (plague victims), Verg. *Aen.* 8.264 (the monster Cacus), Hor. *S.* 2.5.85. It appears only here and at *Pho.* 36 in the tragedies and is on the whole rare in high poetry; the exception is Lucan, who insists on it to make his audience feel the ugliness of civil war. (See R. Mayer's edition of Lucan VIII [Warminster, 1980], 14.)]

725 in patruum cadit: i.e., in a futile gesture of hostility, as Polyxena falls in *Tro.* 1158–59 *cecidit ut Achilli gravem / factura terram, prona et irato impetu.*

726-29 Seneca arranges the deaths as a speaker might the order of points in an argument, with less prominence given to the middle than to the opening and closing sections.

727 adicitque fratri: i.e., he kills him; a typically Senecan way of alluding to an action by its result rather than naming it directly (see on 1044 *liberis detur via*).

percussa amputat: a characteristic Latin use of subordination to describe actions in a temporal sequence (where English would say "he strikes the neck and severs it").

728-29 After the clipped phrases recounting Plisthenes' beheading, the Messenger surveys its effects in two elaborately patterned lines; the neat chiastic arrangement of phrases (*truncus in pronum ruit—cucurrit murmure incerto caput*), the striking use of *cucurrit* for a rolling head, and above all the flamboyant sound-effects (9 *c*'s or *q*'s and 11 *u*'s!) suggest a speaker reveling in his powers of description. (The exuberance of these lines can be gauged by comparing the spare account of a decapitation in *Ag.* 902-903 *hinc trunco cruor / exundat, illinc ora cum fremitu iacent.*)

728 in pronum: adverbial, "downwards," cf. Manil. 3.372, Sen. *NQ* 5.12.1, *Epist.* 123.14 (*per pronum*, "downhill").

729 querulum: i.e., complaining at its death, like the spirits of Camilla and Turnus in the *Aeneid*, *vita . . . cum gemitu fugit indignata sub umbras* (11.831, 12.952); *querulum* is perhaps a reminiscence of Ovid's account of Orpheus' severed head, which murmured *flebile nescioquid* as it floated in the Hebrus, *Met.* 11.52-53 *flebile lingua / murmurat exanimis*. [For examples of tongues and other parts of the body continuing to function after death, see my note on *Ag.* 904, Bömer on Ovid *Met.* 6.560.]

cucurrit: *currere* of severed heads may be original with Seneca; the only parallel cited is from the next generation, *Il. lat.* 480 *deiectum longe caput a cervice cucurrit*. The image might have been suggested by the use of *currere* to describe rotating wheels, cf. Hor. *C.* 3.10.10, Ovid *Pont.* 4.9.10.

incerto: "unclear," i.e., not able to be made out distinctly (*OLD* s.v., #8c).

730-31 Even the Chorus seems swept up in the fervor of the Messenger's speech. These questions are framed in a more florid style than its earlier interventions (especially 690 and 716); note in particular the alliterative flair of *perfunctus facit, puerone parcit,* and *scelus sceleri*.

perfunctus: probably ironic, since *perfungor* commonly implies completing an arduous task or responsibility, cf. Cic. *Dom.* 134 (of the labors of Hercules), *Sen.* 77, Livy 22.26.3.

731 puero: the unnamed third child is presumably younger than his brothers.

732 Silva . . . Armenia: the Armenian lion, like the Indian tigress (707-708), belongs to the exotic regions that symbolize lawless violence, see also on 369-79. [The places chosen for this purpose vary with political conditions: Ko-Ko in *The Mikado* sings "I like to see a tiger / from the Congo or the Niger, / and especially when a-lashing of its tail."] Seneca's geography is here evocative rather than precise: Armenia was usually associated with tigers, not lions, cf. Ovid *Met.* 8.121 with Bömer's note. Seneca might be transposing the elements of Ovid *Met.* 15.86 *Armeniae tigres / iracundique leones.*

733 in caede multa . . . armento: Seneca alludes to the scene by its components, as it were, rather than naming it directly (e.g., by referring to *caesi iuvenci*).

victor: looks both backward to *in multa caede* ("victorious amid much slaughter") and forward, qualifying *incubat* with quasi-adverbial force.

armento incubat: variously interpreted as "falls . . . on the herd" (Miller, similarly Thomann) and "lies stretched on its victims" (cf. *OLD* s.v. *incubo*, #1a). The picture is perhaps instead of the lion "leaning over" the bodies of animals it has already killed (corresponding to the bodies of Tantalus and Plisthenes) and, even though surfeited, still lunging at new victims; for this sense of *incubare* see on 155 above.

734-36 cruore . . . impiger: a loosely appended set of phrases elaborating the general description of the scene in 733; in the tiger-simile 710-11 *flectit . . . tenet* have the same function. (Compare *HF* 283-88, especially 286-88 *pectore . . . via.*)

734 cruore rictus madidus: "its jaws dripping with gore" (*rictus* is acc. of specification or "Greek" acc., AG 397b).

735 non ponit iras: Atreus' true nature emerges, reversing the earlier pretense of harmony, *ponatur omnis ira* 519 (cf. also 509–10).

premens: "charging," "harrassing" (*OLD* s.v., #7).

736 dente iam lasso impiger: "with undiminished vigor even though its teeth are by now exhausted." [*impiger* is a conjecture of Zwierlein for the manuscript reading *piger*; the traditional text asserts that the lion is sluggish, which does not cohere with the violent energy of Atreus' sword-thrust in 740.]

dente: collective singular, see on 232 *lapis*.

737 ira tumet: see on 267–68, 361–62.

738 gemina caede perfusum: echoing *gemina caede perfunctus* (730) at the point when the Messenger begins to answer the Chorus's question.

739 oblitus in quem fureret: a rare glimpse of Atreus without his usual calculating awareness; as with the exercise of control (see on 715–16), the inflicting of pain can be its own reward.

740 exegit ultra corpus: "he drove [i.e., the sword] out through the other side of his body" (lit., "beyond the body," cf. Curt. 4.15.4 *hastae multum ultra temonem eminentes*). The phrase is a good example of Seneca's ability to generate powerful effects from simple and even vague language: its abruptness (heightened by the preparatory clauses *ferrum . . . tenens, oblitus . . . fureret, infesta manu*) conveys the tremendous force of Atreus' thrust, and *ultra corpus* suggests a more devastating impact than the precise terms usually found with *exigere* (e.g., *per costas, per ilia, iugulo*, cf. Verg. *Aen.* 10.682, Ovid *Met.* 4.734, 12.572). For this effect compare Vergil's account of Aeneas killing Lausus *Aen.* 10.815–16 *exigit ensem / per medium Aeneas iuvenem*.

ultra: although a preposition here and an adverb in 745 and 748, all three instances of the word may be related to the idea of "surpassing" or transgressing normal limits, see on 19–20, above, p. 47).

740–41 pueri . . . pectore: in an unsettling displacement, the child is kept in a subordinate syntactical position while attention is focused on the progress of the sword through his body.

741 pectore receptus . . . e tergo exstitit: perhaps a conscious reversal of the detail in Ovid's account of the death of Nessus, *Met.* 9.127–28 *fugientia terga sagitta / traicit; exstabat ferrum de pectore aduncum.* (A fascination with bizarre forms of physical violence and mutilation is part of the *Metamorphoses'* legacy to later poets, cf. Gordon Williams, *Change and Decline* [Berkeley, 1978], 254–61.)

e tergo exstitit: "protruded from his back"; *exstitit* from *exstare*, as is shown by the parallels in Ovid *Met.* 9.128 (previous note) and 6.236 *exstabat nudum de gutture ferrum.* [*e* is my own conjecture; the Mss read *in*, which does not fit as well with *exstare* in this sense (and which may have arisen from taking *exstitit* as from *exsisto*); *e* is equivalent to *de* in the Ovidian passages cited earlier.]

742 aras . . . extinguens: the "altar" implies the sacrificial fires on it, a metonymy for which the closest antecedents I have found are in Propertius, 2.28.36 *iacet extincto laurus adusta foco* (*focus = flamma in foco*), 3.20.25 *qui pactas in foedera ruperit aras* (*arae = foedera ad aras pacta*). The phrasing may imply that this bloodshed extinguishes not only the fire, but also the system of belief and practice that the altar represents.

aras: the plural is standard in high poetry, cf. *Ag.* 166 (n).

743 per utrumque vulnus moritur: another reminiscence of Ovid on the death of Nessus, *Met.* 9.129 *sanguis per utrumque foramen / emicuit*; the combination of the graphic *per utrumque vulnus* and the abstract *moritur* is characteristically Senecan (above, p. 26).

743-53 O saevum scelus! . . . spectet: the Chorus now echoes the horror-struck tones of the Messenger's opening speeches (cf. *tantum nefas* 624, *o domus* 625), while the Messenger enters even further into the mocking spirit of Atreus, meeting each outburst with a pointed *sententia*.

744-45 hactenus si stat nefas, / pius est: "if the crime stops here, he is innocent"; for the ironic linking of *scelus* and *pietas* compare Medea's exhortation, *quidquid admissum est adhuc, / pietas vocetur* (904–905). Both phrases may owe something to Ovid's Procne (*Met.* 6.635): *scelus est pietas in coniuge Terei* (perhaps also the source of ps-Sen. *HO* 986 *hoc erit pietas scelus*).

744 hactenus: "at this point (and not at a farther one)." In post-Augustan Latin *hactenus* often loses the sense of spatial or temporal extent and expresses a general idea of limitation, cf. Sen. *Epist* 88.1 *artificia . . . hactenus utilia* ("useful on condition that"), Tac. *Ann.* 14.42.5 *hactenus Vitellius voluerat* ("this and no more," see Furneaux *ad loc.*); for *hactenus stare* cf. the almost exact parallel in ps-Quint. *Decl. min.* 335 (p. 320 l. 9) *si calamitas mea hactenus stetisset*. [This passage confirms Heinsius' conjecture *si stat*: E reads *sistat*, A *non stat*, an interpolation made necessary by A's corruption of *pius* to *plus* in 744.]

si stat . . . pius est: a contrary-to-fact condition put in the indicative for greater vividness (perhaps a feature of informal speech); compare Juv. 3.257-60 *nam si procubuit qui saxa Ligustica portat / axis . . . , / quid superest de corporibus? quis membra, quis ossa / invenit?*

745 pius est: for the exaggeration see on *innocentem* 20.

maius: recalls Atreus' search for a "greater" form of revenge, cf. 254, 259, 267.

746 natura recipit: the Chorus unwittingly touches on Atreus' highest ambition, a crime that nature *cannot* allow (for *recipere* cf. *Epist.* 82.17 *non recipit rerum natura ut aliquis magno animo accedat ad id quod malum iudicat*, OLD s.v., #9).

746-47 finem . . . gradus: Seneca's most pointed use of a favorite opposition, cf. *HF* 208-209 *finis alterius mali / gradus est futuri, Cons. Helv.* 11.4 *in omni desiderio . . . quidquid illi congesseris, non finis erit cupiditatis, sed gradus.*

747-48 obiecit . . . arcuit: the theme of "surpassing" in its most explicit form, as the Chorus thinks of the worst treatments traditionally inflicted on the dead, only to have the Messenger respond that these would have been acts of mercy (*votum* 752). The progression recurs at 1032-34, with Thyestes and Atreus in the roles here taken by the Chorus and the Messenger.

obiecit feris / lanianda . . . corpora: the language is strong, but conventional, cf. Pollio *ap.* Cic. *Fam.* 10.23.3 *bestiis . . . civis Romanos . . . obiecit*, Val. Max. 1.6.11 *corpus imperatoris . . . avium ferarumque laniatibus obiectum.*

749-51 ne . . . trahat: the Messenger elaborates each of the Chorus's imagined horrors, turning *igne arcuit* into *ne tegat . . . humus / nec solvat ignis* with *obiecit . . . corpora* doubled as *avibus epulandos . . . ferisque . . . pabulum . . . trahat*; the diction also becomes more emotional, cf. *lanianda—epulandos, obiecit—triste pabulum . . . trahat, feris—feris . . . saevis*. The result is to show that, even in their most ghastly forms, the normal extremes of degradation fall short of the present reality.

749 functos: = *morte functos*, see on 15.

750 solvat: perhaps combining the idea of physical dissolution with that of release (*solvere* is often used of a peaceful death, cf. *Epist*. 66.43 *alius inter cenandum solutus est*); these positive overtones would correspond to the hint of protection in *tegat*.

750-51 avibus epulandos . . . ferisque . . . pabulum: "birds and dogs" is a combination going back to Homer (*Il*. 1.4–5); the language here recalls Catullus' Ariadne (64.152–53) *dilaceranda feris dabor alitibusque / praeda, neque iniacta tumulabor harena*.

licet . . . trahat: *licet* is not concessive, but strongly optative ("if only he were dragging them . . ."), a usage found often in Ovid, cf. *Met*. 3.405 *sic amet ipse licet*, 9.480, 12.199, etc.

751 pabulum: perhaps an echo of 12 *plenum recenti pabulum monstro iacet*.

trahat: a brutally graphic detail; compare Hamlet's exit with the body of Polonius, "I'll lug the guts into the neighbour room" (3.4.212).

752 votum . . . solet: a lead-in line to the following *sententia*. Atreus had spoken similarly of his inversion of normal categories, cf. 247–48 *in regno meo / mors impetratur*.

votum: "something wished for," like *metus*, "something feared" (see on 1049).

sub hoc: "under this man's rule" (*hoc* abl.), parallel to *in regno meo* in 247; cf. Sall. *Jug*. 19.7 *Numidae . . . sub Iugurtha erant*, *OLD* s.v., #15c.

753 pater insepultos spectet: Thyestes would wish to see his children unburied because they are in fact "buried" inside his body, cf. 1047, 1050, 1090–92.

753-54 o . . . neget: as the Messenger turns back to his story, the thought of what he is about to describe makes him exclaim in anguish; compare 684 *quis . . . eloqui?*

754 quod . . . posteritas neget: for this horrified denial, cf. *Pho*. 266 [*facinus*] *quod esse factum nulla non aetas neget*. Atreus has surpassed his own ambition, a crime *quod nulla posteritas probat, / sed nulla taceat* (192–93). [Seneca might be alluding to versions of the myth in which the banquet *was* "denied," in that the reversal of the sun's course was instead interpreted as signifying divine approval of Atreus or even symbolizing his calculation of a solar eclipse, see Frazer on "Apollodorus" *Epit*. 2.12.] This awareness of events as a "story" is another trait shared by the Messenger and Atreus, see on 273.

neget: subjunctive in a relative clause of characteristic (AG 535).

755-58 Reverting to his priestly *persona*, Atreus conducts an *extispicium* on the bodies of his victims. He seems to have no serious intention of learning the future but simply to be displaying perverse regard for established form; for the sequence sacrifice-extispicy-banquet, cf. Ovid *Met*. 15.130–39.

755 erepta vivis exta pectoribus: modeled on Ovid *Met*. 15.136 *ereptas viventi pectore fibras*, also echoed in *Oed*. 391 *fibra vivis rapta pectoribus*. Only the organs of freshly-killed victims were thought suitable for divination, cf. Pease on Verg. *Aen*. 4.64.

tremunt: the organs still "quiver" with reflexive muscular contractions, cf. Verg. *Aen.* 4.64 *spirantia consulit exta* (with *spirantia* the probable inspiration for *spirant . . . venae* in 756). The choice of *tremere* may have been influenced by Verg. *Aen.* 1.212 *veribus . . . trementia* [sc. *viscera*] *figunt*, cf. also Ovid *Met.* 6.558 (Philomela's severed tongue) *ipsa iacet terrae . . . tremens.*

756 spirantque . . . salit: based on Ovid's account of the flaying of Marsyas, *Met.* 6.389–91 *trepidaeque sine ulla / pelle micant venae; salientia viscera posses / et perlucentes numerare in pectore fibras*; the detail *cor . . . pavidum* recalls yet another episode of the *Metamorphoses*, the transformation of Daphne; *sentit adhuc trepidare novo sub cortice pectus* (*Met.* 1.554).

spirant: "throb" (= *micant* in Ovid *Met.* 6.390 above).

757 at ille: *at* signals a shift in narrative focus ("as for him"), but may retain some adversative force; Atreus is not troubled by these gruesome sights, but instead pursues his ritual tasks with the calm of a practiced surgeon. The measured tricolon that follows (*fibras tractat, fata inspicit, adhuc . . . notas*) heightens this impression of eerie composure.

758 viscerum venas notat: i.e., he takes account of the *notae*, the markings of the blood-vessels on the organs that were closely scrutinized in divination, cf. *Oed.* 352 *ede certas viscerum nobis notas*, Tib. 2.5.14, Luc. 1.587–88, 618–19.

759 placuere: "have met with approval"; the sacrificial sense is played on by Ovid at *Met.* 15.131 *placuisse nocet*, cf. also Sen. *Ag.* 99–100 *placet in vulnus* (i.e., sacrifice) / *maxima cervix.*

759–60 securus . . . epulis: "he gives full attention to his brother's banquet" (*securus* = without any *curae* to distract him), cf. Val. Max. 3.8 *ext.* 1 *Darium . . . toto animo Hannibalis amicitiae vacantem.* The phrase implies that Atreus will devote the same care to the rôle of chef that he has shown as priest—an expectation borne out by the meticulously detailed lines that follow; also, since *vacare* in this sense normally refers to a pleasurable activity (cf. *Ag.* 183 *Veneri vacat* [n]), it suggests the enjoyment Atreus derives from his preparations (and which the Messenger seems vicariously to share in describing them).

760–61 divisum . . . corpus: family history repeats itself, as Atreus follows the example set by Tantalus, cf. 147 *divisus.* (On the subordination in *divisum . . . corpus* see on 727 *colla percussa.*)

761 amputat trunco tenus: "cuts back as far as the trunk."

762 umeros . . . moras: the children seem to be well-developed adolescents, with broad shoulders and muscular upper arms.

umeros patentes: "spreading shoulders," cf. Ovid *Met.* 13.962 *ingentes umeros*, and for *patens* = "extending widely" cf. Ovid *F.* 3.589, 4.713. [In the only other instances of *umerus patens* I know, Ovid *Ars* 2.504, 3.310, *patens* means "bare," "exposed," but this sense seems out of place here.]

lacertorum moras: "the retarding arms" (Miller), lit., "the delays caused by the *lacerti*," cf. *Cons. Helv.* 11.6 *quantum per moras membrorum . . . licet.* The reference— brilliant in its clinical exactness—is to the sinews of the upper arm (or possibly to the ganglion where the shoulder and arm meet), which slow down the process of dismemberment. For the construction *lacertorum moras* cf. 362 *tumor Hadriae.*

763 denudat artus . . . ossa amputat: each verb applies to both nouns, "he lays bare and cuts out the joints and bones."

artus: "joints," not "limbs" (as in 779); for the combination with *ossa* cf. Pl. *Men.* 855 *membra atque ossa atque artus*, Verg. *Aen.* 5.422–23 *magnos membrorum artus, magna ossa lacertosque / exuit*.

denudat: cf. Pacuvius 200 R², where a ghost's bones have been laid bare, *denudatis ossibus*, also Verg. *Aen.* 1.211 *tergora diripiunt costis et viscera nudant* (preparations for a banquet, a passage drawn on several times in this scene).

764 ora . . . manus: the head and extremities were often reserved in genuine sacrifices, cf. W. Burkert, *Homo necans* (Eng. trans. [Berkeley, 1983], 105). Atreus gives the practice a special motive: the heads serve for identification (hence *ora*, stressing the faces), and the hands as grotesque souvenirs of the pretended reconciliation.

datas fidei manus: "hands given in token of good faith" (*fidei* dat. of purpose, AG 382). The action referred to is implied at 520–21 *obsides fidei accipe / hos innocentes*.

765–66 haec . . . illa: in his choice of cooking styles Atreus is a strict traditionalist: the division of parts into those roasted on spits and those boiled in a cauldron is a fixed element in ancient descriptions of cannibal meals, and may have its origins in ritual practices, cf. Burkert, *op. cit.* (on 764), 89 n. 29, and Acc. 220–22 R² (Atreus), Ovid *Met.* 1.228–29 (Lycaon) 6.645–46 (Procne); it also figures in epic feasting-scenes in Verg. *Aen.* 1.212–13 and Val. Fl. 8.254.

veribus . . . caminis: closest in its detail to Accius 221–22 R² *veribus in focos* [=*caminos*] / *lacerta tribuit*.

lentis . . . caminis: "slow-burning furnaces"; for *lentus* see on 499.

766 stillant: the limbs "drip" as the fat is melted by the fire below; Medea prays that her poisons will have a similar effect on their victims, *Med.* 837 *stillent artus ossaque fument*.

flammatus latex: both *latex* and *flammare* are poeticisms; the combination yields an almost absurdly high-flown expression for "boiling water," far more pompous than Accius' *calida* [*sic*] *latice* (666 R²) or Ovid's *purum laticem* (*Met.* 7.327) and exaggerated in a way that Seneca's other uses of *flammare* are not, cf. *Med.* 387 *flammata facies*, *Tro.* 303–304 *flammatum . . . pectus*. The Messenger seems, like Atreus, to be indulging in conscious stylistic playfulness.

767–75 Once again (cf. 696–702) the external world shows its revulsion at the deed it is forced to experience; the fire burns unwillingly (*invitus ardet* 770), and the smoke from the burning flesh settles ominously on the house.

767–70 impositas . . . ardet: the arrangement of this long sentence mirrors its content, with the action that the fire is reluctant to perform held off until the last possible moment (*ardet*).

768 in . . . trepidantes focos: cf. *Ag.* 168 *recedentes focos* (at the sacrifice of Iphigenia). Atreus characteristically takes no notice of this resistance in his recollections of the scene, *caede votiva focos / placavi* 1058–59.

769 pati iussus moram: i.e., the fire was held in place until it had done its work; another instance of the themes of unwilling action and vain resistance, see above, p. 47.

770 invitus ardet: perhaps suggested by Ovid *Met.* 8.514 (of Meleager) *invitis correptus ab ignibus arsit*.

stridet . . . iecur: a more specific version of Ovid *Met.* 6.646 (the cooking of Itys) *pars* *veribus stridunt*. The verb shifts attention from sight to sound and so leads into the "groaning" of 771–72.

771–72 nec . . . gemuere: another detail inspired by Ovid's account of Meleager, *Met.* 8.513–14 *aut dedit aut visus gemitus est ipse dedisse / stipes*; in each case the noises emitted by burning wood or other objects are likened to groans and interpreted as sounds of mourning. [This application of *gemere* may result from its use for the "creaking" of wood, cf. *OLD* s.v., #3b, Hor. *C.* 1.14.5–6 *mālus celeri saucius Africo / antemnaeque gemant*—a sound which Vergil calls *stridor* in *Aen.* 1.87.] The same sound is referred to with a different metaphor in 1064 *mugire fibras vidi*, cf. *Oed.* 383 *immugit aris ignis*.

771 nec facile dicam: a variation on such prose expressions as *haud facile dixerim*, cf. Cic. *Rep.* 1.6, Tac. *Ann.* 4.34.5, etc. The Messenger seems to be calling attention to the cleverness of his play on *gemere*.

772 gemuere: indicative in an indirect question, common in early Latin and occasionally found later, most often in poetry (AG 575c); good discussion by Austin on Verg. *Aen.* 6.615.

772–75 Divination took careful note of the way the offered victims burned: "it was a good sign if the fire at once seized on the offering, and blazed up in clear flames (Apoll. Rhod. 1.436 . . .). It was a bad sign, if the fire was smothered in smoke" (Jebb on Soph. *Ant.* 1007); cf. also Sen. *Oed.* 307–23, Stat. *Ach.* 1.520–22. The omens here are naturally bad, portending disaster for the house (775).

in fumos abit: *abire in* ("to turn into") is a favorite Ovidian term of metamorphosis, cf. *Met.* 1.236 *in villos abeunt vestes, in crura lacerti*.

773 tristis: "gloomy" (*tristia nubila*, Ovid *Met.* 6.690), but perhaps also implying ill omen, cf. Curt. 7.7.22 *tristia exta*, Juv. 6.569 *quid sidus triste minetur*.

nebula: defining abl. with *gravis*; the *nebula* is a billowing cloud of smoke, cf. *Tro.* 1054–55 *fumus alte / serpit in caelum nebulaeque turpes*. Here, since the smoke does not rise, it appears weighed down by its own mass (*gravis*).

774 non . . . -que: *non* negates *levat* as well as *exit*, with *-que* introducing a more specific restatement of *rectus exit* ("epexegetic" *-que*, cf. *OLD* s.v., #6).

775 Penates . . . obsidet: as the sacrificial fire in *Oedipus* foretells fratricide by dividing in two (321–23), so the "disfiguring cloud" (on *deformis* see 667) settling on the *Penates* symbolizes defilement for the house. The reference to the *Penates* also begins a shift of focus from the grove to the dining hall, completed at 778.

Penates: probably "household gods" rather than a metonymy for *domus*; see on 264 *Lares*.

nube deformi: possibly a reworking of Ovid *F.* 5.505 *tecta senis subeunt nigro deformia fumo*.

776–78 o Phoebe . . . occidisti: the last and most impassioned of the Messenger's prefatory outbursts (cf. 684, 753–54), preceding the most horrific image of all. It is characteristic of Seneca's allusive technique that the Sun's flight, the most famous detail in the entire myth, is not directly narrated but only mentioned in a concessive clause as having already taken place. (See on 120–21.)

776 patiens: "all-enduring" (Miller); the Sun too is made to suffer what it would avoid, cf. 769 *pati iussus moram*, above, p. 47.

777 medio . . . diem: "even though you have drowned the day, broken off in mid-sky"; *rumpere diem* is a more striking equivalent of *rumpere iter* as in Ovid *Ars* 1.329–30 *non medium rupisset iter curruque retorto / Auroram versis Phoebus adisset equis*. The "broken day" is a consequence and a symbol of the severing of all moral law (*fas . . . omne ruptum* 179, see note *ad loc.*). [Some editors replace *ruptum* with *raptum*, a reading found in late Mss; *medio caelo* would then be an abl. of separation, "the day snatched from mid-sky." This reading does not seem superior to the more widely attested *ruptum*; it produces an echo of 637–38 *dies . . . raptus*, but it loses the important notion of fracture.]

medio . . . caelo: almost = "in mid-course," cf. 792 *medio . . . Olympo*.

merseris: alluding to the Sun's chariot sinking into the western ocean (cf. 819–20). Ovid regularly specifies the body of water to which *mergere* relates (cf. *Met.* 7.324, *Ars* 1.410, *F.* 4.388), but Seneca, in his less graphic manner, tends to use the verb absolutely, cf. *Med.* 877–78 *merget diem timendum / dux noctis Hesperus*, *Pha.* 679 *lucem merge et in tenebras fuge*.

778 sero occidisti: i.e., too late to prevent the deed from taking place; in 784–87 the Sun's reason for reversing course is rather to hide the repulsive sight.

778–83 Seneca adroitly ends the Messenger's narrative with the picture of Thyestes at his feast, the starting-point in both time and setting for the next act.

778 lancinat: the shockingly violent word is placed first, its effect heightened still further by the long build-up in 776–78. Thyestes' "rending" and "chewing" (*mandit*) contrast sharply with the antiseptic neatness of Atreus' preparations (cf. 760 *divisum secat*, 761, 763 *amputat*, 763 *denudat*); he seems to be amply fulfilling Atreus' vision, *liberos avidus pater / gaudensque laceret* (277–78).

lancinat: even stronger than *lacerare*, often implying madness or depravity, cf. Sen. *Contr.* 2.5.6 (a frenzied tyrant to his torturers) *seca, verbera, oculos lancina*, also Sen. *Ira* 3.19.5, 40.4, *Clem.* 2.9.2.

natos pater: pointed juxtaposition as in 40–41 *natum parens / natusque patrem* (sc. *expavescat*); see also on 1090.

779 mandit: *mandere* is a neutral description of animal behavior, but often suggests the unnatural when used of humans, cf., e.g., Verg. *Aen.* 3.627 (Polyphemus, so too Ovid *Met.* 14.211), 11.669, Ovid *Met.* 15.92–93 *nil te nisi tristia mandere saevo / vulnera dente iuvat*, 142.

780 nitet . . . comam: an attentive host might offer his guests unguents for their hair (cf. Catullus' *'cenabis bene . . .'*, 13.11, and Nisbet-Hubbard on Hor. *C.* 1.4.9), but the wording of this line (*nitet, madidus, fluente*) strongly implies gross overindulgence; compare *HF* 468–69 *fortem vocemus cuius horrentes comae / maduere nardo?*, *VB* 7.3 (personified *Voluptas*) *mero atque unguento madentem*. See also on 947–48.

madidus: the word occurs only in *Thyestes* among Seneca's plays (734, 948); it tellingly underscores the contrast between Atreus, compared to a lion with dripping jaws (*cruore rictus madidus* 734), and Thyestes, his hair dripping with rich unguents.

781 gravisque vino: somewhat loosely attached to the previous line (as though *nitet* were, e.g., *iacet*); for *gravis vino* cf. 910 *vino gravatum . . . caput* and note on 787.

781–82 praeclusae . . . fauces: "his blocked-up jaws retained the food" (i.e., he could not swallow because the previous mouthfuls had not yet been digested); the image is of a man greedily "bolting" his food. The phrase may have been imitated by Silius 9.511 *fau-*

ces praeclusas pulvere.

782-83 in malis . . . ignoras tua: the plain wording of this phrase is deliberately contrasted with the richness of the previous lines: Thyestes' fantasies of luxury are abruptly brought down to earth.

783 Thyesta: the apostrophe recalls instances of the device in Vergil (cf., e.g., *Aen.* 4.408 *quis tibi tum, Dido, cernenti talia sensus?*, 9.446-49 *fortunati ambo!*, etc.) and especially in Ovid (cf., e.g., *Met.* 1.488-89 *te decor iste quod optas / esse vetat*). The address can both express empathy with a character and also enforce a sense of distance, by reminding the audience of the narrator's presence. The latter effect is prominent here; the Messenger ends his account in the omniscient tone of an author rather than a mere reporter. He shares this feeling of control with Atreus, who addresses the off-stage Thyestes in similar terms: *discutiam tibi / tenebras, miseriae sub quibus latitant tuae* (896-97).

mala ignoras tua: perhaps an echo of *ignotus sibi* (403, and see note *ad loc.*).

784 et hoc peribit: the implacable certainty resembles that of the Fury, cf. in particular 47-48 *et fas et fides / iusque omne pereat.*

784-87 verterit . . . gravis: an elaborate period, whose length and involved syntax parallel the Sun's efforts at concealment. In the end, though, symbolizing the failure of resistance, the language descends to the minimal: *videndum est, tota patefient mala.*

784-86 verterit . . . obruat: *verterit* names a single past action (the Sun's change of direction), *obruat* a present effect of that action (the unnatural darkness).

785 sibi . . . obvium ducens iter: "following a course that will bring him face to face with himself." The notion of "meeting oneself" may have been suggested by descriptions of the winding river Meander, cf., e.g., Ovid *Met.* 8.164 *occurrens . . . sibi venturas aspicit undas*, Sen. *HF* 684 *Maeander . . . cedit sibi.*

ipse Titan: cf. 120.

786 tenebris . . . novis: a perfectly symmetrical line (ABcba, see on 10); the patterning may reflect the Messenger's enjoyment of his own verbal artistry.

novis: "strange," "unheard-of" (*OLD* s.v., #3); together with *alieno* in 787, *novis* underlines the complete breakdown of normal order.

787 nox . . . gravis: placing the subject last in the sentence and qualifying it with three unrelated descriptive phrases represents an inversion of the syntactical norm that corresponds to the unnatural events being described.

missa ab ortu: since night can be thought to proceed from the place where the sun sets, if a backward-moving sun sets in the East (often signified by *ortus* in poetry and high prose), that night can be said to come forth "from the sunrise." The *sententia* combines the literal and figurative meanings of *ortus* in such a way that one (the figurative) is required, while the other (the literal) becomes logically impossible.

tempore alieno: abl. of time; night is usurping the hours that "belong to" day.

gravis: a word insistently repeated at the end of this act, cf. 773 *fumus . . . gravis*, 781 *gravis . . . vino*. These uses relate the oppressive external darkness to its cause, the abnormal heaviness within Thyestes; this link is fully exploited in the last act, cf. 910

gravatum . . . caput, 986 *pondus . . . dextram gravat*, 990 *aether gravis*, 1000 *sentio . . . onus*, 1051 *premor natis*, 1071 *Nox . . . gravis.*

788 tota patefient mala: the prediction is fulfilled (and its latent metaphor made actual) by Atreus in the next scene, cf. 902 *festa patefiat domus.*

CHORUS IV

The Chorus reacts in fear and confusion to the darkness that has suddenly enveloped the scene. The familiar signs of night are missing, and the Chorus wonders if some renewal of primeval conflict between the gods and Giants has annulled the regular sequence of night and day. Even this, though, would be less terrifying than the Chorus's worst dread, that the appointed time has come for the universe to be destroyed, when the sun and moon will veer from their courses and the stars will fall, one by one, from the sky. The Chorus cries out in anguish at being born in such an age—*o nos dura / sorte creatos!* (878–79), then steels itself to embrace death amid the all-encompassing doom.

The ode is closely bound to the dramatic situation, but in one respect it remains oddly detached from its surroundings. At no point does the Chorus seem aware of the actual cause of the phenomena that alarm it, even though the Messenger has just explicitly connected the darkness with the sun's horror at Thyestes' banquet (776–78, 784–88). It is almost as if the Chorus that took part in the previous scene is a different entity from the lyric voice of the ode. Because of this disjunction, the Chorus's fears are conveyed in powerful and immediate terms (see on 828–29), while its attempts to identify their cause all seem unreal and therefore uninvolving; even the ruin of the cosmos emerges as a grandiose pageant rather than an imminent threat. Despite a degree of contrivance, this handling of the Chorus has its roots in a sound dramatic instinct: the mood of bewildered anxiety maintains suspense and allows the revelations of the last act to unfold with their horror undiminished. The Chorus's bewilderment also deepens the pathos of its situation and makes the unflinching composure of its last words all the more impressive.[1]

Since the Chorus is not in a position to interpret what it sees, much of the ode's effect is produced at the unconscious level, through inference and irony. The pictures of the work-day disrupted in heaven as on earth (794–801, 815–24) are saved from being merely witty by their connection to fundamental themes of dislocation and inversion. The evocation of the rebellious Giants (804–12) is unintentionally apt in its suggestion of an unquenched thirst for power and of the intrusion of hellish forces into the world. Finally, the notion of a universe on the point of collapse is a potent metaphor for moral anarchy, both within the play and also in the Roman world to which the play implicitly relates.

The beginning and end of the ode contain striking similarities to Pindar's ninth *Paean*, inspired by a solar eclipse in 478 or 463 B.C. (See notes on 789–93, 883–84.) Direct imitation of Pindar by Seneca would be surprising; the paean may have served as a model for a choral ode in a lost Greek *Thyestes*-play, as Pindar's account of an eruption of Aetna in *P.* 1.15–28 has strongly influenced a passage in the *Prometheus Bound* (351–72). The central section of the ode stands in a different tradition, the astronomical treatise in verse, of which the outstanding example in Greek is the *Phaenomena* of Aratus (3rd century B.C., translated into Latin by Cicero, Ovid, and others), in Latin the *Astronomica* of Manilius (ca. A D. 10–15). In general Seneca's astronomy here is too conventional for his sources to

---

[1] It is significant that the unnatural darkness will be experienced twice more in the play, by Atreus (891–97) and by Thyestes (990–95). The event thus becomes a focal point around which the characters define themselves by their reactions; cf. W. H. Owen, *TAPA* 99 (1968), 297–300.

be evident, but there are interesting parallels with views known to have been held or discussed by Nigidius Figulus, a Neopythagorean sage of Cicero's time who appears as an eminent astrologer in Lucan's *Bellum civile* 1.639–72. (See notes on 856, 860–62).

Meter: Anapests (see above, pp. 32–33, below pp. 245–49).

789–826 The first part of the ode alternates questions and assertions: (a) why has the sun fled? (789–93); (b) the normal signs of night are not present (794–801); (a¹) what catastrophe has driven the sun from its course? (802–12); (b¹) the orderly routine of the heavens has been overturned (813–26). The same themes recur in each part of the sequence, but are repeated in augmented form: a¹ + b¹ are almost precisely double the length of a + b (25 lines to 13) and are also more varied in language. (Compare, for example, the straightforward repetition of *nondum* in 794, 796, 798, 801 with the wider range of negative terms in the corresponding later section: *periere* 813, *nihil . . . nihil* 814, *perversa* 817, *nescit* 818, *nec* 819, *insueto* 821, *nondum* 823, *non . . . nec . . . non* 824–26.) The Chorus's terror grows as it contemplates the chaos that surrounds it.

789–93 Quo . . . quo . . . cur: the questions renew the anxious tone of the prologue (1–4); note in particular repeated *numquid* in 804–12, cf. 6.

789 terrarum superumque parens: a most unusual epithet for the sun, perhaps chosen for the contrast with Thyestes, the impious *pater* (778). [Heinsius emended *parens* to *potens*, but this would be no less peculiar.]

superum: gen. of *supera*, "the high places" or "the heavens," cf. *HF* 423 *inferna tetigit, posset ut supera assequi.*

790–91 cuius . . . fugit: after the opening vocative, this relative clause has the flavor of hymnic invocation, cf., e.g., Hor. *C.* 1.10.1–3 *Mercuri . . . qui feros cultus hominum recentum / voce formasti*, Sen. *Ag.* 400–403 *pater ac rector, cuius nutu simul extremi / tremuere poli* (and my note on *Ag.* 370). Pindar's *Paean* 9 also begins with solemn address to the vanished sun, followed by anxious questions (1–6) and speculations on the cause of the portent (11–20).

791 decus omne fugit: *decus* nearly = *sidus* by metonymy (effect for cause, cf. 50); compare 995 *fugit omne sidus*. It is conventional to say that the stars "flee" at the sun's approach (cf. Hor. *C.* 3.21.24 *dum rediens fugat astra Phoebus*, Bömer on Ovid *Met.* 2.114), but here the cliché is pointedly set against the unnatural flight of the sun itself.

792 medio . . . Olympo: = *medio caelo* or more precisely *medio itinere*; compare Verg. *G.* 1.450 *emenso cum iam decedit Olympo.*

793 tuos . . . aspectus: both active and passive senses of *aspectus* seem at work: the sun averts its gaze, and so can no longer be seen.

794–95 serae . . . Vesper: the picture of Vesper summoning the other stars (perhaps implied in *Med.* 878 *dux noctis Hesperus*) seems not to be conventional; Seneca has perhaps applied to the evening a traditional attribute of the morning star, cf. Ovid *Met.* 4.629–30, 11.97–98, *HF* 128 *cogit nitidum Phosphorus agmen*. In wording the phrase may owe something to Verg. *G.* 1.251 *illic sera rubens accendit lumina Vesper.*

796 Hesperiae flexura rotae: "the turning of the western wheel" is a mannered equivalent of "the western end of the sun's path, where its chariot turns around." The conception may come from the circus, where chariots turned at the *meta*; for this language used of the sun, cf. Ovid *Met.* 3.145 *sol ex aequo meta distabat utraque*, Sen. *Pha.* 288 *ad Hesperias iacet ora metas* (= the far West). This imagery, together with the prominence of *rota* and *currus* (see next note), might recall the unsavory role of racing-chariots in Tantalid history, cf. 660–61 *fracti . . . currus, . . . / iunctae . . . falsis axibus . . . rotae.*

797 emeritos . . . currus: *currus* appears where one might expect *equos*, cf. Verg. *G.* 2.542 *equum fumantia solvere colla*, Ovid *F.* 4.688 *dempserat emeritis iam iuga Phoebus equis*.

798-99 nondum . . . signum: i.e., it is not yet the end of the ninth hour (approx. = 3 p.m. or 15.00), and so of the day's third quarter; this was the point at which "evening" was conventionally thought to begin (cf. Tertullian *De ieiunio* 2.1., perhaps also Hor. *S.* 2.7.32–34), just as in Rome today, "la sera" starts after the mid-day meal. The ninth hour was the favorite time for a Roman *cena* (cf. Cic. *Fam.* 9.26.1, Hor. *Ep.* 1.7.71, Mart. 4.8), so Seneca's chronology is scrupulously exact in Roman terms.

799 tertia . . . bucina: another detail inspired by contemporary Rome, where trumpeters were used to announce the time of day, cf. Sen. *Contr.* 7 *pr.* 1 *saepe declamante illo ter bucinavit*, Petr. *Sat.* 74.2 (figuratively of a cock crowing at dawn). They were probably found in *fora* and other public places (Trimalchio's personal *bucinator* in livery [*Sat.* 26.7] is clearly egregious), and their function may have been semi-official, like that of a *praeco*, cf. *Dig.* 50.6.7(6). I have found no reference to a *bucinator* marking quarters rather than hours, as probably in Vitr. 9.8.5 (of a water-clock), Sen. *Contr.* 7 *pr.* 1 (above; one hopes that Albucius Silo declaimed for three, not nine hours); on the other hand, the Romans attached particular importance to the quarters of the day—the *praetor* at one time was responsible for having them announced, cf. Varro *Ling. lat.* 6.89—and their passage may have been marked with special ceremony. [Earlier commentators saw a reference to the Roman military practice of dividing the night into four watches, cf. Prop. 4.4.63, etc., or else alleged that it was Greek custom to divide the day into thirds, apparently on the basis of the tripartite division of night in Homer, cf. *Il.* 10.252–53, *Od.* 12.312, etc. See also W. Kubitschek, *Grundriss der antiken Zeitrechnung* (Munich, 1928), 187–88.]

800-801 stupet . . . arator: these lines are verbally linked to what precedes by *nondum* (placed differently and modifying an adjective, *fessis*, rather than the verb), but they also look forward to 815-24, since they describe a reaction to the disturbed order of nature; *stupet* is echoed at 815, *nondum* at 823-24, *nondum / nocte parata*. This glimpse of ordinary life may have been introduced partly for the allusion to a *cena*, the only time in the play that Seneca uses the word traditionally associated with Thyestes' meal (cf., e.g., Pl. *Rud.* 508–509 *scelestiorem cenam cenavi tuam / quam quae Thyestae quondam aut posita est Tereo*).

804-12 The Chorus wonders if the Giants, archetypal manifestations of violence and anarchy, have renewed their attacks on the Olympian establishment. These speculations contain an element of truth, hinted at in this section, *aperto / carcere Ditis*: the audience knows that hell's prison-house has indeed opened, first in the prologue (cf. 1-2, 70) and later in the Messenger's account of the secret grove (cf. 669, 678–79). (See also on 1006–19). [Augustan poets used the victory of Jupiter over the Giants to represent the triumphs of Augustus, as Greek writers had done with Alexander, cf. Hor. *C.* 3.4.42–64, Ovid *Tr.* 2.333–36, implicitly in Prop. 2.1.19–20, Ovid *Am.* 2.1.11–18, perhaps Verg. *G.* 1.278–83, *Aen.* 6.580–600. The fear that a Giant revolt may have upset the order of heaven could thus be a negation of Augustan confidence in the stability of the regime.]

804 numquid: "is it possible that . . . ?"; cf. on 6 above.

805-806 victi . . . Gigantes: the legend of the Giants Otus and Ephialtes, who tried to storm heaven by heaping Ossa on Olympus and Pelion on Ossa (*Od.* 11.305–20), was at an early stage conflated with the myth of the Titans (sons of Earth, like the Giants), who fought a pitched battle against the Olympian gods at the Phlegraean fields (Pind. *Nem.* 1.67, cf. 810–11 *Phlegraeos . . . per hostes*) and were cast into Tartarus by Zeus

(Hes. *Theog.* 665-735). The result of the conflation was the "war of the Giants" or Gigantomachy, referred to familiarly by Callimachus (fr. 119 Pf.) and a proverbial topic in Latin (cf. Cic. *Sen.* 5 *Gigantum modo bellare cum dis*); in Vergil's account of Tartarus (*Aen.* 6.577-627) Otus and Ephialtes appear alongside the *Titania pubes* (582-84, 580-81). Tityos and Typhoeus are enemies of the Olympians who have no part in early versions of the Titanomachy or Gigantomachy. Tityos (who attempted to assault Leto) was, however, a Giant and was linked with his heaven-storming fellows by Vergil (*Aen.* 6.595-600, cf. 9-12 above) and Horace (*C.* 3.4.77-78), while Typhoeus, spawned by Earth after the defeat of the Titans (Hes. *Theog.* 820) or Giants ("Apollodorus" *Bibl.* 1.6.3), made a single-handed attempt to overthrow Zeus and met the same fate as his predecessors.

victi temptant / bella: the Chorus makes the Giants resemble the Tantalids, unwilling to abandon violence even in defeat, cf. 37-38, 197-99, 237, 340-41. Thyestes later confirms this association, calling on Jupiter to blast him and Atreus with the thunderbolt once used against the Giants (1082-84).

806-808 Tityos . . . iras: *pectore fesso* and *saucius* allude to the fuller account of his punishment in 9-12.

807-808 pectore fesso renovat . . . iras: probably a significant echo of the lion-simile in 735-36 *non ponit iras . . . minatur dente iam lasso*; in combining weariness and undiminished rage, Tityos, too, resembles the true source of cosmic disorder, the *lassa . . . progenies impia Tantali* (136-37).

renovat veteres . . . iras: an inversion, probably unconscious, of Catullus' beautiful phrase *veteres renovamus amores* (96.3).

808-809 reiecto . . . monte: Hesiod placed Typhoeus simply in Tartarus (*Theog.* 868), but in Pindar he is confined beneath Mt. Aetna (*P.* 1.15-28), whose eruptions represent the Giant's struggles to break free; this detail predominates in later references, e.g., Ovid *Met.* 5.346-53.

809 latus explicuit: "has Typhoeus stretched his body freely?" (*latus* for *corpus*, specifying the part affected); *explicare* of casting off a heavy weight, cf. *Epist.* 65.16 (*animus*) *qui gravi sarcina pressus explicari cupit*. The combination *latus explicare* is unusual; the only other example recorded before late Antiquity is Neronian, Calp. Sic. *Ecl.* 1.5 *vaccae / molle sub hirsuta latus explicuere genista*. There might be an echo of Atreus' words *per nos odia se nostra explicent* (323).

810 struitur: probably based on Ovid *Met.* 1.152-53 *ferunt . . . Gigantas / alta . . . congestos struxisse ad sidera montes*; Ovid's *alta . . . ad sidera* is matched by the less graphic *alta . . . via*.

811 per hostes: "by the enemies," *per* denoting agency (*OLD* s.v., #15).

811-12 Thessalicum . . . Ossa: a familiar detail seen in a new perspective: the contrasting adjectives *Thessalicum / Thressa* (on which cf. *Ag.* 613 [n]) stress unnatural juxtaposition (see above, p. 46), while *premitur* links the image to the theme of oppression (see on 787 *gravis*, and above, p. 46).

812 Thressā premitur Pelion Ossā: i.e., Ossa has been placed on Pelion, and Olympus will presumably be piled onto Ossa, as in *Ag.* 345-46, *HF* 970-71, and Verg. *G.* 1.281-82; in *Tro.* 829-30 the sequence, in ascending order, is Olympus-Ossa-Pelion, as in *Od.* 11.315-16.

813-14 Solitae . . . erit: the Chorus begins to work out the implications of what it is experiencing; the regular cycles of the heavens are no more, and "sunrise" and "sunset" will therefore cease to exist. [These lines are sometimes printed as questions, but the absence of any interrogative signal, after the clear questions of 802–12, makes this unlikely; furthermore, the previous phrase has the weight of a concluding *sententia*; see note on 811–12.]

813 Solitae . . . vices: *solitae* evokes those other *vices* that have overturned the norm, the *scelerum . . . vices* of 133 (cf. also 25–26).

mundi: the primary meaning is "sky," "heavens," as in 834, *Pha.* 973, *Ag.* 827 (n), but the sense "earth," "world" may be present as well, as in 884.

periere: the fulfillment in the external order of the Fury's wish, *ius . . . omne pereat* 48 (a link foreshadowed in 48–49 *non sit a vestris malis / immune caelum*).

815–26 The Chorus imagines the chaotic scene in heaven, with Aurora unable to cope with the sun's exhausted horses and the stars caught unprepared by the premature onset of night. The sense of confusion is vividly conveyed, but it is hard not to find the naturalistic treatment amusing, as it would be in Ovid. (Compare, e.g., *Met.* 2.385–87, 13.587–93, where the sun and Aurora complain that their services are not appreciated by the other gods.) This passage, though, is restrained by comparison with *Agamemnon* 816–23, on the long night of Hercules' conception: there Aurora awakes at the usual time, finds the dawn still far off, and sinks back upon her husband Tithonus.

815 stupet: cf. 800 above, *Ag.* 820 *mirata est*.

Eos: with *frenos* in 816, a novel combination.

815–16 assueta deo (i.e., Phoebo) / tradere frenos: free invention in the spirit of Ovid's story of Phaethon, where the *Horae* yoke and bridle the sun's horses (*Met.* 2.118–21); an even closer parallel is *Ars* 3.180, where Aurora herself yokes the horses (and is called *roscida . . . dea*, cf. 816–17 *genetrix . . . roscida*).

816–17 genetrix . . . lucis: Aurora as *genetrix* of the day is most unusual (the image reverses dawn's Homeric epithet ἠριγένεια "child of morning"); perhaps, as with the sun (see on 789 *parens*), the Chorus is projecting Thyestes' distortion of the parental role onto the heavens.

817–18 perversa sui / limina regni: an odd variation on the notion of "dawn's threshold," cf. Cat. 64.271 *Aurora exoriente vagi sub limina solis*, Sil. 16.230–31. (Vergil's temporal use of *limen* in *Aen.* 6.255 *sub limina solis et ortus* is equally difficult, but in another way.) Aurora's *limen* has apparently been "disordered" by Phoebus' arrival at the wrong time and in the wrong condition. The phrase might recall Tantalus' defilement of the *domus* in 103–104, although the *limen* is not specified there. [The text has been suspected, and *limina* rests only on E, with A reading *lumina* (a common confusion). The conjectures so far proposed—*munia*, *munera*—are not attractive; one might consider *foedera*, which is used of the regular workings of the heavens, cf. Manil. 3.659 *Libra diem noctemque pari cum foedere ducens*, Luc. 1.80 *machina divulsi turbabit foedera mundi*, but I am not confident of its being right, and *limina* is perhaps best accepted as genuine.]

sui . . . regni: Aurora is not commonly a ruler; here too a preoccupation of the drama (perversion of stable government) guides the Chorus's choice of words.

818–20 nescit . . . ponto: Aurora is unequipped to perform the tasks usually carried out by Tethys, goddess of the sea, cf. Ovid *Met.* 2.69 *quae me subiectis excipit undis . . . Tethys*.

818-19 fessos / tinguere currus: *currus = equos*, cf. 797, Ovid *Met.* 15.418-19 *in alto Phoebus anhelos* [= *fessos*] / *aequore tinguet equos.*

819-20 fumantes . . . iubas: based on Vergil's *equum fumantia . . . colla* (*G.* 2.542) but with an unsettling shift of focus: in relation to *fumantes*, *iuba* nearly = *collum* (cf. Ovid *F.* 4.216), but with *mergere ponto*, it suggests *equus*; for a similar displacement cf. Mart. 9.90.12 *fervens iuba saeviet Leonis.* The strain placed on language (cf. also *perversa . . . limina* 817-18) may reflect the distortion of normal experience.

821 insueto novus hospitio: "new to this unfamiliar reception," cf. *Tro.* 67 *rude vulgus lacrimisque novum*; the juxtaposition of *novus* and *insueto* suggests the equal amazement of Sol and Aurora.

823-26 tenebras . . . umbras: the sun compounds the confusion by giving the order for night to begin before it is ready; the "cast," as it were, is not yet in place, so no moon, stars, or other nocturnal light can be seen.

824 succedunt: "take over" (i.e., from the sun), cf. Ovid *Met.* 7.192-93 *quae . . . diurnis / aurea cum luna succeditis ignibus astra*, 10.165, 15.187.

825 nec ullo micat igne polus: cf. 49 *cur micant stellae polo . . .?*, echoed with a neat syntactical inversion.

826 non Luna: mentioned last as the brightest presence in the night sky, cf. Hor. *C.* 1.12.47-48 *velut inter ignis / luna minores.*

gravis . . . umbras: a satisfying conclusion, forming a near-frame with *nox . . . gravis* in 787. The Chorus's fanciful speculations cease, and the darkness closes in once more.

827 quidquid id est: a perplexed expression repeated twice by Thyestes in the next scene, cf. 963, 995; neither the Chorus nor Thyestes realizes the full horror of the situation until it is revealed by Atreus.

utinam nox sit: i.e., let it be *night* (even an unnatural one) rather than something worse.

828-29 trepidant . . . metu: the repeated anapests *trepidant, trepidant*, the breaking of the rhythm by the "half-line" of 829, and the alliteration of *p* and *m* give these words an emotional immediacy unsurpassed anywhere in Seneca.

828 trepidant, trepidant: the only other instances of immediate repetition in Seneca's choral lyrics are *Pha.* 1129 *Euros excipiunt, excipiunt Notos* and *Ag.* 656 *vidi, vidi*; neither carries the same sense of frenzied excitement as this line. (See also on 946 below.) For comparable effects in Greek tragic choruses cf., e.g., Aesch. *Suppl.* 888, *Eum.* 140.

830-35 ne . . . tegat: the cataclysm that the Chorus fears resembles the *ecpyrosis*, or periodic destruction of the world by fire, that was a tenet of early Stoic cosmology. (See J. M. Rist, *Stoic Philosophy* [Cambridge, 1969], 175-76; F. H. Sandbach, *The Stoics* [London, 1975], 78-79; Fantham on *Tro.* 386-92 [although I am not sure that those lines need refer to the concept].) One sign of Stoic thinking is the fact that *natura* is the power behind the event (835), since "nature" (synonymous with "god") was the Stoics' name for the guiding force in all things, cf. *Ben.* 4.7.1 *quid enim aliud est natura quam deus et divina ratio toti mundo partibusque eius inserta?*, *Pha.* 959 *magna parens, natura, deum*; in *Cons. Marc.* 26.7 Seneca explicitly calls god the agent of *ecpyrosis*, *cum deo visum erit iterum ista moliri.* In orthodox Stoic thought *ecpyrosis* brought about purification and renewal (cf. *Cons. Marc.* 26.6 *tempus . . . quo se mundus renovaturus extinguet*, ps-Sen. *Oct.* 394-95), but even in his philosophical writing Seneca can focus exclusively on the prospect of annihilation (cf. *NQ* 3.27, *Ben.* 6.22, *Cons. Pol.* 1.2 *hoc universum, quod omnia divina humanaque complectitur . . . dies aliquis dissipabit et in confusionem veterem tenebrasque demerget*). In this ode there is certainly no hint of a restored world, only the awesome spectacle of universal catastrophe.

Other writers of the period saw the end of the world in explicitly Roman terms: Lucan compares the wars that ended the Republic to the world's final convulsion (1.72–80), and the author of the *Octavia* makes Seneca himself look to the last day, in language recalling Deucalion's flood, to crush the wickedness of his own time (*Oct.* 391–95). In *Thyestes* such a connection with Rome is not stated, but it may be implied by the strongly personal tone of the ode's last lines (875–84).

830–31 ne . . . cuncta ruina / quassata labent: verbally close to Hor. *C.* 3.3.7–8 *si fractus inlabatur orbis, / impavidum ferient ruinae.*

830 fatali: "destined," "decreed by fate," cf. *NQ* 3.27.1 *fatalis dies diluvii.*

831–33 iterum . . . iterum: i.e., that all things might return to the formless state in which they existed before the present world was created, cf. *Cons. Pol.* 1.1 *naturae omnia destruentis et unde edidit eodem revocantis*, Luc. 1.74 *antiquum repetens iterum chaos*, ps-Sen. *Oct.* 391–92 (*Sol*) *in caecum chaos / casurus iterum.*

831–32 deos / hominesque: Seneca can speak thus even as a philosopher, cf. *Cons. Pol.* 1.2 (quoted on 830–35), but in this context there is added point in seeing the gods as suffering the same fate as human beings, cf. 893–94, 1035.

832 premat . . . chaos: chaos is thought of as an oppressive weight, like darkness, cf. Hor. *C.* 1.4.16 *iam te premet nox*, Verg. *Aen.* 6.827 *nocte premuntur*, see above on *nox . . . gravis* 787.

deforme: "lacking form," cf. 667, 775.

833–34 terras . . . mare . . . sidera: the three divisions of the cosmos, whose separation marked the transition from chaos to order, cf. Ovid *Met.* 1.5–7 *ante mare et terras et quod tegit omnia caelum / unus erat toto naturae vultus in orbe, quem dixere chaos.* (Seneca's *tegat* in 835 may be an inverted echo of *Met.* 1.5 *quod tegit omnia.*) Like Ovid, Seneca arranges the regions in a *tricolon abundans* with *terras* unmodified, *mare* joined by *cingens*, and *sidera* given the fullest defining phrase. [In 833 *cingens* is Leo's conjecture for the manuscript reading *et ignes*. The manuscript text has been defended as referring to the four elements—cf., e.g., *Ira* 2.19.1 *cum elementa sint quattuor, ignis aquae aeris terrae*—, but the stars belong to the fiery element and *ignes* would be obviously redundant. In addition the triad "land-sea-sky," and not the four elements, is traditionally associated with thoughts of universal doom, cf. Afranius 9 R[2] *mare caelum terram ruere ac tremere diceres*, Verg. *Aen.* 12.204–205 *non si tellurem effundat in undas / diluvio miscens caelumque in Tartara solvat.*]

833 mare cingens: cf. Ovid *Her.* 10.61 *omne latus terrae cingit mare*, *Met.* 2.6 *aequora . . . medias cingentia terras.*

834 vaga picti sidera mundi: a deceptively simple phrase, which effectively juxtaposes the brightness and motion of the stars.

vaga . . . sidera: *HF* 126–27 *nox . . . vagos / contrahit ignes luce renata*, *Pha.* 962.

picti . . . mundi: "the spangled sky" (Miller), cf. *Med.* 310 *stellis quibus pingitur aether*; the combination is novel, perhaps based on *pingere* used of flowers standing out against a background of grass, as in Lucr. 5.1396 *tempora pingebant viridantis floribus herbas.*

835–74 This vision of celestial ruin proceeds in strict order: first the sun (835–38 *non . . . notas*), moon (838–42 *non . . . currens*), and planets (842–43 *ibit . . . deorum*), then the constellations of the zodiac, in sequence from Aries in early spring to Pisces in late winter (844–66 *hic . . . Pisces*), and finally the circumpolar constellations (867–74). The arrangement of sections is similarly neat, with the long description of the zodiac flanked by smaller panels of almost identical length (835–43, 867–74). In its clarity and balance the passage mirrors the regularity of the heavens, celebrating the cosmic order that is doomed to pass away.

835–36 aeternae / facis exortu: a high-sounding phrase that presents the sun in full splendor, cf. Ennius *sc.* 280 V² (243 J) *Sol, qui candentem in caelo sublimat facem*, Cic. *Div.* 2.17 (from his *De consulatu suo*) *Phoebi fax, HF* 38 *propinqua . . . face*.

836–37 dux astrorum / saecula ducens: a more elliptical version of the picture in *Tro.* 387–88 *quo cursu properat volvere saecula / astrorum dominus*. In both passages *saecula* means "ages" or "generations," i.e., the years seen collectively.

837–38 dabit . . . notas: the sun gives "indications" (*notae*, cf. 758) of summer and winter by varying the length of the day. Hence any change in the sun's behavior can be called by hyperbole an inversion of the seasons, cf. Ovid *Met.* 4.199, Sen. *Ag.* 53–54.

838–39 Phoebeis / obvia flammis: i.e., the moon derives its light from being "exposed to" or "in the way of" the sun's rays (cf. *NQ* 7.27.1). The choice of words is uncommon; it may contrast this normal condition with the sun's present unnatural path, *sibi . . . obvium . . . iter* 785.

840–42 vincet . . . currens: in the geocentric astronomy of the ancient world, the moon's orbit was thought to be closer to the earth than the sun's, which explained why the moon took only a month per revolution as against a whole year for the sun. Ovid's Phaethon loses control of the sun's chariot and so passes closer to the earth than the moon: *inferius . . . suis fraternos currere Luna / admiratur equos* (*Met.* 2.208–209).

841 habenas: a synecdoche for *currus* (compare 820 *iubas*), popular in poetry after Ovid, cf. Manil. 4.834 *cum patrias Phaethon temptavit habenas*, Stat. *Theb.* 6.26, Val. Fl. 6.95.

842 currens: "riding" (*OLD* s.v., #3b); the moon usually rides in a two-horsed chariot or *biga*, cf. *Ag.* 818 (n).

842–43 ibit . . . deorum: the planets (equated with the gods whose name they bear—Mercury, Venus, Mars, Jupiter, Saturn) will fall in a heap into a single huge cavity (= *sinus* cf. *NQ* 6.1.9 *in vasto terrarum dehiscentium sinu*). In this context the fall of the "gods" may have more than an astronomical sense, cf. 1021 *fugere superi*; a *double entendre* would suit this phrase's position at the end of a section.

843 turba: slightly dismissive, sweeping the "gods" into an undifferentiated mass, cf. *Ben.* 6.22 *profunda vorago tot deos sorbeat*. (There may be an allusion to the *turba* of 19: the "brood" of Tantalus has driven the "throng" of the gods from the sky.)

844–47 A general description of the zodiac, the "constellation-bearer" (*signifer*), the band of twelve constellations through which the sun, moon, and planets appear to move.

844 hic: with *signifer* 846.

sacris pervius astris: "allowing passage to the divine stars" (i.e., the sun and the other heavenly bodies that pass through it).

845 secat . . . zonas: the zodiac intersects the celestial zones (for which cf. Verg. *G.* 1.233–38, Ovid *Met.* 1.45–46) at an oblique angle, cf. *G.* 1.238–39 *via secta . . . obliquus qua se signorum verteret ordo,* Ovid *Met.* 2.130–32, Manil. 1.257. (A helpful diagram in G. P. Goold's Loeb edition of Manilius, p. xxxiii.)

846 flectens . . . annos: the zodiac "turns the years" because it carries the sun along in its course, while the sun proceeds in a contrary direction, cf. Manil. 1.258 (*signa quae*) *solem . . . alternis vicibus per tempora* ("seasons") *portant / atque alia adverso luctantia sidera mundo.*

longos . . . annos: the adjective has a vaguely intensifying force, cf. Ovid *Met.* 4.226 *ille ego sum* (sc. *Sol*) *longum qui metior annum.*

848–66 In listing the signs of the zodiac Seneca artfully varies his treatment, alternating straightforward enumeration (e.g., 853–54, 858–59, 864–65) with pointed language or erudite allusion (e.g., 851, 857, 863–64).

848–51 There was no consensus in poetic accounts of the zodiac on where to begin the sequence; Aratus, for example, started with Cancer (*Phaen.* 545), while Quintus Cicero placed Pisces first (*FPL* p. 79 Morel). In beginning with Aries, Seneca agrees with Manilius (1.263).

848 nondum vere benigno: i.e., in very early spring, before the climate has become mild; in *HF* 8 the following sign, the Bull, is associated with spring, *qua tepenti* [A: *recenti* E] *vere laxatur dies.*

849 reddit Zephyro vela: the sun's entry into Aries in mid-March coincided with the opening of the navigation season (cf. Nisbet-Hubbard on Hor. *C.* 1.4.2).

Zephyro . . . tepenti: a standard element in descriptions of spring, cf. Verg. *G.* 2.330 *Zephyri . . . tepentibus auris,* Ovid *Met.* 1.107–108, *F.* 2.220.

851 per . . . Hellen: the constellation of the Ram had long been identified with the ram of golden fleece that transported Phrixus and his sister Helle from Boeotia to Asia; on the journey Helle grew frightened, fell into the sea, and drowned, giving her name to the Hellespont (cf. Ovid *F.* 3.852–76). Helle's fate is an innocent counterpart to that of Myrtilus, who also gave his name to the place where he drowned, cf. 139–42, and note the echo of *vectus* (141) in *vexerat.*

pavidam: the detail may have been suggested by Ovid's description of Europa being carried across the sea by Jupiter disguised as a bull, *Met.* 2.873 *pavet haec.*

852–53 qui . . . Hyadas: "who displays the Hyades in his gleaming horns," closely resembling Ovid *F.* 5.165–66 *ora micant Tauri septem radiantia flammis, / navita quas Hyadas Graius ab imbre vocat.*

854 curvi bracchia Cancri: a reworking of Ovid *Met.* 2.83 *curvantem bracchia Cancrum,* with a typical shift from the naturalistic to the elliptical (*curvi*).

855–56 Leo . . . Herculeus: the constellation Leo was generally thought to represent the Nemean lion overcome by Hercules, cf. Ovid *Ars* 1.68 *cum sol Herculei terga leonis adit,* Manil. 2.531, Pease on Cic. *ND* 2.110.

855 flammiferis aestibus ardens: the sun enters Leo in late July, and the constellation was linked for the Romans with the "dog days" of summer, cf. Hor. *C.* 3.29.19–20 (*furit*) *stella vaesani leonis / sole dies referente siccos, Epist.* 1.10.16.

856 iterum: an allusion to the obscure legend that the Nemean lion originated on the moon, cf. Nigidius Figulus fr. 93 (= *schol. Germ. Phaen.* 72.1), *HF* 83 *sublimis alias Luna concipiat feras.*

857 in terras . . . relictas: Virgo, identified with Astraea, had abandoned the earth in horror at the wickedness of humanity; Seneca reverses the language of Ovid *Met.* 1.149–50 *Virgo caede madentes . . . terras Astraea reliquit.*

860-62 et qui . . . nervo: the Archer (Sagittarius) was depicted as a centaur at least from the time of Eudoxus of Cnidus (4th c. B.C.), but the identification with Chiron is perhaps due to the Roman scholar-mystic Nigidius Figulus (fr. 97 Swoboda). This passage is its first explicit appearance in surviving Latin poetry; cf. also Luc. 9.536, Börner on Ovid *Met.* 2.81. Chiron was more often identified with the constellation of the Centaur, cf. Ovid *F.* 5.379–414, Manil. 5.348–56.

860 nervo . . . Haemonio: based on Ovid *Met.* 2.81 (of Sagittarius) *Haemonios . . . arcus.* Thessaly is the traditional home of centaurs (hence their ill-fated presence at the wedding of Hippodamia, Ovid *Met.* 12.210–14), but the epithet has special point when used of Chiron, teacher of the greatest Thessalian hero, Achilles, cf. *Ag.* 641 (n).

tenet: the Archer is conventionally shown about to shoot an arrow, which he therefore perpetually "holds" in place on the bowstring, cf. Manil. 1.270 *mixtus equo volucrem missurus iamque sagittam.*

861 pinnata . . . spicula: a mannered equivalent for, e.g., *volucres sagittae* (Verg. *Aen.* 12.415, Manil. 1.270 just cited); *pinnata* highlights the artificiality of the phrase by excluding the literal sense of *spiculum* ("arrow-tip"), in contrast to, e.g., Ovid *Pont.* 4.7.37 *spicula cum pictis haerent in casside pennis.*

862 rupto . . . spicula nervo: the near-repetition takes the place of a *sententia.*

perdet: a recurring motif in the ode, cf. 792, 879.

863 pigram . . . hiemem: cf. Ovid *Am.* 3.6.94, *Ars* 3.186.

864 Aegoceros: the Greek form of *Capricornus*, widely used in Latin poetry.

864-65 tuam, quisquis es, urnam: an allusion to competing identifications of the Water-carrier (Aquarius), e.g., Ganymede (Ovid *F.* 2.145, Manil. 5.487), Deucalion (Nig. Fig. fr. 99 Swoboda, Germ. *Phaen.* 562, Luc. 1.653), Cecrops (Hyg. *Astr.* 2.29), and Aristaeus (*schol. Germ. Phaen.* 68); Roscher 6.976–77. (A similar scholarly aside in 378 above.)

865-66 excedent . . . Pisces: the last item carries particular point; *excedent* suggests voluntary departure rather than violent collapse (contrast *praeceps ibit* 850, *cadet* 856, 858, 864, *trahe(n)t* 854, 859), and together with *ultima* almost certainly recalls Justice abandoning the vicious earth, cf. Verg. *G.* 2.473–74 *extrema . . . Iustitia excedens terris,* Ovid *Met.* 1.150 *ultima caelestum terras Astraea reliquit.*

867 monstra . . . numquam perfusa mari: in climactic position come the "fixed" stars which normally never set below the horizon.

monstra: referring to the size and bestial shape of the Bear and the Snake, cf. *Clem.* 1.25.4 (*serpens*) *solitam mensuram transiit et in monstrum excrevit,* Mart. 4.57.5 (of the constellation Leo) *Nemeaei pectora monstri.* [Bentley conjectured *plaustra,* which Leo printed in the form *plostra,* but emendation does not seem required and it is unlikely that the Wain would be separated from its guardian, named in 873–74.]

868 condens omnia gurges: the language suggests the destruction of the world by water that in Seneca's view alternated with the fiery *ecpyrosis*; an exuberant evocation in *NQ* 3.27, cf. 11 *iam omnia, quae prospici potest, aquis obsidentur; omnis tumulus in profundo latet.*

869 et: correlative with *-que . . . -que* in 871, 873 (for *et . . . -que . . . -que* cf. Gratt. 415–16, Stat. *Theb.* 12.232–33); *ruet* is to be understood in all three clauses.

869–870 qui . . . Anguis: cf. Manil. 1.305–306 *has* (sc. *Ursas) inter fusus circumque amplexus utramque / dividit . . . Anguis*, Ovid *Met.* 3.45 *(serpens) geminas qui separat Arctos* (= *Ursas*, Greek form).

medias dividit Ursas: "divides the Bears in two"; *medias* is predicate adj., cf. Manil. 1.451–53 *Arctos / uno distingui medias claudique Dracone / credimus*, Cic. *Div.* 2.92 *illi orbes qui caelum quasi medium dividunt.*

870 fluminis instar: a traditional comparison, cf. Aratus *Phaen.* 45–46, Verg. *G.* 1.244–45 *maximus hic flexu sinuoso elabitur Anguis / circum perque duas in morem fluminis Arctos*, Sen. *Med.* 694.

871–74 The constellations just mentioned are now seen from the opposite perspective: the Snake, the focus of attention in 868–70, recedes into a peripheral position (*magno . . . Draconi*), and the Bears assume the primary role.

871 magno . . . Draconi: Ursa Minor (= Cynosura) is much smaller than the Snake and also much closer to it than is Ursa Major.

872 frigida . . . gelu: the Bears are conventionally linked with the frozen north, cf. Ovid *Met.* 2.171 *gelidi . . . triones* with Bömer's note, Sen. *HF* 129–30 *signum celsi glaciale poli / septem stellis Arcados ursae*, 1139.

873–74 custos . . . plaustri . . . Arctophylax: the same constellation was called Arctophylax (the "Bear-guardian") and Bootes (the "Driver"), according to whether the nearby group of seven stars was thought to represent bears or plough-oxen (*triones*, also *plaustrum* or *plaustra* = the cart drawn by the oxen); cf. Ovid *F.* 3.405 *sive est Arctophylax sive est piger ille Bootes*, Manil. 1.316–17 *a tergo nitet Arctophylax idemque Bootes* (so called) *quod similis iunctis instat de more iuvencis.* Seneca startlingly juxtaposes the conceptions: the *custos plaustri* is also the bear-watcher *Arctophylax*. (Compare *Oed.* 477, where the same stars are called *sidus Arcadium*—i.e., the Greater and Lesser Bear, representing the Arcadians Callisto and Arcas—and *geminum plaustrum*, and *Med.* 315 *Arctica . . . plaustra*, literally "the Wains of the Bears.")

873 custos . . . plaustri: another sign of the conflation of Bootes and Arctophylax: *custos* (= Greek *phylax*) usually describes the bear-watcher, cf. Ovid *F.* 2.153 *custodem . . . Ursae, Tr.* 1.4.1, 11.15.

tardus: i.e., slow in setting, the distinguishing mark of Bootes/Arctophylax from Homer onwards, cf. Ovid *Met.* 2.177 *quamvis tardus eras et te tua plaustra tenebant*, Germ. *Phaen.* 139 *tardus in occasu sequitur sua plaustra Bootes*, Sen. *Med.* 314–15 with Costa's note.

tardus plaustri: the double spondee suggests the slowness of the action.

874 iam non stabilis: "no longer fixed in place" (Miller); *stabilis* seems to imply that Arctophylax never goes below the horizon, which is not true. [In *Ag.* 69–70, if I have understood those lines correctly, Seneca imagines a point so far north that from it Bootes will be a fixed constellation, but there are no such special circumstances here.] Perhaps the fact that Bootes/Arctophylax is visible for at least part of every night in the year made *stabilis* seem an acceptable hyperbole.

875 Nos: an arresting shift of focus; no first-person forms have been used so far in the ode. This immediacy is maintained in the next question (*in nos* . . . 877) and reaches a climax in the despairing cry *o nos dura / sorte creatos* (878–79). As with the introduction of personal language at the end of the second and third odes (393–400, 621–23), it is tempting to see a meaning in these lines that projects beyond the dramatic context.

e tanto . . . populo: i.e., all of humanity, past and present, cf. *NQ* 7.30.5 *venientis aevi populus* (all those yet to be born).

875–77 visi . . . digni . . . mundus: "have we been judged worthy of being crushed by the sky's collapse?"; *premeret* is subjunctive in a relative clause of characteristic or purpose (AG 535f), like *premat* in the parallel lines of *Octavia* (392–93): *adest mundo dies / supremus ille, qui premat genus impium.*

876 premeret: for the theme of oppression see above, p. 46, on 787 *gravis*.

876–77 everso / cardine: "the pole torn from its place." The *cardines* are the two pivots on which the axis of the sky was thought to revolve (*OLD* s.f., #3); *everso cardine* describes, not a mere reversal of position (like *cardine verso* in Manil. 1.449), but an uprooting of the cosmic structure (cf. *Med.* 414 *sternam et evertam omnia*, *Ag.* 912 *eversa domus est funditus*). The Chorus fears that the time may be literally "out of joint" (*Hamlet* 1.5.188).

877–78 in nos . . . venit: "has the last age (of the world) come upon *us*?"; cf. Luc. 7.390 *aevi venientis in orbem*.

879 creatos: almost = *natos*, as often in high poetry (cf. Verg. *Aen.* 10.551, Ovid *Met.* 13.346 *Telamone creatus*). The ablative with *creare* usually specifies the parent or source (as in, e.g., Ovid *Met.* 1.760 *si modo sum caelesti stirpe creatus*); *dura sorte* seems a looser abl. of circumstance.

perdidimus: "lost" (i.e., through the misfortune of being alive at this time); the word recalls *perdis* 792 and *perdet* 862, but with stronger emotional coloring.

881 expulimus: universalizing first person plural ("we human beings"), cf. Ovid *Am.* 3.4.17 *nitimur in vetitum semper cupimusque negata*, Sen. *Ag.* 297 (n).

882 abeant . . . timor: an arresting lead-in to the final *sententia*: the audience must wonder what consolation can have brought strength in the midst of such distress. (*Tro.* 399–400 are similar: *spem ponant avidi, solliciti metum; / tempus nos avidum devorat et chaos.*)

The Chorus's words are unwittingly echoed by Thyestes at the start of his drinking-song, *iam sollicitas ponite curas, / fugiat maeror fugiatque pavor* (921–22); Thyestes' delusion of happiness is undermined by contrast with the Chorus's true *securitas*.

883–84 vitae . . . mori: the thought superficially resembles the commonplace "misery loves company" (cf., e.g., Sen. *Contr.* 9.6.2 *morientibus gratissimum est commori*, Sen. *NQ* 6.2.9 *ingens mortis solacium est terram quoque videre mortalem*, Costa on *Med.* 428), but the language integrates it with the themes of the play and makes it a compelling climax. (The eclipse-passage in Pind. *Paean* 9 ends with a similar thought (21): ὀλοφύρομαι οὐδέν, ὅ τι πάντων μέτα πείσομαι—"I do not bewail what I shall suffer in common with all.")

883 vitae est avidus: Seneca is often most eloquent in denouncing attachment to life (cf., e.g., *Ag.* 589–611, *Brev. vit.* 11.1, *Epist.* 101.8); for *avidus* in this connection see *Epist.* 32.4 *homines avidos futuri*, Cic. *Sen.* 72 (quoted on 471–72). Here *avidus* takes on added meaning from the prominence of hunger in the play (see on *avido* 2); like power and luxury, life itself can be a destructive appetite.

883–84 quisquis . . . mori: a *double entendre*: *mundo pereunte* refers both to destruction of the universe and to the moral extinction envisaged in the prologue (48 *ius . . . omne pereat*); *quisquis non vult* also permits two senses, "whoever is unwilling to die" and "whoever does not wish to die." In a world literally and figuratively on the point of collapse, death is not merely bearable, but attractive.

quisquis non vult . . . mori: recalls *qui . . . occurrit . . . suo libens / fato nec queritur mori* (365–68), but in a stronger form.

884 mundo . . . pereunte: an intensification of *periturum diem* (121) and *mundi periere vices* (813).

mundo: both "heavens" and "world," as in 813.

pereunte mori: two verbs denoting death thrust together in a final image of individual and universal annihilation.

ACT V (885–1112)

As the act opens, Thyestes is still at his ghastly feast within the palace, while Atreus stands outside exulting at the heavenly disorder he has provoked. Atreus orders the palace doors opened to reveal Thyestes, wallowing in newly-regained luxury but at the same time racked by dread of imminent calamity. Atreus joins him, amusing himself at Thyestes' growing unease, then confronts him with the remains of his children, and gradually forces him to recognize the enormity he has committed. Thyestes' first expressions of shock are not violent enough to satisfy Atreus, who bitterly regrets that neither father nor sons were conscious of their act as it was performed; only when Thyestes calls on Jupiter to blast the universe with avenging violence does Atreus admit that his triumph is complete. The play ends as Thyestes threatens Atreus with divine retribution and Atreus coolly reminds him of the torment his own conscience will never cease to exact.

The outcome is a victory for Atreus in more than one sense: he dominates not only on the level of action but also on that of language, on which the struggles between the brothers have been reflected throughout the play. Thyestes' attempts to find suitable words for his grief and outrage are all to a degree thwarted,[1] but Atreus' language is at its wittiest as he toys with his discomfited victim.[2] The final impression, though, is less one of victory or defeat than of a moral vacuity encompassing both brothers, alienating both from an audience's sympathy. Atreus' cleverness is revealed more clearly than before as the febrile brilliance of lunacy,[3] while Thyestes' groundless faith in a just providence and persistent ignorance of his own flawed nature suggest that his sufferings have failed to teach him wisdom.[4]

---

[1] See on 1006–21, 1035–51, 1046–47, 1068–96, 1087–88, 1088, 1089, 1090–92, 1095.
[2] Cf., e.g., 970–71, 972, 976–83, 982–83, 1030–31, 1103, 1112.
[3] See on 885–86, 891–92, 1021–23, 1098–99, 1104–10.
[4] Cf. 1110 (and also on 1024–25, 1027, 1103 *scelere . . . scelus* for other indications of Thyestes' lack of understanding). It is interesting that Thyestes moves from scepticism about the gods' existence (407) to blind trust in their justice, while the Chorus's outlook

885-919 The opening of the palace to display Thyestes is strongly reminiscent of places in Greek drama where a wheeled platform, the *eccyclema*, was used to bring interior scenes onto the stage; cf. probably Aesch. *Ag.* 1372 onwards, Arist. *Ach.* 407–88, etc.; A. M. Dale, "Seen and Unseen on the Greek Stage," *Collected Papers* (Cambridge, 1969), 121–24. As in the third act, the staging acts as a visual equivalent for Atreus' control, since he can observe Thyestes without himself being seen. Here this effect is even more pronounced, since Atreus does not simply note Thyestes' actions but seems almost to be dictating them; he is like a director overseeing a crucial scene, even giving Thyestes the cue, as it were, for his aria (918–19). (It is also appropriate that Thyestes should at this point be literally enclosed by the house that symbolizes the attractions of status he has been unable to resist. [See above, p. 45.])

885-86 Aequalis . . . polum: Atreus proclaims his jubilation with characteristic energy (see on 176–78): except for *gradior*, every word or phrase repeats the notion of exalted height.

Aequalis astris gradior: saying that one can touch the sky is a proverbial expression of felicity (cf. "feeling on top of the world"), cf. Cic. *Att.* 2.1.7 *nostri autem principes digito se caelum putant attingere*, Hor. *C.* 1.1.36 *sublimi feriam sidera vertice* (with Nisbet-Hubbard's note). Atreus gives the commonplace a new twist: *aequalis* means "as high as" (cf. 643) but also implies "of equal status with"; since the stars are divine (cf. 844 *sacris . . . astris*), Atreus is implicitly claiming equality with the gods, as he will do openly in 911 (cf. also 545, 713). (The phrase could take on another sense in light of the previous ode, i.e., that by his crime Atreus has brought the heavens down to his own level.)

886 altum . . . polum: a variant of a "golden line" (abBcA), cf. on 10 above.

887 nunc . . . patris: Atreus means that he has secured his power by eliminating Thyestes' heirs, but his words also imply that only by such an atrocity could he prove his claim to the throne of Pelops. (Compare *Med.* 910 *Medea nunc sum.*)

decora regni: "the adornments of rule," probably the diadem and scepter (see on 341–47).

888 dimitto superos: "I release the gods," explained by *summa votorum attigi*: there is nothing more that Atreus would wish the gods to give him, so he releases them from further obligations. (The phrase, though, is equally true in the literal sense, "I send the gods away," cf. 776, 893.)

889 bene . . . mihi: cf. 279. As in his planning of the crime, so now Atreus enjoys a fleeting moment of satisfaction before his ingrained restlessness returns (*sed cur satis sit?*, cf. 280 *tantisper*, 256).

etiam mihi: "even for me," a wry admission of Atreus' high standards in revenge (compare Tantalus' *nos quoque*, 18).

890 cur satis sit?: "why *should* it be enough?"; *sit* is a deliberative subjunctive (AG 444) repudiating a stated or implied suggestion, cf. Pl. *As.* 47 *cur hoc ego ex te quaeram?*; S. A. Handford, *The Latin Subjunctive* (London, 1947), 67. The usage is found mainly in informal speech.

890-91 implebo . . . suorum: "I shall fill the father with the death of his children," i.e., I shall make Thyestes realize what he has done. The ghoulish play on words resembles that in 282–83 *ingesta orbitas / in ora patris*, and is typical of Atreus' delight in the

develops in almost precisely the opposite direction (compare 122–35 with 621–22 and 804–12, 842–43).

possibilities of language. [Leo bracketed *pergam . . . suorum*, but once the sense of *implebo* is grasped, there is no reason to suspect the phrase, or to emend *implebo* to *impleto*, with M. Müller.]

890 pergam: "I shall go on"; *pergere* implies continuing after a temporary halt, see on 23, 490. For the parataxis *pergam et implebo* cf. 23–24 *perge . . . et . . . age*, HF 75 *perge et . . . opprime.*

891–92 ne . . . recessit: Atreus mischievously pretends that daylight has withdrawn in order not to inhibit him. (Alternatively, the line could be read as the genuine belief of a madman.)

quid: adverbial acc., "in any respect," "at all" (AG 390d).

892 dum caelum vacat: "while the sky is empty" (and there are no witnesses to the deed); for *vacare* cf. *Epist.* 7.5 (of interludes in the amphitheater) *haec fiunt dum vacat harena.*

893–95 utinam . . . viderent: Atreus would like to treat the gods as he does his own subjects, forcing them to do what they most want to avoid (cf. 212 *quod nolunt velint*).

894 ultricem dapem: a bizarre combination of the mundane (*daps*) with the high-flown (*ultrix*), matching the grotesque character of Atreus' revenge. This is Seneca's only use of *ultrix* of an object; a less striking precedent in Ovid *Met.* 3.190 *spargens . . . comas ultricibus undis.*

896–97 etiam . . . tuae: although the gods cannot be forced to return, Atreus can in a sense overcome their resistance by making Thyestes see what they, in the figure of the sun, have tried to conceal. Atreus here fulfills the prediction of the Messenger in 782–88; his abrupt address to Thyestes (*tibi . . . tuae*) parallels the Messenger's apostrophe at 782–83.

discutiam . . . tuae: dispelling darkness usually connotes a return to normal (so with *discutere umbras* in Lucr. 4.341, Verg. *Aen.* 12.669, etc.), but here darkness is a protection and clarity brings ruin; a similar inversion of the norm underlies HF 50 *vidi nocte discussa inferum.*

898–901 Atreus impatiently becomes dissatisfied with the banquet he has himself arranged, and (again like a writer or director) specifies that a "sober Thyestes" is needed for the following scene.

898–99 securo . . . hilarique vultu: Atreus' view of Thyestes is, as before (289–93), one-sided; he sees only the signs of indulgence and does not suspect how divided Thyestes' feelings actually are (cf. 920–69).

899–900 satis . . . Baccho: an elegant periphrasis for *edisti satis atque bibisti* (Hor. *Epist.* 2.2.214); Atreus may employ the poetic clichés *mensa = cibus/cena* (cf. 148) and *Bacchus = vinum* (cf. 467) with conscious irony.

satis . . . datum est: Miller's "enough time has been given" (cf. Ovid *Met.* 7.662–63 *lucis pars ultima mensae / est data*) is perhaps too limiting; *satis* might suggest a tribute or offering (Atreus speaks of the *mensae sacra* below, in 981).

901 turba famularis: a high-flown address to the servants, cf. *Pha.* 725 *fida famulorum manus*, *Ag.* 800 *fida famuli turba*; the adjective *famularis* may recall Republican tragedy, cf. Fantham on *Tro.* 747.

901-902 fores . . . domus: the command is stated twice, with *patefiat domus* giving the result of *fores . . . relaxa*.

902 templi: the "temple" is identical to the palace, as with Latinus' palace in Verg. *Aen.* 7.172–74 (*regia . . . templum*, and cf. 192 *tali . . . templo*). Here the word seems curiously prominent, perhaps to underscore Atreus' pretensions to divinity.

patefiat domus: cf. 788 *patefient mala*. The echo suggests a link between the *domus* and the *mala*, making it appropriate that Thyestes should now be seen actually inside the *domus* that Tantalus has infected (cf. 53, 101–104).

903-907 These lines fill the interval between Atreus' order and its execution; starting at 908 Atreus describes what the audience is supposed to see "within." [In some places in Greek tragedy where the *eccyclema* was used to reveal interior scenes, similar sets of lines cover the time needed to wheel out the device, cf. Soph. *Ajax* 344–47, Eur. *Her.* 1029–38; O. Taplin, *The Stagecraft of Aeschylus* (Oxford, 1977), 442–43.]

This is Seneca's most skillful handling of an interior scene; when Atreus joins Thyestes at 970, the "interior" imperceptibly becomes the setting for the rest of the play. Compare the less accomplished scenes in *Phaedra* (384–86) and *Hercules Furens* (999–1053).

903 libet videre: a strong wish, "I want to see," contrasting with Thyestes' unfulfilled longings in 954–56 (the play's only uses of the present of *libet*).

intuens: modifies the subject of *det* (Thyestes).

904 quos det colores: "what complexion he shows" (i.e., how his face turns red and pale by turns), perhaps based on Verg. *Aen.* 12.69 *talis virgo dabat ore colores*; for alternating blushes and pallor as signs of violent emotion cf. *Med.* 858–61 with Costa's note.

904-905 verba . . . effundat: Thyestes' first horrified words (1006–19) are indeed gratifyingly turbulent.

905-906 aut . . . rigescat: "or how, breathless with shock, his body grows stiff" (like Ovid's Niobe, *deriguit . . . malis*, *Met.* 6.303).

905 spiritu expulso stupens: the reactions Atreus wants to see in Thyestes are similar to those the Chorus has just described in the external world, cf. *stupet* 800, 815, *solem . . . expulimus* 881.

906 fructus . . . operis: "the reward of my hard work," cf. Ter. *Ad.* 870 *hoc fructi pro labore ab eis fero, odium*, Phaedr. 4.20.8 *quem fructum capis hoc ex labore?*

907 miserum . . . miser: a revised version of 246 *de fine poenae loqueris; ego poenam volo*. Atreus constantly sets stricter conditions for his revenge.

908 aperta . . . face: = abAcB (see on 10 above); the symmetrical arrangement could reflect Atreus' pleasure at the smooth working of his plan.

multa . . . face: collective singular, heightening the artifice of the line, cf. ps.-Ovid *Am.* 3.5.4 *in ramis multa latebat avis*, Juv. 4.47–48 *cum plena et litora multo / delatore forent*.

909 resupinus: "on his back," i.e., reclining in Roman style, but perhaps suggesting an abandoned rather than an elegant posture; compare Ovid *Ars* 1.487 *illa toro resupina feretur*, where *resupina* pictures the loved one lying at her ease on her litter.

purpurae atque auro incubat: Thyestes is surrounded by the trappings of wealth. The combination "purple and gold" is conventional (see Pease on Verg. *Aen.* 4.134), but *auro* *incubat* might point to Vergil's rejection of greed and ambition in G. 2.505–507 *hic petit excidiis urbem miserosque penatis, / ut gemma bibat* [cf. 913 *ducit argento*] *et Sarrano dormiat ostro; / condit opes alius defossoque incubat auro.*

incubat: the primary sense is "reclines on," but the notion of "anxiously brooding over" (as in the lines of the *Georgics* just cited) is perhaps also present; Vergil combines both senses in *Aen.* 4.82–83 *sola* (sc. *Dido*) *domo maeret vacua stratisque relictis / incubat.*

910 vino . . . caput: a vivid amplification of the Messenger's *gravis . . . vino* 781.

911 eructat: this revolting detail is not simply a specimen of Senecan crudity; Thyestes' audible signs of pleasure show that he has fulfilled Atreus' wish, *liberos avidus pater / gaudensque laceret* (277–78, cf. also 778–82). Seneca may be turning to more effective use Manilius' description of Thyestes as *ructantem . . . patrem natos* (5.462).

913 argento: i.e., a silver goblet; a significant echo of Thyestes' own maxim *venenum in auro bibitur* (453).

914 ne parce: addressed to Thyestes, ironically encouraging him not to show restraint. The sarcastic aside in the second person recalls the stage-technique of comedy, cf., e.g., Pl. *Amph.* 313, *Most.* 174–75, 183, etc.

potu: dative, cf. Verg. *Aen.* 1.257 *parce metu*, Neue-Wagener 1³.541–46.

915 tot: gloating over the extent of the slaughter, as at 523.

veteris . . . Bacchi: "vintage wine," cf. Hor. *C.* 1.1.19 *veteris pocula Massici*, with a characteristically "Silver" extension of the metonymy (cf. Ovid *F.* 3.301 *odorati . . . pocula Bacchi*). The fact that the wine is of a good year reflects Atreus' scrupulous attention to detail (and perhaps as well Thyestes' weakness for the prerogatives of power).

916 hoc, hoc: for the excited and climactic repetition, cf. 265 above, Hor. *Epod.* 4.20 *hoc, hoc, tribuno militum.*

mensa cludatur: "let the meal be concluded," referring to the custom of a formal toast and drinking-session at the end of a banquet, cf. Verg. *Aen.* 1.723–24.

scypho: the drinking-cup stands by metonymy for the act of drinking, as often with *pocula*, cf. Pl. *Rud.* 362 *magnis poculis hac nocte eum invitavit.*

917–18 Atreus caps his own previous *sententia* (*hoc . . . scypho*), making Thyestes' atrocity the unemphatic lead-in (917) to a still more pointed conclusion (*meum bibisset*). Atreus' recurring dissatisfaction with the revenge he has exacted is matched by his restless striving for ever sharper thrusts of verbal wit.

918 meum bibisset: "my blood" = "the blood of my children," cf. 1043. The inference is crazily logical, given Atreus' conviction that Thyestes has been plotting against him, cf. 201–202, 314–16, 1104–1109. This is the real conclusion of Atreus' speech; the next words introduce Thyestes' monody.

bibisset: apodosis of a contrary-to-fact condition with protasis implied (e.g., "if he had had the chance" or "if I had not acted first").

ecce: Medea's great conjuration-aria is introduced with a similar flourish, 738–39 *sonuit ecce vesano gradu / canitque; mundus vocibus primis tremit.*

919 festas . . . voces: festivity in Senecan drama is consistently deluded or ill-omened, cf. 970 below, *Med.* 300 (the wedding preparations of Jason and Creusa, ironically re-called by Medea in 985–86 *o festum diem, / o nuptialem*), *Ag.* 311, 791 (Greek thoughts of victory and homecoming, set against the short-lived joy of the Trojans, 644–45), *Tro.* 883 (the clothing Polyxena is to wear for her "marriage" to Achilles); cf. also *Oct.* 646.

nec satis menti imperat: almost a stage-direction, a hint that Thyestes will be singing "under the influence," and also that he will betray feelings which he would otherwise suppress. *Pha.* 386 *mente non sana* is similar, although simpler.

920–69 Alone at his lavish table, his inhibitions loosened by wine, Thyestes reveals scorn for the poverty he had claimed to cherish (446–70) and urges himself to accept the pleasures of his regained position. But drink has also released unspoken anxieties, and Thyestes is seized by an impalpable yet terrible fear that reduces his song of celebration to uncontrollable howls of grief (956). The scene is a harrowing portrayal of psychological disintegration, unique in ancient literature and, for all its grotesque exaggeration, uncomfortably real.

920–37 The first part of the song comprises a central generalizing section (925–33 *magis . . . ruinas*), preceded and followed by passages of self-exhortation (920–25, 933–37; note the chiastic balance of *ponite* 921, *pelle . . . dimitte . . . mitte* 934–37, *fugiat . . . fugiat . . . fugiat* 922–23, *redeant* 936). Throughout these lines a sustained irony plays about Thyestes' words; almost every phrase contains a sense beyond the one consciously intended.

921 ponite curas: a pointed echo of 348–49 *res est qui posuit metus / et diri mala pectoris*: since Thyestes lacks *securitas*, his efforts to put aside anxiety are bound to fail.

922–23 fugiat . . . fugiat . . . fugiat: repetition conveys a feeling of drunken eloquence, cf. also 926–28 *magnum . . . magnum*, 942–45 *quid . . . quid . . . quid*, 954–56 *libet . . . libet . . . libet*.

fugiat: the stress on flight reminds the audience of the consequences of Thyestes' actions (776 *fugeris*), just as the fear and grief he is trying to escape recall the reactions of the Chorus to the unnatural darkness (compare 922 *maeror . . . pavor* and 923 *trepidi . . . exilii* with 828 *trepidant pectora*, 882 *questus . . . timor*).

923 comes exilii: in apposition to *egestas*, with *comes* stressing the link between *egestas* and *exilium*, cf. Vell. Pat. 2.102.3 *semper magnae fortunae comes adest adulatio*, Sen. *Pha.* 206–207 *illa magnae dira fortunae comes . . . libido*, OLD s.v., #6b.

924 tristis egestas: this is Atreus' view of poverty (303), sharply at odds with Thyestes' previous statements, cf. 447 *frustra timentur dura*, 449–51, 469.

924–25 rebusque . . . afflictis: a *double entendre* rounding off the first section of the song. The intended meaning is "shame burdensome to poverty" (*rebus afflictis* dat. after *gravis*, see on 612), i.e., the shame that weighs down the poor. At another level, though, the wish "let burdensome *pudor* flee" is all too true of Thyestes' "ruined condition" (*rebus afflictis*, abl. of circumstances); the Fury's curse banished *pudor* (27), and Atreus has interpreted the flight of the sun as a removal of all inhibition (891).

924 gravis: the idea of oppression is especially prominent here, cf. 929 *pressum*, 930 *pondera*.

925–26 magis . . . refert: "it matters (*rĕfert*) more where you fall *from* than what you fall *into*," i.e., the loss of great wealth and status is a greater hardship than exposure to poverty—the reverse of Thyestes' attitude in 447–51.

926–33 magnum . . . ruinas: "it's a great achievement (*magnum*), once having fallen from a lofty pinnacle, to plant one's steps firmly on the lowly earth; it's a great achievement, when weighed down by a huge mass of troubles, to bear the weight of broken rule with one's neck held straight (*non inflexa / cervice*), to endure the disasters forced upon one while remaining upright (*rectum*), not corrupted or overcome by misfortune." With a lack of insight so total as to be frightening, Thyestes congratulates himself on the fortitude with which he has borne the loss of power. The syntax is unusually convoluted, perhaps another sign that Thyestes' speech has been affected by drink; he sounds like a caricature of a sententious moralist.

926-28 magnum . . . figere: cf. *Cons. Marc.* 5.5 *cogita non esse magnum rebus prosperis fortem se gerere.*

926-27 ex alto / culmine . . . in plano: the metaphors recall Thyestes' former pronouncements (cf. 447 *dum excelsus steti*, 451 *humi iacentem*), while reversing the values placed on these opposing conditions; cf. also 391-92 *stet quicumque volet potens / aulae culmine lubrico.*

927-28 stabilem . . . figere gressum: an unfortunate choice of image, since this "firm step" was lost as soon as Thyestes agreed to leave his place of exile, cf. 420 *moveo nolentem gradum.*

929 strage malorum pressum: Thyestes uses *strages* to mean "confused mass" (*OLD* s.v., #3), cf. Livy 42.63.4 *ex ipsa ruinae strage congestis saxis*; it is, however, impossible not to hear the more common sense "slaughter," especially since Thyestes is literally "weighed down" by an *ingens strages* of this kind (910 *gravatum . . . caput*, 1000 *sentio . . . onus*, 1051 *premor . . . natis*).

929-30 fracti / pondera regni: i.e., the crushing burden of having his reign shattered; for *fracti* see on *ruptum* 179. (This phrase too might conceal a grim allusion to the bodies of the children, a dead weight that shatters Thyestes' hopes of dynastic succession.)

930-32 non inflexa / cervice . . . rectum: these complacent descriptions are undermined by Thyestes' present position, *resupinus* (909) and with his lolling head propped up on his hand (910).

931 pati: even clearer in its assumptions than 470 *immane regnum est posse sine regno pati* (see note *ad loc.*).

nec: = *et non*, with *et* linking *pati* and *ferre*, and *non* opposing *degenerem* and *victum* to *rectum*; see note on 926-33 above.

degenerem: Thyestes uses the word loosely to mean "ignoble," "debased," but he is also *non degener* in the strict sense, in that his actions are all that might be expected of a Tantalid; for a similar point compare Ovid *Met.* 6.636 *degeneras; scelus est pietas in coniuge Terei.*

932 victum . . . malis: Thyestes here comes close to fulfilling Atreus' suspicions of him, cf. 196-97 *quid esse tam saevum potest / quod superet illum? numquid abiectus iacet?*

932-33 impositas . . . ruinas: a pointed echo of 542, *regni nomen impositi feram*: by choosing to "bear" rule, Thyestes has in fact exposed himself to disaster (*ruina*).

934 nubila fati: the "clouds" of destiny recall the *nubes deformis* (775) that has settled on the house.

935 temporis . . . notas: another innocent phrase given point by the preceding choral ode, where "all indications of time" have indeed been sent away (cf. 813 *solitae mundi periere vices*, 837-38 *aestatis / brumaeque notas*, also 888 *dimitto superos*).

936 vultus . . . boni: "cheerful faces," cf. Ovid *Met.* 8.677–78 *vultus / accessere boni nec iners pauperque voluntas* (at the meal that Baucis and Philemon prepared for Jupiter and Mercury).

ad laeta: "at/in response to my good fortune," cf. *Ira.* 3.10.1 *ad primum mali sensum mederi sibi.*

937 veterem . . . Thyesten: the "old Thyestes" is the austere character Thyestes assumed in exile, the ostentatiously gloomy figure mocked by Atreus (505–507). But Thyestes' words again turn against him, reminding us of a yet older Thyestes, hungry for comfort and status, who was never fully discarded and who reasserted himself when temptation was put in his way.

938–41 Thyestes notices that his advice to be cheerful is not working; still pompously generalizing, he claims that the unfortunate are perversely reluctant to accept a change for the better.

938 Proprium hoc . . .vitium: i.e., this "defect" is "unique," "peculiar" to the wretched, cf. Cic. *Div* 2.109 *ipsa varietas quae est propria fortunae,* Sen. *HF* 1220–21 *quod . . . habet proprium furor, / in se ipse saevit.*

sequitur: possibly ironic, since at several earlier points the "following" is in the other direction (i.e., Tantalus or Thyestes pursue their *vitium* to their own misfortune, cf. 100, 174, 489).

939 numquam rebus credere laetis: what Thyestes calls a *vitium* is to the clear-sighted Chorus a norm of prudence, *nemo confidat nimium secundis* (615).

942 quid me revocas: as Thyestes' fears grow, his tone shifts from the confidently gnomic to the urgent and personal.

revocas: i.e., from the happiness I seek; the address is to *dolor* (944), which Thyestes experiences as an external force (*vetas . . . iubes . . . prohibes*). Tantalus is similarly "ordered" by his hunger, cf. 165 *iubet.*

942–43 festum . . . diem: cf. 970–71.

944 nulla . . . causa: this "uncaused" grief matches Thyestes' earlier apprehension, cf. 434–35 *causam timoris ipse quam ignoro exigis;* Thyestes is morally alert enough to be uneasy, but not sufficiently aware to understand the reason for his fears.

945 [quid me prohibes: a conjecture of Heinsius for the manuscript reading *quis me prohibet.* The manuscript text is not intolerable—*quis* has no obvious referent, but in this passage it would be perverse to insist on absolute clarity—, but all other agents in the surrounding lines are aspects of Thyestes himself, either his emotions (*dolor* 944, *maeror* 951, *cupido* 952, *mens* 958, *terror* 966, *dolor . . . metus . . . voluptas* 968–69) or parts of his body (*capiti . . . rosae* 947, *crinis* 948, *imber* 950, *gemitus* 951, *oculi* 957), and this consistent focus makes it likely that the *dolor* of 944 is still being addressed here.]

945–46 flore decenti / vincire comam: garlands were a standard item at elegant dinners and symposia, cf. Hor. *C.* 1.4.9–10 *viridi nitidum caput impedire myrto / aut flore, terrae quae ferunt solutae,* 4.1.31–32 *nec certare iuvat mero / nec vincire novis tempora floribus.* The metaphor in *vincire,* though conventional (as the Horatian passages show), applies with special force to Thyestes, who has assumed the *vincla* of rule (544).

945 flore decenti: a generically phrased equivalent of *vernae . . . rosae* 947; for *decens* ("fair," "attractive") cf. *Pha.* 764 *prata novo vere decentia.* [Some late manuscripts have the more obvious variant *recenti*, perhaps a reminiscence of Hor. *C.* 3.27.43–44 *recentis / carpere flores*.]

946 prohibet, prohibet!: Thyestes seems about to break down in terror; his language touches the boundaries of articulate speech. (Compare Lear's "howl, howl, howl!" 5.3.258.)

947–51 Thyestes enumerates the symptoms of his *malaise* like a horrified spectator; this alienation from one's own body is found in every scene of the play, cf. 96–99, 165–66, 267–70, 419–20, 436–37, 496–505, 634–36, 985–86, 999–1001.

947–48 rosae . . . amomo: garlands and unguents are a natural combination, cf. Lucr. 4.1132, Hor. *C.* 2.7.7–8 *coronatus nitentis / malobathro Syrio capillos*, Ovid(?) *Her.* 21.165–66, Petr. *Sat.* 65.7, Juv. 9.128. Martial 5.64.3–4 seems a clear imitation of this passage: *pinguescat nimio madidus mihi crinis amomo / lassenturque rosis tempora sutilibus*.

947 Vernae . . . rosae: cf. Prop. 3.5.21–22 *me iuvat et multo mentem vincire Lyaeo / et caput in verna semper habere rosa*.

capiti fluxere: "have slipped from my head"; *capiti* is dat. of separation (AG 381) where prose would use *de* or *ex*, cf. Cic. *Phil.* 12.8 *fluent arma de manibus*.
In Hellenistic poetry slipping garlands are a sign of drinking to assuage the sorrow of a difficult love affair, cf. Call. *Ep.* 43.3–4 Pf., *AP* 12.135, Gow on Theocr. 7.64. Here the loss of the garland portends Thyestes' imminent loss of power (perhaps symbolized earlier by the toppling diadem at 701–702); the link between garland and diadem is strengthened by the use of *vincire* of both (see on 945–46 above).

948–49 madidus crinis . . . inter subitos stetit horrores: a characteristic "Silver" treatment of a cliché (hair standing on end), with emphasis on the novel or unexpected detail; compare *Ag.* 712 (of Cassandra) *stetere vittae, mollis horrescit coma*, and contrast the almost formulaic regularity of this motif in Vergil and Ovid, cf. Pease on *Aen.* 4.280, Börner on *Met.* 3.100, *F.* 3.332. (The line is also a neat inversion of *HF* 468–69, on Hercules in service to Omphale, *cuius horrentes comae / maduere nardo*).

inter subitos . . . horrores: "with sudden bristling"; *inter* denoting circumstance, as in Ovid *Pont.* 4.4.21 *dilapsis inter nova gaudia curis*, Sen. *Ira* 3.29.1 *inter cotidiana pervigilia fessum*.

950 imber: = *lacrimae*, a neoteric coinage (cf. Catullus 68.56) that had become part of the common stock of high poetic diction by the end of Ovid's life, cf. *Tr.* 1.3.18, 4.1.98.

vultu nolente: cf. 420 *moveo nolentem gradum*, 985–86 *nolunt manus / parere*.

951 in medias voces: "into the middle of my words."

952–53 Another attempt, as at 938–41, to explain these troubling signs by a generalization. Here there is an undertone of desperation; Thyestes himself seems aware that he is clutching at straws.

952 lacrimas amat: stronger then 941 *afflictos gaudere piget* or 427 *esse iam miserum iuvat*.

953 flendi . . . est: probably an echo of Verg. *Aen.* 6.721 *quae lucis miseris tam dira cupido?* In both passages *dira cupido* is a "strange/incomprehensible longing."

954 infaustos: lamentation would be ill-omened on a *festus dies* (942–43, 970–71).

mittere: = *emittere*, as in 957; *OLD* s.v. *mitto*, #11.

955-56 saturas ostro . . . vestes: probably a reminiscence of Verg. *G.* 4.334–35 *vellera . . . saturo fucata colore*, where *satur* denotes a "rich," "full" dye. Thyestes sees his purple garments as "replete," like himself (*satur est* 913); this form of satiety is opposed to that hoped for by the Chorus, *me dulcis saturet quies* (393).

956 ululare: "to howl," like a wild animal (cf. *Oed.* 179), a much stronger word than, e.g., *gemere*. (The sounds Thyestes makes or wants to make—*gemitus* 951, *ululare*—are also those emitted by the ghosts who haunt the grove inside the palace, cf. 668–69 *gemere ferales deos / fama est*, 670 *ululant . . . manes*. The parallel might suggest that Thyestes is being haunted by the *manes*, i.e., the spirits of the murdered children within him, cf. 1001 *meum . . . gemitu non meo pectus gemit*.)

957-60 A brief moment of lucidity, in which general reflection (959–60) clarifies rather than clouds Thyestes' vision.

957 luctus: genitive with *signa*.

958 mens . . . sui praesaga mali: almost a quotation from the *Aeneid* (10.843), *agnovit longe gemitum preasaga mali mens*, when Mezentius realizes that his son Lausus has been killed. The echo exposes the dullness of Thyestes' perceptions: unlike Mezentius, he is unable to interpret the signals of disaster that surround him.

ante: adverbial, "beforehand."

959-60 instat . . . tument: swelling seas were an obvious sign of an approaching storm, cf. Arat. *Phaen.* 909–10, translated by Cicero as *ventos praemonstrat saepe futuros / inflatum mare, cum subito penitusque tumescit* (*Div.* 1.13), Sen. *Ag.* 469 *agitata ventis unda venturis tumet* (n). Even at his most clear-headed, Thyestes does not advance beyond the commonplace.

960 tranquilla: neut. pl. as substantive, "calm seas."

961 tumultus: taken up at 999, when the disturbance can no longer be disregarded.

962-63 credula . . . fratri: Thyestes here conforms in part to Atreus' view of him (cf. 295 *credula est spes improba*), but not in the way Atreus suspected. He seems almost to be his brother's willing victim, and the gullible spirit he urges on himself is the pathetic counterpart to Atreus' calculated show of trustworthiness, cf. 507 *praestetur fides*.

963 iam: "by now," as in 305.

quidquid id est: see on 827.

964 vel sero times: as before (cf. 485), Thyestes feebly consoles himself with the thought that it is too late to turn back.

965-69 At the end of the song Thyestes lapses back into undefined foreboding, no closer than at the start to a knowledge of his actual situation.

965 Nolo infelix: "wretched that I am, I do not want [this]" (i.e., the *terror* and *fletus* about to be mentioned); this elliptical use of *nolle* is generally confined to the idiom *velim nolim* ("whether I want [it] or not"), but cf. also Pers. 1.11–12 *nolo, / quid faciam?* The syntax underscores Thyestes' inability to control his feelings.

965-66 vagus intra / terror oberrat: Atreus' revenge has not yet come to rest (cf. *errare* in 282 and 473), but its wanderings are now restricted to Thyestes' body.

967 nec causa subest: Thyestes' choice of *subest* (for which cf. *Ag*. 246 [n]) betrays his ignorance; the cause of his fear and grief is precisely an "underlying" one.

968 habet: "entail," "involve," cf. Hor. *Epod*. 2.37 *quas amor curas habet* and the especially close parallel in Petr. *Sat*. 89.17 (the *Troiae Halosis*) *mentis . . . pavidae gaudium lacrimas habet*.

969 magna voluptas: the song ends weakly, trailing off with a bemused question; overwhelmed by events, Thyestes is equally at a loss to control words. There is also a painful irony in having this despairing outcry end with a reference to "great happiness."

970-71 Festum diem . . . celebremus: Atreus breaks in with deliberately grating heartiness: he mockingly echoes Thyestes' troubled words *quid me . . . festum . . . vetas / celebrare diem?* (942–43), and with *consensu pari* he seems to be amusing himself at Thyestes' expense, knowing how far Thyestes is from internal harmony.

971 hic: sc. *dies*.

sceptra qui firmet mea: ostensibly because no further strife will threaten it, but with a private allusion to the removal of Thyestes' heirs, cf 887.

firmet: subj. in a relative clause of characteristic (AG 535).

972 solidam . . . fidem: a pompous and sonorous line (with interlocked word-order aBcbA, see on 10), whose wording hints at its real meaning for Atreus, cf. 239 *imperi quassa est fides*, 240–41 *certi nihil / nisi frater hostis*, 327–28 *pacis incertae fides / ex hoc petatur scelere*. The metaphor of binding in *alliget* may also have a sinister undertone (see following note).

973 Satias . . . me . . . tenet: a more elevated way of saying *satis habeo*; *me tenet* expresses complete satisfaction (cf. Verg. *Ecl*. 5.58–59 *silvas et cetera rura voluptas / . . . tenet*), but unwittingly implies captivity (cf. *Med*. 550 *bene est, tenetur*) or the grip of a passion or disease (*OLD* s.v., #10, cf. Sen. *Epist*. 74.11 *vitae nos odium tenet, timor mortis*).

Satias: perhaps an archaism; the word is found in the older Latin dramatists (cf. Acc. 176 R², Ter. *Hec*. 594–95), not in Cicero or Augustan poetry.

974-75 augere . . . datur: the language is extremely deferential, as befits a pampered guest asking yet another favor of his host. True to his own precept (*credula praesta / pectora fratri* 962–63), Thyestes gives no hint of his uneasiness.

974 cumulus: "addition," cf. Cic. *Att*. 4.19.2 *ad summam laetitiam meam . . . magnus illius adventus cumulus accedit, Fam*. 13.62.

975 meis: "my children."

felici: sc. *mihi*.

976-83 Prolonging the pleasure of his revelation (cf. 907 *miserum videre nolo, sed dum fit miser*), Atreus indulges in a series of ghastly *double entendres* (a more elaborate version of the taunt used by Ovid's Procne at a similar moment, '*intus habes quem poscis*,' *Met*. 6.655).

978 ora: Thyestes will understand *ora* as a synecdoche (as in "longing to see your face" or "showing one's face in public," cf. Verg. *Aen*. 5.576, Cic. *Verr*. 1.1), but Atreus means it literally, since the faces (and hands) are all that remain (764).

979 totum . . . patrem: Atreus seems so pleased with his own earlier witticism (cf. 890–91) that he nearly repeats it, amusing himself by coming dangerously close to the truth; a less fuddled victim would find this a distinctly odd phrase.

totum: almost = *plenum*, "full and complete," cf. Prop. 2.15.28 *masculus et totum femina coniugium*. The adjective is proleptic, i.e., it anticipates the result produced by the verb (here a condensation of "I shall fill the father and make him complete"), cf. Verg. *G*. 4.400 *doli frangentur inanes*, Ovid *Met*. 1.183–84 *quisque parabat /inicere . . . captivo bracchia caelo*.

980 mixti meis: "in company with my own children," with a glance at another sort of "mixing," cf. 917.

981 iucunda . . . colunt: the royal children dine at a separate table, just as they did at Nero's court, cf. Tac. *Ann*. 13.16.1 (the poisoning of Britannicus) *mos habebatur principum liberos cum ceteris idem aetatis nobilibus sedentes vesci in adspectu propinquorum propria et parciore mensa*. In Accius (217–18 R²) and Ovid *Met*. 6.648–49, subterfuge is used to isolate the prospective victim, but Atreus simply places his fictitious *mensa iuvenilis* in another room. Atreus grandiloquently describes the children's meal as a ritual (*sacra . . . colunt*), perhaps recalling the "rite" of their murder (685–758).

982–83 poculum . . . Baccho: Atreus' last play on words is especially brilliant. The ostensible meaning is "a cup that belongs to our family ["an heirloom" Miller, cf. Verg. *Aen*. 1.729–30] filled with wine," but also present is the sense "a drink consisting of your *gens*, with wine poured upon it" (cf. 914–16). [Watling takes *gentile* with *Baccho* by hypallage, "wine from our ancestral vintage"; this would give an equally good *double entendre*, but *gentilis* of wine seems unlikely.]

983 Capio: an echo of 542 *accipio*; compare also *dapis / donum* 983–84 and *dona fortunae* 536. The stage-picture is another link between the scenes; in each Atreus stands before Thyestes holding out an object—a diadem, a drinking-cup—and urging him to take it, knowing that it will be ruinous for him to do so. The parallelism points up the connection between Thyestes' attraction to power and his inability to resist Atreus' deception.

984–85 vina . . . hauriantur: Thyestes begins to follow the correct procedure for after-dinner drinking, cf. Verg. *Aen*. 1.736–37 *in mensam laticum libavit honorem / primaque, libato, summo tenus attigit ore*.

985–95 sed quid hoc? . . . fugit omne sidus: as Thyestes attempts to drink, a wave of revulsion sweeps through the world, beginning with the objects closest to the unnatural act—his hands, the cup, the wine—spreading to the table and floor beneath him, the light in the room, and the sky above, and finally taking in the shaken heavens and the fleeing stars. The passage recalls several earlier episodes in which the outside world has reacted in horror at the evil being planned or executed (106–21, 262–65, 700–702, 789–826). It also weaves together several leading motifs and images, e.g., unwillingness (985–86 *nolunt manus / parere*), oppressive weight (986 *pondus . . . gravat*, 990 *gravis*), flight and escape (987, 991 *desertus*, 994 *se . . . abdidit*, 995 *fugit*), deception (988 *ore decepto*), fear (989 *trepido*), darkness (990 *vix lucet ignis*, 993–94 *densis coit / caligo tenebris*), and rupture (992–93 *concussi labant / convexa caeli*). This heaping-up of thematically loaded terms, like a crescendo in music, produces a sense of approaching crisis and signals that the moment of discovery is near.

987–88 admotus . . . fluit: a re-enactment of the punishment of Tantalus, cf. 171–74—itself the consequence of a ghastly banquet (149–51).

987 ipsis . . . a labris: virtually the same phrase in 69 *labrisque ab ipsis* (of Tantalus).

988 ore decepto: used of Tantalus in *HF* 754, *Ag.* 20; see note on 2.

989 trepido . . . solo: the shaking of the ground makes the table jump, cf. 696–97 *tota succusso solo / nutavit aula*.

990 ignis: probably the torches mentioned at 908 *multa tecta conlucent face*; Thyestes' awareness of disorder proceeds steadily outward, reaching the sky in the following phrase (*quin* marks a significant step).

gravis: "sluggish"; the *aether* was normally the fastest-moving of the elements, cf. Ovid *Met.* 1.67–68 *imposuit liquidum et gravitate carentem / aethera*, 15.242–43.

991 inter diem noctemque . . . stupet: it is too dark to be called "day," yet neither is it a normal night, cf. 813–14, 824–26.

desertus: "abandoned," i.e., by the heavenly bodies, cf. 892 *caelum vacat*.

stupet: cf. 800–801 *stupet . . . arator*, 815 *stupet* (sc. *Aurora*). Personification of *aether* is quite unusual; even the elements are stunned by the evil being committed. (The play's other uses of *stupere* or *stupefacere* cluster around the brothers: of Thyestes at his first entrance, *incessu stupet* 421 and as Atreus wants to see him, *spiritu expulso stupens* 905; Atreus, on the other hand, chides himself with *quid stupes?* 241 and counterfeits amazement at the sight of Thyestes, *stupefactus haesit* 547.)

992–93 magis . . . caeli: Thyestes means that violent rumblings shake the heavens, but his words recall the Chorus's fears of the sky's actual collapse, cf. 830–31 *ne . . . cuncta ruina / quassata labent*, 847 *lapsa videbit sidera labens*.

992 magis magisque: with *concussi*.

993 convexa caeli: "the vaulted sky," as in Verg. *Aen.* 4.451, a more elevated equivalent of *caelum convexum* (Ovid *Met.* 1.26) or *convexum caeli . . . orbem* (Cic. *Arat.* 314); *caeli* is a partitive gen., and the construction resembles, e.g., *adversa montium* in Livy 9.3.1 or *angusta viarum* in Verg. *Aen.* 2.332 (see Austin *ad loc.*).

993–94 spissior . . . tenebris: "a mist gathers, thicker than the dense shadows." This mysterious *caligo* sounds like the mists that figure in accounts of disastrous storms, cf. *Ag.* 472–73 *densa tenebras obruit / caligo*, *Pha.* 955–56 *atra ventis nubila impellentibus / subtexe vultum*. [The phrase could also be rendered "a thicker mist gathers with dense shadows," making *densis tenebris* abl. of description and equating *tenebrae* with *caligo*, cf. Juv. 12.18–19 *densae caelum abscondere tenebrae / nube una*. The following *sententia* (*nox . . . abdidit*), though, seems to require two kinds of darkness.]

993 spissior . . . coit: possibly an unconscious reminiscence of Prop. 3.5.36 *Pleiadum spisso cur coit igne chorus*.

994 nox . . . abdidit: a variation on pointed expressions in storm-scenes, cf. Pacuvius 412 R² *tenebrae conduplicantur*, Ovid *Met.* 11.521 *nox premitur tenebris hiemisque suisque*, 550 *duplicata . . . noctis imago est*, Sen. *Ag.* 472 *nec una nox est*, but with a new emphasis that makes night actively seek the concealment of its "double." (See on 896–97.)

995 fŭgit: present, "is in flight."

quidquid est: cf. 827, 963.

995–97 fratri . . . procella: Thyestes comes closest to evoking sympathy just before his shattering discovery; his dominant thoughts are concern for his brother and children and a conviction of his own worthlessness. The fact that his generous wish has already been fulfilled adds to the pathos.

996 vile hoc caput: a strong expression, showing that Thyestes feels guilt for his past crimes (cf. also 513–14, 532–33); his son Aegisthus in *Agamemnon* has a similarly low estimate of his worth, cf. 231 *oppone cunctis vile suppliciis caput*. Thyestes' words may carry the added suggestion that he is offering himself as an expiatory victim in place of his children; for *vile caput* in this sense cf. Livy 9.9.19 *vilia haec capita luendae sponsioni feramus*, Oed. 521 *mitteris Erebo vile pro cunctis caput*.

997 redde iam natos mihi: this anguished cry is far removed from the suave politeness of 974–75, where the request was first made; Atreus has had the pleasure he desired (907), of seeing Thyestes reduced to desperate anxiety.

998 Reddam . . . dies: a brilliant depiction of deranged joy: the bright *i* and *e* sounds and the lingering double *ll*'s of *illos* and *nullus* let us hear Atreus' exquisite delight.

tibi illos nullus eripiet dies: this perverted union is the counterpart to unnatural separation, cf. 755 *erepta vivis exta pectoribus*, 1086 *lumen ereptum polo*. (For earlier phases of this motif cf. 428, 503, 625).

999 Quis . . . tumultus viscera exagitat mea: possibly linked to the play's other use of *exagitare*, 339 *quis vos exagitat furor?* Thyestes' "upheaval" is the physical result of his desire for power. (Atreus too experiences inner *tumultus*, cf. 260, 1041–42.)

1000 impatiens . . . onus: "a restless weight," a paradox, since an *onus* would normally be inert. [A milder pointed use of *onus* in Ovid *Met.* 13.624–25 (Aeneas) *patrem / fert umeris, venerabile onus* (based on Verg. *Aen.* 2.729 *oneri . . . timentem*).] Seneca links unrelated ideas, the weight of undigested food (cf. Suet. *Cal.* 58.1 *pridiani cibi onere*) and the thought that Thyestes' children protest at their confinement, to produce a jarring combination.

1001 meum . . . non meo: the juxtaposition has an Ovidian neatness, cf., e.g., *Met.* 10.197 *video . . . tuum, mea crimina, vulnus*, 13.495 *tuum, mea vulnera, pectus* (text uncertain).

gemitu: the inexplicable sobs that interrupted Thyestes' drinking-song (951) have assumed a more tangible form.

1003 visis . . . dolor: "this grief will flee at the sight of you"; 922 *fugiat maeror fugiatque pavor*. Thyestes' choice of metaphor is again inept, cf. 776.

1004 unde obloquuntur?: Thyestes interprets the rumblings within as his children's voices "breaking in" on his words; for *obloqui*, often implying unfriendly interruption, cf. Sen. *Contr.* 9 *pr.* 3 *nemo ridet, nemo ex industria obloquitur*, Pliny *NH* 36.126 *(natura) dederat vocem saxis . . . respondentem homini, immo vero et obloquentem*. The prosaic word seems shockingly anti-climactic, as it is meant to be: Seneca does not dignify Thyestes' situation by treating it with tragic decorum, but instead makes it seem mundane and even banal. (It is also appropriate that Thyestes, who is consistently unable to control words, should be discomfited at this crucial moment by an unseen "interruption.")

Expedi amplexus, pater: this is the moment Atreus has longed for, *ingesta orbitas / in ora patris* (282–83). He leads up to it with a mild pun on *expedire* ("get ready your embraces," i.e., spread your arms to embrace your sons, cf. *OLD* s.v., #1b) and a cruelly mocking *pater*, cf. Ovid *Met.* 8.231 (Daedalus after the death of Icarus) *at pater infelix nec iam pater*.

1005 venere: servants now bring in the heads of the children.

natos ecquid agnoscis: *ecquid* suggests eager impatience: "well, don't you recognize your own sons?"

1006-21 The first of three impassioned speeches by Thyestes as the full horror of the crime comes home to him (the others are 1035-51 and 1068-96). Each appeals for a response to this enormous evil: this speech invokes Earth and the underworld, the second turns to Atreus and Thyestes himself (1043-47), and the third calls on every realm of the world (1068-72) before addressing itself to Jupiter (1077-92). These appeals are all unheard or thwarted, and each of the speeches consequently ends in frustration and incompleteness, reflected in the weak rhetoric of their closing lines. Thyestes is denied the verbal satisfaction of a powerful *sententia* as he is the emotional support of seeing the world react as he would want it to. (The cosmos *has*, of course, recoiled in shock, but Thyestes, who was already aware of this as a mysterious and threatening phenomenon— cf. 985-95—cannot now take comfort from it; there is something almost matter-of-fact in his recognition, *hoc est deos quod puduit, hoc egit diem / aversum in ortus* 1035-36).

1006 Agnosco fratrem: i.e., Atreus has now shown himself in his true form; compare Medea's taunt to Jason, *coniugem agnoscis tuam?* (1021 and cf. 923 *ultimum agnosco scelus*) and Hecuba's rueful "recognition" of her fellow-captives in *Tro.* 94-95 *placet hic habitus, / placet; agnosco Troada turbam.* For the loaded use of *frater* cf. 24, 425, 476.

sustines tantum nefas: before *gestare* completes the sense, these words suggest Earth "bearing up" under a crushing weight; this conception is reversed in 1020, where Thyestes calls the unmoving Earth itself an "inert weight."

1007-1009 non . . . abripis?: a version of the wish, uttered at moments of intense shame or disgrace, that the earth might open and consume one (see Pease on Verg. *Aen.* 4.24), but stated in typically intense and violent language (*rupta, ingenti via*).

1007-1008 non . . . mergis: *tantum nefas* (1006) is the object.

ad infernam Styga / tenebrasque: almost a hendiadys for "to the Stygian darkness below"; for the connection cf., e.g., Verg. *G.* 3.551 *Stygiis emissa tenebris*, Sen. *Epist.* 24.18 *nemo tam puer est ut Cerberum timeat et tenebras et larvalem habitum.* [This text incorporates B. Schmidt's conjecture *tenebrasque* for the manuscript reading *te nosque*. With the manuscript text, *te* would refer to *Tellus*, and Earth would be asked to plunge itself, along with Atreus and Thyestes, into Tartarus—a physical impossibility which it is hard to attribute even to Seneca's mannerist imagination. Furthermore, *te nosque* places Earth on the same footing as the guilty brothers, which clashes with the basic assumption of the speech, that Earth should express outrage at their crime. Finally, *nos* does not cohere well with *rege* in 1009, while with *tenebrasque* the progress of Thyestes' thoughts becomes clear: he first calls Atreus the guilty one (*rege*), then makes himself bear equal blame (*uterque* 1012, *nos* 1015), then focuses on his own punishment (*caput . . . nostrum* 1017).]

1008 mergis: often used by Ovid of violent descent to the underworld, cf. *Met.* 10.697 *an Stygia sontes dubitavit mergeret unda*, Luck on *Tr.* 4.5.21, but here recalling the appearances of *mergere* in the preceding cosmic upheaval, cf. 777, 820, 868.

rupta: nom. modifying *Tellus*. The language is again conventional (cf. Ovid *Met.* 13.442 *exit humo late rupta*, of the ghost of Achilles; Sen. *Oed.* 160-61 *rupere Erebi claustra profundi / turba sororum*, *Oct.* 136), but it gains in force from the prominence of "sundering" metaphors in the play, see on 179, also 88 *tellure rupta*.

ingenti via: i.e., the "path" opened by the fissure in the earth's surface; *ingens via* is an unusual combination (*via lata* would be normal, cf. *HF* 237, *Prov.* 2.10), and the intensifying *ingens* might have been suggested by Verg. *Aen.* 7.568–70 *spiracula Ditis / monstrantur, ruptoque ingens Acheronte vorago / pestiferas aperit fauces.*

1009 ad chaos inane: *chaos* is often applied to the underworld (cf. Verg. *Aen.* 6.265, Sen. *Med.* 9, 741, *Pha.* 1238, *Oed.* 572–73 *rumpitur caecum chaos / iterque . . . ad superos datur*), and so is *inanis*, "insubstantial" (*OLD* s.v., #10, Ovid *Met.* 4.510 *inania . . . regna Ditis*), but *inane chaos* must carry cosmological overtones, recalling the "void" which Atomist philosophers placed before the formation of the universe, cf. Verg. *Ecl.* 6.31, Ovid *Ars* 2.470, Sen. *Epist.* 72.9 *in Epicureum illud chaos decidunt, inane sine termino.*

1010 tota . . . tecta: "[*totus*] eventually develops into a synonym of *omnis* and indeed replaces it (cf. French 'tout'). But most seeming instances in classical Latin . . . are intelligible in the proper sense; [*tecta*] is treated as a collective, undifferentiated noun [= *urbs*], not as a number of separate units." (Courtney on Juv. 8.255, *mutatis mutandis*; see also D. R. Shackleton Bailey, *Propertiana* [Cambridge, 1956], 48–49).

Seneca was probably thinking of Verg. *Aen.* 2.445–46, *Dardanidae contra turris et tota domorum / culmina convellunt*: note also 464–65 [*turrim*] *convellimus altis / sedibus* [= *ab imo . . . solo*]. [In *Aen.* 2.445 *tecta* is a widely attested ancient variant for *tota*; Seneca may just possibly have conflated the readings to produce *tota . . . tecta*.]

1010–11 ab imo . . . solo / vertis Mycenas: another echo of Vergil's description of the fall of Troy, *Aen.* 2.625 *ex imo verti Neptunia Troia.*

1011–12 stare . . . iam debuimus: "we ought by now to have been standing."

1012 uterque: Thyestes now realizes, as Atreus had foreseen (271–72), that he is as deeply tainted as his brother. (He also makes explicit the connection with Tantalus that is implied in the Prologue, see above p. 85).

compagibus: the links holding the earth in place and thereby closing off the lower world; for the idea of their rupture, cf. *NQ* 6.32.4 *securus aspiciet ruptis compagibus dehiscere solum, illa licet inferorum regna retegantur* and the closely parallel lines *Oed.* 579–83 *sive ipsa tellus, ut daret functis viam, / compage rupta sonuit . . . subito dehiscit terra et immenso sinu / laxata patuit.* [The imitation of this passage in *HO* 1135–36 transposes it to a heavenly setting: *hinc et hinc compagibus / ruptis uterque debuit frangi polus.* Note the reworking of *uterque . . . debuimus* in *uterque debuit*, typical of the way Senecan phrases are handled by the author of *HO*.]

1013 si quid infra Tartara est: i.e., Tartarus is not sunk far enough below the earth to be a suitable place of confinement for Atreus and Thyestes. (For the thought cf. Ovid *Pont.* 4.14.11–12 *Styx quoque, si quid ea est, bene commutabitur Histro, / si quid et inferius quam Styga mundus habet*, Sen. *HF* 1223–25 *si quod exilium latet / ulterius Erebo, Cerbero ignotus et mihi, / hoc me abde, Tellus.*) Thyestes here transcends Tantalus' prediction that his descendants would fill the region of the damned (21–23)— another example of the Tantalid urge to surpass previous levels of wickedness (cf. 19, 195–96).

1014 avosque nostros: one of Thyestes' rare *sententiae*: Tartarus is ironically defined as nearly synonymous with "our ancestors" because of the eminent place Tantalus holds among the inmates.

avos: generalizing plural, cf. Acc. 207 R² *matres conquinari regias* [= Aerope], Verg. *Aen.* 7.359 *exulibusne datur . . . Lavinia Teucris* [= Aeneas], K-S 1.86–87.

1014-15 hoc . . . vallem: "to this place let your chasm descend in an enormous cavity"; *hoc* is adverbial (= *huc*, cf. 710 above), *immani sinu* is abl. of manner defining how the action of *demitte vallem* is to be performed (compare *immenso sinu* in *Oed.* 582, quoted on 1012 *compagibus*), and *vallis* is the fissure spoken of in 1008 *rupta* (similarly *Tro.* 178 *scissa vallis aperit immensos specus*). The phrasing is unusually knotty, perhaps because Seneca is straining to recall other depressions in the play: the abyss (*sinus*) into which the planets will fall on the last day (843) and the *vallis* that surrounds the grove of the palace (651).

1015 demitte: of the personified earth in Verg. *Ecl* 9.7-8 *qua se subducere colles / incipiunt mollique demittere clivo*.

1016 Acheronte: = the underworld, as in 17, Verg. *Aen.* 7.312 *flectere si superos nequeo, Acheronta movebo*.

1016-19 noxiae . . . fluat: the emotional level of Thyestes' speech changes, as he elaborates the notion of a sub-Tartarean prison in graphic but essentially fanciful terms; the seclusion of this retreat may even have an attraction for him (see on 1018).

1016-17 caput . . . nostrum: not a likely collective singular; Thyestes is now thinking of his own punishment (cf. *vile hoc caput* 996).

1017 vagentur: an unexpected detail, since the famous sinners are usually shown in strict confinement; the only "wandering" in Vergil's underworld, for example, is by Aeneas and Anchises—*Aen.* 6.886 *tota passim regione vagantur*—and by the spirits of the unburied at the banks of the Styx, *Aen.* 6.329 *centum errant annos volitantque haec litora circum*. (It is perhaps a sign of Thyestes' passivity that even in his fantasies others possess a freedom of motion that is denied to him.)

ardenti freto: Thyestes again "outdoes" Tantalus, who had offered to stand in the middle of Phlegethon, cf. 72-73.

1018 Phlegethon . . . agens: = ABabc (see on 10), a refined arrangement suggesting a certain pleasure in the act of description.

Phlegethon: the border of Tartarus in Verg. *Aen.* 6.550-51, Sen. *Pha.* 1226-27.

tostas: if this is the correct reading (see below), the grains of sand are "roasted" by the fiery river, like lupines (Ovid *Med. fac.* 69), beans (Col. 8.11.6), or chestnuts (Mart. 5.78.15) over a fire—a unique and ingenious detail. [The reading printed here is a 16th-century conjecture for *totas*, which seems to lack point, unlike the intensifying uses of *totus* in 1010 and 1016. Another early conjecture is *tortas*, which would describe the sand "twisted" by the violent flow of the river; this can be more closely paralleled—cf. Verg. *Aen.* 7.567 *torto vertice torrens*, Luc. 4.767 *quantus Bistonio torquetur turbine pulvis*—but does not cohere as neatly with the stress on fire in *ardenti* and *igneus*.]

1019 exilia: "place of exile," cf. Ovid *Tr.* 4.4.51 *mitius exilium paulumque propinquius opto*, *HF* 93 *ultra nocentum exilia*, 1223-24 *si quod exilium latet / ulterius Erebo*; a fitting term for the Tantalids, no strangers to exile as the consequence of wickedness, cf. 32-38, 237. [The manuscripts read *exitia*, which yields no satisfactory sense; *exilia* is an emendation by Gronovius.]

1020 immota . . . iaces?: Thyestes disconsolately realizes that his appeal has produced no effect. [The manuscripts divide between *iaces* (A) and *iacet* (E); the former balances *sustines* in 1006 and so provides an effective frame for the speech.]

1021–23 Iam . . . tribus: Atreus acts as if nothing untoward had happened, and pretends that Thyestes' children are present, waiting for their father to embrace them. Though understated in its language, this is one of the play's most deeply disturbing moments.

1021 potius: i.e., rather than lamenting; Atreus disregards Thyestes' speech as irrelevant to his "reunion."

1022 diu expetitos: referring to Thyestes' repeated request to see them (974–75, 997); perhaps also a mocking echo of his earlier invitation to Thyestes, *complexus mihi / redde expetitos* (508–509).

nulla . . . mora: "your brother's not stopping you," a phrase with colloquial overtones, cf. Juv. 6.333, 12.111.

1023 divide: the word provokes echoes of more sinister "divisions," cf. 147, 760.

1024–25 Hoc . . . ponis?: the bewildered questions give an impression of naive credulity; one could easily imagine Atreus meeting each query with a delighted nod. Accius' Thyestes may have been more forceful in his protests, if the words *fregisti fidem* (227 R²) come from the corresponding scene in the *Atreus*.

gratia: "good will," "friendship," cf. Ovid *Met.* 1.145 *fratrum quoque gratia rara est*.

1025 sic odia ponis?: recalling Atreus' words *animis odia damnata excidant* (511) and Thyestes' reply *ponatur omnis ira* (519).

1025–30 non peto . . . perditurus: Thyestes assumes an almost deferential tone, striking evidence of his submission to Atreus' will.

1026–27 scelere . . . salvo . . . odioque: "without harm to your crime and hatred," a courteous idiom like "saving your reverence" in older English, cf. *Epist.* 117.1 *salva conscientia*, Luc. 7.378 *salva . . . maiestate*, Quint. 6.3.35 *salva verecundia*. The use of *scelus* and *odium* in such a phrase is an inversion like that in 203–204 *in medio est scelus / positum occupanti* (see note *ad loc.*).

1027 frater hoc fratrem rogo: a curious emphasis; can Thyestes still think that Atreus feels any respect for the claims of brotherhood? (For Atreus' view, cf. 240–41 *certi nihil / nisi frater hostis*, and note Thyestes' own suspicions, 425, 476–82). Seneca's depiction of a perverted world is so successful that a belief in traditional moral values seems in this context laughably out of place.

1028–29 redde . . . uri: "give me back what you may see burned without delay" (*quod cernas . . . uri* is a relative clause of characteristic).

1029–30 nihil te . . . habiturus rogo, / sed perditurus: "I ask you for nothing in order to possess it, but in order to lose it" (i.e., since the remains would be destroyed as soon as they were handed over); the future participles express intention, cf. *Ira.* 1.3.5 *irascimur . . . iis qui laesuri sunt* ("those who mean to do us harm"), *Ag.* 101 *ruitura* (n).

1030–31 Quidquid . . . habes: another Atrean *jeu de mots*. At one level he is using a "polar expression" only one element of which is logically applicable: the meaning would be "you see before you all that remains of your children" (lit., "what there is and is not"). (For other such expressions—perhaps colloquial in origin—cf. Pl. *Trin.* 360 *comedit quod fuit quod non fuit*, Catullus 76.16 *hoc facias, sive id pote sive non pote*, Verg. *Aen.* 12.810–11 *nec tu me . . . videres / digna indigna pati*, Sen. *Med.* 566–67 *incipe / quidquid potest Medea, quidquid non potest*.) But Atreus also intends a sense in which both parts of the phrase are relevant: "you have [on this platter] what is left and you have [within you] what is not."

1032–33 Utrumne . . . feras?: not having grasped the hidden sense of Atreus' words, Thyestes asks what has become of the rest of the bodies; as with the Chorus's similar question to the Messenger (747–48 and see note), his worst imaginings fall far short of the truth.

1032 pabulum . . . iacent: an echo of 12 *pabulum monstro* [= *vulturi*] *iacet*.

1033 beluis scinduntur: "are they being torn apart by beasts?"; for *scindere* cf. Ovid *Ibis* 168 *scindent avidi perfida corda canes*, 1067 below (of Thyestes himself). [*scinduntur* is my conjecture; the Mss read *servantur*, "are they being reserved for wild animals?" (cf. *Oed.* 31 *cui reservamur malo?*), which seems too vague to cohere with the other possibilities mentioned. Axelson's *vorantur* is attractive—it would make all three questions turn on forms of eating—but *beluis vorantur* and *pascunt feras* are too close to tautology for comfort.]

1034 Epulatus . . . dape: dropping his playful ambiguity, Atreus reveals the truth in a formal, perhaps slightly archaic style (note the pleonasm of *epulatus es* and *dape*).

impia: a neat reminder that Thyestes bears responsibility for the deed.

1035–51 An oddly disjointed speech, consisting largely of rhetorical gestures that fail to cohere or develop. The appearance of the *'tale quis vidit nefas?'* motif near the end (1047–50) testifies to a lack of progression, and the feeble attempts at *sententiae* in 1046–47 and 1050–51 strengthen the impression of a botched performance.

1036 aversum: "turned away" in disgust, cf. Ovid *Am.* 3.12.29 *aversum . . . diem mensis furialibus Atrei*, *Tr.* 2.392 *aversos Solis . . . equos.*

1036–37 quas . . . mihi?: a version of the "inexpressibility topos" (see on 684), creating the expectation of a formal lament.

1037 questusque quos: the unusual word-order and repeated *qu-* sounds suggest speech broken by sobs.

1038 cerno: another introductory motif in lamentation, cf. Verg. *Aen.* 9.481 *'hunc ego te, Euryale, aspicio?'*, Ovid *Met.* 13.495 *'nate, iaces, videoque tuum, mea vulnera, pectus'* (text uncertain), Sen. *Pha.* 1168–69 *'Hippolyte, tales intuor vultus tuos / talesque feci?'*

1038–39 abscisa . . . avulsas . . . rupta fractis: the appalling climax of the play's many instances of "breaking" and "sundering" language, see on 179 *ruptum.*

1038 capita . . . manus: cf. 764.

1039 vestigia: = *pedes*, a coinage inspired by Greek ἴχνος and first found in neoteric poetry, cf. Catullus 64.162, Verg. *Aen.* 5.566, Ovid *Met.* 1.536 with Bömer's note. The feet, which would be as hard to disguise as the heads and hands, were probably not mentioned earlier (764) because they do not lend themselves to pointed comment.

1040 hoc . . . pater: the sight of these fragments makes Thyestes guiltily aware of the eagerness with which he consumed the rest of the bodies. The line is unusual in having three resolved long syllables (*ăvĭdŭs, căpĕrĕ, pŏtŭĭt*)—Thyestes' excited words come tumbling out in a rush.

hoc est: echoing 1035 and rounding off the speech's phase of recognition.

avidus . . . pater: Thyestes has played to perfection the role for which Atreus had cast him, cf. 277–78.

capere: "take in," "find room for," cf. 255.

1041-42 volvuntur . . . fugam: a restatement of the disorder felt at 999–1001, with fear (*tremuit*) and lament (*gemitu*) replaced by a more vigorous struggle to escape. Thyestes is experiencing the counterpart of Atreus' "seizure" in 260–61 *tumultus pectora . . . quatit / penitusque volvit.*

volvuntur: passive with middle force, "heave," "toss," cf. Luc. 8.272 *mille . . . volvuntur in aequore puppes.*

1041 viscera: the flesh of the children, immediately redefined in abstract terms as *clusum nefas.*

1042 quaerit fugam: even the children seek to join the universal flight from Thyestes; an unfortunate extension of the motif of "escape."

1043-44 da . . . via: Thyestes' first impulse is to kill himself. The reaction of Tereus in Ovid *Met.* 6.663–64 is similar (*et modo, si posset, reserato pectore diras / egerere inde dapes semesaque viscera gestit*), but with characteristic abstractness Seneca only alludes to the act by naming its metaphorical result, "releasing" the children (*liberis detur via*); compare *Med.* 970–71 *victima manes tuos / placamus ista* (as Medea kills one of her children).

sanguinis . . . ille: i.e., Thyestes can rightly lay claim to the weapon because it has already shed "his" blood.

1044 detur via: the image of a "path" may suggest the freedom Thyestes knows he lacks; see also 1008 *ingenti via,* note on 1017 *vagentur.* [The A manuscripts read *demus viam* in a misguided attempt to make the language more vivid.]

1045-46 pectora . . . planctu: "let my battered breast resound with smashing blows of grief." The language is hyperbolical (in the style parodied in Petr. *Sat.* 87.2 *verberabam aegrum planctibus pectus*), perhaps in order to convey the violence of Thyestes' self-hatred; its effect, though, is undercut by the following *sententia.*

1046 contusa: stronger than *tundere,* the standard Augustan term for beating one's breast (cf., e.g., Verg. *Aen.* 1.481, Ovid *Am.* 3.9.10); in time, however, *contundere* loses its original sense of battering (cf. Ovid *Met.* 12.85 *ut . . . pectus tantummodo contudit ictu* [i.e., "merely struck" rather than pierced], Luc. 2.38 *contundite pectora, matres*). Here *contusa* is reinforced by *illiso* and *sonent.*

1046-47 sustine . . . umbris: this dreadful specimen of misplaced cleverness has only one equal in the tragedies: the blind Oedipus, about to leave the stage on which Jocasta lies dead, says (1051) *i profuge vade—siste, ne in matrem incidas.* Here at least the tastelessness of the point serves a dramatic purpose, subverting Thyestes' attempts at tragic dignity, and so preventing him from fully engaging an audience's sympathy even when his situation might most warrant it. (See on 1004 *obloquuntur.*)

1047-50 tale . . . Procrustes: for the motif see on 627–32.

1048 inhospitalis: = ἄξενος, the term originally applied to the Black Sea (later euphemistically called the Euxine); *inhospitalis* was by Seneca's time a conventional epithet of the Caucasus (cf. Hor. *Epod.* 1.12, *C.* 1.22.6, Sen. *Med.* 43), but here it could have its literal sense ("unfriendly to strangers"), since the Heniochi were notorious pirates, cf. Ovid *Pont.* 4.10.26, Strabo 12.2.12.

1049-50 quis . . . Procrustes?: Procrustes (also called Damastes) was an Attic brigand (hence *Cecropiis . . . terris*, high-poetic idiom for "the land of Attica") who waylaid travelers and fitted them to a bed either by stretching or amputation, cf. "Apollodorus" *Epit.* 1.4 with Frazer's note. He too may be cited as a violator of hospitality: "Apollodorus" speaks of him inviting passers-by to be his guests, a motif almost certainly taken from an earlier Greek treatment. [It is also possible that Thyestes invokes Procrustes as a dismemberer of bodies, but, if so, this would be the one place in Latin apart from the late compilation called "Hyginus" where this aspect of Procrustes' legend is alluded to; Ovid and Seneca are the only writers who mention him, and elsewhere in their work he appears simply as a name along with other figures of egregious cruelty, cf. Ovid *Her.* 2.69, *Met.* 7.438, *Ibis* 405, Sen. *Pha.* 1170, *Clem.* 2.4.1.]

1049 metus: "cause of fear," cf. 670, *OLD* s.v., #5b, *HF* 230 *taurum . . . centum non levem populis metum.*

1050 en: marks a new recognition and leads into the final *sententia*; Thyestes is obviously pleased with the point he is about to make.

1050-51 genitor . . . natis: "I weigh heavily on my sons and in turn they weigh heavily on me," a poor attempt at a striking phrase. (Perhaps not in Seneca's eyes, however: Andromache frames a nearly identical antithesis in *Tro.* 690-91 *ne pater natum obruat / prematque patrem natus.*

1051 modus: "proper measure," because of the equal balance of oppression.

1052-68 Ever responsive to the ambiguities of language, Atreus takes *modus* to mean that his crime contains some "limitation" or "restriction." The thought re-awakens his feelings of dissatisfaction (cf. 252-54, etc., 890); he reviews his atrocities in a slighting, concessive tone, ending with the play's most horrifying line: his revenge has been in vain, since Thyestes may have eaten his children, but at the time neither he nor they knew it.

1052 Sceleri modus debetur: "a limit is owed to crime," a financial metaphor which makes *scelus* a half-personified entity (like *ira* in 1056).

facias: generalizing second person, cf. 925 *cadas*, 195-96 *scelera non ulcisceris / nisi vincis.*

1054-56 ex vulnere ipso . . . cruorem: this missed opportunity is sketched almost absently—one feels that Atreus' thoughts are elsewhere—and then forgotten.

1056-57 verba . . . propero: "through haste my anger has been tricked"; Atreus speaks of his *ira* as something independent of himself, to which he owes a loyalty he has failed to honor. (Compare 712-13, where the children are victims *devota impiae . . . irae*, and also Medea's apology to her *dolor: plura non habui, dolor, / quae tibi litarem* 1019-20.)

1056 verba sunt . . . data: *verba dare* ("to deceive," cf. *OLD* s.v. *verbum*, #6) is generally avoided in high poetry; Ovid, for example, has it only in elegiacs (cf. *Ars* 2.166, 558, etc.), not in the *Metamorphoses.*

1057 dum propero: *dum* is causal: Atreus blames haste for his anger's deception, cf. *OLD* s.v., #4a, Ter. *And.* 822 *dum studeo obsequi tibi, paene inlusi vitam filiae*, Verg. *Aen.* 12.735-37 *fama est praecipitem . . . dum trepidet, ferrum aurigae rapuisse Metisci, HF* 35-36.

1057-65 ferro . . . flammas: a point-by-point digest of the Messenger's account. Atreus at first dwells on the details as evidence of thoroughness, but in the end the emphasis on his own involvement (1064–65 *manu / mea, ipse*) shows him the reason for his disappointment: *he* did all of this, and not Thyestes.

Specific parallels: 1057 *ferro* . . . *impresso*/722 *ensem premens*; 1058 *cecidi ad aras*/ 693 *stat ipse ad aras*; *caede votiva*/712 *capita devota*, 714 *caede immolet*; *focos*/768 *trepidantes focos*; 1059 *corpora* . . . *amputans*/760–62 *secat* . . . *corpus, amputat* . . . *umeros*, etc.; 1060–62 *haec* . . . *iussi*/765–67 *haec* . . . *iactat*, 769 (*ignis*) *iussus*; 1062 *membra nervosque abscidi*/763 *denudat artus* . . . *ossa amputat*; 1063 *viventibus*/755 *erepta vivis exta pectoribus*; 1063–64 *traiectas veru* . . . *fibras*/765 *veribus haerent viscera*; 1064 *mugire*/764 *gemuere*; 1064–65 *aggessi* . . . *flammas*/769 (*ignis*) *bis ter regestus*.

1057 vulnera . . . dedi: "I dealt wounds"; *dare vulnera* is high style, cf. Verg. *Aen.* 10.733, Ovid *Met.* 1.458, 3.84, etc. (On periphrases with *dare* cf. Bömer on *Met.* 2.165.)

1059 placavi: Atreus' idiosyncratic view of the event foreseen by the Fury, *patrios polluat sanguis focos* (61).

1060 in . . . frusta: probably a borrowing from Verg. *Aen.* 1.212 *pars in frusta secant veribusque trementia figunt*.

carpsi: unlike Vergil's *secant* (previous note), *carpere* suggests pulling the flesh into pieces with bare hands. The intention is not to stress Atreus' cruelty, but his care: he thoughtfully does for Thyestes what a guest would normally do for himself, cf. Ovid *Ars* 3.355 *carpe cibos digitis* (i.e., rather than gnawing a joint of meat).

1063 gracili: almost the only detail not mentioned by the Messenger; it demonstrates the precision of Atreus' recollections.

1064 mugire: see on 772 *gemuere* (and for the close connection of the two words, cf. Stat. *Theb.* 6.28 *gemitu iam regia mugit*).

1066 cecidit in cassum: "has proven fruitless," cf. Pl. *Poen.* 360 *bene promittis multa* . . . ; *omnia in cassum cadunt*, Sen. *Brev. vit.* 11.1 *quam in cassum ceciderit omnis labor cogitant*; *cadere* may originally have retained its sense of motion (compare Livy 2.6.1 *ad irritum cadentis spei*), but as used here the expression is simply a fixed idiom.

1067 scidit ore natos impio: a concessive lead-in combining elements of 778–79 *lancinat natos pater / artusque mandit ore funesto suos* and 1034 *epulatus ipse es impia natos dape*; the play's previous high points of horror are recalled, then impatiently dismissed.

1067–68 sed nesciens, / sed nescientes: what galls Atreus is that, if his victims were unaware of what was happening, they cannot be said to have taken part in the action; Atreus has thus failed to make Thyestes "will what he would not" (212), and has not fully met the goal he set himself, to have Thyestes "rejoice" in eating his children (*gaudens* 278). It is characteristic of Seneca that bloodshed and violent death count for little compared to mental anguish; similar reasoning lies behind Medea's reply when Jason begs to be killed instead of his child: '*hac qua recusas, qua doles, ferrum exigam*' (1006) and Aegisthus' refusal to kill Electra in *Ag.* 994 '*concede mortem*' '*si recusares, darem.*'

1068–96 Thyestes' third speech is rhetorically his most ambitious and, in its first part, his most successful (see on 1077–87). Like its predecessors, though, it ends in futility and impotence, a feeling reflected in some jarring shifts of stylistic level (see on 1088 *si minus*, 1095 *nil queror*), the proliferation of *si*-clauses in the closing section (1088, 1090, 1092, 1096), and the weak final *sententia* (*nil, Titan, queror, / si perseveras*).

1068-76 Clausa . . . mea: Thyestes calls on the realms of nature as the only witnesses of his misery (*tibi sum relictus* 1073). The gesture recalls the isolated heroes of Greek tragedy, for example Sophocles' Philoctetes (*Phil.* 936–38) or Prometheus in *Prometheus Bound* (88–92, with Griffith's note); here the convention is seen from a fresh angle, since Thyestes is concerned for the stability of the natural order he invokes (1076 *vobis vota prospicient mea*).

1068 litoribus vagis: "winding shores," an expression for which *OLD* s.v. *vagus* cites only later parallels (cf. Stat. *Theb.* 5.494–95 *vaga litora furtim / incomitata sequor*), though Seneca comes close in *Tranq.* 2.13 *peregrinationes suscipiuntur vagae et litora pererrantur* and Ovid *Met.* 9.450 speaks of the windings of Meander's banks, *curvamina ripae*. (The conventional use of *vagus* is with rivers, cf. Hor. *C.* 1.34.9 with Nisbet-Hubbard's note.) This novel combination, which evokes the motif of "wandering" (see on 1017), is even more remarkable for being joined to an image of confinement (*clausa . . . maria*); the word-order depicts an enclosure—*clausa . . . maria* surrounding *litoribus vagis*—that inverts the reality described. The resulting tension between motion and restraint is a variant of the idea of flight or escape that haunts Thyestes in this act (see on 922–23, 987, 1003, 1008, 1017, 1042, 1044).

1071 nox . . . gravis: see on 787.

Tartarea: abl. with *nube*, parallel to *atra*; *Tartareus* is not a mere synonym for "black," and may suggest the presence of infernal matter in the upper world (cf. 678–79).

1072 vaca: "pay heed," cf. Prop. 4.6.14 *Caesar dum canitur, quaeso, Iuppiter ipse vaces.* (Seneca may be punning at Thyestes' expense on the basic sense "be empty," a condition that has already been met, cf. 892 *caelum vacat.*)

1073 tibi sum relictus: "I have been abandoned to you" (i.e., only night is present to hear him), cf. Verg. *Aen.* 12.382 *truncum . . . reliquit harenae.* Ovid *Met.* 14.217 *leto poenaeque relictus.*

1074 tu quoque sine astris: i.e., night too has been "abandoned" (cf. 990–91 *aether . . . desertus*). This is a third member of a tricolon (after *tibi sum relictus* and *sola tu miserum vides*) and exhibits the slight twist typical of a *sententia*, but without the impact of the best Senecan examples.

vota . . . improba: presumably as opposed to Atreus' *vota* (888, 912), although Thyestes did not actually hear these being made. The phrase also points to a contrast with the traditional "curse of Thyestes," see on 1110–11.

1075 pro me: "for my own benefit."

1076 vobis . . . prospicient: "will look out for your interests," cf. Cic. *Cat.* 4.3 *consulite vobis, prospicite patriae, Fam.* 3.2.1,

1077-87 tu . . . exple: for the address to Jupiter, Seneca lends Thyestes all his own rhetorical skill: the language is rich and powerful, the phrases long but fully controlled, the forward impetus unflagging. (By comparison, the other places in Seneca where Jupiter is called on to hurl his thunderbolt—*HF* 1202-1205, *Med.* 531-37, *Pha.* 672-83—seem unimpressive or hysterical.)

1077-79 rector . . . potens / dominator aulae: Jupiter is addressed as a sovereign, the lord of a heavenly court (for *rector* cf. 607, and for *aula* see on 392); the following reference to l..s battle against the Giants implies that Jupiter's authority is again being threatened (cf. 804–12). What Thyestes is calling for—and failing to obtain—is a clear vindication of the gods' power.

1078 dominator: first used by Cicero, *ND* 2.4 *illum . . . et Iovem et dominatorem rerum et omnia regentem*, cf. also *Eleg. in Maec.* 1.87 *fudit Aloidas postquam dominator Olympi*.

1078–80 totum . . . undique . . . omni parte: a variety of "universalizing" terms, punctuating the threefold invocation (*convolve . . . committe . . . intona*).

1079 bella ventorum: a passing glance at a well-worn topic, the warfare of opposing winds, cf., e.g., Verg. *G.* 1.318 *omnia ventorum concurrere proelia vidi*, Ovid *Met.* 11.490–91 *omni . . . e parte* [compare 1080 *omni parte*] *feroces / bella gerunt venti* (with Bömer's note), Sen. *Ag.* 476 (n), *Med.* 940.

1080 omni . . . intona: cf. *HF* 1202 *nunc parte ab omni, genitor, iratus tona, Med.* 531 *nunc summe toto Iuppiter caelo tona.*

violentum: adverbial acc. (AG 390b).

1081–84 manuque non qua . . . hac arma expedi: "not with that hand with which you attack innocent homes and dwellings, using a lesser weapon, but with that hand by which the threefold mass collapsed and [with it] the Giants who equaled the mountains in stature—with *this* hand get ready your weapons." [The text is disputed in two places: in 1081 the manuscripts divide between *manumque* (E P) and *manuque* (T CS) and in 1084 *hac* is Scaliger's conjecture for *haec*. The combination *manuque . . . hac* gives a smooth and coherent text, and I have therefore adopted it—although with some misgivings, since *manuque* could easily have arisen by false attraction to *qua*, as *haec* has probably been drawn into agreement with *arma*. Leo (*Obs.*, 40) defended *manumque . . . haec*, arguing that the thought begun with *manumque* is forgotten after the parenthetical clause *non . . . Gigantes*, and so a new object, *haec arma*, is introduced with the main verb *expedi*. This shift seems unlikely in view of the continued stress on *manus* in *non qua . . . sed qua*, but the hypothesis of a change in construction could be used to support *manumque . . . hac*; the swerve would then be from the expected *hanc manum expedi* to *hac arma expedi*.]

1081 manuque. *manus* implies the force with which the weapon is to be hurled, cf. *OLD* s.v., #8, Sall. *Hist.* 2.64 *parietes . . . templorum ambusti manus Punicas ostentabant.*

tecta et immeritas domos: a poetic condensation of *immerita tecta et immeritas domos*; the adjective appears only once but is to be taken in common with both nouns. (The construction is often called ἀπὸ κοινοῦ.) The adjective is more often attached, as here, to the second of the nouns to which it applies.

1082 telo . . . minore: for the idea that the innocent or obscure receive milder treatment from the gods cf. *Pha.* 1124–25 *minor in parvis Fortuna furit / leviusque ferit leviora deus*, 1132–33 *raros patitur fulminis ictus / umida vallis*; the notion of thunderbolts coming in a range of sizes, however, seems to be a whimsical inspiration of Ovid, cf. *Met.* 3.303–307 *nec, quo centimanum deiecerat igne Typhoea, / nunc armatur eo; nimum feritatis in illo est. / est aliud levius fulmen, cui dextra Cyclopum / saevitiae flammaeque minus, minus addidit irae; / tela secunda vocant superi. capit illa*, etc. Ovid's lines may be the basis for the balanced clauses *non qua . . . sed qua*; as often, the model is both evoked and altered, as Thyestes calls on Jupiter to use precisely the weapon that his Ovidian counterpart had rejected.

1082–83 montium / tergemina moles: the mass produced by piling Pelion, Ossa, and Olympus one above the other; see on 810–12 above.

1083 cecidit: in Ovid *Met*. 1.154–55 Jupiter's thunderbolt shakes the mountains free, *misso perfregit Olympum / fulmine et excussit subiectae Pelion Ossae*.

1083-84 qui montibus / stabant pares Gigantes: apparently an original twist, a sign of the unusual rhetorical fluency Thyestes shows in this passage.

1084 arma expedi: the echo of Atreus' *expedi amplexus* (1004) is surely intentional.

1084-87 expedi . . . exple: the invocation ends with a surge of energy, the appeals hammered out in short phrases and the insistent imperatives (*expedi . . . torque . . . vindica . . . iaculare . . . exple*) urgent and even commanding.

1086-87 lumen . . . exple: the lightning-flash will replace the natural souces of light that have fled. The point resembles a clever touch in an unnamed declaimer's handling of a sea-storm, cf. Sen. *Contr*. 8 *exc*. 6 *demissa nox caelo est et tantum fulminibus dies redditus*; compare also Ovid *Met*. 2.330–32 (after Phaethon's disastrous ride) *unum / isse diem sine sole ferunt; incendia lumen / praebebant*, Sen. *Ag*. 494, 496–97 (nn). The *sententia* may sound forced to modern taste, but for Seneca and his audience it could have seemed an effective variation on a familiar theme.

1087-88 causa . . . sit: "so that you don't need to think it over at length, let the justification be the evil done by both of us"; i.e., if Jupiter considers Atreus and Thyestes together, his decision to punish them should be an easy one. (Compare Medea's argument at 534–37, that Jupiter need not take care to aim his thunderbolt at herself or Jason; both are guilty, so he cannot fail to hit someone deserving punishment.) Thyestes' language slips into near-informality, and his reasoning begins to sound merely clever.

1087 causa: see on 276.

ne dubites diu: an implicit recognition of Jupiter's failure to heed Thyestes' appeal.

1088 utriusque mala: cf. 272 *uterque faciat* (sc. *facinus*).

si minus: "if not," cf. *OLD* s.v. *minus*, #4b. The expression is strikingly undignified for this context; it also signals another stage in the frustration of Thyestes' hopes.

1089 trisulco flammeam telo facem: an abrupt return to the grand style, with two alliterative periphrases intertwined in the order abAB (see on 10). It is as if Thyestes, having formulated a new request for Jupiter, looks for a suitably august tone of voice in which to make it; the shift is too sudden to be effective, and the diction suggests bluster rather than real power. (This ornate style is reminiscent of early tragedy, cf., e.g., Accius 581–82 R² *Soli, qui micantem candido curru atque equis / flammam citatis fervido ardore explicas. . . .*)

trisulco . . . telo: cf. Ovid *Am*. 2.5.52, *Met*. 2.848 *trisulcis . . . ignibus*, Sen. *Pha*. 681 *trisulca . . . face*; compare Varro *Sat*. 54 Buecheler *trisulcum fulmen*, Sen. *Pha*. 189, ps-Sen. *HO* 1994.

flammeam . . . facem: cf. Prop. 4.6.29–30 *nova flamma / luxit in obliquam . . . facem*, Sen. *Pha*. 681 (previous note); see also on 835–36 *aeternae / facis exortu*.

1090-92 si . . . cremandus: Thyestes is struck by a sudden inspiration, that being blasted by Jupiter's thunderbolt is the only way the children can receive a proper funeral; this strained point is a weak variation on an older motif, in which Thyestes is the tomb of his children, cf. Accius 226 R² *natis sepulchro ipse est parens*, applied to Tereus in Ovid *Met*. 6.665 *se . . . vocat bustum miserabile nati*.

1090 natos pater: for the juxtaposition see on 40–41, 90; here it makes relatively little impact.

1091 humare: used in a general sense, "to give funeral rites to," which may involve cremation and burial of the ashes, cf. (perhaps) Lucr. 6.1281, Verg. *Aen.* 6.161 and 226–35, 11.2 and 211–12, Nepos *Eum* 13.4.

1092-93 si . . . petit: Thyestes retreats another step; *nihil* and *nullus* show that he has given up looking for any response from the gods.

1095 nil . . . queror: used several times by Cicero, usually as a lead-in line (cf. *Cluent.* 188–89 *nihil de alteris Oppiciani nuptiis queror . . . illud primum queror de illo scelere*, etc., *Verr.* 2.111, *Phil.* 2.79); in final position it sounds jarringly flat (almost like "it's all right with me").

1096 si perseveras: "if you keep to your present course" (since the Sun has already turned and fled).

1096-1112 The pace now accelerates, and the play ends with a set of quick, pointed exchanges. Greek tragedy contains some superb examples of this type of finale, e.g., Aesch. *Ag.* 1649–73, Soph. *El.* 1491–1507. The nearest Senecan parallels are in *Agamemnon* 978–1012, *Phoenissae* 645–64, and *Medea* 982–1027; of these only the end of *Medea* equals these lines in concentration and power. Atreus, like Medea, remains in control throughout; he begins and ends the dialogue and has the only speech of any length (1104–1110), while Thyestes is allowed just one complete line, the lead-in to Atreus' concluding *sententia*.

1096-99 Nunc . . . toris: Atreus is delighted to have provoked Thyestes' long outburst and at last professes himself satisfied with his work.

1096 manus: "handiwork," as in *Med.* 977 *approba populo manum*. Atreus may be opposing his *manus* to that of Jupiter, cf. 1081–84.

1097 parta . . . est: "has been obtained"; the word was so often used with *victoria, pax, laus*, etc. (*OLD* s.v., #5) that its connection with birth may not have been any longer felt.

palma: the victory-palm, cf. 410 above, *Ag.* 918–19 (n). (By speaking of a *vera palma*, Atreus may be placing his triumph on a higher level than the mundane athletic victories Thyestes looks back to in 410.)

1097-98 perdideram . . . doleres: "I would have wasted my crime if you were not lamenting in this way"; *perdideram* is indicative for subjunctive in the apodosis of a contrary-to-fact condition (AG 517b).

1097 perdideram: compare *Med.* 976–77 *non in occulto tibi est / perdenda virtus* (where *virtus* is used ironically of murder). It is a typical Senecan inversion to regard *scelus* as precious and not to be "squandered"; cf. *Ag.* 519 *perdenda mors est?*, *Cons. Helv.* 3.2 *perdidisti enim tot mala, si nondum miseram esse didicisti*.

1098-99 liberos . . . toris: Atreus had said that his paternity of Agamemnon and Menelaus would be assured if they cooperated in his plan (cf. 327–30); he now concludes that the success of his revenge has resolved his doubts. His second phrase (*castis . . . toris*) has a logical meaning, i.e., his marriage is saved from the disgrace of bastardy, but it goes beyond the rational in suggesting that Thyestes' adultery with Aerope has been undone. Medea too claims that revenge has annulled her past, 982–84 *iam iam recepi sceptra germanum patrem, / . . . rediere regna, rapta virginitas redit*. It is in passages like these, with their unsettling mixture of logic and sheer delusion, that Seneca's understanding of madness is most clearly revealed.

1101 Natos parenti—: Thyestes means to complete the sentence with some phrase like *epulandos dedisti?*

1102 certos: "legitimate"; contrast 240 *dubius sanguis*, 327 *prolis incertae fides*. If Atreus can now be sure that Agamemnon and Menelaus are his own children, he feels he can be equally confident that Tantalus and Plisthenes were Thyestes'.

Piorum: objective gen. with *praesides* ("guardians of the just"), cf. *Ira* 6.3 *legum praesidem civitatisque rectorem*. Thyestes' claims to be considered *pius* are, of course, open to dispute, as Atreus is quick to point out.

1103 Quid coniugales?: "What about the gods of marriage?" (i.e., do you call upon them as well, seeing that you have violated the marriage-bond?), cf. *Rhet. Her.* 2.34 '*duae res sunt, iudices, quae omne ad maleficium impellant, luxuires et avaritia*' '*quid amor*' *inquiet quispiam* '*quid ambitio?*' [Heinsius proposed reading *quin* for *quid*, which would give the sarcastic question a different point: "why not invoke the gods of marriage?" (i.e., if you are going to be a hypocrite, why not do it properly by calling on the very gods whose laws you have abused?). This is attractive, and has been supported by Zwierlein in *Gnomon* 41 (1969), 769, but it does not seem decisively superior to *quid*, and the parallels cited are not closely relevant.]

Scelere . . . scelus: an astonishingly naive question, which Atreus does not even deign to notice.

pensat: "repays," cf. *Oed.* 937–39 *tam magnis breves / poenas sceleribus solvis atque uno omnia / pensabis ictu?*, Val. Max. 4.3.3.

1104–10 Atreus assumes that Thyestes is the mirror image of himself (cf. 314–16, 917–18), and so attributes to him the reaction he would have had in Thyestes' position, anger at having been anticipated.

1104 scelere praerepto: abl. with causal force, "because the crime was snatched away from you"; *praeripere* is here close in meaning to *occupare* in 204, 270.

1105–1106 nec . . . pararis: "nor is it the fact that you consumed the lawless feast that torments you, [but] the fact that you did not prepare it [for me]"; the absence of an adversative word between the clauses produces a strikingly harsh effect.

1105 hauseris . . . dapes: a post-Augustan usage, cf. *OLD* s.v. *haurio*, #5b.

hauseris: the last syllable is scanned as long *in arsi* (i.e., because it occupies a place in the iambic metron where a metrical ictus falls), cf. *HF* 463 *quemcumque miserum videris, hominem scias*.

angit: i.e., *te*; cf. Livy 24.2.4 *ea cura angebat* (sc. *eos*), Tac. *Ann.* 1.47.1 *multa quippe et diversa angebant* (sc. *Tiberium*). [E reads *angit*, A *tangit*; Giardina has conjectured *te angit*, which would remove the unusual lengthening in *hauseris* and supply *angit* with its object (for the elision in *te angit*, cf. *Ag.* 199 *si aliter*, *Pho.* 443 *in me omnis ruat*). Giardina's proposal is quite elegant, but the features of E's text that it would remove are not true flaws; indeed, the omission of the object with *angit* seems of a piece with the more difficult absence of a connective between *nec quod . . .* and *quod non pararis*. See also Zwierlein, *Gnomon* 41 (1969), 765.]

1106 pararis: = *paraveris*.

1106–1107 fuerat . . . animus . . . instruere similes: the rush of short syllables reflects Atreus' excitement.

1106 animus: "intention," "design" (*OLD* s.v., #7b).

1108 matre: i.e., Aerope, see above, p. 39.

aggredi: "attack," cf. *Med.* 565, *Ag.* 207.

1110 tuos putasti: again Atreus ascribes his own anxieties to Thyestes.

1110–11 Vindices . . . mea: this is Seneca's closest approach to a curse pronounced by Thyestes on Atreus, a central element of the story from Aeschylus onward (cf. *Ag.* 1601–1602) and a memorable episode in earlier Latin dramatic versions, cf. Cic. *Pis.* 43, *Tusc.* 1.107 (quoting Ennius). The restraint of this prayer may be intended to set Thyestes apart from Atreus, but it cannot avoid suggesting as well his weakness and ignorance. Thyestes' confidence in divine justice seems misplaced, especially after the failure of his appeal to Jupiter; his prediction is also colored by irony, since the punishment he wishes for Atreus will be brought about only after he has committed a second unnatural crime, incest with his daughter (above, p. 39). In his last line, as in his first (404), Thyestes fails to recognize the full import of his own words.

1111 his . . . mea: a line of lapidary dignity; it would be impressive were it not for Atreus' reply.

1112 te . . . tuis: in a final display of his verbal control, Atreus mockingly turns Thyestes' words against him; Thyestes' punishment will be the constant awareness of his own crimes (cf. *premor . . . natis* 1051). Atreus clearly gets the better of this last exchange, since the punishment he speaks of is not a hope (*vota te tradunt mea*), but a reality (*te . . . trado*).

As usual, Seneca provides no resolution at the end, no choral comment to set the action in a wider context, no uninvolved minor characters to give a sense of life continuing in its normal course. At its most powerful, here and in *Medea*, Senecan drama seems to negate the very concept of a normally functioning world; the passions that have driven the protagonists have left the order of things radically and permanently disjointed.

APPENDIX I: ANAPESTIC COLOMETRY

The lyric sections of Seneca's tragedies composed in stichic meters (e.g., asclepiads, glyconics, or hendecasyllables) pose no difficulties of colometry, i.e., division into lines: a single metrical unit coincides exactly with a single verse. This is not the case with anapests: ancient writers on metrics recognized several lengths of anapestic verse, from the monometer to the pentameter, and the manuscripts of Seneca exhibit considerable variety in presenting anapestic sections. For example, the two main manuscript families, E and A, often disagree in the placement of monometers, and in a number of passages either E or A offers trimeters where the other arranges the lines as dimeters.

This diversity is not reflected in current texts of the tragedies, since for the past hundred years editors have concurred in regarding the dominant form, the dimeter, as the standard anapestic unit, with monometers normally introduced only at the end of a section or ode. As a consequence, the trimeters transmitted by the manuscripts have been generally discounted as mere scribal errors (with the exception of *Ag.* 642–44 and 647).[1]

Where the manuscripts disagree in their colometry, scholars have usually supported a preference for one of the alternatives by invoking two recognized principles of Seneca's practice: hiatus and *syllaba brevis in longo* are not found within a verse, and there is a marked tendency for verses and units of sense to coincide.[2] Where the manuscripts agree on a division into dimeters, however, editors have been unwilling to alter the resulting arrangement except on the basis of gross metrical irregularity (e.g., hiatus). As a consequence, modern texts are curiously inconsistent in their colometry, generally maintaining coincidence of sense- and metrical units, but admitting many departures from this pattern for which no artistic motive or benefit can be made out. (Contrast, for example, *Thy.* 793–802 and 803–808.)

The prevailing consensus has recently been challenged by Otto Zwierlein,[3] on the grounds that manuscript colometry is too unreliable to

---

[1] This view was first expounded by Leo, *Obs.* 98–110; for typical restatements in recent editions see my *Agamemnon*, pp. 369–70; Fantham's *Troades*, pp. 110–13; above, pp. 32–33.

[2] As noted by G. Richter, *Kritische Untersuchungen zu Senecas Tragödien* (Jena, 1899), 32–47.

[3] *Prolegomena*, 182–202.

merit the authority that has been attributed to it. Zwierlein argues instead that coincidence of meter and sense is the most secure criterion of line-arrangement, and that editors ought to preserve this correspondence as consistently as possible, subject only to the need to avoid hiatus and *brevis in longo*. In the numerous places where a unit of sense fills three anapestic metra, Zwierlein's proposal would thus entail printing either a trimeter or a dimeter + monometer.[4] For example, *Thy.* 803–12, which appear in all editions as pure dimeters:

> quae causa tuos limite certo
> deiecit equos? numquid aperto
> carcere Ditis victi temptant
> bella Gigantes? numquid Tityos
> pectore fesso renovat veteres
> saucius iras? num reiecto
> latus explicuit monte Typhoeus?
> numquid struitur via Phlegraeos
> alta per hostes et Thessalicum
> Thressa premitur Pelion Ossa?

might be re-arranged as follows:

> quae causa tuos limite certo deiecit equos?
> numquid aperto carcere Ditis
> victi temptant bella Gigantes?
> numquid Tityos pectore fesso
> renovat veteres saucius iras?
> num reiecto latus explicuit monte Typhoeus?
> numquid struitur via Phlegraeos alta per hostes
> et Thessalicum Thressa premitur Pelion Ossa?

This passage well illustrates the main attraction of Zwierlein's approach, namely that it gives due prominence to the word-patterning which is frequent in Seneca's anapests as in his iambics; note, e.g., *via Phlegraeos alta per hostes* (= AbaB) and *Thessalicum Thressa—Pelion Ossa* (= ab AB). More subjectively, it could also be argued that variety of verse-length does much to reduce the impression of monotony that Senecan anapests often convey when printed as virtually unbroken series of dimeters.

Since it will be some time before a new consensus on this question has emerged, I have thought it best to retain the conventional colometry in the text and to present here my own suggested alternative. I have admitted trimeters where a sense-unit seemed to extend without a break over three metra, and have generally restricted monometers to sense-units filling a single metron (e.g., *quo vertis iter* 791, *ululare libet* 956)

---

[4] See *Prolegomena*, 195–98 for discussion of cases where an editor might hesitate between these alternatives. [Professor Zwierlein now informs me that he proposes to employ only dimeter + monometer combinations in his forthcoming edition of all the tragedies.]

and phrases serving a clausulating function (e.g., *mergere ponto* 820,
natura tegat 835).

The traditional line-numbering is appended for ease of reference.

CHORUS

Quo, terrarum superumque parens,   789
cuius ad ortus noctis opacae decus omne fugit,
quo vertis iter
medioque diem perdis Olympo?
cur, Phoebe, tuos rapis aspectus?
nondum serae nuntius horae
nocturna vocat lumina Vesper,   795
nondum Hesperiae flexura rotae
iubet emeritos solvere currus,
nondum in noctem vergente die
tertia misit bucina signum;
stupet ad subitae tempora cenae   800
nondum fessis bubus arator.
quid te aetherio pepulit cursu?
quae causa tuos limite certo deiecit equos?
numquid aperto carcere Ditis
victi temptant bella Gigantes?   805
numquid Tityos pectore fesso
renovat veteres saucius iras?
num reiecto latus explicuit monte Typhoeus?
numquid struitur via Phlegraeos alta per hostes   810
et Thessalicum Thressa premitur Pelion Ossa?
    Solitae mundi periere vices.
nihil occasus, nihil ortus erit.
stupet Eoos assueta deo tradere frenos   815
genetrix primae roscida lucis
perversa sui limina regni;
nescit fessos tinguere currus,
nec fumantes sudore iubas
mergere ponto.   820
ipse insueto novus hospitio
Sol Auroram videt occiduus,
tenebrasque iubet surgere nondum nocte parata;
non succedunt astra, nec ullo micat igne polus,   825
non Luna gravis digerit umbras.
    Sed quidquid id est, utinam nox sit!
trepidant, trepidant pectora magno percussa metu,
ne fatali cuncta ruina quassata labent   830
iterumque deos hominesque premat deforme chaos,
iterum terras et mare cingens
et vaga picti sidera mundi
natura tegat.
non aeternae facis exortu   835
dux astrorum saecula ducens
dabit aestatis brumaeque notas,
non Phoebeis obvia flammis
demet nocti Luna timores

vincetque sui fratris habenas,   840
curvo brevius limite currens;
ibit in unum congesta sinum turba deorum.
hic qui sacris pervius astris
secat obliquo tramite zonas,   845
flectens longos signifer annos,
lapsa videbit sidera labens;
hic qui nondum vere benigno
reddit Zephyro vela tepenti,
Aries praeceps ibit in undas,   850
per quas pavidam vexerat Hellen;
hic qui nitido Taurus cornu praefert Hyadas,
secum Geminos trahet et curvi bracchia Cancri;
Leo flammiferis aestibus ardens   855
iterum e caelo cadet Herculeus;
cadet in terras Virgo relictas,
iustaeque cadent pondera Librae,
secumque trahent Scorpion acrem;
et qui nervo tenet Haemonio   860
pinnata senex spicula Chiron
rupto perdet spicula nervo;
pigram referens hiemem gelidus
cadet Aegoceros frangetque tuam, quisquis es, urnam;
tecum excedent ultima caeli sidera Pisces.   865
monstraque numquam perfusa mari
merget condens omnia gurges;
et qui medias dividit Ursas
fluminis instar lubricus Anguis   870
magnoque minor iuncta Draconi
frigida duro Cynosura gelu,
custosque sui tardus plaustri
iam non stabilis ruet Arctophylax.
    Nos e tanto visi populo   875
digni, premeret quos everso cardine mundus?
in nos aetas ultima venit?
o nos dura sorte creatos,
seu perdidimus solem miseri, sive expulimus!   880–81
abeant questus, discede, timor;
vitae est avidus quisquid non vult
mundo secum pereunte mori.   884

THYESTES

Pectora longis hebetata malis,   920
iam sollicitas ponite curas.
fugiat maeror fugiatque pavor,
fugiat trepidi comes exilii
tristis egestas,
rebusque gravis pudor afflictis.   925
magis unde cadas quam quo refert.
magnum, ex alto culmine lapsum
stabilem in plano figere gressum;
magnum, ingenti strage malorum
pressum fracti pondera regni   930

non inflexa cervice pati,
nec degenerem victumque malis
rectum impositas ferre ruinas.
sed iam saevi nubila fati
pelle, ac miseri temporis omnis dimitte notas;   935
redeant vultus ad laeta boni,
veterem ex animo mitte Thyesten.
     Proprium hoc miseros sequitur vitium,
numquam rebus credere laetis;
redeat felix fortuna licet,   940
tamen afflictos gaudere piget—
quid me revocas festumque vetas celebrare diem,
quid flere iubes,
nulla surgens dolor ex causa?
quid me prohibes flore decenti vincire comam?   945
prohibet, prohibet!
     Vernae capiti fluxere rosae,
pingui madidus crinis amomo
inter subitos stetit horrores,
imber vultu nolente cadit,   950
venit in medias voces gemitus.
maeror lacrimas amat assuetas,
flendi miseris dira cupido est;
libet infaustos mittere questus,
libet et Tyrio saturas ostro rumpere vestes,   955
ululare libet.
     Mittit luctus signa futuri
mens, ante sui praesaga mali;
instat nautis fera tempestas,
cum sine vento tranquilla tument—   960
quod tibi luctus quosve tumultus fingis, demens?
credula praesta pectora fratri;
iam, quidquid id est,
vel sine causa vel sero times.
     Nolo infelix, sed vagus intra terror oberrat,   965
subitos fundunt oculi fletus,
nec causa subest.
dolor an metus est?
an habet lacrimas magna voluptas?   969

APPENDIX II: VARIANTS AND CONJECTURES

The following manuscripts only are reported:

E   Florence, Bibl. Laurenziana plut. lat. 37.13 ("codex Etruscus"), s. XI (late)
P   Paris, Bibl. nat. lat. 8260, s. XIII (middle)
T   Paris, Bibl. nat. lat. 8031, s. XV
C   Cambridge, Corpus Christi College 406, s. XIII (first half)
S   El Escorial, Real Bibl. de S. Lorenzo 108 T.III.11, s. XIII (late)
[For brief discussion of the manuscripts and their affiliations, see pp. 36–38.]

Other symbols:

A   Consensus of PTCS
δ   Consensus of PT
β   Consensus of CS
recc. Reading found in later Mss (s. XIV–XV)
Mss Reading of all manuscripts for which evidence is on record
Edd. Emendation made in editions before Gronovius
E¹   Reading of E (or PTCS) before correction
E²   Reading of E (or PTCS) after correction by a later hand
Ec   Reading of E (or PTCS) after correction, when the hand responsible for the correction cannot be specified
Ev   Reading entered in E (or PTCS) as a marginal or interlinear variant

This list is highly selective, comprising only places where there is some question about the original reading; for fuller accounts of the manuscript variants, see the editions of Giardina and Zwierlein.

3 visas *E* : vivas *A* : invisas *Heinsius*   9 qui specu vasto patens
E : semper accrescens iecur *A*   10 visceribus *Avantius* : vulneribus
Mss   15 addi *Gronovius* : adde *Mss*   18 quaere *Ascensius* : quare
Mss   23 Furia *E* : Meg(a)era *A* (*also* 83, 101)   44 omnis *E* : omnes
A   47 facinus *Bentley* : fratris *EA*   51 alta *PT* : alia *E* : atra
*CST*ᵛ*recc.*   53 accerse *E S* : arcesse *PTC*   58 *deleted by*
Tarrant   59 ecquando *Baden* : et quando *Mss*   60 spument aena
E : spumante aeno *A*   61 patrios *EA* : patruos *recc.*   87 mittor
Mss : mittar *Zwierlein* (*in app.*)   94 violate *edd.* : violatae *E* : violata

A   99 cor *Mss* : iecur *Bentley*   100 sequor *del. Bentley*   107
fontis *E* : fontes *A*   116 sacer *Gronovius* : sacras *Mss*   139 aut
EA : at *recc.* : ad *Bothe*   152 lassus *E* : lusus *A*   161 inclusisque
Mss : inclusamque *Heinsius, Bentley*   180–82 iratus Atreus? fremere
iam totus tuis / debebat armis orbis et geminum mare / utrimque
classes agere, iam flammis agros *E* : iras? at Argos fremere iam totum
tuis / debebat armis, omnis et geminum mare / innare classis, iam tuis
flammis agros *A*   204 Satelles *E* : Servus *A* (*throughout the scene*)
219 puta *A* : puto *E*   227 effuso *E* : infuso *A*   233 saxeo *E* : sacro
A   237 erravi *E* : erravit *A*   238 generis *E* : nostri *A*   240 est
Mss : et *Heinsius*   255 modum *Mss* : modus *Madvig*   267 animus
Mss : animo *Leo*   272 uterque *A* : quod uterque *E*   281 versatur
Mss : servatur *Axelson*   289 291 292 290 293 *F* : 289 291 292 293 290
E : 289 290 291 292 293 *A*   300 eius *Mss* : aevi *Heinsius*   302
praecommovebunt *A* : prece commovebo *E* : preces movebunt
recc. : prece commovebunt *L. Müller*   303 ac *Bothe* : hinc *Mss*
321 meo *A* : meos *E*   325 illis *E* : illi *A*   326 fratri sciens
Bentley : patri sciens *E* : patris cliens *A*   333 occule *A* : occules *E*
336–38 *deleted by Richter*   344 regem *E, Lactantius Placidus schol.*
Stat. Theb. 4.530 : reges *A*   346 regia *Lactantius* : regiae *Mss*   347
trabes *A, Lactantius* : fores *E*   361 rabidus *E* : rapidus *A*   388
deleted by Leo   metuit *Mss* : metuet *Bentley*   389 *omitted by* A,
deleted by Leo   404–90 *lines spoken by Tantalus in E are given to*
Plisthenes in A   406 tractum *Kapp* : tactum *Mss*   452 scyphus
Axelson : cibus *Mss*   454 licet *Mss* : libet *Heinsius*   456
imminentem *Bentley* : eminentem *Mss*   467 iungenda *E* : ducenda
A   469 magna *E* : alta *A*   486 cautus *Madvig* : captus Mss   487
given to Thyestes by S²recc., *to Tantalus/Plisthenes by* E A   563
natos tenuere matres *E* : matres t. natos *A* : natis timuere matres
Bentley   571 noctis *E* : nocti *A*   572 *deleted by Tarrant*   580 in
portu *E* : in totum *A* : intortum *recc.* : inflatum *Tarrant*   585 aeternis
EA : Aetnaeis *recc.*   590 *comma after* secare *recent editions* : *after*
velis (591) *early eds.*   591 speciosa *E PST*¹ : spatiosa *CT*²   616 lassis
EA : lapsis *recc.* (*T*²)   624 involvet *O recc.* : involvit *E* : volvet *A*
650 iacet *E* : patet *A* : latet *Richter*   652 qua *recc.* : quae *E PT* : -que
CS   658 lassis *EA* : lapsis *recc.*   668 ferales *A* : feralis *E*   672
loco *A* : ioco *E*   673 tota *Mss* : tuta *Heinsius* : taetra *Bentley* : tecta
Richter   685 revocat *A* : religat *E* : renodat *recc.*   694 ferro parat
Tarrant, Zwierlein (ferrum parat *Koetschau*) : ferro admovet *Mss* (*from*
690?) : arae admovet (*and* atque *for* et) *Bentley*   731 puerone
recc. : puerisne *A* : querone *E*   732 in *Mss* : iam *Damsté*   736
impiger *Zwierlein* : piger *Mss*   741 e *Tarrant* : in *Mss*   744 si stat
Heinsius (sistat *E*) : non stat *A*   745 pius *E* : plus *A*   767 candente
E : querente *A*   771 dicam *Mss* : dicas *Heinsius*   magis *E* : gemant

A   777 ruptum *EA* : raptum *recc.* (*C¹P*)   781 tenuere *Mss* : renuere
Gronovius   789–884 *on arrangement of lines see p. 247*   789
parens *Mss* : potens *Heinsius*   813/14 vices? . . . erit? *M. Müller*
818 limina *E* : lumina *A* : munera *Garrod* : foedera *Tarrant*   829/30
percussa metu / ne fatali etc. *E* : percussa metu ne fatali etc. *A*   833
cingens *Leo* : et ignes *Mss*   835 aeternae *Mss* : alternae *Heinsius*
 : alterno *Bentley*   843/44 congesta sinum turba deorum / hic
E : congesta sinum turba deorum / hic *A*   864 frangetque
Mss : frangesque *Wakefield*   867 monstraque *Mss* : plaustraque
Bentley   877–81 cardine mundus / in . . . venit? / o . . . creatos /
seu . . . miseri / sive expulimus! / abeant *A* : cardine . . . aetas /
ultima . . . dura / sorte . . . perdidimus / solem . . . expulimus! /
habeant *E*   890/91 pergam . . . suorum *deleted by Leo*   911 o me
Avantius : omne *Mss*   920–69 *given to Thyestes in A* : 920–37,
942–44, 961–64 *given to Chorus*, 938–41, 945–60, 965–69 *to Thyestes in*
E (*on arrangement of lines see p. 248*)   930–32 pondera . . . inflexa /
cervice . . . degenerem / victumque . . . impositas
A : pondera . . . pati / nec . . . impositas *E*   945 quid me prohibes
Heinsius : quis me prohibet *Mss*   decenti *EA* : recenti *recc.*   956
rumpere . . . libet *E* : rumpere vestes / ululare libet *A*   1008
tenebrasque *Schmidt* : te nosque *Mss*   1012–14
uterque . . . compagibus / et . . . est / avosque . . . sinu *E* : avosque
nostros, si quis intraTartara est / uterque iam debuimus; hinc
compagibus / et hinc revulsis, huc tuam immani sinu *A*   1018 tostas
Raphelengius : totas *EA* (totus *S*) : tortas *Delrio*   1019 exilia
Gronovius : exitia *Mss*   1020 iaces *A* : iacet *E*   1032 scinduntur
Tarrant : servantur *Mss* : vorantur *Axelson*   1070 di fugistis
recc. : diffugistis *EA* (defugistis *P*)   1081 manuque *CST* : manumque
E P   1084 hac *Scaliger* : haec *Mss*   1103 quid *Mss* : quin
Heinsius   1105 angit *E* : tangit *A* : te angit *Giardina*

SELECT BIBLIOGRAPHY

I. EDITIONS
  A. *Editions of all the tragedies* [only the most important are listed]
      J. F. Gronovius. Leiden, 1661 [second edition by Jacob Grono-
        vius, Amsterdam, 1682].
      J. C. Schroeder. Delft, 1728 [a variorum edition with notes of
        many sixteenth- and seventeenth-century scholars].
      F. H. Bothe. Leipzig, 1819 [with short textual notes].
      F. Leo. Berlin, 1879.
      R. Peiper and G. Richter. Leipzig (Teubner), 1902.
      G. C. Giardina. Bologna, 1966.
      O. Zwierlein. Oxford (Oxford Classical Texts), forthcoming.
  B. *Editions with commentaries of single plays*
      Agamemnon. R. J. Tarrant. Cambridge, 1976 [see reviews by
        C. J. Herington, *Phoenix* 32 (1978), 270–75; O. Zwierlein,
        Gnomon 49 (1977), 565–74].
      Hercules Furens. H. M. Kingery. New York, 1908, reprinted
        Norman, Okla., 1966 [brief notes].
      Medea. H. M. Kingery [as above]; C. D. N. Costa. Oxford, 1973.
      Phaedra. P. Grimal. Paris, 1965; G. and S. Lawall and
        G. Kunkel. Chicago, 1982.
      Troades. H. M. Kingery [as above]; E. Fantham. Princeton, 1982.
II. TRANSLATIONS OF *THYESTES*
      J. Heywood. London, 1560 (collected in *Seneca His Tenne Tra-
        gedies*, ed. T. Newton, London, 1581 [reprinted 1927, 1966]).
      F. J. Miller. Cambridge, Mass. (Loeb Classical Library), 1917
        [essentially a reprint of F. Leo's Latin text, with a serviceable
        English prose rendering].
      T. Thomann. Zürich, 1961 and 1969 [German prose, with short but
        useful notes].
      E. F. Watling. Harmondsworth (Penguin Classics), 1966 [rather flat
        blank verse; introduction good on Seneca's influence in the
        Renaissance].
      J. Elder. Ashington/Manchester, 1982 [in a modern poetic idiom].
III. LEXICA
      Oldfather, W. A. (with A. S. Pease and H. V. Canter). *Index ver-
        borum quae in Senecae fabulis necnon in Octavia praetexta*

reperiuntur. Urbana, 1918 (Univ. of Illinois Studies in Language and Literature, vol. 4, n. 2).

Busa, R. and A. Zampolli. *Concordantiae Senecanae*. Hildesheim, 1975 [includes prose works as well as tragedies].

IV. OTHER WORKS

This selection concentrates on studies of *Thyestes* and works of general relevance to Senecan drama, with greater attention to scholarship in English since about 1960. An excellent critical survey of earlier work is available in *Lustrum* 2 (1957), 113–86 (by Michael Coffey, covering 1922–55); a similar digest of more recent scholarship would be very welcome.

Anliker, K. *Prologe und Akteinteilung in den Tragödien Senecas*. Bern, 1960.

Axelson, B. *Korruptelenkult: Studien zur Textkritik der unechten Seneca-Tragödie Hercules Oetaeus*. Lund, 1967.

Bonner, S. F. *Roman Declamation*. Berkeley, 1949.

Boyle, A. J. "*Hic epulis locus*: The Tragic Worlds of Seneca's *Agamemnon* and *Thyestes*." *Seneca Tragicus: Ramus Essays on Senecan Drama*, ed. A. J. Boyle (Berwick [Australia], 1983), 199–228.

Calder, W. M. (III). "The Size of the Chorus in Seneca's *Agamemnon*." *CP* 70 (1970), 32–35.

_____. "*Secreti loquimur*: An Interpretation of Seneca's *Thyestes*." *Seneca Tragicus* [see under Boyle], 184–98.

Canter, H. V. *Rhetorical Elements in the Tragedies of Seneca*. Urbana, 1925 (Univ. of Illinois Studies in Language and Literature, vol. 10).

Coffey, M. "Seneca and his Tragedies." *Proc. African Class. Assoc.* 3 (1960), 14–20.

Dingel, J. *Seneca und die Dichtung*. Heidelberg, 1974.

Eliot, T. S. "Seneca in Elizabethan Translation." *Collected Essays*. London, 1951, 65–105.

Fantham, E. "Virgil's Dido and Seneca's Tragic Heroines." *Greece and Rome* 22 (1975), 1–10.

Fitch, J. G. "Sense-Pauses and Relative Dating in Seneca, Sophocles and Shakespeare." *AJP* 102 (1981), 289–307.

Friedrich, W.-H. *Untersuchungen zu Senecas dramatischer Technik*. Borna-Leipzig, 1933.

Giancotti, F. *Saggio sulle tragedie di Seneca*. Rome, 1953.

Gigon, O. "Bemerkungen zu Senecas Thyestes." *Philologus* 93 (1938), 176–83.

Griffin, M. "Imago vitae suae." *Seneca*, ed. C. D. N. Costa (London, 1974), 1–38.

_____. *Seneca. A Philosopher in Politics*. Oxford, 1976.

Heldmann, K. *Untersuchungen zu den Tragödien Senecas.* Wiesbaden, 1974 ("Hermes" Einzelschriften, 31).

Henry, Elisabeth. "Seneca the Younger." *Ancient Writers: Greece and Rome. II: Lucretius to Ammianus Marcellinus,* ed. T. J. Luce (New York, 1982), 807–32.

Herington, C. J. "Senecan Tragedy." *Arion* 5 (1966), 422–71. (Reprinted in *Essays on Classical Literature,* ed. N. Rudd [Cambridge, 1972], 170–219.)

——————. "The Younger Seneca." *The Cambridge History of Classical Literature. II: Latin Literature* (Cambridge, 1982), 511–32.

Herrmann, L. *Le théâtre de Sénèque.* Paris, 1924.

Hine, Harry. "The Structure of Seneca's *Thyestes.*" *Papers of the Liverpool Latin Seminar* 3 (1981), ed. Francis Cairns (*ARCA* 7), 259–75.

Knoche, U. "Senecas Atreus. Ein Beispiel." *Das Antike* 17 (1941), 60–76.

Lefèvre, E. *Der Thyestes des Lucius Varius Rufus: Zehn Überlegungen zu seiner Rekonstruktion.* Mainz, 1976 (Akademie der Wissenschaften und der Literatur, Abhandlungen der geistes- und sozialwissenschaftlichen Klasse. 1976, no. 9).

——————. (ed.). *Senecas Tragödien.* Darmstadt, 1972. [A collection of essays by several scholars, mostly German.]

——————. "A Cult without God or the Unfreedom of Freedom in Seneca Tragicus." *CJ* 77 (1981/2), 32–36.

——————. "Die philosophische Bedeutung der Seneca-Tragödie am Beispiel des 'Thyestes'." *ANRW* II.32.1 (forthcoming in 1985).

Leo, F. *De Senecae tragoediis observationes criticae.* Berlin, 1878.

——————. "Die Composition der Chorlieder Senecas." *Rheinisches Museum* 52 (1897), 509–18.

——————. *Der Monolog im Drama. Ein Beitrag zur griechisch-römischen Poetik* (Abhandlungen d. Göttingischen Gesellschaft d. Wissenschaften, Phil.-Hist. Kl. N.F. 10.5 [1908]).

Lesky, A. "Die griechischen Pelopidendramen und Senecas Thyestes." *Wiener Studien* 43 (1922/3), 172–98.

Liebermann, W.-L. *Studien zu Senecas Tragödien.* Meisenheim am Glan, 1974.

Lucas, F. L. *Seneca and Elizabethan Tragedy.* Cambridge, 1922.

Maguinness, W. S. "Seneca and the Poets." *Hermathena* 88 (1956), 81–98.

Marti, B. L. "Seneca's Tragedies: A New Interpretation." *TAPA* 76 (1945), 216–45.

MacGregor, A. P. "The Manuscripts of Seneca's Tragedies: A Survey." *ANRW* II.32.1 (forthcoming).

Owen, W. H. "Commonplace and Dramatic Symbol in Seneca's Tragedies." *TAPA* 99 (1968), 291–313.

Philp, R. H. "The Manuscript Tradition of Seneca's Tragedies." *CQ* N.S. 18 (1968), 150–79.

Poe, J. P. "An Analysis of Seneca's *Thyestes*." *TAPA* 100 (1969), 355–76.

Pratt, N. T. *Dramatic Suspense in Seneca and his Greek Predecessors.* Diss. Princeton, 1939.

_____. "The Stoic Base of Senecan Drama." *TAPA* 79 (1948), 1–11.

_____. "Major Systems of Figurative Language in Senecan Melodrama." *TAPA* 94 (1963), 199–234.

_____. *Seneca's Drama.* Chapel Hill, 1983.

Regenbogen, O. "Schmerz und Tod in den Tragödien des Seneca." *Vorträge der Bibliothek Warburg* 1927/8, 167–218. (Reprinted in *Kleine Schriften* [Munich, 1961] 411–64.)

Ribbeck, O. *Die römische Tragödie im Zeitalter der Republik.* Second edition. Berlin, 1875.

Rist, J. M. *Stoic Philosophy.* Cambridge, 1969.

Sandbach, F. H. *The Stoics.* London, 1975.

Segal, C. P. "Boundary Violation and the Landscape of the Self in Senecan Tragedy." *Antike und Abendland* 29 (1983), 172–87.

Seidensticker, B. *Die Gesprächsverdichtung in den Tragödien Senecas.* Heidelberg, 1969. [See review by R. J. Tarrant, *Phoenix* 26 (1972), 194–99.]

Shelton, J.-A. "Problems of Time in Seneca's *Hercules Furens* and *Thyestes*." *California Studies in Classical Antiquity* 8 (1975), 257–69.

_____. "Seneca's *Medea* as Mannerist Literature." *Poetica* 11 (1979), 38–82.

Staley, G. A. "Seneca's *Thyestes: quantum mali habeat ira*." *Grazer Beiträge* 10 (1981 [1983]), 233–46.

Steele, R. B. "Some Roman Elements in the Tragedies of Seneca." *AJP* 43 (1922), 1–31.

Steidle, W. "Bemerkungen zu Senecas Tragödien." *Philologus* 96 (1944), 250–64.

Strzelecki, L. *De Senecae trimetro iambico quaestiones selectae.* Cracow, 1938.

Tarrant, R. J. "Senecan Drama and its Antecedents." *HSCP* 82 (1978), 213–63.

_____. "The Younger Seneca: Tragedies." *Texts and Transmission*, ed. L. D. Reynolds (Oxford, 1983), 378–81.

Trabert, K. *Studien zur Darstellung des Pathologischen in den Tragödien des Seneca.* Diss. Erlangen, 1953.

Williams, G. *Change and Decline: Roman Literature in the Early Empire.* Berkeley, 1978.

Winterbottom, M. (ed.). *The Elder Seneca: Declamations.* Cambridge, Mass. (Loeb Classical Library), 1974.

Zwierlein, O. *Die Rezitationsdramen Senecas.* Meisenheim am Glan, 1966.

_____. *Prolegomena zu einer kritischen Ausgabe der Tragödien Senecas.* Mainz, 1984 (Akademie der Wissenschaften und der Literatur, Abhandlungen der geistes- und sozialwissenschaftlichen Klasse. 1983, no. 3).

_____. "Der Schluss der Tragödie 'Atreus' des Accius." *Hermes* 111 (1983), 121–25.

INDEXES

The indexes are selective: they do not register all matters mentioned in the book, but only those on which specific comment is offered. The numbers refer to pages.

I. WORDS

II. SUBJECTS